Starmont Reference G
ISSN 0738-012?

FUTURE AND FANTASTIC
WORLDS:

A Bibliographical Retrospective of DAW Books
(1972–1987)

by
Sheldon Jaffery

BORGO PRESS / WILDSIDE PRESS

www.wildsidepress.com

Library of Congress Cataloging-in-Publication Data

Jaffery, Sheldon.

Future and fantastic worlds.

(Starmont reference guide, ISSN 0738-0127 ; # 4)
Includes indexes.
1. DAW Books Inc. 2. Science fiction--Bibliography--
Catalogs. 3. Fantastic fiction--Bibliography--Catalogs.
4. Science fiction--Stories, plots, etc. 5. Fantastic
fiction--Stories, plots, etc. 6. Paperbacks--
Bibliography--Catalogs. I. Title. II. Series: Starmont
reference guide, ISSN 0738-0127 ; no. 4.
Z473.D29J33 1987   016.80883'876   87-9901
ISBN 1-55742-003-3
ISBN 1-55742-002-5 (pbk.)

CONTENTS

iii

This book is a gift to my daughter,
Kimberly Hallie Jaffery,
to commemorate her 21st birthday
on
January 21, 1987
and her graduation from the
University of Michigan
on
May 2, 1987

What more can a proud father say?

ACKNOWLEDGMENTS AND REFERENCES

A work of this nature can only be successfully accomplished by using other reference works for assistance in one way or another. To further my ends, the following reference books, some of which have been cited extensively in the bibliographical portion of this book, where appropriate, were used.

Barron, Neil ed. *Anatomy of Wonder: A Critical Guide to Science Fiction*. Second edition. R.R. Bowker Company, New York (1981).

Barron, Neil ed. *Anatomy of Wonder: A Critical Guide to Science Fiction*. Third edition. R.R. Bowker Company, New York (1987).

Contento, William. *Index to Science Fiction Anthologies and Collections*. First edition. G.K. Hall & Co., Boston (1978).

Cottrill, Tim, Greenberg, Martin H. and Waugh, Charles G. *Science Fiction and Fantasy Series and Sequels*. First edition. Garland Publishing, Inc., New York (1986).

Magill, Frank N. ed. *Survey of Science Fiction Literature: Five Hundred 2,000-Word Essays of World-Famous Science Fiction Novels with 2500 Bibliographical References*. First edition. Five volumes. Salem Press, Englewood Cliffs (1979).

Magill, Frank N. ed. *Survey of Modern Fantasy Literature*. First edition. Five volumes. Salem Press, Englewood Cliffs (1983).

Nicholls, Peter ed. *The Science Fiction Encyclopedia*. First edition. Doubleday, New York (1979).

Reginald, R. *Science Fiction and Fantasy Literature: A Checklist 1700-1974*. First edition. Two volumes. Gale, Detroit. (1979).

Rock, James A. *Who Goes There?: A Bibliographic Dictionary of Pseudonymous Literature in the Fields of Fantasy and Science Fiction*. First edition. James A. Rock and Company, Bloomington (1979).

Sampson, Robert. *Yesterday's Faces. Volume 2: Strange Days*. First edition. Popular Press, Bowling Green (1984).

Schlobin, Roger C. *The Literature of Fantasy: A Comprehensive, Annotated Bibliography of Modern Fantasy Fiction*. First edition. Garland Publishing, Inc., New York. (1979).

Smith, Curtis C. ed. *Twentieth Century Science Fiction Writers*. Second edition. St. James Press, Chicago (1986).

Tuck, Donald H. *The Encyclopedia of Science Fiction and Fantasy*. First edition. Three volumes. Advent, Chicago (1974-1983).

Tymn, Marshall B., Zahorski, Kenneth J. and Boyer, Robert H. *Fantasy Literature: A Core Collection and Reference Guide*. First edition. R.R.

Bowker Company, New York (1979).

Tymn, Marshall B. ed. *Horror Literature: A Core Collection and Reference Guide*. First edition. R.R. Bowker Company, New York (1981).

Wells, Stuart W. III. *The Science Fiction and Heroic Fantasy Author Index*. First edition. Purple Unicorn Books, Duluth (1978).

Additional acknowledgments to:

Lloyd W. Currey for the immense amount of bibliographical material that is contained in each and every one of his catalogues, which, by the way, are indispensable to the serious collector of fantasy and science fiction. The catalogues were of immense help in the preparation of this book. A special thanks is also appropriate for Lloyd's suggestion to use the Smith and Cottrill et al. books. They were invaluable.

Neil Barron for providing me with material from his not-yet-as-of-this-writing-been-published third edition of *Anatomy of Wonder*. For anyone who didn't notice, some of my citations have been to that august volume, scheduled for August 1987 publication. I'm writing this in February 1987. Neil warned me that Bowker could renumber Chapter 4, in which case all of my citations to the third edition would be wrong. What a bummer. In case anyone didn't know it, the chapter in Neil's book, labeled as the modern period (from 1964-1986), was prepared by Brian Stableford, a hell of a science fiction writer in his own right, and whose novels are liberally represented in the DAW Book list.

Roy Preece of The Village Bookshelf for his unstinting aid in filling some major holes in my Daw Book collection.

Don Wollheim for his cooperation in supplying me with missing copies of DAW Books so that this book could be completed, as well as for his gracious consent to the use of DAW back cover blurb material and, of course, adding a touch of class to this book by writing a preface. And I won't forget Don's lovely and gracious wife, Elsie, who was also an important factor in the ultimate equation of this book.

Last and, perhaps, best, all of the writers, artists, and, especially, readers who have had a hand in making DAW Books an institution in our favorite genre.

PREFACE

1971 was a bad year for science fiction paperback books. Ace Books, whose editor-in-chief I had been for nineteen and a half years, was in deep financial straits under its post-Wyn management. Ballantine Books, with whom Ace shared the SF market, was also in trouble and more or less marking time. That was when it became apparent to me that my wisest course was to become a publisher myself—and hence DAW Books came into official existence November 8th, 1971.

In my anthology, *The 1974 Annual World's Best SF*, I printed a dedication opposite the Table of Contents. It read, "In memory of three who were there at the right time: John T. Barr, Melville Harris, Edward John Carnell." Let me, in this the sixteenth year of DAW's successful life, enlarge on that.

John "Jack" Barr had been the typesetter and layout man for Ace Books for many years. He it was who first suggested getting out of what he termed "a sinking ship." He bolstered my own thoughts, and our conferences helped solidify the project. He lived long enough to set type for DAW's first four books. His sudden death was an unexpected tragedy which caused us to turn to New American Library's facilities which has ever since stood us in good stead.

Melville Harris was an attorney for whom my wife had once worked and who had remained a friend of the family ever since. He advised us, set up the corporation, did the legal necessities, and further bolstered our confidence. He, too, died early in 1972, after a short illness.

Edward "Ted" Carnell was one of my longest SF fan friends and close correspondent. We had known each other for over a third of a century, and he had become the major science fiction literary agent of Britain and a power in all the SF world. He was a great help in establishing our earliest titles and resolving some editorial problems. I knew that he had been ill. He died early in the spring of 1972.

None of these three lived to see a finished DAW book. But they were there when they were most needed and DAW owes a perpetual debt to all three, as well as to my wife, Elsie, who joined me at the start as my business manager and has remained at that highly responsible task ever since. Now, too, I must include my daughter, Betsy, who grew up in the world of science fiction writers and fans, who has become editor-in-chief of DAW Books since 1985.

—Donald A. Wollheim

vii

Introduction

Man, am I excited! I've found something I've been searching for all my life: the perfect book collectible. Sure, I collect Arkham House and have just about a complete collection. And I've got substantial numbers of Gnome Press and Fantasy Press, among the early specialty publishers. Lots of Don Grant books. Scarce horror and supernatural novels, anthologies and collections. Shelves full of first editions. Pulps of every description: horror, detective, western, sports, adventure, hero, air, and, of course, science fiction and fantasy, including complete runs of *Unknown* and *Fantastic Adventures*; mostly representative selections and broken runs of somewhere between 300 and 400 different titles. Lots of things. They're good, too.

Okay, then, let's analyze my quest for perfection. The perfect collectible, books or otherwise, should have the following qualities:

SIZE. Small for easy portability. Who needs to hire a truck every time you buy another one for the collection? Or rent a warehouse to contain it? That eliminates Eighteenth Century Dutch Provincial Sideboards and John Deere tractors from consideration.

AVAILABILITY. There should be sufficient quantities available so that a collector has a reasonable chance of completing the collection. After all, who ever collected one of something? Like, "I'm a Mona Lisa collector." Big deal, so you're the Louvre. On the other hand, there should be a good shot at getting an entire collection, so the collectible, in the abstract, should be of finite number.

SCARCITY. There should be some element of unavailability of some items, in order to titillate the collector's palate and not make it too easy to complete the collection. If it's all over quickly, think of all the dusty bookshelves in out-of-the-way bookstores in remote cities that won't see you again. The necessity of obtaining 700 of something, for example, creates that element, particularly if you shoot for first printings. Notice that we're back to talking about books again, not other types of collectibles. Hey, 700 of anything, if you think about it, is a lot of anything.

COST. The collectibles should be within the average collector's means. You're not all rich lawyers like me.

APPEARANCE. The collectibles should look nice for display purposes. That makes sense. Who wants to collect ugly things?

UTILITY. The collectible should be useful, and what's more useful than a book? It can be read. And read. And read. At home, on airplanes, on buses to work, on the can, on spacecraft to the Moon.

So, what fits the bill? DAW Books! Or haven't you been paying attention?

What is a DAW Book, anyway? Well, it's 4 1/4" wide and 7" long, and somewhere around 1/2" to 3/4" thick, depending on the book, and, for a number of years, it was mostly yellow (especially on the spine), which makes it pretty distinctive when you're searching the stacks of used paperback stores to complete your collection. That changed in June 1984; since then, the front cover art has wrapped around to the spine, and, in many cases, all around the book.

Used copies of DAW Books can generally be found for a buck or two, even in excellent condition. The prices could go higher, as they become collected by more people. Therefore, the early collector may be getting in on a good thing: a collection that appreciates in value. Ever hear of Arkham House? Some titles have become more expensive already, especially for Philip K. Dick, Marion Zimmer Bradley or, perhaps, Philip Jose Farmer, Tanith Lee and C.J. Cherryh first editions, among others. First editions, you gasp in disbelief. Sure, first editions; you don't think I'm going to collect junk, do you? (Maybe you ought to re-read *Horrors and Unpleasantries*, my book about Arkham House, or, if you haven't read it, find a copy and do so. Now.)

Since DAW Books are mass market paperbacks, there are plenty of copies available to the collector. It's somewhat more difficult to obtain the first printings of some titles, but they're out there, too, and that's part of the fun of collecting. Upgrading until perfection is achieved. For those of you who need a bibliographical brushup on recognition points, keep on reading. If you're a smartass, skip the next few paragraphs.

On the copyright page of each DAW Book, after the first couple of years that the company was in business, can be found the following information, as an example:

FIRST PRINTING, JANUARY 1975
1 2 3 4 5 6 7 8 9

That's a first printing. A later printing would look like this:

FIRST PRINTING, JANUARY 1975
3 4 5 6 7 8 9

See? It's simple. Each time DAW reprints the title in its original form (with the possible exception of a price change), a number gets knocked off. The second example above would indicate the third printing of the title. Now, you're an expert on that phase of this fascinating lesson. Don't gloat, however; it gets a little more complicated. Later on, DAW reprinted some of its more popular titles with different cover art by artists other than the original ones. Only the logo numbers aren't the same. Logo number; that's the same as a DAW Collector's Number, as it's referred to in more recent books. Simple. Sure, but DAW also reprinted some titles with the same covers and no changes in any way except to indicate a later printing and a price change. Instead of a new logo number, the code number was changed. That's the little combination of two letters followed by four numbers that appears on every book, such as UE1659.

If you want to make any sense of the code numbering system, assuming that you pay any attention to it in the bibliographical section of each entry to follow in this book, heed this. It works this way. You'll notice that the code numbers of the first printings aren't sequential. That's because the numbers themselves (not the letters—those refer to the price) reflect a running account of all DAW books as they were published, reprints and all. For example, DAW Books No. 1 had code number UQ1001 and showed a $.95 price. If you're still with me, you'll realize that the 482nd book to be published by DAW, including original publications and all reprints, would show the code number number UE1482, but is Logo No. 349, Tanith Lee's *Electric Forest*. Sexy stuff, eh?

But wait. There's another complicating factor exemplified by Philip Jose Farmer's *Hadon of Ancient Opar*. I mentioned this before. There are two different logo numbers for this title; the first is number 100, with a cover by Roy Krenkel. The second, number 442, has a cover by Clyde Caldwell, although it retains Roy Krenkel's interior illustrations as they appeared in the first publication. This phenomenon occurs on more than one occasion. Watch for it. So you thought collecting DAW Books was going to be easy, did you. Silly you.

A DAW Books collection is extensive and impressive. More than 700 new titles from April 1972 have been published as you read this, and the number is increasing at a clip of about three per month as of April 1987. (Compare Arkham House with about 180 titles since 1939). Compare any imprint. Yet the whole collection can fit nicely into a decent-size bookcase or two, even though such a collection looks like a giant egg yolk splattered against the wall (that's one of its attractions), and the collector will never lack reading material.

Finally, the art work. Unbelievable! A DAW collector will have acquired and have available, at his fingertips, a major sampling of the work of some of the top artists working in our beloved genre. People like Frank Kelly Freas, George Barr, Jack Gaughan, Roy Krenkel, Boris Vallejo, Victoria Poyser, Michael Whelan, Don Maitz, Ken W. Kelly, Carl Lundgren, Ron Walotsky, and more. Many, many more.

You may have noticed a certain measured enthusiasm on the part of this writer as you have read this introduction. It's genuine. Trust me on this. I'm really excited about DAW Books.

Now let's get serious for a moment. Aside from being, in essence, a collector's guide to DAW Books, this book is a tribute to Don Wollheim, a giant in our field for so many years and in so many ways: fan, author, editor and publisher. I believe that Don has long been underrated, and that he can be numbered among other giants in our genre. Men like John W. Campbell, August Derleth, Farnsworth Wright, Hugo Gernsback.

Born in 1914 in New York City, Don was a science fiction fan in the genre's infancy. He was the founder of the concept of science fiction conventions, a now traditional part of fandom. He helped inaugurate the Fantasy Amateur Press Association. He has one of the world's most complete collections of science fiction and associated materials. In comparison, my collection doesn't compare. In 1941, Don founded *Stirring Science Stories* (I just bought a copy of the first issue of this magazine for my collection) and its companion pulp, *Cosmic Stories*, both of which flopped after a few issues. Undaunted, he joined Avon Publishers after the war and edited *Avon Fantasy Reader*, a great weird reprint series which is, itself, a sought-after collectible. Then, in the early fifties, as pulps were on their way out, Don edited *Out of This World Adventures, Ten Story Fantasy*, and *Avon Science Fiction Reader*. He also selected the stories for *Saturn SF* and *Orbit SF*.

In 1952, Don left Avon to become editor-in-chief for Ace Books, where he developed Ace Books into a major line of paperbacks, which included the publication of westerns, mysteries, romances, mainstream novels, humor and non-fiction, as well as science fiction. Don's proud of that accomplishment. In 1967, he became a vice-president of Ace. Finally, Don founded his own science fiction and fantasy line, DAW Books, and the rest is history.

For any who are unaware of the deed, Don Wollheim has the further distinction of having edited the first science fiction anthology in history, *The Pocket Book of Science Fiction*, published by Pocket Books in 1943.

As an author, Don wrote many novels for Winston's juvenile series and also another juvenile series of "Mike Mars" adventures for Doubleday. He has also written non-juvenile novels under the pseudonym of David Grinnell and has two short story collections to his credit. His strength, however, has been as an anthologist and an editor. This is reflected in his exquisite taste in selecting the stories for inclusion in all of the anthologies with which he has been involved, as well as what eventually led to the success of the DAW line, a success which is unique in science fiction history. I think that it can be said that Don Wollheim and DAW Books brought modern science fiction and fantasy into respectability. Racks in bookstores throughout the nation abound with genre literature, more so than at any time in the history of American popular culture. Don Wollheim, more deservingly than any other single figure, can be called the father of "popular" science fiction and fantasy. I better stop now. I could go on and on, and Don Wollheim doesn't even know that I admire and respect him this much. I guess he does now.

Okay. As for the format of *Future and Fantastic Worlds*. The first paragraph of each logo number gives bibliographical information and a brief publishing history, where warranted. It also includes the cover artist, the number of pages, and original price. Where appropriate, citations have been made to scholarly references which have analyzed or noted the book as important in the genre. Following that, for most of the books, is a short summary of the novel's plot, being composed, in most instances, of the back cover blurbs, sometimes modified, for each of the novels. They were originally written by an anonymous editorial assistant at DAW, or maybe by Don Wollheim himself. I'll get back to you on that. Hey, give me a break. You don't think I've read every one of those 700 books, did you? This book doesn't pretend to be a critical survey. It's a bibliographical review at heart: the rest is a bonus to amuse you while you do your collecting and research. Oh, did I forget to tell you? It's a research tool, too. In any event, reading all the books beforehand would have taken me forever, and you wouldn't be holding this book in your hands right now. But I digress. To continue: in the case of single-author collections and anthologies, I've listed the contents. Interspersed throughout the book are bibliographer's comments, wry, irreverent, sometimes inane, and otherwise, that are mine, all mine, and not cribbed lazily from the books themselves. I had to do something to amuse myself while getting this tome in shape to go to Starmont House. Then, so you won't feel cheated by the enormous price that Ted Dikty's going to charge for this great bibliography (I'm being serious again, since I truly believe that this is an important book, as much as *Horrors and Unpleasantries*, which used to be my favorite until this one), I've included an Author-Title Index and a Cover Artist-Title Index. Also Ted talked me into doing a Title Index for brain-damaged readers who remember a book's title and can't remember who wrote the damned thing. If you don't think that was boring and a real pain in the ass, you ain't really cogitating. Merde.

So—have I missed anything? Probably. I never claimed to be perfect. Well, there you have it. I hope the book is useful to the many DAW Book collectors in America and Great Britain, because, God willing, a number of copies will find their way overseas.

Oh, one more thing. For those skeptics who want to know what good the god-damned book is, in the first place, I'll tell you how I'm going to use it. A copy of the hardcover will go on my reference shelf to be used periodically as needed. A copy of the paperback will be used as a checklist for several purposes. First, a lot of the DAW Books that I have in my own collection aren't first printings. It didn't matter to me when I got them, because I needed to use them to bring you this book. Now, I want to correct that minor deficiency. Therefore, I'll have to carry the book around with me (for I'll have cunningly identified and marked off those later printings for this very purpose), and, when I go to strange cities for conventions, or, even in my own city, which is pretty strange, I can look for firsts, buy them and substitute them for my later printings. What a clever dodge. Secondly, and, more importantly, I'll make margin notations about plots and even critical commentary as I gradually make inroads on reading all the rest of my DAW Books, which ought to take me into my dotage. Like the punch line of Arthur C. Clarke's "The Nine Billion Names of God," maybe I won't blink out until I've read them all. That's probably cheating, since they're still being published at the rate of three new books a month. What the hell, reading DAW Books instead of working is a small price to pay for immortality. Now I need to explain that to my wife, the char, my daughter, the little match girl, and my two sons, the indentured servants.

Happy collecting, friends, and, above all, happy reading.

Sheldon Jaffery
Beachwood, Ohio 1987

BIBLIOGRAPHIC RETROSPECT, 1972-1987

Logo No. 1. Norton, Andre. *Spell of the Witch World*. Code No. UQ1001. First edition. First printing, April 1972. 159 pp. Cover and interior art by Jack Gaughan. Later published by Gregg Press (1977). See Schlobin, *The Literature of Fantasy* 838 (1979). $.95.

Somewhere in the infinite spaces beyond the galaxy that we know lies a planet with a strange affinity to the Earth, for Earthling blood had crossed that incomprehensible vastness to mingle with the human-but-alien civilizations of that untracked world, having been brought through an ancient "door" set down between the worlds in times unknown.

(Bibliographer's note: The seventh book of the Witch World saga, and, of course, notable as having been the very first DAW Book.)

Logo No. 2. Green, Joseph. *The Mind Behind the Eye*. Code No. UQ1002. First U.S edition. First printing, April 1972. 191 pp. Cover art by Josh Kirby. Originally published in U.K. by Gollancz (1971) under the title, *Gold the Man*. $.95.

"In the fairly near future, genetic engineering has produced two super-intelligent men: Gold in the U.S.A. and Petrovna in the U.S.S.R. Meanwhile the solar system has been visited by aliens who seem to want to eliminate homo sapiens. An alien ship comes to grief, but its occupant survives with extensive brain damage. He is—wait for it—a 300-foot humanoid giant. Petrovna has a good idea: scoop the damaged brain section out, install computer control of muscles plus a chamber to contain a human being, then return said giant to his own planet so that the spy in his head can find out what's cooking. Petrovna is killed, but Gold and Petrovna's female assistant carry out the mission . . ."—London *Sunday Times*

Logo No. 3. Hall, Brian N. *The Probability Man*. Code No. UQ1003. First edition. First printing, April 1972. 175 pp. Cover art by Kelly Freas. Later published in U.K. by Sidgwick & Jackson (1973). $.95.

He had forgotten his real name, so they called him "Spingarn" after the last role he had played. He was the man the directors of the Frames regarded as their major headache—for he was guilty of two unforgivable arrogances. He had programmed himself into every one of the vast world-staged dramas he had directed, and he had reactivated the forbidden Frames of the pre-human planet of Talisker.

In those days of an overcrowded colonized cosmos, a thousand years from now, the Frames were the major means of diversion. Employing historical re-creations and fictional dramas played out with planets as stages and whole populations as actors, the Frame directors and their robot assistants had become the masters of all life.

They couldn't destroy Spingarn, the Probability Man, but they could

1

sentence him to undo the damage he had done. So he was sent to the mad Frames of Talisker to unravel the secret of their origin a billion years before the Universe.

Logo No. 4. Van Vogt, A.E. *The Book of Van Vogt*. Code No. UQ1004. First edition. First Printing, April 1972. 191 pp. Cover art by Karel Thole. Later published in U.K. by New English Library (1980) as *Lost: Fifty Suns*. $.95.
   Contents:

The Timed Clock	Ersatz Eternal
The Confession	The Sound of Wild Laughter
The Rat and the Snake	Lost: Fifty Suns
The Barbarian	

Logo No. 5. Wollheim, Donald A., with Saha, Arthur W., eds. *The 1972 Annual World's Best SF*. Code No. UQ1005. First edition. First printing, May 1972. 302 pp. Cover art by John Schoenherr. See *Anatomy of Wonder* 3-911 (1981). $.95.
   Contents:

Introduction	The Editor
The Fourth Profession	Larry Niven
Gleepsite	Joanna Russ
The Bear with the Knot on His Tail	Stephen Tall
The Sharks of Pentreath	Michael G. Coney
A Little Knowledge	Poul Anderson
Real-Time World	Christopher Priest
All Pieces of a Silver Shore	R.A. Lafferty
With Friends Like These	Alan Dean Foster
Aunt Jennie's Tonic	Leonard Tushnet
Timestorm	Eddy C. Bertin
Transit of Earth	Arthur C. Clarke
Gehenna	Barry Malzberg
One Life, Furnished in Early Poverty	Harlan Ellison
Occam's Scalpel	Theodore Sturgeon

Logo No. 6. Geston, Mark S. *The Day Star*. Code No. UQ1006. First edition. First printing, May 1972. 126 pp. Cover art and illustrations by George Barr. $.95.
   Once, at the height of Earth's fabled history, there was a city called Ferrin. Compared to Ferrin, all the cities of Earth that ever were or ever would be, from imperial Rome and towering New York before, to the city called R afterwards, paled into insignificance. In the long twilight centuries that followed the fall of Ferrin, memories faded and men's ambitions waned, and, by the time that the young man Thel heard of Ferrin, no one was sure it was anything but a myth.
   But part of an abandoned highway still passed near Thel's home, and, when a starry fragment from Ferrin came into Thel's possession, he knew

there could be no rest for him until he had followed the ruined roadway that still spanned time and space to find the truth about the Rise and Fall of Ferrin, and also of all humanity's hopes.

Logo No. 7. Stableford, Brian M. *To Challenge Chaos.* Code No. UQ1007. First edition. First printing, May 1972. 160 pp. Cover art by Kelly Freas. $.95.

They named the planet Chaos X, because one hemisphere was not in this universe, and no one who ventured there would ever return. They named the other universe Ultra, because it was beyond the laws of the Milky Way galaxy. It was only by means of Ultra's non-Euclidean physics that men could travel the starways. They named the ruler of that "immobile" planet Fury, because that was the effect of his power on people.

But they were afraid to call Craig Star Gazer by any other name, because he was the space captain who was going to cross into Fury's domain and wrench his loved one from Ultra's power, and this was something that no one had ever done before except the legendary Orpheus.

Logo No. 8. Sutton, Jeff. *The Mindblocked Man.* Code No. UQ1008. First edition. First printing, May 1972. 159 pp. Cover art by Jack Gaughan. $.95.

The fish eye! The distorted sky! The blob that ate the stars! Those were the first memories he had when he opened his eyes in a strange room in a strange sector of the city. Who he was he did not know, where he came from was an enigma. But in those nightmare visions lay the only clues to his past.

There were mighty forces and dangerous agents seeking him; this he learned quickly enough. There was a hospital in orbit missing one patient; that added to the crisis that involved all the powers that contended within the 22nd Century's intricate society. But was there anybody on his side? And was he good, or was he really everyone's enemy?

Logo No. 9. Dickson, Gordon R. *Tactics of Mistake.* Code No. UQ1009. First paperback edition. First DAW printing, June 1972. 222 pp. Cover art by Kelly Freas. Published earlier by Doubleday (1971) as *The Tactics of Mistake.* Published later in U.K. by Sphere (1975). See *Anatomy of Wonder* 3-275 (1981) and *Survey of Science Fiction Literature I*, pp. 330-336 (1979). $.95.

The two superpowers of future Earth had learned to fight their wars among the colonized planets rather than on the home world, and, if they could do it with paid mercenaries, so much the better. The best were the men of the Dorsai, soldiers born and bred, who commanded the greatest military respect.

But, in the battle going on on Kultis, something extra was involved. A very personal contest between the brash theoretical tactician Cletus Grahame, for the Western Alliance, and his challenge to the most ambitious statesman of the Eastern Coalition. Grahame was no Dorsai, but he did have a set of untested theories, a style of physical wizardry, and what he called the "tactics of mistake."

(Bibliographer's note: This novel comprises a portion of the Childe Cycle.)

Logo No. 10. Elgin, Suzette Haden. *At the Seventh Level*. Code No. UQ1010. First edition. First printing, June 1972. 142 pp. Cover art and illustrations by George Barr. See *Anatomy of Wonder* 3-300 (1981). $.95.

Coyote Jones had never heard of Abba until he was assigned there. It was a remotely beautiful world, but one which had been admitted to the society of civilized planets only after it had made concessions on its degrading treatment of women. Until then, women were considered as not human, as a sort of necessary beast, but not more.

The concessions had been slight, but, as a result, one brilliant female, Jacinth, had risen to the very top of that strange society, to the Seventh Level. Thereby, she had become the spiteful target of male fury, female envy, and, finally, of a deviously evil plot that might cost the world its status.

(Bibliographer's note: The fourth novel of the Communipath Worlds series.)

Logo No. 11. Klein, Gerard. *The Day Before Tomorrow*. Code No. UQ1011. First U.S. and first English language edition. First printing, June 1972. 128 pp. Translated by P.J. Sokolowski. Original edition entitled *Le Temps N'a Pas D'odeur* and published by Editions Denoel, Paris, France (1967). Cover art by Josh Kirby. See *Anatomy of Wonder* 4-302 (1987). $.95.

The Federation considered itself a technological Utopia, and the innumerable planets under its sway were guaranteed stability by virtue of the time-change teams. For, whenever a planetary historian located evidence in the past of any newly found world that suggested it might evolve into a possible menace, a team of seven would be sent to tamper with that world's history. But the seven men that went to Ygone encountered a fate no theorist had projected. They met with immediate ambush, they met with a strangely peaceful culture that could not be fathomed, and they finally were confronted with all the contradictions and temporal knots that the whole system of time-change had to imply.

Logo No. 12. Koontz, Dean R. *A Darkness in My Soul*. Code No. UQ1012. First edition. First printing, June 1972. 124 pp. Cover art by Jack Gaughan. Later published in the U.K. by Dobson (1979). $.95.

Although Simeon Kelly was the first successful product of the Artificial Creation laboratory, he would work for them only under compulsion. And the efforts they made to get him to probe the mind of their latest gene-construct, a thing called Child, were the greatest.

Because Child was anything but a child. In that incredibly monstrous infant appeared to be the potential for whole oceans of inventions and an entire cosmos of total creativity. But Child was vicious, insane and short-lived.

Logo No. 13. Davis, Richard, ed. *The Year's Best Horror Stories No.1.*
Code No. UQ1013. First edition. First printing, July 1972. 174 pp. Cover
art by Karel Thole. See *Horror Literature* 4-252 (1981). $.95.

Contents:

Double Whammy	Robert Bloch
The Sister City	Brian Lumley
When Morning Comes	Elizabeth Fancett
Prey	Richard Matheson
Winter	Kit Reed
Lucifer	E.C. Tubb
I Wonder What He Wanted	Eddy C. Bertin
Problem Child	Peter Oldale
The Scar	Ramsey Campbell
Warp	Ralph Norton
The Hate	Terri E. Pinckard
A Quiet Game	Celia Fremlin
After Nightfall	David Riley
Death's Door	Robert McNear

(Bibliographer's note: The first of what has proven to be one of, if not,
arguably, the best annual horror anthologies published over the years.)

Logo No. 14. Dick, Philip K. *We Can Build You.* Code No. UQ1014. First
edition. First printing, July 1972. 206 pp. Cover art by John Schoenherr.
Later published in U.K. by Fontana (1977). $.95.

They began as manufacturers of electronic mood organs and player
pianos. Then they improved the line; they started building exact simulcra
of famous men. They thought that people would pay a good price to have
anyone they wanted made to order: to talk with, befriend, and eventually
utilize for any purpose they wanted.

But they ran into trouble. For one thing, an exactly programmed
reconstruction of a famous man is going to be as obstinate and as
character-complex as the real man was—and nobody's puppet. For another,
they got involved with a project for settling the moon with their creations.
And, finally, they got tangled up with their own personal identities.

Logo No. 15. Biggle, Lloyd Jr. *The World Menders.* Code No. UQ1015.
First paperback edition. First printing, July 1972. 192 pp. Cover art by
Kelly Freas. Published earlier by Doubleday (1971). Published later in
U.K. by Elmfield Press (1973). $.95.

On the world Branoff IV live the RASCZ, an artistic, superbly civilized
race. Few of them are aware that their prosperous civilization is totally de-
pendent upon the OLZ, a race of slaves owned by their god-emperor. The
OLZ till the fields and work the forests and mines, and their reward is
starvation and the whip.

Cultural Survey trainee Cedd Farrari receives a routine assignment to
Interplanetary Relations Bureau headquarters on Branoff IV. His delight

with the culture of the RASCZ is shattered when he becomes aware of the horrible plight of the OLZ. He dedicates himself to their liberation, and, to achieve that, he must become one of them. He must share their body-destroying labor and their starvation and torture.

As he pursues his quest, he leads the OLZ in the strangest rebellion ever described in truth or fiction; the RASCZ, the master race, don't know their slaves are rebelling. Neither do the slaves!

(Bibliographer's note: A novel in the Cultural Survey series.)

Logo No. 16. Phillifent, John T. *Genius Unlimited.* Code No. UQ1016. First edition. First printing, July 1972. 141 pp. Cover art by Jack Gaughan. $.95.

If you had a high IQ, a yen to do the science-thing in your own way, then Iskola was your place. Iskola was an island on the colony planet Martas, and it was owned and controlled by the man who had led the colonists.

To qualify for Iskola, besides talent, you needed something else; you had to mind your own business about the other experimenters and the rest of the world. That was for certain kinds of mental wizards and do-it-yourself idealists.

It was also quite perfect for another sharp-eyed type, the kind that perfected villainy to a complex science. That's where Interstellar Agents Rex Sixx and Roger Lowry came into the picture, because something very, very evil was coming to a boil in Utopia.

Logo No. 17. Edmondson, G.C. *Blue Face.* Code No. UQ1017. First paperback edition. First printing, August 1972. 128 pp. Originally published by Doubleday (1971) under the title *Chapayeca* and later published in U.K. under the same title by Hale (1973). $.95.

When Nash Taber found the alien living among the Yaqui Indians, he was certain that this was the sensational discovery that would end his search for the badly-needed bolster to his sagging academic reputation.

Crippled in mind and body, from a wrong marriage and a severe motor accident, the anthropologist had made this last do-or-die trip to Mexico, never thinking that this discovery would mean not only an end to pain and hunger, but also the beginning of immortality and power beyond his wildest imaginings.

But, before he can announce his discovery, he finds that his situation is very much that of the legendary man who caught a mountain lion alone and with his bare hands. The only time he really felt the need of help was when he tried to turn it loose.

(Bibliographer's note: For some strange reason, the identity of the cover artist isn't disclosed on the copyright page.)

Logo No. 18. Tubb, E.C. *Century of the Manikin.* Code No. UQ1018. First edition. First printing, August 1972. 142 pp. Cover art by Jack Gaughan. Later published in U.K. by Millington (1975). $.95.

Dale Tulliver was his name, and he was a product of the 21st Century, the era of non-violence, permanent peace, and the drugs that controlled warlike emotions. He was a police agent of the Peace Committee that controlled the world.

Naomi Constance Fisher was her name, and she had been a crusading writer of the 20th Century. She had been a vigorous advocate of world peace, women's liberation, and social progress. She had been frozen in near-death all those decades, and then they brought her back to life to enjoy the fruits of her thinking. But, instead of augmenting the forces of peace, it turned out that what Dale's world meant by peace and what Naomi meant by peace were two different and violently conflicting things. The mixture could shatter civilization.

(Bibliographer's query: So where's Earl Dumarest already?)

Logo No. 19. Ball, Brian N. *The Regiments of Night*. Code No. UQ1019. First edition. First printing, August 1972. 188 pp. Also published in U.K. by Sidgwick & Jackson (1972) as *Night of the Robots*. Cover art by Kelly Freas. $.95.

Archeologists considered the legend superstition and poked about among the surface ruins. Tourists regarded the tales as tourism ads to glamorize a burned-out world. Robots believed only what they saw, and none had ever seen such an army.

But, when a combination of all three tripped the alarm by accident, they found reality turned suddenly into nightmare, as the Black Army awoke to march against the universe!

Logo No. 20. Hubbard, L. Ron. *Ole Doc Methuselah*. Code No. UQ1020. First paperback edition. First printing, August 1972. 190 pp. Cover art by Josh Kirby. Published earlier by Theta Press (1971). $.95.

Contents:
Ole Doc Methuselah (October 1947)
The Expensive Slaves (November 1947)
Her Majesty's Aberration (March 1948)
The Great Air Monopoly (September 1948)
Plague (April 1949)
A Sound Investment (June 1949)
Ole Mother Methuselah (January 1950)
(Bibliographer's note: The "Doc Methuselah" stories all originally appeared in *Astounding Science Fiction* under the pseudonym of Rene Lafayette. The issue of first publication appears above next to the story title.)

Logo No. 21. Laumer, Keith. *Dinosaur Beach*. Code No. UQ1021. First paperback edition. First printing, September 1972. 151 pp. Cover art by Kelly Freas. A shorter version of this novel first appeared in the August 1969 issue of *Analog* under the title, "The Time Sweepers." Originally published by Scribner (1971). Later published in U.K. by Hale (1973). $.95.

Appearing from the remote future, Nexx Central agent Ravel is emplaced in America of 1936. His mission: to undo successive tamperings of the time stream which threaten the survival of mankind. He falls in love with a charming, simple girl, Lisa, but, in the midst of his happiness, is

7

called away to Dinosaur Beach.

Dinosaur Beach is a Nexx Central station located millions of years in the past, in the Jurassic Age. Shortly after Ravel's arrival, the station is attacked and destroyed, and Ravel begins a terrifying odyssey through time. The attackers were another time-tampering team from a still different future era. Not only is Ravel himself in growing danger, but all the human world as we know it.

Logo No. 22. Friedell, Egon. *The Return of the Time Machine.* Code No. UQ1022. First U.S. edition and first English language edition. First printing, September 1972. 127 pp. Cover art and illustrations by Karel Thole. Translated by Eddy C. Bertin. Originally published as *Die Reise mit der Zeitmaschine* (1946) by R. Piper & Co., Munich. $.95.

H.G. Wells' world-famous novel, *The Time Machine*, the story of the inventor of a time-travelling machine and his trip in it to the far future, is a classic that has thrilled the world in books and films since the turn of the century. But there had never been a known sequel to it.

Now such a sequel has been found, and this book is the presentation of its first appearance in English. Written by an admirer and correspondent of Wells, the critic, Egon Freidell, it was available during Wells' lifetime, but only in a limited U.S. Military Government German-language edition published right after the war.

This is the rest of the story of Wells' Time Traveller, of his further visits to the future, and of the Time Machine's desperate entanglement with the past. Like the original classic, it contains thought-provoking theories of time and society.

(Bibliographer's note: At the 1986 Pulpcon, at which Don Wollheim was a guest of honor, he stated that he believed *The Time Machine* was the best science fiction novel ever written. If memory serves me, he called it a "gem," and he's the gemologist who would know.)

Logo No. 23. Brunner, John. *The Stardroppers.* Code No. UQ1023. First edition thus. First printing, September 1972. 144 pp. Cover art by Jack Gaughan. A much shorter and different version of this novel was published by Ace (1963) under the title, *Listen! The Stars!.* The DAW version was later published in the U.K. by Hamlyn (1982). $.95.

A stardropper got its name from the belief that the user was eavesdropping on the stars. But that was only a guess; nobody really knew what the instrument did.

The instrument itself made no sense scientifically. A conventional earpiece, an amplifier, and a power source were all attached to a small vacuum box, an alnice magnet, and a calibrated "tuner." What you got from all this was some very extraordinary noises and the conviction that you were listening to beings from space and could almost understand what you were hearing.

What brought Special Agent Dan Cross into the stardropper problem was the carefully censored news that users of the instrument had begun to disappear. They popped out of existence suddenly, and the world's leaders began to suspect that, somehow, the fad had lit the fuse on a bomb that would either destroy the world or change it forever.

Logo No. 24. Trimble, Louis. *The City Machine.* Code No. UQ1024. First edition. First printing, September 1972. 143 pp. Cover art by Kelly Freas. $.95.

The entire population of that colonized planet was crowded into one all-enclosed, self-functioning city construction. For the majority, the situation was like living forever in the steerage of an immigrant freighter. For a few, there were some privileges, and, for the Highs, power and luxury had been secured by a change of language and the destruction of the old books.

That was where the man Ryne came in. For he was the last who could read the original language, and, if they could ever locate the machine that could build new cities, he'd be the only one to read the instructions.

Logo No. 25. Jakes, John. *Mention My Name in Atlantis.* Code No. UQ1025. First edition. First printing, October 1972. 142 pp. Cover art by H.J Bruck; frontispiece by Jack Gaughan. See Schlobin, *The Literature of Fantasy* 555 (1979). $.95.

The continent of Atlantis had troubles enough before Conax the Barbarian washed ashore. For Hoptor the Vintner, who considered himself a citizen of importance, things were going from bad to worse. The king was on his last legs, his generals were plotting, there were those scary lights in the sky, and Hoptor's favorite girl was being put up for auction on the slave block.

Then Conax, the self-styled king of Chimeria, a place nobody ever heard of, turned up at the auction with his broadsword, his barbaric manners, and his hair-trigger temper.

That was the last straw. From then on Atlantis was doomed!
(Bibliographer's note: Robert E. Howard's Conan, parodied.)

Logo No. 26. Brunner, John. *Entry to Elsewhen.* Code No. UQ1026. First edition. First printing, October 1972. 172 pp. Cover art and illustrations by Jack Gaughan. "Host Age" first appeared in *New Worlds SF* (1955). "Lungfish" first appeared in Great Britain in *Science Fantasy* (1957) and in the U.S. in *Fantastic Universe* (under the title "Rendezvous with Destiny) (1958). "No Other Gods But Me" first appeared in shorter and substantially different form as "A Time to Rend" in *Science Fantasy* (1956) and in its present form in *No Other Gods But Me*, Compact Books (1966). $.95.

Contents:
Host Age
Lungfish
No Other Gods But Me
(Bibliographer's note: First U.S. publication of "Host Age" and "No Other Gods But Me.")

Logo No. 27. Swann, Thomas Burnett. *Green Phoenix*. Code No. UQ1027. First edition. First printing, October 1972. 141 pp. Cover art by George Barr. See Schlobin, *The Literature of Fantasy* 1017 (1979). $.95.

"Phoenix, said the Lady of the Bees, I'm going to live for a long time. When you're an old, old man and your father is dead, I'll still be much as you see me now. That city he's going to build—it may not be the one. The Second Troy, I mean, predestined by the gods. But in time there will be such a city, and somehow I'm going to be there to see it built. Who knows, I may help to consecrate the ground or lay the first stone!

Anyway, I'll be keeping a watchful eye on your great-great-great grandchildren, and I can tell you now that they need never fear the forest, neither lions nor vengeful queens."

That was a brief idea of the way the past was prior to the dawn of history, when the Earth did not belong solely to humanity, and there were other intelligent species still fighting a last-stand battle against extinction. These are the beings remembered today only in legend, creatures of the trees and water, beings that combined beast and man, with strange lore of their own and sciences lost to the human victors.

(Bibliographer's note: A sequel to *Lady of the Bees*.)

Logo No. 28. Dickson, Gordon R. *Sleepwalker's World*. Code No. UQ1028. First paperback edition. First printing, October 1972. 158 pp. Cover art by Kelly Freas. Originally published by J.B. Lippincott (1971). Later published in U.K. by Hale (1973). $.95.

Shafts driven deep into the Earth's hot core utilized that buried energy to run the world's power station. That broadcast energy alone kept the food factories running. Without those factories and that power, the hungry, overpopulated planet couldn't survive. But the cost was high, for the power broadcasts had a terrifying side-effect. While they were on, the human race was unable to stay awake.

Among the rare few with immunity to the sleep compulsion was the astronaut Rafe Arnaul Harald, one of six who had been training on the Moon for the first star voyage. But now, unless humanity could conquer the dark power that was using the sleep phenomenon to paralyze society, that flight might never be made. To defeat the unknown masters of the sleeping world, Rafe had only the help of a crippled girl, a wolf with a very special ability, and the unique talents of his own mind and body.

(Bibliographer's note: The only SF novel selected by *The New York Times* as one of the "Hundred Best Books of the Year.")

Logo No. 29. Aldiss, Brian W. *The Book of Brian Aldiss*. Code No. UQ1029. First edition. First printing, November 1972. 191 pp. Cover art by Karel Thole. Published later in the U.K. by New English Library (1973) as *The Comic Inferno*. $.95.

Contents:

Introduction	All the World's Tears
Comic Inferno	Amen and Out
The Underprivileged	The Soft Predicament

10

Logo No. 30. Carter, Lin. *Under the Green Star.* Code No. UQ1030. First edition. First printing, November 1972. 144 pp. Cover art and illustrations by Tim Kirk. $.95.

On Earth, life held for him the fate of a recluse, confined to daydreams and the lore of ancient wonders, destined never to share them, until he found the formula that enabled him to cross interstellar space.

It was then that the world that revolved around an unnamed green star drew him, and, as the usurper of the body of the tree-city of Phaolon's fabled hero, he was to experience in flesh-and-blood all that his heroic fantasies had yearned for. For there was a princess to be saved, an invader to be thwarted, and other-world monsters to be faced.

(Bibliographer's note: The first novel in the Green Star saga. The book concludes with an author's note on the "Burroughs Tradition.")

Logo No. 31. Coney, Michael G. *Mirror Image.* Code No. UQ1031. First edition. First printing, November 1972. 174 pp. Cover art by Kelly Freas; frontispiece by Jack Gaughan. Later published in U.K. in hardcover by Gollancz (1973). $.95.

They named the planet after the pretty wife of the corporation's boss. The planet itself seemed not so pretty; the first impression of the indentured worker colonists was that it was dull. Then they met the native creatures they called "amorphs."

These changelings had a weird, but effective, defense technique; they changed shapes until they had the form of the most desirable object of any potential predator they encountered. When they met the humans, what happened altered the whole future of the new planet. For, suddenly, the colonists found themselves in possession of a free labor reserve of slaves, fetishes, wives, husbands, and pets, until the time came to pay for their fun. At that point, the mirror image became a vision out of nightmare.

(Bibliographer's note: The author's first book.)

Logo No. 32. Stableford, Brian M. *The Halcyon Drift.* Code No. UQ1032. First edition. First printing, November 1972. 175 pp. Cover art by Jack Gaughan. See *Anatomy of Wonder*, 3-710 (1981); *Survey of Science Fiction Literature II*, pp. 936-939 (1979). Later published in U.K. by Dent (1974). $.95.

Grainger had acquired a second mind; he didn't want it, and it had never asked him for permission. But the disembodied mentalism had invaded his brain during the crack space pilot's castaway months on the edge of the Halcyon Drift.

The Halcyon Drift was a dark nebula within whose electronic chaos the laws of physics were so distorted that space ships could not explore within its vast borders without near-certain catastrophe. But somewhere within the cosmic darkness was the steady distress signal of a vessel lost many years before, a vessel laden with a treasure cargo that could make its finders powerful and wealthy. And it could be that Grainger's mental parasite might be the means by which he alone could penetrate the impenetrable.

(Bibliographer's note: First book of the *Hooded Swan* series.)

Logo No. 33. Akers, Alan Burt (pseud. Kenneth Bulmer). *Transit to Scorpio*. Code No. UQ1033. First edition. First printing, December 1972. 190 pp. Cover art and illustrations by Tim Kirk. Later published in U.K. by Futura (1974). $.95.

On the planet Kregen that circled the brightest star of the Constellation of the Scorpion, two forces contended for that world's destiny. One of them, the Savanti, called in a human pawn from far-away Earth.

His name: Dray Prescot. His role: only the Savanti knew. Dray Prescot confronted a fabulous world: barbaric, unmapped, peopled with both human and inhuman races. But there were always the mysterious Star Lords to watch and check the Savanti's plans. It soon turned out that Dray Prescot himself had to make such decisions as would change him from a mere pawn to a bolder piece on that planetary chessboard.

(Bibliographer's note: The first in the saga of Prescot of Antares (The Delian Cycle).)

Logo No. 34. Trimble, Louis. *The Wandering Variables*. Code No. UQ1034. First edition. First printing, December 1972. 158 pp. Cover art by Kelly Freas; frontispiece by Jack Gaughan. $.95.

Dr. Tandy Venner was an irreplaceable asset to the Charter Worlds Union. When she decided to take a mind-bending vacation with a Euphor Trek team, Jano Kegan was sent along to keep an eye on her. To qualify for the safari across that mad planet, he, too, had to submit to the Trekkers' mental conditioning. What was not on the tour program was the unwritten sidetrack their guide had prepared for Tandy. What was not on the guide's secret detour was the planet's out-of-bounds programming. What was not on either of them was the eccentricity of two brilliant vacationeers breaking all the rules to find out what Euphor was really all about.

Logo No. 35. Barbet, Pierre (pseud. Claude Avice). *Baphomet's Meteor*. Code No. UQ1035. First U.S. and first English language edition. First printing, December 1972. 144 pp. Cover art by Karel Thole. Translated by Bernard Kay. Original edition entitled *L'Empire du Baphomet* (1972), Editions Fleuve Noir, Paris, France. $.95.

Are there parallel dimensions in which history turned out differently? Are there other universes with other Earths where the alternates became the realities? What would have happened had the Knight Templars really made the demoniac alliance claimed by their royal rivals?

The "demon" was Baphomet, a stranded extra-terrestrial, and his alliance gave the Templars the atomic arms and scientific equipment to create the empire that Baphomet needed for his own outer-space motives, an empire upon which our sun never rose.

Logo No. 36. Bradley, Marion Zimmer. *Darkover Landfall.* Code No. UQ1036. First edition. First printing, December 1972. 160 pp. Cover art by Jack Gaughan. See *Anatomy of Wonder* 3-127 (1981); *Survey of Science Fiction Literature I*, pp. 488-492 (1979). Later published in U.K. by Arrow (1978). $.95.

Darkover, planet of wonder, world of mystery, is a truly alien sphere, a world of strange intelligences, of brooding skies beneath a ruddy sun, and of powers unknown to Earth. In this novel, we learn of the original coming of the Earthmen, of the days when Darkover didn't know humanity. This is the flashback in the saga as to what happened when a colonial starship crashlanded on that uncharted planet to encounter, for the first time in human existence, the impact of the Ghost Wind, of the psychic currents that were native only to that world, and of the price that every Earthling must pay before Darkover can claim him for itself.

(Bibliographer's note: Chronologically, the first Darkover novel, although the seventh to be published sequentially.)

Logo No. 37. Goulart, Ron. *A Talent for the Invisible.* Code No. UQ1037. First edition. First printing, January 1973. 144 pp. Cover art and illustrations by Jack Gaughan. $.95.

In 2020 A.D., even 20-20 vision wouldn't help you to see Jack Conger when he was working, because Jack was an operative of the Wild Talents Division of the U.S. Remedial Functions Agency, and his particular specialty was making himself invisible. The RFA sent him where nobody else was able to go.

Another one whom nobody else was able to set eyes upon was the scientist known as the Sandman. The legendary sandman of childhood myth used to put people to sleep. This one woke them up, much to the chagrin of the governments and plotters who had assassinated them.

So they sent the Invisible Man to find the Unseen Resurrectionist.

(Bibliographer's note: And neither could tell who was doing what to whom.)

Logo No. 38. Schmitz, James H. *The Lion Game.* Code No. UQ1038. First edition. First printing, January 1973. 157 pp. Cover art by Kelly Freas. A serial version of this novel appeared in *Analog* in 1971. See *Anatomy of Wonder* 3-644 (1981). Later published in the U.K. by Sidgwick & Jackson (1976). $.95.

Telzey Amberdon was just a college girl, but she was one of the most valuable assets that the human-colonized worlds had. Besides her sharp mind and warm personality, she possessed a most unusual mutant accumulation of talents.

So, when she found herself being hounded by a psi-powered killer, she was not too worried. But, when that incident turned out to be merely the opening gambit in a game of mental chess with a planet of beast-masters who were challenging humanity for the grand-mastery of the universal board, Telzey was put to her full capacity. After all, she was never sure whether she was just someone else's mind-pawn, or really the queen on the human side of the lion game.

(Bibliographer's note: The second Telzey Amberdon novel, following *The Universe Against Her*.)

Logo No. 39. Herbert, Frank. *The Book of Frank Herbert*. Code No. UQ1039. First edition. First printing, January 1973. 189 pp. Cover art by Jack Gaughan. Published later in U.K. by Panther (1977). $.95.

Contents:

Seed Stock	The Gone Dogs
The Nothing	Passage for Piano
Rat Race	Encounter in a Lonely Place
Gambling Device	Operation Syndrome
Looking for Something?	Occupation Force

Logo No. 40. Ball, Brian N. *Planet Probability*. Code No. UQ1040. First edition. First printing, January 1973. 188 pp. Cover art by Kelly Freas. Later published in U.K. by Sidgwick & Jackson (1974). $.95.

The Frames were only a realization of the ultimate form of escape. Books, films, sensors, complete total experience, and, finally, the Frames. The saviors of civilization had shown the way: move the tribes of Americans to Europe, the tribes of Germans to Spain, the tribes of the English to Switzerland and permutate the combinations endlessly. Use trains, then aircraft, then spaceships. The Frames of the Thirtieth Century were a logical extension of the Mechanical Age's exploitation of the means of mass travel. Now, whole populations moved to new areas of experience. New worlds, new re-created worlds, were manufactured for them, and it had all begun on Talisker. But, whatever had left the monstrous scenery on Talisker's desert, had not begun anywhere in our Universe.

(Bibliographer's note: Second novel in the Frames Sequence.)

Logo No. 41. Saberhagen, Fred. *Changeling Earth*. Code No. UQ1041. First edition. First printing, February 1973. 176 pp. Cover art and frontispiece by Tim Kirk. $.95.

The planet was Earth. The time was fifty thousand years from now. Magic and witchcraft worked, and the Old Science didn't.

Why this was nobody knew; it had always been that way during the long tyranny of the Empire of the East. During that same period, there had always been little bands of rebels using fragments of white magic against the demonic armies. Rolf was the latest of these rebels, and he had on his side the mysterious power known as Ardneh.

(Bibliographer's note: Third novel in the *Empire of the East* series, following *The Broken Lands*, Ace (1968) and *The Black Mountains*, Ace (1971). All three, in a greatly revised version, were published under the collective title, *Empire of the East*, by Ace (1979).

Logo No. 42. Pournelle, Jerry. *A Spaceship for the King*. Code No. UQ1042. First edition. First printing, February 1973. 157 pp. Cover art by

Kelly Freas. A serial version of this novel appeared in *Analog* in 1972. $.95.

They had struggled upwards for a thousand years to reach the point that Earth had reached in the early 20th Century, and then the revived Galactic Empire took them over as a colony. There was one condition under which the planet's people could achieve freedom: they had to prove they could build themselves a spaceship on their own know-how. The plans for such a starship existed on an even more backward world, heavily guarded as taboo documents.

So the puppet king called on his former foeman, Nathan MacKinnie, to go and bring back the "sacred" blueprints, without bringing a world-destroying Imperial fleet on his heels.

(Bibliographer's note: While a part of the Co-Dominium series, chronologically, the novel is Post-Falkenberg, the key character in two other Co-Dominium tales, *West of Honor*, Laser (1976) and *The Mercenary*, Pocket Books (1977).)

Logo No. 43. Bayley, Barrington J. *Collision Course.* Code No. UQ1043. First edition. First printing, February 1973. 175 pp. Cover art by Chris Foss. Later issued in hardcover in the U.K. by Allison & Busby (1977) as *Collision with Chronos.* $.95.

The ruins were getting younger. They were thought to be the ruins of an invading force of space monsters that man had defeated during the Dark Ages centuries before. But the ruins were visibly getting newer, apparently rebuilding themselves.

The militarists who had reconstructed society after the supposed invasion were getting panicky. Until they found a complete invader vehicle and learned it traveled through time.

But what was Time? What was Now?

Could there be more than one Time Front, one going forward, one in reverse? And what would happen when two such fronts met in the inevitable collision course?

(Bibliographer's query: Could one then remember the future?)

Logo No. 44. Dick, Philip K. *The Book of Philip K. Dick.* Code No. UQ1044. First edition. First printing, February 1973. 187 pp. Cover art by Karel Thole; frontispiece by Jack Gaughan. Published later in the U.K. by Coronet (1977) as *The Turning Wheel and Other Stories.* $.95.

Contents:

Nanny	The Commuter
The Turning Wheel	A Present for Pat
The Defenders	Breakfast at Twilight
Adjustment Team	Shell Game
Psi-Man	

Logo No. 45. Norton, Andre. *Garan the Eternal.* Code No. UQ1045. First paperback edition. First printing, March 1973. 156 pp. Cover art and frontispiece by Jack Gaughan. Originally published by Fantasy Publishing Co.,

Inc. (1972). $.95.

In our world, he was Garin, jet pilot and explorer. In the lost land of Tav, he was Garan who would supply the link with their most ancient past.

And, in a world far distant in space and time, he was Garan of Yu-Lac, who would stand alone between a planet's doom and the ones he loved.

This is the story of three lives tied by a recurrent destiny: Kepta the Ambitious, Thrala the Divine, and Garan himself, man of three worlds.

Logo No. 46. Phillifent, John T. *King of Argent*. Code No. UQ1046. First edition. First printing, March 1973. 191 pp. Cover art by Kelly Freas. $.95.

They told John Lampart that he would have to have his entire bodily metabolism altered to survive on Argent. Because that unknown planet was his most valuable find, he agreed.

He landed on Argent, golden-skinned and different. He had expected to find himself on a barren world, destined for two years of hard work. But Argent had life of its own of a different kind, weird, wild and endlessly challenging.

Not the least challenge to him was the discovery that his Earthly bosses regarded him as expendable; his work would end in his death while they got rich.

(Bibliographer's note: Some great job.)

Logo No. 47. Gordon, Stuart (pseud. Richard Gordon). *Time Story*. Code No. UQ1047. First U.S. edition. First printing, March 1973. 160 pp. Cover art by Josh Kirby. Originally published in U.K. by New English Library (1972). $.95.

Her name was Hawisa. She died in 1992 in an effort to kill Kitson. Her name was Hawinda. She risked her life in 1996 to save Kitson. His name was Kitson. He got away with the theft of the Moongem reactor stones. His name was Denzil Amiss. As Twilight Journeyman 356, he couldn't get his hands on the Moongems.

But Hawisa and Hawinda were the same person! Kitson and Amiss were the same person!

(Bibliographer's note: The author's first book.)

Logo No. 48. Farmer, Philip Jose. *The Other Log of Phileas Fogg*. Code No. UQ1048. First edition. First printing, March 1973. 191 pp. Cover art and illustrations by Jack Gaughan. Published later in U.K. by Hamlyn (1979). $.95.

This is the story Jules Verne did not tell in *Around the World in Eighty Days*. Who was Phileas Fogg really, this man whose origins were shrouded in mystery and whose actions were guided as if by clockwork? How could he compute the probabilities of future events so accurately?

The Other Log of Phileas Fogg tells what went on behind the scenes during Fogg's unprecedented trip, in which not only do two alien races contend for Earth's mastery, but there appear some even more famous characters one never suspected were involved in the globe-girdling race!

Logo No. 49. Akers, Alan Burt (pseud. Kenneth Bulmer). *The Suns of Scorpio.* Code No. UQ1049. First edition. First printing, April 1973. 192 pp. Cover art and illustrations by Tim Kirk. Published later in U.K. by Futura (1974). $.95.

Slave of the Colossus builders or scourge of the inland sea? Both roles awaited Dray Prescot on his return to Kregen. Torn between two contending forces, the Star Lords and the Savanti, Prescot himself wanted only to find his beloved, the Princess Delia of the Blue Mountains. But the powers that had drawn him across interstellar space to the world that orbited the two suns of the brightest star in the Constellation Scorpio had set him a task, the nature of which even he could not fully estimate.

(Bibliographer's note: The second book in the saga of Prescot of Antares (The Delian Cycle).)

Logo No. 50. Lafferty, R.A. *Strange Doings.* Code No. UQ1050. First paperback edition. First printing, April 1973. 192 pp. Cover art and illustrations by Jack Gaughan. Published earlier by Scribner (1971). $.95.

Contents:

Rainbird	World Abounding
Camels and Dromedaries, Clem	Dream
Continued on Next Rock	Ride a Tin Can
Once on Aranea	Aloys
Sodom and Gomorrah, Texas	Entire and Perfect Chrysolite
The Man with the Speckled Eyes	Incased in Ancient Rind
All But the Words	The Ugly Sea
The Transcendent Tigers	Cliffs That Laughed

Logo No. 51. Herck, Paul Van. *Where Were You Last Pluterday?* Code No. UQ1051. First U.S. and first English language edition. First printing, April 1973. 159 pp. Cover by Karel Thole. Original edition entitled *Sam, of de Pluterdag*, published by Meulenhoff Nederland N.V. (1968). Translated by Danny De Laet and Willy Magiels. $.95.

The day they banned science fiction was the day that Sam, sf writer, encountered the enigma of Pluterday. Looking for a new way of making a living, he had met the daughter of a millionaire and made a date with her. She said, "Meet me next Pluterday."

But when was Pluterday? Sam's efforts to find out became a quest that turned his world upside down several times over. For it took him back and forth in time, it took him through several incarnations, it made him the biggest laughingstock of the little green Martians that infested the Earth.

(Bibliographer's note: Winner of the 1972 Europa Award as the best SF novel from its part of the world.)

Logo No. 52. Biggle, Lloyd Jr. *The Light That Never Was.* Code No. UQ1052. First paperback edition. First printing, April 1973. 192 pp. Cover art by Kelly Freas. Published earlier by Doubleday (1972). Published later in U.K. by Elmfield Press (1975). $.95.

Art critics are notoriously inhuman, and, on Donov, many of them were physically inhuman as well. Donov was a planet devoted to the arts. People came from all over the galaxy to attend its galleries and meet its artists. And many of its best artists were not human either.

But, when a rising tide of anti-alien pogroms and riots began zeroing in on Donov from outer space, it became clear that there was a plot afoot that had nothing to do with art criticism. It had to do with planetary genocide.

Logo No. 53. Wollheim, Donald A. with Arthur W. Saha eds. *The 1973 Annual World's Best SF.* Code No. UQ1053. First edition. First printing, May 1973. 253 pp. Cover art by Jack Gaughan. See *Anatomy of Wonder* 3-911 (1981). $.95.

Contents:

Introduction	The Editor
Goat Song	Poul Anderson
The Man Who Walked Home	James Tiptree, Jr
Oh, Valinda!	Michael G. Coney
The Gold at the Starbow's End	Frederik Pohl
To Walk a City's Street	Clifford D. Simak
Rorqual Maru	T.J. Bass
Changing Woman	W. Macfarlane
"Willie's Blues"	Robert J. Tilley
Long Shot	Vernor Vinge
Thus Love Betrays Us	Phyliss MacLennon

Logo No. 54. Tubb, E.C. *Mayenne.* Code No. UQ1054. First edition. First printing, May 1973. 159 pp. Cover art by Kelly Freas. Published later in U.K. by Arrow (1977). $.95.

The planet was without a star of its own. It was from another galaxy, it was uninhabited, and it was sentient. In its own way, it might have been the most powerful single intelligent entity in the universe. But it knew nothing about humanity.

So, when it picked up the survivors of a wrecked space-liner, it was confronted by mysteries. What were men? What were women? What was emotion? What, especially, was love?

Whether any of the desperate handful could survive the devilish series of planet-wide laboratory tests the alien world devised to solve these mysteries would depend on whether any single one of them could answer such eternal riddles.

Dumarest—and Mayenne—thought they could.

(Bibliographer's note: The eighth Dumarest novel.)

Logo No. 55. Dickson, Gordon R. *The Book of Gordon Dickson.* Code No. UQ1055. First paperback edition. First printing, May 1973. 205 pp. Cover art by Karel Thole. Original title: *Danger-Human*, published by Doubleday (1970). $.95.

Contents:

Danger-Human	An Honorable Death
Dolphin's Way	Flat Tiger

And Then There Was Peace	James
The Man from Earth	The Quarry
Black Charlie	Call Him Lord
Zeepsday	Steel Brother
Lulungomeena	

Logo No. 56. Coney, Michael G. *Friends Come in Boxes*. Code No. UQ1056. First edition. First printing, May 1973. 160 pp. Cover art by John Holmes. Published later in the U.K. by Gollancz (1974). $.95.

The problem of immortality was solved in the 21st Century. It was a matter of successful brain transference. When you reached forty, your brain was removed and transferred to the head of a six-months-old infant. In that way, you got another forty years of life, until you could do it all over again. It solved the population crisis as well. After all, who wanted to have a baby that would soon become a total adult stranger mentally?

So there was a growing waiting period between transfers, and, in the interim, the disembodied brains were conscious in special boxes known as Friendship Boxes. If you would be companion to such a box, you would be truly charitable. But, as the old saying might have it, if you had a Friend in a Box, you didn't need any enemies.

(Bibliographer's note: It's something like Janitor in a Drum.)

Logo No. 57. Clement, Hal (pseud. Harry Clement Stubbs). *Ocean on Top*. Code No. UQ1057. First edition. First printing, June 1973. 141 pp. Cover art by Jack Gaughan. Magazine serial version appeared in *Worlds of If* (1967). Later published in U.K. by Sphere (1976). $.95.

The world's energy was limited, and, with overpopulation and a high level of technology, the Power Board had virtually become the real government of the world. Power was rationed, it was guarded, it was sacred.

Thus, when three of the Power Board's agents disappeared at sea, and there was evidence that something irregular was happening to the energy quota in that area, it was cause for real alarm.

Logo No. 58. Lundwall, Sam J. *Bernhard the Conqueror*. Code No. UQ1058. First edition. First printing, June 1973. 159 pp. Cover art and frontispiece by Tim Kirk. $.95.

What's a hundred thousand years more or less to the universe? To ex-private Bernhard breaking rocks on a prison planet, every day felt like an eternity. To the myriads of people, robots and self-thinking servo-mechanisms aboard the twenty-thousand mile long spaceship *Refanut*, it seemed like just another day on their endless trip.

But, when Bernhard escaped to the *Refanut*, things changed sharply. For all the machinery on the fabulous starship, pride of a long forgotten galactic empire, had been accidentally programmed to adore Bernhard, and all its people would just as gladly cut his throat.

Logo No. 59. Stableford, Brian M. *Rhapsody in Black*. Code No. UQ1059.

First edition. First printing, June 1973. 157 pp. Cover art by Kelly Freas. Later published in U.K. by Dent (1975). $.95.

The planet was a sponge of stone and metal, honeycombed with millions of narrow passages, hidden lightless caves, and scurrying pale colonists who hated the stars and the men who came from them. Somewhere amid the lightless maze, there was a newly found treasure: a thing, nobody knew just what, that would make its owner either richer than any emperor had ever dreamed or give its finder power beyond any imperial army's weapons.

Grainger, pilot of the starcraft *Hooded Swan*, was down there in the darkness hunting. Not for himself, but for the unscrupulous men who held his soul in bondage. But the alien second mind that was parasitic to Grainger's owed no other human allegiance. To its inscrutable way of thinking, the potency of the unknown discovery could move a universe.

(Bibliographer's note: Second book in the *Hooded Swan* series.)

Logo No. 60. Goulart, Ron. *What's Become of Screwloose? And Other Inquiries.* Code No. UQ1060. First paperback edition. First printing, June 1973. 157 pp. Cover art by Josh Kirby. Published earlier by Scribner (1971). $.95.

Contents:

What's Become of Screwloose?	Confessions
Junior Partner	Monte Cristo Complex
Hardcastle	The Yes-Men of Venus
Into the Shop	Keeping an Eye on Janey
Prez	Hobo Jungle

Logo No. 61. Brunner, John. *The Wrong End of Time.* Code No. UQ1061. First paperback edition. First printing, July 1973. 160 pp. Cover art by Chris Foss. Published earlier by Doubleday (1971). Later published in U.K. by Methuen (1975). $.95.

The time is the future. The place, an America so isolated by fear that it is cut off from the rest of the world by a massive defense system. Into this armed, barricaded state comes a young Russian scientist bearing a strange, and almost unbelievable, story.

Superior, intelligent life of a far higher order than any on earth has been detected near the planet Pluto. Immune themselves by virtue of their far greater intelligence, these Aliens are about to destroy the planet Earth.

The only person who can provide the solution is a brilliant and clairvoyant young American Black, hunted by the ever-present police, hidden far within the turbulent, festering slum of one of America's jungle cities. Somehow he must be found, and found before the planet melts in one final holocaust.

Logo No. 62. Carter, Lin. *When the Green Star Calls.* Code No. UQ1062. First edition. First printing, July 1973. 176 pp. Cover art and illustrations by Luis Dominguez. $.95.

To him, his native Earth was a prison of the mind and body. For him, only the lure of the wonder world that revolved in the rays of the nameless green star was worth the struggle to live. Finally the call came.

But awaiting him there was only the body of a primitive youth, while the city of his beloved princess was far away. Once revived, he found himself the puppet of a half-mad experimenter in immortality and the companion of the last living monster of a race that had once been ruler of that world.

(Bibliographer's note: The second book in the Green Star saga.)

Logo No. 63. Farmer, Philip Jose. *The Book of Philip Jose Farmer.* Code No. UQ1063. First edition. First printing, July 1973. 239 pp. Cover art by Jack Gaughan. Later published in U.K. by Elmfield Press (1976). $.95.

Contents:

Foreword	The Voice of the Sonar in my
My Sister's Brother	Vermiform Appendix
Skinburn	Brass and Gold
The Alley Man	Only Who Can Make a Tree?
Father's in the Basement	An Exclusive Interview with
Toward the Beloved City	Lord Greystoke
Polytropical Paramyths	Sexual Implications of the Charge
Totem and Taboo	of the Light Brigade
Don't Wash the Carats	The Obscure Life and Hard Times
The Sumerian Oath	of Kilgore Trout
Thanks for the Feast	by Leslie A. Fiedler

Logo No. 64. Snyder, Guy. *Testament XXI.* Code No. UQ1064. First edition. First printing, July 1973. 144 pp. Cover art by Kelly Freas. $.95.

When Astronaut Williamson returned after the longest flight ever made, he found that the great civilization that had launched him was gone, destroyed in a chaos of its own creation. But, somewhere in what had once been Michigan, the Republic welcomed him back. The Republic that was a kingdom: the Republic that consisted of one underground city ruled by a weakling monarch and a power-hungry priesthood.

Logo No. 65. Akers, Alan Burt (pseud. Kenneth Bulmer). *Warrior of Scorpio.* Code No. UQ1065. First edition. First printing, August 1973. 190 pp. Cover art and illustrations by Tim Kirk. Published later in U.K. by Futura (1975). $.95.

Once again in the grip of the Star Lords of the Constellation Scorpio, Dray Prescot found himself torn from the battles of the Inner Sea for a mission in the air. For it was now his duty to carry his betrothed Delia by airboat to that far kingdom from whence she had come. But the route lay across the gaunt mountains and shadowy jungles of the Hostile Territories, and, there, Dray was to be plunged among stranger peoples and more fantastic challenges than even his Kregen princess had known.

(Bibliographer's note: The third adventure in the saga of Dray Prescot.)

Logo No. 66. Anvil, Christopher (pseud. Harry C. Crosby). *Pandora's*

Planet. Code No. UQ1066. First paperback edition. First printing, August 1973. 192 pp. Cover art by Kelly Freas. This novel was developed from a short story entitled "Pandora's Planet," which was first published in *Analog* in 1956. Published earlier in book form by Doubleday (1972). $.95.

"If you can't lick 'em, join 'em" is an old rule of politics and warfare. So, when the various armies of Earth, divided as they were between suspicious nations, were unable to lick the single-minded invading Centrans who ruled a complacent galactic empire, they surrendered and decided to give their leonine conquerors everything that humans could wholeheartedly grant.

So they exported installment payments, loan sharks, communism, fascism, planned obsolescence, food fads, religious cults, and all the other delights we are so accustomed to on our own world. Out there among the orderly stars, all these goodies were received with gaping jaws and open arms, until the Terrestrial tail was very soon wagging the Centran lion, and the military might of the conquerors faced the unprecedented problem of how to turn their glorious victory into a secure defeat if only their victims would let them!

Logo No. 67. Walker, David. *The Lord's Pink Ocean.* Code No. UQ1067. First paperback edition. First printing, August 1973. 160 pp. Cover art by Josh Kirby. Published earlier by Houghton Mifflin (1972). $.95.

This novel is the story of two feuding families isolated in the last fertile valley of North America after the world's oceans have turned toxic and the lands gray with total death.

(Bibliographer's note: Eerily, this book was published at the same time that newspapers were reporting a "red tide" of mutated algae that had destroyed millions of fish along the sea coast. The red tide slowly went away—then. What might the future bring?)

Logo No. 68. Klein, Gerard. *Starmasters' Gambit.* Code No. UQ1068. First U.S. and first English language edition. First printing, August 1973. 172 pp. Cover art by Kelly Freas. Translated by C.J. Richards. Original edition entitled *Le Gambit des Etoiles,* published by Librairie Hachette (1958) and Biblioteque Marabout (1971). See *Anatomy of Wonder* 3-435 (1981). $.95.

As colonists penetrated the galaxy, a series of strange legends accumulated about the worlds just beyond the rim of our exploration. These legends told of vast black citadels built by pre-human intelligences that dominated certain deserted planets. The legends agreed that these colossal structures were not only impenetrable to explorers, but were still, in some mysterious way, activated.

This is the story of Jerg Algan, into whose restless hands fell the key to the citadels. This is the story of Jerg Algan, whose fate it was to be a "knight" on a cosmic chessboard, leaping from planet to planet as a gambit, a chess sacrifice move, to check the dark monarch who ruled the farther half of the Milky Way.

(Bibliographer's note: Winner of the Prix Jules Verne for 1958.)

Logo No. 69. Dickson, Gordon R. *The Pritcher Mass.* Code No. UQ1069. First paperback edition. First printing, September 1973. 158 pp. Cover art by Kelly Freas. Published earlier by Doubleday (1972). $.95.

The only hope for mankind's survival after the contamination of the Earth lay in the Pritcher Mass, a psychic forcefield construction out beyond the orbit of Pluto. Created by the efforts of individuals with extraordinary paranormal powers, the Mass was designed to search the universe for a new habitable planet.

Chaz Sant knew he had the kind of special ability to contribute effectively to the building of the Mass, but, somehow, the qualifying tests were stacked against him. Then he learned that he had become the special target of an insidious organization that fattened on the fears of the last cities of the world. His confrontation with this organization, their real motives and his unexpected reactions, were to touch off the final showdown for mankind's last enterprise.

Logo No. 70. Coney, Michael G. *The Hero of Downways.* Code No. UQ1070. First edition. First printing, September 1973. 188 pp. Cover art by Josh Kirby. Later published in U.K. by Futura (1974). $.95.

Once there was a Hero who confronted the dreaded Daggertooth and slew it. Unfortunately he was also slain by it, but the legend persisted. If it could be done once, then another Hero could be raised to do it again, because the Daggertooth was dangerous to hibernating humanity. All people--all that anyone knew of--lived far underground in tunnels built for safety and hibernation. The Daggertooth was a mass killer, more so even than the hideous Oddlies, the outcasts of the darker tunnels.

This is the story of John-A, the "vatkid" who was trained to be a second Hero; the story of "trukid" Shirl who taught John-A what to do; Threesum, the Oddlies' leader, who scoffed at heroes; and the Elders who frowned at all the risky goings-on.

Logo No. 71. Bradley, Marion Zimmer. *Hunters of the Red Moon.* Code No. UQ1071. First edition. First printing, September 1973. 176 pp. Cover art by George Barr. Published later in U.K. by Arrow (1979).

The hunters were fair by their standards, but their standards were utterly inhuman. They kidnapped intelligent beings from many far-off planets as prey for their hunt. They gave them their choice of the best weapons available, allowed them plenty of time to practice, gave them a "chance."

If the prey could survive until the next eclipse of the red moon, wealth and freedom would be theirs. The catch was this: nobody knew what the hunters looked like. How then do you outwit an enemy who might look like your best friend, your comrade-in-arms, or like a monster that could slay an army?

Logo No. 72. Brunner, John. *From This Day Forward.* Code No. UQ1072. First edition. First printing, September 1973. 176 pp. Cover art by Kelly Freas. Published earlier by Doubleday (1972). $.95.

Contents:

The Biggest Game	The Vitanuls
The Trouble I See	Factsheet Six
An Elixer for the Emperor	Fifth Commandment
Wasted on the Young	Fairy Tale
Even Chance	The Inception of the Epoch of
Planetfall	Mrs. Bedonebyasyoudid
Judas	The Oldest Glass

(Bibliographer's note: All of the above stories were revised by the author for this book.)

Cap Kennedy #1. Kern, Gregory (pseud. E.C. Tubb). *Galaxy of the Lost.* Code No. UT1073. First edition. First printing, September 1973. 125 pp. Cover art by Jack Gaughan. Later published in U.K. by Mews (1976). $.75.

Free Acting Terran Envoy: Throughout the inhabited galaxy, that spelled FATE. FATE meant Earth's troubleshooter against the unknown sciences and alien psychologies of a thousand worlds. It meant: Cap Kennedy, Free Acting Terran Envoy, Secret Agent of the Spaceways, a man of courage facing a hostile universe.

Logo No. 73. Gunn, James. *Breaking Point.* Code No. UQ1074. First paperback edition. First printing, October 1973. 173 pp. Cover art by Michael Gilbert. Published earlier by Walker (1972). $.95.

Contents:

Introduction	The Man Who Owned Tomorrow
Breaking Point	Green Thumb
A Monster Named Smith	The Power and the Glory
Cinderella Story	The Listeners
Teddy Bear	Translations

Logo No. 74. Tubb, E.C. *Jondelle.* Code No. UQ1075. First edition. First printing, October 1973. 159 pp. Cover art by Kelly Freas. Published later in U.K. by Arrow (1977). $.95.

Ourell was the closest planet to legendary Earth that Earl Dumarest had reached. There, the legend of the Original People persisted among the several strange races that populated this world out along a far arm of the Milky Way.

Somehow, the boy named Jondelle held the key to further data in Earl's quest, but, before he could obtain it, the child was kidnapped. The pursuit of the kidnappers led directly to the weirdest, most vicious race of all, to a city of paranoiac killers in a country of madmen whose hair-trigger tempers and erratic violences terrified the rest of that world.

But it was there and there alone that Dumarest could pick up the trail that led to Jondelle and to long-lost Terra.

(Bibliographer's note: The tenth Dumarest book.)

Logo No. 75. Norton, Andre. *The Crystal Gryphon.* Code No. UQ1076. First paperback edition. First printing, October 1973. 192 pp. Cover art by

Jack Gaughan. Published earlier in U.S. by Atheneum (1972) and in the U.K. by Gollancz (1973). See *Fantasy Literature*, pp. 152-153 (1979); Schlobin, *The Literature of Fantasy* 835 (1979). $.95.

This novel relates the story of Kerovan, half-human, half-something-else, who sought his rightful heritage to the throne of Ulm at a time when strange sea invaders were shattering the old kingdoms, and equally enig-matic manifestations of the Old Ones were coming again to interfere with humanity.

(Bibliographer's note: A Witch World novel.)

Logo No. 76. Gordon, Stuart (pseud. Richard Gordon). *One-Eye.* Code No. UQ1077. First edition. First printing, October 1973. 224 pp. Cover art by Tim Kirk. Later published in U.K. by Sidgwick & Jackson (1974). $.95.

They fought for racial purity in Phadraig. All around were monsters, but the stern hierarchy of the old city was ruthless. Patrick Cormac was their great defender; where he stood, the mutants would be halted.

But the long-heralded birth of the one-eyed babe broke the tradition. Not only was it impossible to slay this god-to-be, but Patrick himself became its first convert.

Beyond the walls of Phadraig lay the route to the new era that was to be, and, there, Patrick and his brave companions brought One-Eye to the mutants and to the tower where the last of the old science-wizardry still held the centuries in thrall.

(Bibliographer's note: First book in The Eye trilogy.)

Cap Kennedy #2. Kern, Gregory (pseud. E.C. Tubb). *Slave Ship from Sergan.* Code No. UT1078. First edition. First printing, October 1973. 127 pp. Cover art by Jack Gaughan. Published later in U.K. by Mews (1976). $.75.

To the reptilian mind, especially the intelligent type on planets like Sergan and Obrac, the lives of others were as nothing to the need for status. To the feline mind, especially to the clever advisor of the master of Sergan, the agonies of others were not only of no consequence, they could even be a source of joy.

So when these two types of inhuman intelligences got together to defy the Terran orders against interplanetary kidnapping, space hijacking, and human slavery, it was definitely a case for a top-notch secret agent.

The secret agent was Cap Kennedy, Free Acting Terran Envoy, because Earth could not afford a showdown with more than one alien species at a time.

Logo No. 77. Wylie, Philip. *The End of the Dream.* Code No. UQ1079. First paperback edition. First printing, November 1973. 206 pp. Cover art by Podium II. Published earlier, posthumously, by Doubleday (1972). Published later in U.K. by Elmfield Press (1975) $.95.

"The superb imagination of Philip Wylie, plus his burning desire to save mankind from its own wilful, unheeding poisoning of the air, land, sea and rivers, plus his very deep knowledge of the environment and its perils, make this novel of the near-destruction of a world seem like factual history rather than a look into the future . . .

"The incidents that take place as a world turns to waste and its population perishes are spectacular. The heroics of the scattered leaders and geniuses, scholars and helpers, struggling to restore bands of people turned wild, and to nurse humanity back to life, are gripping. Wylie's simple, straightforward writing strikes home, as it has in so many of his dozens of books." —Long Beach *Press-Telegram*

Logo No. 78. Rackham, John (pseud. John T. Phillifent). *Beanstalk.* Code No. UQ1080. First edition. First printing, November 1973. 158 pp. Cover art by Kelly Freas. $.95.

Behind every folktale there is a true story, and behind every legend a lost fact of history, distorted by word of mouth of people who did not understand what was really happening. In the case of the infiltration of the highly strategic space station upon which the battle between the Salviar Federation and the Hilax Combine pivoted, the account of Earth's role in the affair has become greatly distorted. Because that was eight hundred years ago, and the men of Olde England never even knew the world was round, let alone that it was a planet.

Earth still doesn't know which side we were on, and, because we are out on a far limb of Galactic Sector Seven, they haven't contacted us yet. But our very position in the Milky Way, just that once, made our little planet strategic, and, when Salviar's scout, Jasar-am-Bax, had to enlist the aid of a clever young yeoman to launch his kamikaze attack, the result became legend.

Logo No. 79. Franke, Herbert W. *The Orchid Cage.* Code No. UQ1082. First U.S. and first English language edition. First printing, November 1973. 174 pp. Cover painting by Vincent DiFate. Translated by Christine Priest. Original edition entitled *Der Orchideenkafig,* published by Wilhelm Verlag Munchen (1961). See *Anatomy of Wonder* 3-328 (1981). $.95.

On a distant planet, not too different from Earth, there stands a mechanized city with no visible inhabitants. Obviously of a highly developed civilization, the questions are who built it, where are they, and what can humans learn from them?

Two teams of explorers enter into a competition to find the answers. There are no holds barred; almost anything goes to win the contest. But the city is capable of meeting trickery with trickery, violence with violence, and murder with justice.

Logo No. 80. Goulart, Ron. *The Tin Angel.* Code No. UQ1083. First edition. First printing, November 1973. 144 pp. Cover art and illustrations by Jack Gaughan. $.95.

Start with some medical transplants, add a dash of cybernetic engineering, and a talking dog can be a commonplace. But Bowser was no commonplace; he was the top-rated star of 1999's television: comedian, commentator, actor, and temperamental headache of the media masters. But he was still a dog, man's best friend to the vast gaping audience of watchers, and a cur, mutt, and son of a five-letter-word to Bert Schenley, his agent and guardian.

So when Bert got two assignments at once, both taking him and Bowser to the battle front in Lower California where the various guerillas and rebels were making news, history and hysterics, it was the climax. Bowser was determined to keep on grabbing the headlines, Bert was determined to keep a grip on his own life, and the rest were equally set on blotting them both out.

(Bibliographer's query: Is Ron Goulart zany, or what?)

Cap Kennedy #3. Kern, Gregory (pseud. E.C. Tubb). *Monster of Metelaze.* Code No. UT1084. First edition. First printing, November 1973. 125 pp. Cover art by Jack Gaughan. $.75.

"Destiny awaits the world of Metelaze. Mighty will be our future. To us will come the races of the galaxy. To us will come the wealth of a universe. "Too long have we rested beneath the Terran heel. Very soon now, we shall strike off the chains of our oppressors. Metelaze shall be free!"

This sort of propaganda was always common among demagogues of backward planets that had received help from Terra. But Metelaze was different. There, the promise held out was that secrets of the ancient pre-galactic science were becoming available, and that an offer was being made that "could not be refused."

To Cap Kennedy fell the task of finding out if there were unknown scientific marvels available on Metelaze? Who was behind these offers of total power and absolute wealth? What, in fact, was the monster of Metelaze? And how could such a monster out of time and space be stopped?

Logo No. 81. Akers, Alan Burt (pseud. Kenneth Bulmer). *Swordships of Scorpio.* Code No. UQ1085. First edition. First printing, December 1973. 191 pp. Cover art and illustrations by Tim Kirk. Later published in U.K. by Futura (1975). $.95.

What does a man do when fate makes him the protector of the royal head of the land of his enemies? If it is Dray Prescot, Earthman on Antares, he sets aside his quest to do his duty.

His quest was to reach Vallia and his princess and help her claim her throne. His duty was to defend Vallia's ancient foe and place its rightful heir on its throne, who was sworn to attack Vallia.

So, when the third force, the pirate fleets known as the swordships, came between the two contending demands, Dray saw that only by following his own personal star could the contradiction be resolved.

(Bibliographer's note: The fourth book in the saga of Dray Prescot of Antares.)

Logo No. 82. Schmitz, James H. *The Telzey Toy.* Code No. UQ1086. First edition. First printing, December 1973. 175 pp. Cover art by Kelly Freas. The four parts of this book appeared individually as novelettes in *Analog* in 1970 and 1971. Later published in U.K. by Sidgwick & Jackson (1975). See *Anatomy of Wonder* 3-644 (1981). $.95.

One Telzey Amberdon was usually more than a match for any ill-intentioned mentalist or alien psi-power, but two? Two might cancel each other out. Or two could mean double the control for whoever could enslave that mutant teen-age potential.

The master operator of the most advanced puppet show on Orado had just such a plan, and, when he created the Telzey Toy, the scheme was set into motion. But which was the real Telzey, and which the perfect duplication? Even the real Telzey did not know, but, when the time came, she was going to put on the act of a lifetime, or that lifetime would be exceedingly short!

(Bibliographer's note: The third Telzey Amberdon book.)

Logo No. 83. Barbet, Pierre (pseud. Claude Avice). *Games Psyborgs Play.* Code No. UQ1087. First U.S. and first English language edition. First printing, December 1973. 158 pp. Cover by George Barr. Translation by Wendayne Ackerman. Original edition entitled *A Quoi Songent les Psyborgs?*; published by Editions Fleuve Noir, Paris, France (1971). $.95.

Captain Setni, of all the officers of space, was the most immune to hypnotic suggestion and psychological delusions. Therefore, when reports reached the Great Brains of a strange new planet in the Hydra group, Setni was the logical astronaut to check it out, because, by all accounts, the planet seemed a double of Old Earth, but of Earth as it had been in the far past, and legendary beings were alive and well there.

Setni was specially trained for the task, but even the best training in disbelief was not sufficient. For, on that pseudo-Earth, not only was Charlemagne in power and knighthood in flower, but the pagan gods were visible, physically real, and devilishly active. Setni knew it was no illusion, but, then, what was the reality?

Logo No. 84. Ball, Brian N. *Singularity Station.* Code No. UQ1088. First edition. First printing, December 1973. 176 pp. Cover art by Chris Foss. Later published in U.K. by Sidgwick & Jackson (1974). $.95.

Robotic minds made interstellar travel possible, but human minds still controlled the destination and purpose of such flight. Conflict develops only when a programmed brain can't evaluate beyond what is visible and substantial, whereas the human mind is capable of infinite imagination, including that which is unreal.

Such was the problem at the singularity in space in which the *Altair Star* and a hundred other vessels had come to grief. At that spot, natural laws seem subverted, and some other universe's rules impinged.

For Buchanan, the station meant a chance to observe and maybe rescue his lost vessel. For the robotic navigators of oncoming spaceships, the meaning was different, and, at Singularity Station, the only inevitable was conflict.

Logo No. 85. Brunner, John. *Polymath.* Code No. UQ1089. First revised edition. First printing, January 1974. 156 pp. Cover art by Vincent DiFate. A shorter and substantially different version of this novel was published in 1963 as one-half of an Ace Books double, under the title, *Castaway's World*. $.95.

Colonizing a new planet requires much more than just settling on a newly discovered island of Old Earth. New planets were different in thousands of ways, different from Earth and from each other. Any of those differences could mean death and disaster to a human settlement.

When a ship filled with refugees from a cosmic catastrophe crash-landed on such an unmapped world, their outlook was precarious. Their ship was lost, salvage had been minor, and everything came to depend on one bright young man accidentally among them.

He was a trainee planet-builder. It would have been his job to foresee all the problems necessary to set up a safe home for humanity. But the problem was that he was a mere student, and he had been studying the wrong planet.

(Bibliographer's note: First book of the Zarathustra Refugee Planet series.)

Logo No. 86. Trimble, Louis. *The Bodelan Way*. Code No. UQ1090. First edition. First printing, January 1974. 158 pp. Cover art by Kelly Freas. $.95.

Margil was not exactly human. She wasn't exactly inhuman either. She was sort of feline, but you couldn't quite call her a pussycat. She could be brilliant when she wanted to be. She could be moody. Her purr was deafening, her love-taps could bowl over an elephant, and her furies were of earthquake intensity.

It was lucky that her instructor in the ideals of peaceful unity, the Earthman, Endo Leduc, was liked by her. Because the things he was teaching Margil went against the principles of Margil's Bodelan home world and especially against the thoughts of her father, who was twice her size and many times more formidable. It was also lucky for the inhabited galaxy that Endo was where he was, because the Bodelan Way was rapidly undermining humanity's grip on the stars, and Margil was the key to it all.

Logo No. 87. Leiber, Fritz. *The Book of Fritz Leiber*. Code No. UQ1091. First edition. First printing, January 1974. 173 pp. Cover art by Jack Gaughan. See *Survey of Science Fiction Literature IV*, pp. 1958-1962 (1979). Later collected with *The Second Book of Fritz Leiber* and published by Gregg Press (1980). $.95.

Contents:

Foreword	King Lear
The Spider	Yesterday House
Monsters and Monster Lovers	After Such Knowledge
A Hitch in Space	Knight to Move
Hottest and Coldest Molecules	Weird World of the Knight
Kindergarten	To Arkham and the Stars
Those Wild Alien Words	The Whisperer Re-examined

Crazy Annaoj
Debunking the I Machine
When the Last Gods Die

Beauty and the Beasts
Masters of Mace and Magic
Cat's Cradle

Logo No. 88. Shea, Michael. *A Quest for Simbilis*. Code No. UQ1092. First edition. First printing, January 1974. 159 pp. Cover art by George Barr. See Schlobin, *The Literature of Fantasy* 949 (1979). $.95.

Cugel the Clever was seeking revenge when he met Mumber Sull who was seeking justice. Revenge and justice may seem phantom concepts when the sun may flicker and go out at any moment, but such is the eternal nature of man as it has always been since the dawn of time.

Mumber Sull owed his loyalty to the long-vanished overlord Simbilis, whose knowledge and science were legendary, whose domains had extended over vast terain, and whose whereabouts had been lost for centuries. He persuaded Cugel that if they could but find Simbilis, they would both gain their just rewards.

(Bibliographer's note: The author's first book. A Cugel the Clever pastiche. Cugel the Clever is one of my favorite characters.)

Cap Kennedy #4. Kern, Gregory (pseud. E.C. Tubb). *Enemy Within the Skull*. Code No. UT1093. First edition. First printing, January 1974. 127 pp. Cover art by Jack Gaughan. $.75.

Within the buried recesses of the human brain, there lurk the ravening beast instincts of a million years ago. Thousands of years of growing intelligence and social culture had buried this deadly strain, until an alien science learned how to release the killer impulse of the Earth-born psyche.

The aliens were willing to sell their know-how to the highest bidder in exchange for an alliance against Terra. This was a serious problem for FATE's Free Acting Terran Envoys, and their top man, Cap Kennedy, was assigned to it. But Cap realized rapidly that the enemy within the skull lurked inside his own mind too, and that cancelling the plot might mean first releasing the demon, thereby turning himself and his friends into monsters that would no longer be men.

Logo No. 89. Blish, James. *Midsummer Century*. Code No. UQ1094. First enlarged edition. First printing, February 1974. 159 pp. Cover art by Josh Kirby. Published earlier by Doubleday (1972) and in the U.K by Faber (1973) without "Skysign" and "A Style in Treason." $.95.

Contents:
Midsummer Century
Skysign
A Style in Treason

Logo No. 90. Conway, Gerard F. (pseud Wallace Moore). *Mindship*. Code No. UQ1095 First edition. First printing, February 1974. 191 pp. Cover art by Kelly Freas. $.95.

The mindship was the break-through to the stars. In spite of work on Faster Than Light, hyperdrives, and such, it was the power of the mind that turned out to be the most certain directing force between the worlds. So the mindships came into being, driven forward by the lines of mental energy, directed by trained crews, and held together not by the navigator or the captain, but by the man they called the cork. He was just another man, but he had the ability to siphon out the discords which could wreck a ship and to create the harmony without which starflight would be disastrous.

Kilgarin was such a "cork," but he had deliberately grounded himself until they forced him to take up the mental reins again. It was their risk, and they should have known better, because Kilgarin had ulterior motives that no ship's cork had a right to harbor.

Logo No. 91. Lumley, Brian. *The Burrowers Beneath.* Code No. UQ1096. First edition. First printing, February 1974. 160 pp. Cover art by Tim Kirk. See *Horror Literature* 4-164 (1981). $.95.

Were humans the first intelligent beings to make themselves masters of this world? Before man emerged from the primeval jungles, might not other beings have dominated this planet, utilized it, contacted the stars, and called Earth theirs?

H.P. Lovecraft's answer was yes, and his famous novels and stories have all been based on that frightening premise: that there are Older Ones who have a prior claim to Earth; that man is but a newcomer who has moved in only by virtue of the indifference of the world's original owners.

(Bibliographer's note: The first of the Titus Crow series in an extension of the Lovecraftian Cthulhu Mythos.)

Logo No. 92. Stableford, Brian M. *Promised Land.* Code No. UQ1097. First edition. First printing, February 1974. 160 pp. Cover art by Kelly Freas. Later published in U.K. by Dent (1975). See *Anatomy of Wonder* 3-710 (1981). $.95.

They had set out from Earth in search of the promised land, and, after centuries of flight, they believed they had found it. It was already inhabited, but by a peaceful and primitive humanoid race that gave them no opposition.

This was the situation when the *Hooded Swan* landed on its information-seeking mission for the vast interstellar libraries of New Alexandria. Grainger, man of the double-mind, realized early that there was something odd about the truce between the xenophobic colonists and the docile natives. It took a fleeing wide-eyed native child to bring the Promised Land suddenly to critical mass. What was there about this little girl that could so take an entire planet to the edge of Kingdom Come? That was what Grainger's minds had to find out—and quickly.

(Bibliographer's note: The third book of the *Hooded Swan* series.)

Cap Kennedy #5. Kern, Gregory (pseud. E.C. Tubb). *Jewel of Jarhen.* Code No. UQ1098. First edition. First printing, February 1974. 143 pp. Cover art by Jack Gaughan. Later published in U.K. by Mews (1976). $.95.

The fate of a terror-ridden world brought all of Cap Kennedy's fabulous team into action, when Cap Kennedy himself was put out of action. Cap's body hung between life and death, while his mind had been thrown back a million miles into the past.

This left his remarkable team members to break the mystery of the pre-galactic artifact on which all horror hinged. Saratov would use his high-G muscles to tear the secret out. Chemile would use his chameleon powers to go where no human had ever been. Luden would seek the answer in super-science.

Between the three, there had to be a way to bring Kennedy back to life—and the Jewel of Jarhen under control. But a world and an aeon were working against them.

Logo No. 93. Klein, Gerard. *The Overlords of War.* Code No. UQ1099. First English language edition. First printing, March 1974. 189 pp. Cover art by Karel Thole. Translated by John Brunner. Original edition entitled *Les Seigneurs de la Guerre*, published by Editions Robert Laffont, S.A., Paris, France (1971). $.95.

This novel focuses on George Corson, an Earthman on a secret mission which, if it comes off, will bring victory to Earth in its long smoldering war with the birdlike inhabitants of the planet Uria.

Central to the scheme is the wild pegasone, the most deadly beast in the known universe, which is just about to bear its horde of young that, between them, could lay waste to an entire planet. But what Corson takes to be a strange accident transporting him 6000 years into the future proves to be nothing of the kind, and he soon finds himself used as a pawn in a cosmic game played by beings as close to gods as any may dare imagine.

Logo No. 94. Swann, Thomas Burnett. *How Are the Mighty Fallen.* Code No. UQ1100. First edition. First printing, March 1974. 160 pp. Cover art and illustrations by George Barr. See Schlobin, *The Literature of Fantasy* 1018 (1979). $.95.

Cyclops and sirens, halfmen and godlings: the stuff of which myths are made and from which worship arises. This tale is of a queen of ancient Judea who was more than human, of her son who became legend, and of their cyclopean nemesis whose name became synonymous with Colossus.

Logo No. 95. Lory, Robert. *Identity Seven.* Code No. UQ1101. First edition. First printing, March 1974. 155 pp. Cover art by Kelly Freas. $.95.

Hunters Associated was the simple name of the organization. Who was behind it and what its ultimate purpose was were never told its agents. All they needed to know was that they covered the galaxy, that their real identities had been buried, and that, once in Hunters, they could be anybody.

He was Seven. That was all. Identity Seven. He had a new assignment. Identity Six had just been slain, lasered down on a far world by enemies unknown. But the death had been kept secret long enough for Seven to be sent to take his place.

To take his place, to take his features, to take his task, and to be a target to be slain once again. If he failed, there would be an Identity Eight to step into his burned-out shoes—and a Nine and a Ten. Seven was determined to see that the progression stopped with him, even if he had to go to the bottom af an alien sea and hobnob with horror.

Logo No. 96. Norman, John (pseud. John Lange). *Hunters of Gor*. Code No. UW1102. First edition. First printing, March 1974. 320 pp. Cover art by Gino D'Achille; interior illustrations by Jack Gaughan. Later published in U.K. by Tandem (1975). See Schlobin, *The Literature of Fantasy* 613 (1979). $1.50.

Three lovely women were keys to Tarl Cabot's career on Gor, Earth's orbital counterpart. They were: Talena, daughter of Gor's greatest ruler and once Tarl's queen; Elizabeth Cardwell, who had been Tarl's comrade in two of his greatest exploits; and Verna, haughty chief of the untamed panther women of the Northern forests. *Hunters of Gor* finally reveals the fate of these three, as Tarl Cabot ventures into the wilderness to pit his skill and his life against the brutal cunning of Gorean outlaws and enemy warriors.

(Bibliographer's note: The eighth book of the Tarl Cabot saga.)

Cap Kennedy #6. Kern, Gregory (pseud. E.C. Tubb). *Seetee Alert!* Code No. UQ1103. First edition. First printing, March 1974. 126 pp. Cover art by Jack Gaughan. Later published in U.K. by Mews (1976). $.95.

Contra-terrene matter, seetee, as the astronauts call it, is the most dangerous substance in the universe. Reversely charged, when brought into contact with even the most stable of normal material, it will instantly disintegrate with a 100% energy diffusion.

So when Cap Kennedy's scout vessel, *Mordain*, brushed against a cloud of seetee dust that was being gathered and moved by unknown ships, it was not only a narrow escape for Cap and his friends, but signaled an emergency of the highest urgency. Such a swarm could cause the destruction of an entire solar system, and there was reason to suspect that its ultimate target was our sun and all its planets, including, particularly, the Earth.

Logo No. 97. Akers, Alan Burt (pseud. Kenneth Bulmer). *Prince of Scorpio*. Code No. UY1104. First edition. First printing, April 1974. 223 pp. Cover art and illustrations by Jack Gaughan. $1.25.

Dray Prescot had fought long and hard through perilous lands to claim the hand of the heiress of mighty Vallia. Yet, when finally he set foot in that long-sought empire, it was not as a hero or noble, it was as an unknown, a mendicant, and, finally, as a condemned slave. For the combatant fates that had interfered continually with his quest on the planet of the twin suns of Antares had yet more tests for the man they had selected as their agent. But, for Dray, there could be but one goal, already in sight, and he would not be turned aside any longer no matter what dangers that Vallian intrigues and quasi-human mysteries might have in store for him.

(Bibliographer's note : This book, the fifth in the saga of Prescot of Antares (The Delian Cycle), contains, as a supplement, a map of a part of

Kregen and an extensive glossary of persons, places and things in the saga.)

Logo No. 98. Chilson, Robert. *As the Curtain Falls.* Code No. UQ1105. First edition. First printing, April 1974. 174 pp. Cover art by Hans Ulrich and Ute Osterwalder. $.95.

In the old age of the once great planet Earth, the oceans have long since dried up, and, in their empty sea bottoms, stand the last cities of mankind, for the once mighty continental heights are barren and frigid.

The world is strewn with the ruins of the star-faring civilizations of the Dawn ages, and, somewhere in those ruins, lies the legendary Kingsworld Legacy, which may yet save humanity.

Trebor of Amballa possesses the key to the Legacy. But can he use it, and will the remnants of a myriad lost nations let him?

(Bibliographer's note: The author's first book.)

Logo No. 99. Sheckley, Robert. *Can You Feel Anything When I Do This?* Code No. UQ1106. First paperback edition. First printing, April 1974. 160 pp. Cover art by Hans Arnold. Published earlier in the U.S. by Doubleday (1971) and in the U.K. by Gollancz (1972). Also published by Pan (1974) as *The Same to You Doubled and Other Stories.* See *Anatomy of Wonder* 3-657 (1981). $.95.

Contents:
Can You Feel Anything When I Do This?
Cordle to Onion to Carrot
The Petrified World
Game: First Schematic
Doctor Zombie and His Little Furry Friends
The Cruel Equations
The Same to You Doubled
Starting from Scratch
The Mnemone
Tripout
Notes on the Perception of Imaginary Differences
Down the Digestive Tract and into the Cosmos with Mantra, Tantra, and Specklebang
Pas de Trois of the Chef and the Waiter and the Customer Aspects of Langranak
Plague Circuit
Tailpipe to Disaster

Logo No. 100. Farmer, Philip Jose. *Hadon of Ancient Opar.* Code No. UY1107. First edition. First printing, April 1974. 224 pp. Cover art and illustrations by Roy Krenkel. Later published in the U.K. by Magnum (1977). $1.25.

Opar: the Atlantean colony in the heart of Tarzan's Africa.

Opar: in the words of Edgar Rice Burroughs, a hidden city of "gold and silver, ivory and apes, and peacocks."

Opar: the starting point of this novel of twelve thousand years past, when Africa had an inland sea, and a high civilization bloomed along its forgotten shores, when lost empires flew their time-vanished banners, and deeds of daring were commonplace.

(Bibliographer's note: Second book of the Ancient Africa series.)

Cap Kennedy #7. Kern, Gregory (pseud. E.C. Tubb). *The Gholan Gate.* Code No. UQ1108. First edition. First printing, April 1974. 124 pp. Cover art by Jack Gaughan. $.95.

"Beyond that curtain of darkness lies paradise."

That was the promise of the doorway known as The Gholan Gate, a doorway so ancient that its makers had vanished millions of years before the first Earthly life crawled out of the primeval oceans. It was still functioning in the possession of its discoverers.

To go through it was to enter a universe where all your dreams came true, where your every wish was obeyed, every fantasy became reality, and where you could play God to your heart's content.

But there was a price, for, once beyond The Gholan Gate, you would live only in hopes for a second visit, and a third. To get the right for that return to paradise, a man would sell his soul, his people, his world.

Cap Kennedy entered The Gholan Gate once, and the result became cosmic history.

Logo No. 101. Wollheim, Donald A. ed. with Arthur W. Saha eds. *The 1974 Annual World's Best SF.* Code No. UY1109. First edition. First printing, May 1974. 280 pp. Cover art by Jack Gaughan. $1.25.

Contents:

Introduction	The Editor
A Suppliant in Space	Robert Sheckley
Parthen	R.A. Lafferty
Doomship	Frederik Pohl and Jack Williamson
Weed of Time	Norman Spinrad
A Modest Genius	Vadim Shefner
The Deathbird	Harlan Ellison
Evane	E.C. Tubb
Moby, Too	Gordon Eklund
Death and Designation	
Among the Asadi	Michael Bishop
Construction Shack	Clifford D. Simak

Logo No. 102. Compton, D.G. *The Unsleeping Eye.* Code No. UY1110. First U.S. edition. First printing, May 1974. 221 pp. Cover art by Karel Thole. Issued in U.K. by Gollancz (1974) entitled *The Continuous Katherine Mortenhoe.* Later published by Magnum (1981) as *Death Watch.* See *Survey of Science Fiction Literature V*, pp. 2366-2369 (1979); *Anatomy of Wonder* 3-219 (1981). $1.25.

Katherine Mortenhoe was going to die. She was going to do it slowly, painfully, and before the eyes of millions.

It was to be on a television program of the highest rating. The crises and problems of the closing years of the 20th Century had forced the entertainment industry to ever more escalating needs to hold its audiences. And fatal illness, once so common, had become such a rarity that Katherine's doom was a magnet for all eyes.

Katherine thought she had evaded the television ghouls. She had been helped to do so by her newfound friend, Roddie. He was sensitive, he was understanding, he helped her flee the morbid metropolis. But Roddie was the "Unsleeping Eye": what Roddie saw and heard, the whole world saw and heard. What Roddie thought and sought, only Katherine was to learn.

Logo No. 103. Snyder, Cecil III. *The Hawks of Arcturus.* Code No. UQ1111. First edition. First printing, May 1974. 159 pp. Cover art by Kelly Freas. $.95.

Somewhere out there among the stars, there had to be a greater intelligence than man's. Though mankind had spread out, none had yet contacted such an intelligence. The first of the now fiercely competitive planetary empires to do so might gain power over all the others, assuming it survived at all.

Arcturus was ambitious. Its emblem was the hawk, and its leaders thought of themselves as birds of prey. When they were first to reach an alien powerhouse, the hawks of Arcturus prepared to pounce. Only Chen the Earthman stood in their way. Arcturus may have considered itself to be an irresistible force, but this despised, imprisoned, and insignificant Earthling turned out to be the immovable object.

Logo No. 104. Dickinson, Peter. *The Weathermonger.* Code No. UQ1112. First paperback edition. First printing, May 1974. 158 pp. Cover art by George Barr. Originally published in the U.K. by Gollancz (1968) and in the U.S. by Little, Brown (1969). $.95.

From the Twentieth Century to the Dark Ages overnight; such was the fate that befell Britain five years from now. Machines were shunned, and witchcraft had become the order of the day. Superstition and all the narrowness of the medieval era was the way of the populace, and those who believed in science and mechanics fled the island.

To this strangely changed land, two return to seek the source of the blight that had so altered the natural laws. Geoffrey, the condemned weathermonger of Weymouth, and his sister slip back, take over a still-functioning Rolls Royce Silver Ghost and follow the lightning to a terrifying confrontation between myth and science.

(Bibliographer's note: The first book of The Changes trilogy.)

Cap Kennedy #8. Kern, Gregory (pseud. E.C. Tubb). *The Eater of Worlds.* Code No. UQ1113. First edition. First printing, May 1974. 126 pp. Cover art by Jack Gaughan. $.95.

On a far semi-desert world, shunned by trade routes, and unattractive to star travelers, there is a barren and isolated valley. Dominating this valley is a great time-eroded Sphinx-like construction, a mass known to the few who have looked upon it as the Skull of Sykoris.

Cap Kennedy followed a dangerous trail across many worlds, a trail of murder, duels, and evil, to find that it ended there, before the Skull, confronting a mystery older than all mankind.

Beneath that Sphinx lay something desired by Earth's old enemies. Beneath it lay something that lured the criminal minds of many worlds. But what it was, none knew, until Cap Kennedy himself released the frightful power of the Eater of Worlds.

Logo No. 105. Bayley, Barrington J. *The Fall of Chronopolis.* Code No. UQ1114. First edition. First printing, June 1974. 175 pp. Cover art by Kelly Freas. Later published in U.K. by Allison & Busby (1979). See *Anatomy of Wonder* 3-70 (1981). $.95.

There is real time, and there is potential time. By controlling the difference, the Chronotic Empire came into existence and maintained itself over a thousand years of human history. Its Time Fleets, armadas of time-traveling fortresses, patrolled its temporal borders relentlessly, blotting out potential-time deviations, erasing errors of history that might undermine the empire. Nevertheless, the empire's days were numbered, for somewhere in its own future was the century of the Hegemony, its implacable enemy.

Logo No. 106. Biggle, Lloyd Jr. *The Metallic Muse.* Code No. UY1115. First paperback edition. First printing, June 1974. 220 pp. Cover art by George Barr. Published earlier by Doubleday (1972). See *Anatomy of Wonder* 3-82 (1981). $1.25.

Contents:

The Tunesmith	Well of the Deep Wish
Leading Man	In His Own Image
Spare the Rod	The Botticelli Horror
Orphan of the Void	

Logo No. 107. Goulart, Ron. *Flux.* Code No. UQ1116. First edition. First printing, June 1974. 159 pp. Cover art by Jack Gaughan. $.95.

There was a youth protest movement on the planet Jasper, which should not have been anything new. There were always youth protest movements, and a planet like Jasper with its mixed colonies was entitled to them too. The difference was that these boys and girls had been made into human bombs; they blew up on contact.

That was good enough reason to call in Ben Jolson of the galaxy-famous Chameleon Corps. Jolson could disguise himself as just about everything; doctor, lawyer, Indian Chief, or even icebox.

But Jasper strained him to the limit. Not only did it house a mad combination of mad cultures, but someone else was doing the chameleon trick too, and, besides, how do you go about looking like an exploding bomb?

(Bibliographer's note: Third book in the Chameleon Corps series.)

Logo No. 108. Eklund, Gordon. *All Times Possible.* Code No. UQ1117.

First edition. First printing, June 1974. 191 pp. Cover art by Charles Gross. See *Anatomy of Wonder* 3-299 (1981). $.95.

Do you remember Tommy Bloome, our beloved leader who led the revolution that kept America out of World War II and established the workers' state? No? Perhaps you may remember Tommy Bloome, the alienated kid who tried to assassinate our heroic General Norton in 1947? Not him either?

Well, never mind. This account is of still another Tommy Bloome, an ambitious, idealistic young man who tried to make our country and our world "better," and what happens when he bucks the invisible tides that sweep relentlessly through the courses of human events.

Cap Kennedy #9. Kern, Gregory (pseud. E.C. Tubb). *Earth Enslaved.* Code No. UQ1118. First edition. First printing, June 1974. 128 pp. Cover art by Jack Gaughan. $.95.

It could have been a black hole, but wasn't. That it was artificial in origin didn't make it any less deadly. Worst of all, that strange extra-galactic torus was drifting into an intersect with Earth in its orbit. The result would be devastation beyond concept.

Cap Kennedy and his three companions were considered expendable in such a cause. Then Cap himself volunteered to dare the impossible: to turn that cosmic hole aside. What he fell into was an adventure utterly different than anything he had expected.

Logo No. 109. Davis, Richard ed. *The Year's Best Horror Stories: Series II.* Code No. UY1119. First edition. First printing, July 1974. 207 pp. Cover art by Hans Arnold. See *Horror Literature* 4-253 (1981). $1.25.

Contents:

Foreword	Christopher Lee
David's Worm	Brian Lumley
The Price of a Demon	Gary Brandner
The Knocker at the Portico	Basil Copper
The Animal Fair	Robert Bloch
Napier Court	J. Ramsey Campbell
Haunts of the Very Rich	T.K. Brown III
The Long-Term Residents	Kit Pedler
Like Two White Spiders	Eddy C. Bertin
The Old Horns	J. Ramsey Campbell
Haggopian	Brian Lumley
The Events at Poroth Farm	T.E.D. Klein

Logo No. 110. Carter, Lin. *By the Light of the Green Star.* Code No. UQ1120. First edition. First printing, July 1974. 175 pp. Cover art and illustrations by Roy Krenkel. $.95.

Miscast in the role of assassin, inhabiting the stolen body of a stalwart savage, the star-wanderer from Earth found himself in dangers beyond even his wildest imaginings. His friends had fled, his princess with them, and awaiting him were the islands of the sky with their merciless masters, the prowlers of the dark tree bottoms with their horrible steeds, and the treachery of his comrades in captivity.

But this is what he had left his safe home on Earth for, and his adventures by the light of the Green Star, however knife-edge, were the very staff of life to him!

(Bibliographer's note: The third novel of the Green Star saga. Included, as an appendix, is a glossary of Green Star people and beasts of the Green Star world.)

Logo No. 111. Stableford, Brian M. *The Paradise Game.* Code No. UQ1121. First edition. First printing, June 1974. 158 pp. Cover art by Kelly Freas. Later published in U.K. by Dent (1976). $.95.

Everyone seeks paradise. If the explorers of the planets could find a world that answered the description, it could be a holiday world beyond price.

When the *Hooded Swan* landed on Pharos, it was, indeed, all that paradise could be. They came to investigate, they stayed to protect. For, unless they played the role of the angel with the flaming sword, very soon this softest and gentlest of all men's dreams would become another gaudy hellhole of exploitation.

But, as Grainger and the crew of the *Hooded Swan* were to learn, this world, like the original paradise, had a serpent of its own. And the apple of its tree of knowledge might be found too late to save its star-borne invaders, including its would-be defenders.

(Bibliographer's note: The fourth in the series of novels about Star-Pilot Grainger and the *Hooded Swan.*)

Logo No. 112. Brunner, John. *Give Warning to the World.* Code No. UQ1122. First printing, July 1974. 158 pp. Cover art by Jack Gaughan. A shorter and substantially different version of this novel was published by Ace Books in 1959 under the title *Echo in the Skull* and was bound with *Rocket to Limbo* by Alan E. Nourse. This version was later published in the U.K. by Dobson (1981). $.95.

Are there aliens among us? Are the chariots of the gods returning? If so, are they for us or against us?

This is a tale of the man who discovers that the vanguard of the aliens are, indeed, among us, and that the human species has but a few hours left before our time runs out.

Cap Kennedy #10. Kern, Gregory (pseud. E.C. Tubb). *Planet of Dread.* Code No. UQ1123. First edition. First printing, July 1974. 126 pp. Cover art by Jack Gaughan. $.95.

Of all possible enemies, Cap Kennedy had yet to cross swords with the legendary master of galactic villainy, Dr. Kaifeng. In the struggle for the mind of the tyrant of Papan, they finally met, and Kennedy was the loser.

There was only one chance to save the situation, and that was to pay the price of the enigmatic super-surgeons of the Kraid. He would have to take a role in their eternal play-acting.

The stage would be the past, a barbaric world of swords and sorcery. Kennedy would be just a sword-wielding freebooter with a crew of murderous puppets at his back. And, if he survived, Kaifeng would be waiting at the stage door.

Logo No. 113. Akers, Alan Burt (pseud. Kenneth Bulmer). *Manhounds of Antares.* Code No. UY1124. First edition. First printing, August, 1974. 185 pp. Cover art by Jack Gaughan. $1.25.

Dray Prescot, Earthman on the planet Kregen of Antares; was he to remain a prince of proud Vallia, or just one more human victim of the hunters and manhounds of the mysterious Southern Continent?

For that was the enigmatic fate that the Star Lords had suddenly confronted him with. They wanted someone freed from the terrified pack of human prey among which Prescot found himself. But who it was and how it was to be done, they left to him.

In unknown Havilfar, there were other mysteries to be solved and other discoveries to be made, yet Prescot knew there could be no return to his princess and his newly won homeland until he had done the bidding of his all-powerful tormentors.

(Bibliographer's note: The first book in The Havilfar Cycle and the sixth adventure in the saga of Prescot of Antares.)

Logo No. 114. Van Vogt, A.E. *The Man with a Thousand Names.* Code No. UQ1125. First edition. First printing, August 1974. 159 pp. Cover art by Vincent DiFate. Later published in U.K. by Sidgwick & Jackson (1975). $.95.

Although thirty light years distant, Mittend was Earth's nearest habitable planet. So the bored young heir, Steven Masters, contrived to join the first manned expedition just for a bit of excitement.

When he found himself suddenly back on Earth in another man's body, it was more than he had expected. What then followed was a veritable kaleidoscope of events that was to involve him in multiple personalities, in more expeditions to Mittend, and in the affairs of the entity called Mother, for whom Mittend itself was just a means to an end, and Steven Masters the handy next step in a galactic program.

Logo No. 115. Tubb, E.C. *Zenya.* Code No. UQ1126. First edition. First printing, August 1974. 157 pp. Cover art by Kelly Freas. Later published in U.K. by Arrow (1978). $.95.

Earl Dumarest was on his way back to his home world, the mythical homeland of cosmic humanity he called Earth. Gradually, dangerously, he had picked up clue after clue to its galactic whereabouts as his quest moved outward from the crowded center of the Milky Way.

In the course of his desperate trek, he had learned the one secret that the far-flung cyborg cult of The Cyclan required to assure their control over the thousands of inhabited spheres.

Always the Cyclan pursued, plotted, searched. Always Dumarest managed to slip past their clutches, until he found himself obligated to

Zenya of Paiyar and forced to lead an army for her faction, while the Cyclan used the time to weave its web around him tighter and tighter.

(Bibliograper's note: This is the eleventh adventure of Dumarest of Terra, although only the third published by DAW Books. Never fear. There's more to come. Many more.)

Logo No. 116. Dickson, Gordon R. *The Star Road.* Code No. UY1127. First paperback edition. First printing, August 1974. 208 pp. Cover art by Eddie Jones. Published earlier by Doubleday (1973) and later by Hale (1975) as first U.K. edition. $1.25.

Contents:

Whatever Gods There Be	On Messenger Mountain
Hilifter	The Catch
Building on the Line	Jackal's Meal
The Christmas Present	The Mousetrap
3-Part Puzzle	

Logo No. 117. Zelazny, Roger. *To Die in Italbar.* Code No. UQ1129. First paperback edition. First printing, September 1974. 174 pp. Cover art by Carl Lundgren. Published earlier by Doubleday (1973). Later published by Faber & Faber (1975) as first U.K. edition. $.95.

H was the name he was known by.

H was unique in the galaxy, for he had the healing touch. Where there was plague, sickness, pain, H was the universal cure.

But H also had the slaying touch. Where he went, death and disaster often followed. Where there had been health, there would be left desolation.

The talent alternated. It reversed itself, and H always warned people of this. To live in Italbar or to die in Italbar, that was always the question.

(Bibliographer's note: Sequel to *Isle of the Dead.*)

Logo No. 118. Anthony, Piers (pseud. P.A.D. Jacob). *Triple Detente.* Code No. UQ1130. First edition. First printing, September 1974. 175 pp. Cover art by Jack Gaughan. A portion of this novel is derived from the novelette, "The Alien Rulers," which first appeared in the March 1968 issue of *Analog.* Later published in U.K. by Sphere (1975). $.95.

Victory! Our invincible space fleet has occupied the monsters' worlds!

Victory! Our mighty space force has seized the aliens' home planet!

Victory! Our triumphant space warriors have captured the enemy system!

But, then, why are we suffering so beneath the tread of those heartless conquerors from the stars?

Logo No. 119. Bradley, Marion Zimmer. *The Spell Sword.* Code No. UQ1131. First edition. First printing, September 1974. 158 pp. Cover art by George Barr. Later published in U.K. by Arrow (1978) and in first hardcover edition by Gregg Press (1979). See *Anatomy of Wonder* 4-77 (1987). $.95.

Although Darkover was a world inhabited by humans as well as semi-humans, it was primarily forbidden ground to the Terran traders. Most of the planet's wild terrain was unexplored, and many of its peoples seclusive and secretive.

But, for Andrew Carr, there was an attraction he could not evade. Darkover drew him, Darkover haunted him, and, when his mapping plane crashed in unknown heights, Darkover prepared to destroy him. At last, however, the planet's magic asserted itself, and his destiny began to unfold along lines predicted only by phantoms and wonder workers of the kind Terran science could never acknowledge.

(Bibliographer's note: The eighth Darkover novel.)

Logo No. 120. Coney, Michael G. *Monitor Found in Orbit.* Code No. UQ1132. First edition. First printing, September 1974. 172 pp. Cover art by Kelly Freas. $.95.

Contents:

Introduction	The Unsavory Episode of Mrs.
The True Worth of Ruth Villiers	Hector Powell-Challenger
The Manya	Monitor Found in Orbit
Hold My Hand, My Love!	The Mind Prison
Beneath Still Waters	R26/5/PSY and I
	Esmerelda

Cap Kennedy #11. Kern, Gregory (pseud. E.C. Tubb). *Spawn of Laban.* Code No. UQ1133. First edition. First printing, September 1974. 127 pp. Cover art by Jack Gaughan. $.95.

The planet was fine for big game hunters. It was the tradition there that one must have a trophy before one could call oneself truly a man.

If that were all, it would hardly have interested Cap Kennedy; his trophies consisted of planets saved for Terra and missions accomplished. But there was something on Eriadne which was not just a hunt trophy—something which required the presence of Kennedy and his men to check on. One of these things was a fragment of Zheltyana construction which outdated all civilizations.

But the hunt proved to be a double one: Kennedy against an invincible monster, and a lost world of monsters against Kennedy. If he lost, it would be Terra itself that would be the trophy on some alien's hunting lodge wall.

Logo No. 121. Norton, Andre. *Here Abide Monsters.* Code No. UY1134. First paperback edition. First printing, October 1974. 205 pp. Cover art by Jack Gaughan. Published earlier by Atheneum (1973). $1.25.

"Have you ever wondered how much of ancient folklore is grounded in fact? Are there really unicorns, elves, magic cities?

"*Here Abide Monsters* is a fresh approach to myth. Most people have heard of the 'Bermuda Triangle,' but Andre Norton uses a similar situation to show the possibility of a two-way door that opens both on this world and on another quite unlike our own. Nick Shaw and Linda Durant pass through the door into a world where their nightmares are real and deadly. They band together with an English group, some of whom have been on

the planet since before the turn of the century...."
—*Chattanooga Daily Times*

Logo No. 122. Gordon, Stuart (pseud. Richard Gordon). *Two-Eyes*. Code No. UY1135. First edition. First printing, October 1974. 240 pp. Cover art by Peter Manesis. Later published in U.K. by Sidgwick & Jackson (1975). $1.25.

Somewhere the infant god had been born. The ripples of power emanating from the mutant messiah were shaking the complex societies that had mushroomed from the world's ashes.

For Tschea, the Red Feather of Ussian, the vibrations of One-Eye meant confrontation with the final meaning of her rites. For Liam of Phadraig, one of the original apostles, the vision meant spreading a psychic plague wherever he wandered. For the brotherhood of the Zuni Bird, it meant the day had come for the "bird" to sing the redemption of Science. For everyone in the world, the Book of Two-Eyes was to be the testament for the millenium to come.

(Bibliographer's note: The second book of The Eye trilogy.)

Logo No. 123. Franke, Herbert W. *The Mind Net*. Code No. UQ1136. First U.S. and first English language edition. First printing, October 1974. 173 pp. Cover art by Kelly Freas. Translation by Christine Priest. Original edition entitled *Das Gedankennetz*, published by Wilhelm Goldmann Verlag Munchen (1963). $.95.

This novel centers around a vast spacefleet exploring the cosmos. Organic remnants are found in the lifeless soil of an ancient world, but, when the space explorers test these mysterious objects, they suddenly find their ship trapped in an alien mental web and face a menace never allowed for on their computers.

But that's only the beginning, and, thereafter, there are encountered seemingly isolated scenes on alien worlds with unearthly growths, in mechanical civilizations, and in rebel cities where everyday people face extraordinary problems.

Logo No. 124. Fast, Howard. *A Touch of Infinity*. Code No. UQ1137. First paperback edition. First printing, October 1974. 172 pp. Cover art by Charles Gross. Published earlier in U.S. by Morrow (1973) and later in U.K. by Hodder & Stoughton (1975). $.95.

Contents:

The Hoop	The Talent of Harvey
The Price	The Mind of God
A Matter of Size	UFO
The Hole in the Floor	Cephes 5
General Hardy's Profession	The Pragmatic Seed
Show Cause	The Egg
Not with a Bang	

Cap Kennedy #12. Kern, Gregory (pseud. E.C. Tubb). *The Genetic Buc-*

cancer. Code No. UQ1138. First edition. First printing, October 1974. 125 pp. Cover art by Jack Gaughan. $.95.

Tampering with the genes of humanity to create a super-race was an ideal of many scientific Utopians. Tampering with the genes of humanity to create a super-army was a dream of many military commanders. Tampering with the genes of humanity to create a horde of obedient, but brilliant, monsters was the scheme of Dr. Kaifeng.

For Cap Kennedy, the abduction of a dozen leading geneticists spelled trouble for Earth. Their trails led not to some idealist or some would-be Napoleon, but pointed only at the one man in the galaxy who might prove to be more powerful than the legions of Terra themselves.

Logo No. 125. Carter, Lin. *The Warrior of World's End.* Code No. UQ1140. First edition. First printing, November 1974. 160 pp. Cover art by Vincent DiFate. $.95.

I see Gondwane as it shall be in the untold ages of dim futurity, near the time when the Earth shall be man's habitation no more, and the great night shall enfold all, and naught but the cold stars shall reign. The first sign of the end ye shall see in the heavens, for Lo! the moon is falling, falling. And there shall come a man into the lands, a man not like other men, but sent from Galendil.

(Bibliographer's note: The name of the man is Ganelon Silvermane, and this is the first book of the Gondwane epic. A glossary of unfamiliar names and terms is included.)

Logo No. 126. Strugatski, Arkadi & Boris. *Hard To Be a God.* Code No. UY1141. First DAW printing, November 1974. 205 pp. Cover art by Kelly Freas. Translated by Wendayne Ackerman. Originally entitled *Trudno Byt Bogom,* published by Vsesojuznoje Objedinenije, "Mezhdunarodnaja Kniga," Moscow, Russia (1964). Also published in the U.S. by Seabury (1973). See *Anatomy of Wonder* 3-717 (1981); *Survey of Science Fiction Literature,* pp. 950-955 (1979). $1.25.

"My personal penchant in s-f is more its fiction than its science. The story the Strugatski brothers have to tell is profligate and wildly generous. Beginning with a rather Marxist premise (that history must follow a course through feudalism to some sort of democracy before the brown-shirt, black-shirt, Red Guard phenomenon can occur) we have a situation in which the bad guys turn up at the wrong time—in the feudal stage. What to do, if you are an observer sent from a distant Earth to observe, to save what is worth saving, but not to interfere?

"Lord Rumata is the masquerading Earthman, a most noble nobleman, a dueler, a brawler if necessary, who is never defeated but never kills. Rumata is a man full of doubts and passions and compassions, and you'll remember him for a long, long time."
—Theodore Sturgeon in the *New York Times*

Logo No. 127. Wallace, Ian (pseud. John Wallace Pritchard). *A Voyage to Dari.* Code No. UY1142. First edition. First printing, November 1974. 239

pp. Cover art by Peter Manesis. $1.25.

There's a trip between galaxies. There's a parallel universe which may or may not be the one in which we all dwell. There's a man named Croyd. And there's something which seeks to control all the galaxies for its own inscrutable purposes.

The man named Croyd stands in this something's way. This is possible because Croyd is a lot more than what he seems. He has, for instance, an identical twin somewhere out there who may or may not have similar powers. As to what those powers are, perhaps even Croyd doesn't know their full extent.

(Bibliographer's note: Third book in the Croyd series.)

Logo No. 128. Barrett, Neal Jr. *Stress Pattern.* Code No. UQ1143. First edition. First printing, November 1974. 160 pp. Cover art by Josh Kirby. See *Anatomy of Wonder* 4-39 (1987). $.95.

Consider the problem of this marooned astronaut. His spaceship and supplies are swallowed in one gulp by something from beneath the featureless plain of an unknown world. The natives aren't hostile, but they seem incurious. He's welcome to use their free railroad system, the "alimentary express" of a world-girdling Wormway. Those he regards as sane are considered to be crazy.

The culture techniques he is sure are crazy turn out to be quite rational by that world's standards.

He fathers a child without ever touching the mother. It's when he does physically create his true offspring that he gets his most startling surprise.

(Bibliographer's note: He discovers that doing it the right way is fun.)

Cap Kennedy #13. Kern, Gregory (pseud. E.C. Tubb). *A World Aflame.* Code No. UQ1144. First edition. First printing, November 1974. 128 pp. Cover art by Jack Gaughan. $.95.

Millions of years before humanity and other intelligent races learned to roam the Milky Way, the Zheltyana had created an empire among the stars, had risen, triumphed and vanished. All that remained were a few ruins, some artifacts, and the knowledge that their powerful scientific secrets awaited rediscovery.

One such secret had been found on the feudal planet, Naxos, under the tyranny of the half-mad Idalia Ancanette. Her scientists had tapped its mystery to create a pillar of energy which promised to make Idalia mistress of a hundred worlds, if it didn't destroy Naxos before it could be harnessed. Such an event called for the attention of Earth's master agent, Cap Kennedy, and his scientific crew. because that column of atomic fire was a beacon that could either herald a millennium or end in a world aflame.

Logo No. 129. Akers, Alan Burt (pseud. Kenneth Bulmer). *Arena of Antares.* Code No UY1145. First edition. First printing, December 1974. 207 pp. Cover art and illustrations by Jack Gaughan. $1.25.

Never a man to leave something half done, even when the powerful Star Lords commanded otherwise, the Earthman, Dray Prescot, knew his task on the mysterious continent of Havilfar was far from completed. There were cruel conquerors to be overthrown; there was pursuit of the man-hounds and their masters; and there was Delia, his princess.

Delia was coming with an airfleet from Vallia, but, before Prescot could hope for help, there was to be the arena. Could he survive the life of a gladiator against the killers and monsters of a spoiled queen, while the Star Lords waited for his mission to be resumed?

(Bibliographer's note: Seventh book of The Saga of Dray Prescot and the second in The Havilfar Cycle. Also included is a glossary of places and things in The Havilfar Cycle.)

Unnumbered. Norman, John (pseud. John Lange). *Imaginative Sex*. Code No. UJ1146. First edition. First printing, December 1974. 269 pp. Cover designed by One Plus One Studio. $1.95.

A guide to the advancement of sexual fantasies: fifty-three bedroom scenarios and recipes for pleasure designed to expand the reader's sensual horizons.

The author's outlines include:

The Capture-in-the-Dark Fantasy

The Rites-of-Submission Fantasy

The Captured-by-Pirates Fantasy

The Male-Slave-of-the-Imperious-Queen Fantasy

The Helpless-Maid Fantasy

The I-Am-His-Slave-Girl Fantasy

The Husband-As-Wife Fantasy

The I-Am-a-Love-Prize Fantasy

The Common-Chain Fantasy

The Wife-As-Pickup Fantasy

(Bibliographer's note: This is fun stuff, but he left out The Sex-With-a-Slave-While-Standing-Up-in-a-Hammock Fantasy.)

Logo No. 130. Stableford, Brian M. *The Fenris Device*. Code No. UQ1147. First edition. First printing, December 1974. 156 pp. Cover art by Kelly Freas. Later published in U.K. by Pan (1978). $.95.

The oldest spacefaring race in the galaxy were the secretive Gallacellans. The most difficult type of planet to explore is the heavy gas giant, the Jovian-Saturnian type planet with which all star systems abound.

Somewhere on the storm-ridden, unapproachable surface of such a monstrous gas giant, an abandoned Gallacellan warship was lying. It was reputed to be armed with the device known to legend as the Fenris weapon.

Such stories attract adventurers thirsting for power. Such tales also attracted the masters of the *Hooded Swan* who sought knowledge rather than power, and, when they gave orders, Grainger of the double-mind had no choice but to obey.

It was up to Grainger, therefore, to take a little walk where no man had ever gone before: into a hell of nature's making and man's ambitions.

(Bibliographer's note: Fifth novel in the *Hooded Swan* series with Star-

Pilot Grainger of the double-mind.)

Logo No. 131. Green, Joseph. *Conscience Interplanetary.* Code No. UY1148. First paperback edition. First printing, December 1974. 204 pp. Cover art by Kelly Freas. Originally published in U.K. by Gollancz (1972) and in the U.S. by Doubleday (1973). This novel incorporates, in revised form, the following stories: "The Decision Makers," "The Shamblers of Misery," The Butterflies of Beauty," and "The Cryer of Crystal." $1.25.

Armed with your required five masters' degrees, among other outstanding accomplishments, you are a member of the elite Practical Philosopher Corps, a handful of galactic roamers trained to detect intelligent life-forms on the hundreds of newly colonized planets. As mankind's "Conscience," you are a brilliant blend of scientific realism and unfettered imagination; you must perceive the often subtle and always unexpected manisfestations of the alien mind.

And, of course, your life is a tightrope walk between twin duties to planetary conservation and your own aggressive, expanding race, for when Conscience declares a world to cradle intelligent life, man must, regardless of cost, abandon it to its own destiny.

Your name is Allen Odegaard. You probably have more enemies than friends. But the job has compensations; in your wanderings it is said you have met the final intelligence.

Logo No. 132. Goulart, Ron. *Spacehawk, Inc.* Code No. UQ1149. First edition. First printing, December 1974. 160 pp. Cover art by Hans Arnold. $.95.

In the Barnum system, Malagra was considered to be the most uninviting planet of them all. In fact, among the engineers and androids of Kip Bundy's set, it was known as the pesthole of the universe, which made things quite sticky when Kip's rich uncle assigned him to Malagra to make certain top secret reforms. Kip was no Hercules, and this task would have balked even that mythical fixer. But, then, there were compensations, if you could call them that: a sex-mad photographer, a couple of lovely maidens in distress, and the ardent guerrillas of the Boy Scout Liberation Army.

(Bibliographer's note: A novel in the Barnum System series.)

Logo No. 133. Brunner, John, *The Stone That Never Came Down.* Code No. UY1150. First paperback edition. First printing, January 1975. 191 pp. Cover art by Kelly Freas. Published earlier by Doubleday (1973). Later published in U.K. by New English Library (1976). $1.25.

There was a cure for depression and unemployment.

There was a cure for war, madness, and national hatreds. There was a cure for prejudice, crime and mass hysteria. But there were those that wanted the cure suppressed until the world collapsed.

(Bibliographer's note: Some people are never satisfied.)

Logo No. 134. Klein, Gerard. *The Mote in Time's Eye.* Code No. UY1151.

First U.S., first paperback, and first English language edition. First printing, January 1975. 173 pp. Cover art by Josh Kirby. Translated by C.J. Richards. Original edition entitled *Les Teures de Temps*, published by Editions Fleuve Noir, Paris, France (1965). $1.25.

Shangrin was the captain of the most advanced starliner of a thousand thousand centuries from now. His vessel was between the Magellanic galaxies when it became a casualty of a war between the ultimate powers of the Last Days.

But, far from being destroyed, Shangrin's vessel became the digit that threw off everyone's calculations. Then, Shangrin, himself, determined to return home to his own time and sphere, and, refusing to be a pawn for sacrifice, took his own hand in the cosmic game.

Logo No. 135. Foster, M.A. *The Warriors of Dawn*. Code No. UY1152. First edition. First printing, January 1975. 278 pp. Cover art by Kelly Freas. Later published in U.K. by Hamlyn (1979). $1.25.

The human race had divided into two species. One had created the other; normal humans had experimented in forced evolution and had produced the ler, a sort of superman race, but pacifistic and contemplative.

The ler fled from the turbulent worlds of homo sapiens and established their own quiet planetary colonies. That made it all the more inexplicable when reports came in of fierce planetary marauders, looting and burning, who were of ler ancestry.

The existence of barbarian lers was a contradiction in terms, and the search for their reasons for existence was to take a human male and a ler female on an expedition into strange worlds and the unsuspected bypasses of all the systems of science and philosophy.

(Bibliographer's note. The author's first novel. Chronologically, the second novel of the Ler trilogy.)

Logo No. 136. Saberhagen, Fred. *The Book of Saberhagen*. Code No. UY1153. First edition. First printing, January 1975. 172 pp. Cover art by Jack Gaughan. $1.25.

Contents:

The Long Way Home	Pressure
Planeteer	Starsong
Volume PAA-PYX	Calendars
Seven Doors to Education	Young Girl at an Open Half-Door
Deep Space	What Do You Want Me To Do To Prove I'm Human Stop

Logo No. 137. Dickson, Gordon R. *The R-Master*. Code No. UY1155. First paperback edition. First printing, February 1975. 157 pp. Cover art by Jack Gaughan. Published earlier by Lippincott (1973). Later published in U.K. by Hale (1975). $1.25.

The World Economic Council said the world had become Utopia. There should have been no cause for dissatisfaction. But, for those who were still restless, there was the new mind-stimulating drug R-47. The kicker was that those who took R-47 were engaging in a sort of lottery whose rare winners would be super-geniuses and whose losers might be fit only for asylums. Etter Ho, whose brother was one of the losers, took the drug on the chance that, if he won, he could cure his brother. Yet what he became when he emerged from the mainlining was something none expected: a menace to Utopian order, a danger to those who knew him, and the only man who might, just possibly, diagnose the real illnesses of the world.

Logo No. 138. Carter, Lin. *As the Green Star Rises.* Code No. UY1156. First edition. First printing, February 1975. 172 pp. Cover art by Roy Krenkel; illustrated by Roy Krenkel and Michael Kaluta. $1.25.

Has there ever been a situation such as befell the Earthling who found his way to the world under the Green Star? While his real body lay crippled and silent under the sun of old Earth, his mind occupied the vigorous body of a young primitive on that alien planet of mighty trees, floating cities, and unmapped limits. In that guise, he found incredible friends, a royal love, and inhuman and superhuman enemies.

But no matter what predicament he was in, even though alone and abandoned on an uncharted sea, his courage never flagged, though the greatest of risks would confront him.

(Bibliographer's note: The fourth novel of the Green Star saga.)

Logo No. 139. Chandler, A. Bertram. *The Big Black Mark.* Code No. UY1157. First edition. First printing, February 1975. 224 pp. Cover art by Kelly Freas. $1.25.

The career of John Grimes, a futuristic Captain William Bligh (to whom this book is dedicated), from ensign in the Galactic Federation to admiral of the Rim Worlds, has been chronicled over the years in many novels and short stories. But the pivotal account of Grimes' career, the big black mark on his service record that forced him to change his loyalties, has never been recorded.

This novel is the key story of Commander Grimes and of the voyage of the *Discovery,* a spaceship which bore an uncanny resemblance to a certain legendary vessel called the *Bounty.*

(Bibliographer's note: A novel in the John Grimes: Federation Survey Service series.)

Logo No. 140. Swann, Thomas Burnett. *The Not-World.* Code No. UY1158. First edition. First printing, February 1975. 160 pp. Cover, illustrations by George Barr. See Schlobin, *The Literature of Fantasy* 1022 (1979). $1.25.

One would not have expected to find the last hideout of the ancient weird folk of legend and prehistory in an English forest of two centuries ago. Yet, in that land which has always been haunted by the lore of little folk, there had to be some truth behind such universal belief.

Here is the story of Dylan and Deirdre, of Thomas Chatterton, and of the balloon flight that brought them into an older and more enchanted land to mingle their fates with those of Arachne and the Night Mares in whom a rising industrial materialism could no longer believe.

Cap Kennedy #14. Kern, Gregory (pseud. E.C. Tubb). *The Ghosts of Epidoris.* Code No. UQ1159. First edition. First printing, February 1975. Cover art by Jack Gaughan. $.95.

The world was haunted. Every sunset, the natives went home, locked their doors, and pulled down the window blinds. Ghosts didn't scare Cap Kennedy. As an agent of FATE, it took more than superstition to shake him. But Epidoris was the real thing. Monsters did appear in the darkness, people did vanish at night; in fact, a whole MALACA barracks had vanished, garrison, weapons, and building.

That's what brought Kennedy to Epidoris. That and one thing more, a creature of the infamous Dr. Kaifeng had turned up. A beautiful woman, a princess she called herself, but Kennedy had seen her before, lying in a processing vat on a Kaifeng planetoid of warped genetics. Between the scientific machinations of the galaxy's most perverted mind and the spectral realities of a disputed world, there had to be a meaning that boded no good for Terra, and that's where Kennedy came in.

Logo No. 141. Norman, John (pseud. John Lange). *Marauders of Gor.* Code No. UW1160. First edition. First printing, March 1975. 296 pp. Cover, illustrations by Kelly Freas. Published later in U.K. by Universal (1977). See Schlobin, *The Literature of Fantasy* 614 (1979). $1.50.

Tarl Cabot's efforts to free himself from the directive of the mysterious priest-kings of Earth's orbital counterpart were confronted by frightening reality when horror from the northland finally struck directly at him.

Somewhere in the harsh lands of transplanted Norsemen was the first foothold of the alien Others. Somewhere up there was one such who waited for Tarl. Somewhere up there was Tarl's confrontation with his real destiny. Was he to remain a rich merchant-slaver of Port Kar, or become again a defender of two worlds against cosmic enslavement?

(Bibliographer's note: The ninth book of the saga of Tarl Cabot.)

Logo No. 142. Lundwall, Sam J. *2018 A.D. or the King Kong Blues.* Code No. UY1161. First U.S., first English language, and first paperback edition. First printing, March 1975. 160 pp. Cover art by Josh Kirby. Later published in U.K. by Wyndham (1976). See *Anatomy of Wonder* 3-502 (1981); *Survey of Science Fiction Literature V*, pp. 2339-2342 (1979). $1.25.

They needed the first girl born in the first minute of the first day of the first year of the Twenty-first Century.

They needed her for an ad campaign that would put millions into the largest cosmetics company in Sweden, and, from there, into the accounts of the giant conglomerate that owned it, and, from there, into the unpublicized holding company that controlled that, and then into the secret Swiss bank account that directed the holding company, and from there to the numbered box that ran the account, and from there to—nobody knew, not even the Swiss bankers.

But, though the life of everyone in the world was supposed to be on taped computerized credit records down to the smallest detail, hers was ıot. They knew her name, and that was all.

Logo No. 143. Tubb, E.C. *Eloise.* Code No. UY1162. First edition. First ɔrinting, March 1975. 156 pp. Cover art by George Barr. Later published n U.K. by Arrow (1978). $1.25.

The Cyber Prime had a problem. The vast combination of disembodied ntelligences he controlled was in trouble. There was a solution, but it ·emained as an equation in the mind of just one man, the wanderer Ɔumarest, and Dumarest hated the Cyber.

To locate Dumarest and to gain his secret had become an exercise in ;heer intellect. The exercise had been conducted before, but without ;uccess. Now there was an emergency; the Cyber had to have the answer ʍithout further delay.

The Cyber Prime weighed the known factors of Dumarest's movements, ıis desperate questing efforts to find the lost Earth. An answer came up: Ɔumarest must soon arrive on the world Tynar. The Cyber mobilized to in-:ercept him there.

But the girl, Eloise, intercepted him first, and she was the random fac-:or that the Cyber had not counted on.

(Bibliographer's note: The twelfth novel in the saga of Dumarest of Ierra.)

Logo No. 144. Coney, Michael G. *The Jaws That Bite, The Claws That Ɔatch.* Code No. UY1163. First edition. First printing, March 1975. 191 pp. Ɔover art by Kelly Freas. Later published in U.K. by Elmfield Press 1975) as *The Girl with a Symphony in Her Fingers.* $1.25.

Call them the spare parts people. They chose the risk: jail for convicted :rimes, or semi-freedom as someone's bonded servant for the same term. Ihe price was that they were body insurance. If their master lost a leg or ın internal organ, they would have to supply the missing part. That was he risk. Sagar used bondsmen in his other-world farm where he raised ex-ɔtic alien pelts to sell to the rich. He had no thoughts about the bondsman ɔroblem, pro or con, but when Carioca Jones, 3-V star, visited him, he net her bonded companion, the lovely girl with the musical talent.

It's dangerous to fall in love with a bondsmaiden. Doubly so when her nistress is in love with you. Triply so when it might set off the social ex-ɔlosion that had been smouldering beneath the delicately balanced surface ɔf their post-cataclysmic Peninsula.

(Bibliographer's inane comment: Damn the social explosion. Full speed ıhead!)

Logo No. 145. Akers, Alan Burt (pseud. Kenneth Bulmer). *Fliers of An-ares.* Code No. UY1165. First edition. First printing, April 1975. 207 pp. Ɔover art and illustrations by Jack Gaughan. $1.25.

Dray Prescot, the Earthman who had been brought across interstellar pace as the tool of the mysterious Star Lords, confronted his most baffling ask as a hunted and harried wanderer on the continent of Havilfar. His ask was to discover the means by which the aircraft of that continent's most advanced civilization operated.

Prescot was no scientist, for he was a fighting man from the days before the Twentieth Century. But, fulfill his task he must, or he would never return to the princess and homeland he had won. For Prescot, therefore, there was but one course; with a whole continent against him, with time itself conspiring to balk him, the secrets of an unknown science must be made his!

(Bibliographer's note: The eighth novel in the saga of Dray Prescot and the third in the Havilfar Cycle.)

Logo No. 146. Dick, Philip K. *Flow My Tears, The Policeman Said*. Code No. UW1166. First paperback edition. First printing, April 1975. 208 pp. Cover art by Hans Ulrich and Ute Osterwalder. Published earlier in U.S. by Doubleday (1974) and in U.K. by Gollancz (1974). See *Anatomy of Wonder* 3-267 (1981); *Survey of Science Fiction Literature II*, pp. 797-801 (1979). $1.50.

Jason Taverner woke up one morning to find himself completely unknown. The night before he had been the top-rated television star with millions of devoted watchers. The next day he was just an unidentified walking object, whose face nobody recognized, of whom no one had heard, and without the I.D. papers required in the near future.

When he finally found a man who would agree to counterfeiting such cards for him, that man turned out to be a police informer. Then Taverner found out not only what it was like to be a nobody, but also to be hunted by the whole apparatus of society. It was obvious that Taverner had become the pea in some sort of cosmic shell game. But how? And why?

(Bibliographer's note: Winner of the John W. Campbell Memorial Award for the best science fiction novel of the year and nominated for both the 1974 Nebula and 1975 Hugo awards.)

Logo No. 147. Saberhagen, Fred. *Berserker's Planet*. Code No. UY1167. First edition. First printing, April 1975. 173 pp. Cover art by Jack Gaughan. See *Anatomy of Wonder* 3-633 (1981); *Survey of Science Fiction Literature I*, pp. 168-172 (1979). $1.25.

The invincible weapons of a war that had gone on long before the first life stirred on Earth's primeval seas still ranged the galaxy, though its war was long over and its masters extinct. These were the computer-robots known as the Berserkers; they were totally programmed to implacably destroy all life everywhere. Thus far, humanity had managed to hold its own against these murderous constructs, but the Berserkers further developed as their data tapes added information about this life form.

There was a planet on which humanity seemed to thrive, on which life went on, and, on that world, a Berserker was master. It was a contradiction, and it had to be solved. Such a contradiction was theoretically impossible; therefore, there must be a special factor in that world's equation which had to be negated if life was to continue in the universe.

(Bibliographer's note: Third book in the Berserker series.)

Cap Kennedy #15. Kern, Gregory (pseud. E.C. Tubb). *Mimics of Dephene.* Code No. UY1168. First edition. First printing, April 1975. 126 pp. Cover art by Eddie Jones. $1.25.

"On Dephene, the native life-form is peculiar and unique. All protoplasmic life is equal to and one with the Mimics." On the screen, the shape changed, altered in the shape of a man. Then it changed. It shrank, dropped, lifted a snouted head in the semblence of a dog. It grew, spread wings and became a large bird which hopped and pecked. The wings vanished, and a tall and lovely woman smiled from where the bird had halted. A dozen changes, a score until the mind reeled.

"These Mimics represent a threat to every world in the entire galaxy. Their power of mimicry would enable them to adopt the outward form of rulers and high officials. A man could never be certain that his companion was what he seemed to be."

When Cap Kennedy went to Dephene, the speculation became pure nightmare, for both he and his crew were being duplicated over and over, and so was the worlds-conqueror he sought to block.

(Bibliographer's note: The last book in the unnumbered Cap Kennedy series.)

Logo No. 148. Wollheim, Donald A. ed. with Arthur W. Saha. *The 1975 Annual World's Best SF.* Code No. UW1170. First edition. First printing, May 1975. 269 pp. See *Anatomy of Wonder* 3-911 (1981). Cover art by Jack Gaughan. $1.50.

Contents:

Introduction	The Editor
A Song for Lya	George R.R. Martin
Deathsong	Sydney J. Van Scyoc
A Full Member of the Club	Bob Shaw
The Sun's Tears	Brian M. Stableford
The Gift of Garigolli	Frederik Pohl and C.M. Kornbluth
The Four-Hour Fugue	Alfred Bester
Twig	Gordon R. Dickson
Cathadonian Odyssey	Michael Bishop
The Bleeding Man	Craig Strete
Stranger in Paradise	Isaac Asimov

Logo No. 149. Stableford, Brian M. *Swan Song.* Code No. UY1171. First edition. First printing, May 1975. 158 pp. Cover art by Kelly Freas. Later published in U.K. by Pan (1978). $1.25.

Grainger's time of service was nearly up. Pilot of the marvel spaceship *Hooded Swan,* the strange double-mind that occupied his brain had pulled him out of difficulties that would have doomed anyone else. But now Grainger had been warned.

This trip could be the end, because nobody knew what a newly created reality meant in terms of physics and chemistry; nobody but that alien parasitic mentality, and it knew one thing: that it could not survive that kind of flight. Yet the existence of the *Hooded Swan* might depend on exactly such a survival.

(Bibliographer's note: The sixth adventure in the saga of Grainger of the *Hooded Swan*.)

Logo No. 150. Carter, Lin. *The Enchantress of World's End*. Code No. UY1172. First edition. First printing, May 1975. 192 pp. Cover art by Michael Whelan. $1.25.

Gondwane: In the last days of Earth, the continents drifted together again after aeons' seperation, and that was Gondwane.

Gondwane: When all the kingdoms of all the peoples of Earth had come and gone, and new ones arose, it was on Gondwane they created their ephemeral glories.

On Gondwane, amid the turmoil of the last wars and the last quests and the last efforts of scientists and alchemists, there arose one final hero, the mighty Ganelon Silvermane.

(Bibliographer's note: The second book of the Gondwane epic. Includes a glossary of unfamiliar names and terms.)

Logo No. 151. Lumley, Brian. *The Transition of Titus Crow*. Code No. UW1173. First edition. First printing, May 1975. 253 pp. Cover art by Michael Whelan. See *Horror Literature* 4-169 (1981). $1.50.

The author of this Lovecraftian pastiche was born exactly nine months after the death of H.P. Lovecraft. Although he steadfastly maintains that he is not the reincarnation of the originator of the Cthulhu Mythos, we who know him are convinced otherwise.

This novel chronicles the ordeal of the occultists, Henri-Laurent de Marigny and Titus Crow, against the ever-rising power and enmity of the Elder Gods and the Chaos from Outer Space, as well as the ever-ominous Cthulhuoid menace.

(Bibliographer's note: The book is an excellent companion to Lumley's Arkham House contributions, and, like *The Burrowers Beneath*, is an extension of H.P. Lovecraft's Cthulhu Mythos. It's the second book in the Titus Crow series.)

Logo No. 152. Norton, Andre. *Merlin's Mirror*. Code No. UY1175. First edition. First printing, June 1975. 205 pp. Cover art by Jack Gaughan. Later published in U.K. by Sidgwick & Jackson (1976). $1.25.

This novel is a new look at the Arthurian legend in the light of modern knowledge of a lost period of history and today's understanding of science and interplanetary communication.

Here is Merlin, half star-born and gifted with the advice of an alien intelligence, given the task of renewing civilization and starting humanity again up the ladder to the stars.

Here is Arthur, unaware of his stellar heritage, and the Lady of the Lake, akin to Merlin in that she is also a listener to the music of the spheres and obedient to a celestial command post.

Logo No. 153. Anderson, Poul. *The Book of Poul Anderson*. Code No.

UW1176. First paperback edition. First printing, June 1975. 284 pp. Cover art by Jack Gaughan. Published earlier by Chilton (1974) as *The Many Worlds of Poul Anderson*, edited by Roger Elwood. See *Anatomy of Wonder* 3-25 (1981). $1.50.

Contents:
Tomorrow's Children
The Queen of Air and Darkness
Her Strong Enchantments Failing   by Patrick McGuire
Epilogue
The Longest Voyage
Challenge and Response   by Sandra Miesel
Journey's End
A World Named Cleopatra
The Sheriff of Canyon Gulch (with Gordon R. Dickson)
Day of Burning

Logo No. 154. Lee, Tanith. *The Birthgrave*. Code No. UW1177. First edition. First printing, June 1975. 408 pp. Cover art by George Barr. See *Anatomy of Wonder* 3-470 (1981), *Survey of Modern Fantasy Literature I*, pp. 116-121 (1979); Schlobin, *The Literature of Fantasy* 625 (1979). Later published in U.K. by Futura (1977). $1.50.

The place: the heart of a rumbling volcano.
The person: a woman awakening from a deathlike sleep.
The time: unknown, far from today.
The problem: her identity. Who is she? What are her powers? Where is her lover and who or what is he? What is to be her relation to the world in which she finds herself: slave girl, goddess, nomad, or warrior?
(Bibliographer's note: 1975 Nebula nominee. First book of the Birthgrave trilogy.)

Logo No. 155. Davis, Richard ed. *The Year's Best Horror Stories: Series III*. Code No. UY1180. First edition. First printing, July 1975. 173 pp. Cover art by Michael Whelan. See *Horror Literature* 4-254 (1981). $1.25.

Contents:
Introduction	Richard Davis
The Whimper of Whipped Dogs	Harlan Ellison
The Man in the Underpass	J. Ramsey Campbell
S.F.	T.E.D. Klein
Uncle Vlad	Clive Sinclair
Judas Story	Brian M. Stableford
The House of Cthulhu	Brian Lumley
Satanesque	Allan Weiss
Burger Creature	Steve Chapman
Wake Up Dead	Tim Stout
Forget-Me-Not	Bernard Taylor
Halloween Story	Gregory Fitz Gerald
Big, Wide, Wonderful World	Charles E. Fritch
The Taste of Your Love	Eddy C. Bertin

Logo No. 156. Barbet, Pierre (pseud. Claude Avice). *The Enchanted Planet.* Code No. UY1181. First U.S. and first edition in English. First printing, July 1975. 159 pp. Cover art by Michael Whelan. Translated by C.J. Richards. Original edition entitled *La Planete Enchantee*, published by Editions Fleuve Noir, Paris, France (1973). $1.25.

Planets cannot appear and disappear; especially not in a galaxy that had been mapped, colonized and controlled by the united Great Brains of the many intelligent races. Thus, when a new planet popped up out of nowhere, it was an unprecedented phenomenon.

When the planet turned out to be identical with one of the fantasy epics of the ancient Earth, it was cause for alarm, because it contradicted too many laws of science.

Where the problem of sorcery versus technology is concerned, there was only one man in the space service experienced enough to cope with it. That was Captain Setni, and it fell to him to explore this enchanted planet of dragons and demons and damsels in distress—and return alive with the scientific truth.

Logo No. 157. Kurland, Michael. *The Whenabouts of Burr.* Code No. UY1182. First edition. First printing, July 1975. 158 pp. Cover art by Kelly Freas. See *Anatomy of Wonder* 3-451 (1981). $1.25.

Someone had taken the original document of the U.S. Constitution and substituted another. The substitute was identical, it was just as old, it was equally authentic, except that it had been signed by Aaron Burr! It contradicted history, but it was real, and it was there for everyone to see!

And it called for some out-of-this-world detective work. There must be alternate Americas, and one of them must be an American union that Burr had shaped. With a few impossible coins, the way was pointed, and the search for the "whenabouts" of Burr began a hunt through all the Americas that might have been, with Alexander Hamilton to point the way and Aaron Burr to block it!

Logo No. 158. Cowper, Richard (pseud. John Middleton Murry, Jr.). *The Twilight of Briareus.* Code No. UW1183. First paperback edition. First printing, July 1975. 208 pp. Cover art by Kelly Freas. Issued earlier in U.S. by John Day Company (1974) and in the U.K. by Gollancz (1974). See *Anatomy of Wonder* 3-230 (1981). $1.50.

It took the light of the supernova Briareus Delta one hundred and thirty-two years to cross space to the Solar System. But the night it exploded in our sky was a night that would never be forgotten in the history of the world.

For, in that bath of cosmic particles, all things changed. Not only the weather and the flora and the fauna, but humanity itself received what seemed to be its death sentence. Sterility signalled the end of man, until the strange children known as the Zeta-mutants began to appear.

Logo No. 159. Akers, Alan Burt (pseud. Kenneth Bulmer). *Bladesman of*

Antares. Code No. UY1188. First edition. First printing, August 1975. 208 pp. Cover art and illustrations by Jack Gaughan. $1.25.

The problem with being a spy is that you have to make friends with the enemy to learn anything. And Dray Prescot, Earthman who had become prince of Vallia, was the kind of man who always stood by his friends. So, in his quest to learn the war secrets of Hamal, empire of the aircraft-makers, Dray found himself not only becoming blade-comrade to some of its greatest warriors, but of championing the very life of its cruelly beautiful queen.

And, though Dray's devotion to his glorious Vallian princess never flagged, his mission, and his life, was perilously balanced upon the razor-edged blades of loyalty versus duty.

(Bibliographer's note: The ninth book in the saga of Dray Prescot and the fourth in the Havilfar Cycle.

Logo No. 160. Bradley, Marion Zimmer. *The Heritage of Hastur.* Code No. UW1189. First edition. First printing, August 1975. 381 pp. Cover art by Jack Gaughan. Later published in U.K. by Arrow (1979). See *Anatomy of Wonder* 3-127 (1981). $1.50.

For many years, the Darkover novels of Marion Zimmer Bradley have built up an audience of devoted followers. No standard series this, for each novel spelled out a different epoch of the long history of that dark and mysterious world, taken from different eras and different aspects of its human and non-human cultures.

In this, the longest and most intricate of the Darkover books, is an epic of the most pivotal event in the strange love-hate relationship between the Terran worlds and this semi-alien offspring of forgotten peoples.

(Bibliographer's note: This, the ninth book in the Darkover series, was a 1975 Nebula nominee.)

Logo No. 161. Chilson, Robert. *The Star-Crowned Kings.* Code No. UY1190. First edition. First printing, August 1975. 188 pp. Cover art by Kelly Freas. $1.25.

Race Worden was his name, and he was a human being trying to live peacefully in his alloted niche on the colony world Mavia. One day he moved a stone slab by mental projection. Until that moment, he had regarded himself as a simple pawn on the vast social board. The feat raised him to a higher status at once: possibly a castle or bishop or knight. The kings of the board, they who ruled the human cosmos, had the telekinetic-telepathic power. They had crowned themselves with the stars, and all the rest of humanity were theirs to move or sacrifice as they wished.

But a maverick, even one like Race who didn't even know the rules of their games nor the extent of his place, was not to be tolerated. He had to be removed from the board before he broke up their cozy zodiac.

(Bibliographer's note: The author's second book.)

Logo No. 162. Brunner, John. *Total Eclipse.* Code No. UY1193. First paperback edition. First printing, September 1975. 206 pp. Cover art by

Christopher Foss. Published earlier in U.S. by Doubleday (1974) and in U.K. by Weidenfeld & Nicolson (1975). See *Anatomy of Wonder* 3-144 (1981). $1.25.

Sigma Draconis, nineteen light years from Earth, had once harbored a world with a high civilization. That world had died, and only certain mysterious artifacts had remained: wonderful creations, but just one of each kind.

By the year 2028, humanity was facing its own final crisis, and the starship *Stellaris* was sent to find out the cause of that neighboring race's extinction. If they could discover why, it might mean saving our own world from a similar disaster.

Logo No. 163. Tubb, E.C. *Eye of the Zodiac.* Code No. UY1194. First edition. First printing, September 1975. 176 pp. Cover art by George Barr. Later published in U.K. by Arrow (1978). $1.25.

Working for his next passage in his desperate quest, Earl Dumarest befriended a young man who said his home world was called Nerth. Nerth? Earth? New Earth, perhaps? Or even the old and original world, the one that Dumarest sought.

In any case, a vital clue had to be investigated, so Dumarest came to Nerth. The Cyclan, his cosmos-spanning enemy, was already there. So was mystery and terror and an initiation that defied the imagination. It was a life and death challenge, but, for Dumarest, the hunt was at last getting warm, if Nerth was indeed the world that lay in the eye of the Zodiac.

(Bibliographer's note: The thirteenth book in the saga of Dumarest of Terra.)

Logo No. 164. Leiber, Fritz. *The Second Book of Fritz Leiber.* Code No. UY1195. First edition. First printing, September 1975. 204 pp. Cover art by Jack Gaughan. Later published in combination with *The Book of Fritz Leiber* by Gregg Press (1980) as the first hardcover edition of both titles. See *Survey of Science Fiction Literature IV* pp. 1958-1962 (1979). $1.25.

Contents:

Foreword	Ingmar Bergman: Fantasy Novelist
The Lion and the Lamb	Scream Wolf
The Mighty Tides	Those Wild Alien Words
Trapped in the Sea of Stars	The Mechanical Bride
Fafhrd and Me	Through Hyperspace with Brown Jenkin
Belsen Express	A Defense of Werewolves

Logo No. 165. Norton, Andre. *The Book of Andre Norton.* Code No. UY1198. First paperback edition. First printing, October 1975. 221 pp. Cover art by Jack Gaughan. Edited by Roger Elwood. Earlier issued by Chilton (1974) under the title *The Many Worlds of Andre Norton.* See Schlobin, *The Literature of Fantasy* 826 (1979). $1.25.

Contents:

Introduction by Donald A. Wollheim	The Long Night of Waiting
The Toads of Grimmerdale	The Gifts of Asti

London Bridge
On Writing Fantasy
Mousetrap
All Cats Are Gray

Long Live Lord Kor!
Andre Norton: Loss of Faith by
    Rick Brooks
Norton Bibliography by
    Helen-Jo Jakusz Hewitt

Logo No. 166. Carter, Lin ed. *The Year's Best Fantasy Stories: I.* Code No. UY1199. First edition. First printing, October 1975. 175 pp. Cover art by George Barr. See *Fantasy Literature*, pp. 191-192 (1979). $1.25.
Contents:
The Year in Fantasy: An Introduction

The Jewel of Arwen	Marion Zimmer Bradley
The Sword Dyrnwyn	Lloyd Alexander
The Temple of Abomination	Robert E. Howard
The Double Tower	Clark Ashton Smith
Trapped in the Shadowland	Fritz Leiber
Black Hawk of Valkarth	Lin Carter
Jewel Quest	Hannes Bok
The Emperor's Fan	L. Sprague de Camp
Falcon's Mate	Pat McIntosh
The City of Madness	Charles R. Saunders
The Seventeen Virgins	Jack Vance

The Year's Best Fantasy Books: An Appendix

Logo No. 167. Defontenay, C.I. *Star (Psi Cassiopeia).* Code No. UY1200. First U.S. and first English language edition. First printing, October 1975. 191 pp. Cover art and illustrations by George Barr. Translated by P.J. Sokolowski. Originally published under the title *Star ou Psi Cassiopee: Histoire Merveilleuse de l'un des Mondes de l'Espace,* by Ledoyen, Paris, France (1854). $1.25.
"Defontenay invented the novel of the future, of science fiction and of interplanetary voyages far in advance of Jules Verne." —Jean Marchand
"In reading Defontenay, one occasionally feels that he had been preceded by a whole school of science fiction—by SF anthologies, magazines, and—why not?—fan publications; in short by numerous writers whose works could have influenced him, for the reader will come across many inventions that were rediscovered afterward, often long afterward....And when one thinks that Defontenay pushed audacity in his epic—because it is an epic—to the point of giving examples of Star poetry and theater...!" —Pierre Versins
(Bibliographer's note: Preceded Jules Verne's moon voyages and blurbed by DAW as the first modern "space opera.")

Logo No. 168. Anvil, Christopher (pseud. Harry C. Crosby, Jr.) *Warlord's World.* Code No. UY1201. First edition. First printing, October 1975. 207 pp. Cover art by Kelly Freas. $1.25.
Vaughan Roberts of the almighty Interstellar Patrol was literally riding a roller coaster when he got the appeal for help from a damsel in distress.

Being a gallant space hero with time on his hands, he fell for it.

She was a princess of Festhold, a planet addicted to soldiery, military adventure, and hairy-chested heroics, where, unfortunately for the maiden, her side was being outfoxed and outsoldiered by a combination of treachery and armed might.

When Roberts found himself the odd-man-out in that perpetual war game, he realized that he was still on a roller coaster, only, this time, with his life and the Interstellar Patrol as the unwilling patsies.

Logo No. 169. Norman, John (pseud. John Lange). *Time Slave.* Code No. UW1204. First edition. First printing, November 1975. 380 pp. Cover art by Gino D'Achille. $1.50.

What has happened to man since the days when his rugged ancestors battled the mastodon and the saber-toothed tiger and wrested a living from the raw nature of an untamed world? This was the directive that brought a dedicated group of scientists to devise a means of sending one of their number back into the Old Stone Age when the great hunters of the Cro-Magnon days ripped the world away from the Neanderthals and their savage clan rivals.

(Bibliographer's note: If you're hooked on Tarl Cabot, you won't find him in this novel. You'll find his philosophy, though.)

Logo No. 170. Coney, Michael G. *Rax.* Code No. UY1205, First U.S. edition. First printing, November 1975. 189 pp. Cover art by Josh Kirby. Published earlier in U.K. by Gollancz (1975) as *Hello Summer. Goodbye.* See *Anatomy of Wonder* 3-222 (1981). $1.25.

It was an alien planet, yet not too alien from Earth. It had its differences: its ice-goblins, its curious furry lorin, its thickening water, and its unearthly tides. But, for a young man like Alika-Drove, thinking of a vacation by the sea, these oddities were the norm.

But this vacation was to be different. Rax was coming into the ascendent, and Rax, that cold second sun, was the equivalent of evil, of Satan, and of Hell. As its time grew near, everything began to get warped and sinister, until, for Alika-Drove, it would be either the harsh brutal end of his innocence or the end of his world forever.

(Bibliographer's note: Some great choice.)

Logo No. 171. Gordon, Stuart (pseud. Richard Gordon). *Three-Eyes.* Code No. UW1206. First edition. First printing, November 1975. 268 pp. Cover art by Michael Whelan. Later published in U.K. by Sidgwick & Jackson (1976). $1.50.

In a warped world, Scarbloom Valley seemed an exception. There, crops grew tall, and the superstition-ridden farmers gave thanks to the unseen Elder Ones with a human sacrifice each year.

Then the golem came over the mountain and seized their virgin offering. After the golem, all the troubles that were shaking the outside lands flooded in: the mutant godling, the mirror-masters, the dancing monsters, and those who would awaken the sleeping powers of the past. For

Scarbloom was the key, and, beneath its unnaturally fertile soil, lay the mind-blowing magma of a world's destruction.

(Bibliographer's note: The third book of The Eye trilogy.)

Logo No. 172. Dickson, Gordon R. *Soldier, Ask Not.* Code No. UW1207. First printing, November 1975. 223 pp. Cover art by Kelly Freas. Published earlier in U.S. by Dell Books (1967) and in U.K. by Sphere (1975). See *Anatomy of Wonder* 3-275 (1981). $1.50.

When mankind burst into the stars, the human psyche splintered, and humanity became many species, each a specialized overdevelopment of a single trait.

Tam Olyn was a trained news observer from Old Earth: a complete man. To him, the conflict between the fissuring worlds was at first a challenge, then a personal vendetta.

The Friendlies were his enemy. In them, blind, fanatical Faith had become an all-abiding obsession. The Dorsai were warriors, born and bred, but they had not used their talents for self-glory. Instead, they had placed them, for a price, at the service of others. When these two driving destructive talents of humanity met head on, Tam Olyn had a plan of his own for which cosmic humanity was not prepared.

(Bibliographer's note: Third Dorsai novel; part of the Childe Cycle. One-third of the book originally appeared as a novella in the October 1964 issue of *Galaxy Science Fiction* under the title, "Soldier, Ask Not" and was a 1965 Hugo Award winner.)

Logo No. 173. Akers, Alan Burt (pseud. Kenneth Bulmer). *Avenger of Antares.* Code No. UY1208. First edition. First printing, December 1975. 176 pp. Cover art and illustrations by Jack Gaughan. $1.25.

For a brief, but wonderful, moment, it seemed as if Dray Prescot was on the road to victory, for he was aboard a Vallian ship bound for home with the secret of Vallia's enemies in his possession. But Dray, the Earthman sent to the planet Kregen of the double-star Antares in Scorpio, had not fulfilled the mission of the unseen Star Lords, and, until he did, there could be no escape from peril!

And peril came: in the form of hideous sea raiders, in the sharp edges of the dueling blades of a swordsman enemy, and in the horrid rites of the underground cult of the Silver Leem.

(Bibliographer's note: The tenth book of the saga of Dray Prescot of Antares and the fifth in the Havilfar Cycle.)

Logo No. 174. Dickinson, Peter. *The Green Gene.* Code No. UY1209. First printing, December 1975. 176 pp. Cover art by John and Anthony II Gentile. Published earlier in U.S. by Pantheon Books (1973) and in U.K. by Hodder & Stoughton (1973). $1.25.

The Irish were having green-skinned babies, until they all were "wearing of the green" permanently! The Scots kept right up with them and turned green too! And the Welsh, being fellow Celtics, also became grass-colored! In all the world, only one meek little Indian genius had tracked down the wild gene that was doing it. So they called him to the British Isles, and thereby upset the whole delicately balanced green-apple cart!

Logo No. 175. Goulart, Ron. *When the Waker Sleeps.* Code No. UY1210. First edition. First printing, December 1975. 157 pp. Cover art by Michael Whelan. $1.25.

You've heard of the mad scientist's beautiful daughter? Well, Nat Kobean made the mistake of making a pass at the mad scientist's beautiful wife and thereby became a guinea pig for Dr. Dumpus's Dose.

The dose was a serum that would enable one to travel into the future by naps of fifty years duration. The unsolved part of the experiment was that the sleepers would only stay awake a limited time before falling asleep again for another half century.

So when Nat woke up fifty years later, he had to act fast to find an antidote. But an antidote in a world so changed was a problem that required too much time to solve. So, it was back to sleep and up again and back to sleep and up again.

(Bibliographer's note: That happens to me a lot.)

Logo No. 176. Kern, Gregory (pseud. E.C. Tubb). *Beyond the Galactic Lens.* Code No. UY1211. First edition. First printing, December 1975. 156 pp. Cover art by Eddie Jones. $1.25.

Three times had the scientific genius, Kaifeng, slipped through the hands of the men of FATE, and three times those equally fanatic guardians of the fragile structure of interworld peace had tracked him down again. But now Kaifeng had something that the Free Acting Terran Envoys had never met before. He had a ship beyond all previous capacities, he had a crew of dedicated devils, and he had FATE's finest operative as his hostage. And when FATE pursued him beyond the very Milky Way itself, beyond the Galactic Lens, things changed very rapidly, for, out there, Kaifeng had the means to enforce a stop to human progress, and he would not hesitate to use it!

(Bibliographer's note: The sixteenth Cap Kennedy novel.)

Logo No. 177. Brunner, John. *The Book of John Brunner.* Code No. UY1213. First edition. First printing, January 1976. 159 pp. Cover art by Jack Gaughan. $1.25.

Contents:
Premumble
Crossword
Limerick #1
A Different Kick, or How To Get High without Actually Going into Orbit.
"Lullaby for the Mad Scientist's Daughter" Bloodstream
Domestic Crisis 2017
Hide and Seek (*Cache-Cache* By Gerard Klein)
Limerick #2
The Technological Folk Hero: Has He a Future?

"The Ballad of Teddy Hart"
Who Steals My Purse
Excerpt from a Social History of the 20th Century
Feghoot I
Die Spange (by Stefan George)
Limerick #3
Them As Can, Does
"Faithless Jack the Spaceman"
When Gabriel...
What We Have Here
Feghoot II
The Spartans' Epitaph at Thermopylae (from The Greek Anthology)
Limerick #4
The Educational Relevance of Science Fiction
"The Spacewreck of the Old 97"
Manalive (excerpt)
Matthew XVIII, 6
Feghoot III
Corrida (by Rainer Maria Rilke)
Limerick #5
The Evolution of a Science Fiction Writer
"The H-Bombs' Thunder"
The Atom Bomb Is Twenty-five This Year Epigrammata LXV (by Decimus Magnus Ausonius)
Solution to crossword

Logo No. 178. Moorcock, Michael. *The Land Leviathan.* Code No. UY1214. First printing, January 1976. 174 pp. (and one unnumbered). Cover art by Michael Whelan. Published earlier in the U.K by Quartet (1974) and in the U.S. by Doubleday (1974). $1.25.

Set on a world in which events defy the laws of Space and Time, this novel tells the tale of Oswald Bastable, a man trapped forever by Time.

The desperation of Bastable's bizarre fate runs deep, for an unpredictable time warp thrusts him into strange worlds, all parallel to his own, and yet different. Throughout all this, Bastable can remain steadfast in his determination to reach his own time because of his faith in one woman, inextricably bound to him in all dimensions of Time, and his belief in the existence of a secret Utopian citadel.

But there is one thing that may have the power to come between Bastable and his goal: a battle of Armageddon so horrifying in its believability that it almost obliterates his ability to keep searching.

(Bibliographer's note: Second book in the Oswald Bastable, Nomad of Time, sequence, the first being *The Warlord of the Air*.)

Logo No. 179. Vinge, Vernor. *The Witling.* Code No. UY1215. First edition. First printing, January 1976. 173 pp. Cover art by George Barr. Later published in U.K. by Dobson (1976). $1.25.

In the eyes of the inhabitants of Giri, the scientific explorers from outer space were witlings. In the context of that primitive-seeming planet, they were. On Giri, a peculiarity of evolution had given a special talent to all living things, and this talent made unnecessary most of the inventions associated with intelligent life elsewhere. Roads and planes, engines and doors: these were the products of witlings, not of "normal people." So, when the little band from Earth's exploration team fell into Giri hands, their problem was unprecedented. How could they demonstrate that science is worthwhile, and how could they keep the medieval masters of Giri from realizing their potential for cosmic mischief.

Logo No. 180. Carter, Lin. *In the Green Star's Glow*. Code No. UY1126. First edition. First printing, January 1976. 192 pp. Cover art and illustrations by Michael Whelan. $1.25.

He was Karn, the savage of the sky-high trees. He was protector and defender of the princess Niamh, whose very city was lost in the mapless jungles of the world under the Green Star.

But he was also an Earthling, whose helpless body lay in suspended animation in a guarded mansion in New England. It was his alien mind that drove Karn through perils no other would dare. But dare he must, for, though that alien planet was replete with dangers and treachery, with lost castles of forgotten science and armies of mindless monsters, there was a cause to be won and a love to be rescued.

(Bibliographer's note: The fifth and concluding novel in the Green Star saga.)

Logo No. 181. Dickson, Gordon R. *Dorsai!*. Code No. UW1218. First separate printing of an enlarged version of the paperback edition published in 1960 under the title, *The Genetic General*. First printing, February 1976. 236 pp. Cover art by Paul Lehr. See *Anatomy of Wonder* 3-275 (1981); *Survey of Science Fiction Literature I*, pp. 330-336 (1979). A magazine version was serialized in *Astounding Science Fiction* in 1959. Published later in U.K. by Sphere (1976). $1.50.

Donal Graeme, Dorsai of the Dorsai, was the final link in a long genetic train, the ultimate soldier, whose breadth of vision made him a master of space war and strategy—and something even greater. He was the focus of centuries of evolution, the culmination of planned development, and, through him, a new force made itself felt.

The Dorsai were renowned throughout the galaxy as the finest soldiers ever born, trained from birth to fight and win, no matter what the odds. With Donal at their head, they embarked upon the final, impossible venture: they set out to unify the splintered worlds of Mankind.

(Bibliographer's note: A novel in the Childe Cycle masterwork.)

Logo No. 182. Swann, Thomas Burnett. *The Minikins of Yam*. Code No. UY1219. First edition. First printing, February 1976. 156 pp. Cover art and illustrations by George Barr. See Schlobin, *The Literature of Fantasy* 1020 (1979). $1.25.

"Swann's neo-romantic fantasies of the past are unique. He uses the stuff of myth but with twists and inventions of his own." —The Village Voice.

This is the story of a young Pharaoh in Ancient Egypt, of his journey to the jungles and kingdoms of whispers and legend, and of his meeting with ghosts, gods and the minikins.

(Bibliographer's reverie: I wonder what it would be like to be an Egyptologist and say words like "minikin" out loud.)

Logo No. 183. Kurland, Michael. *Tomorrow Knight*. Code No. UY1220. First edition. First printing, February 1976. 156 pp. Cover art by Douglas Beekman. $1.25.

Somewhere out there in the dark, with both moons in hiding, the Saracen Horde was preparing for a night attack on the Holy Crusade. You could always tell because the Guests were gathering in their flitterboats.

For the men in the field, that didn't count. It was warfare, it was deadly, and there was a Sacred Cause to be won. That was the real thing. Or so it had been for Corporal Allan until his accident. Then he found he had a dozen warring epochs to fight through before he could win his own sacred cause, the *real* real thing.

Logo No. 184. Lee, Tanith. *Don't Bite the Sun*. Code No. UY1221. First edition. First printing, February 1976. 158 pp. Cover art by Brian Froud. $1.25.

It's *jang* to be wild and sexy and reckless and teen-age.

It's *jang* to do daredevil tricks and even get killed a few times. You could always come alive again.

It's *jang* to change your body, to switch your sex, to do anything you want to keep up with the crowd.

But there comes a time when you begin to think about serious things, to want to do something valid. That's when you find out there are rules beyond the rules, and that the world is something else than all they'd taught you.

(Bibliographer's note: First book of the *Don't Bite the Sun* sequence. What's the second book? You'll find out later.)

Logo No. 185. Norman, John (pseud. John Lange). *Tribesmen of Gor*. Code No. UW1223. First edition. First printing, March 1976. 364 pp. Cover art by Gino D'Achille. See Schlobin, *The Literature of Fantasy* 615 (1979). $1.50.

The Others were on the move! The Priest-Kings had received a message: "Surrender Gor." The date had been set for conquest or destruction. Tarl Cabot could no longer linger in Port Kar. Now he must act on behalf of the Priest-Kings, on behalf of Gor, and on behalf of Gor's teeming, unsuspecting, twin world known as Earth.

Evidence pointed to the great wasteland of the Tahari, the desert known only to the clannish, militant tribes of desert-wanderers. There must Cabot go. There among the feuds, along the trail of slavers, beyond the forbidding salt mines to a rendezvous with treachery, with a woman warlord, with a bandit chief, and with the monster intelligences from the worlds of steel.

(Bibliographer's note: The tenth book of the saga of Tarl Cabot.)

Logo No. 186. Rohmer, Sax (pseud. Arthur Sarsfield Ward). *The Wrath of Fu Manchu.* Code No. UW1224. First U.S. edition. First printing, March 1976. 240 pp. Cover art by Jack Gaughan. Published earlier in U.K. by Stacey (1973). $1.50.

Contents:

Introduction	by Robert E. Briney
The Wrath of Fu Manchu	The Mystery of the Fabulous Lamp
The Eyes of Fu Manchu	A Date at Shepheard's
The Word of Fu Manchu	The Mark of Maat
The Mind of Fu Manchu	The Treasure of Taia
Nightmare House	Crime Takes a Cruise
The Leopard-Couch	A House Possessed

(Bibliographer's note: Fifteenth and final Fu Manchu book, published, of course, posthumously. Only the first four stories, however, are Fu's.)

Logo No. 187. Rosny, J.H. *Ironcastle.* Code No. UY1225. First U.S. edition and first English language edition. 175 pp. Cover art and illustrations by Roy Krenkel. Translated and retold in English by Philip Jose Farmer. Originally entitled *L'Etonnante Aventure de Hareton Ironcastle*, published by Librairie Ernest Flammarion, Paris, France (1922). $1.25.

Somewhere in the unexplored heart of Africa, a part of this Earth has been taken over by an intelligence from outer space. Such was the message that reached the explorer, Hareton Ironcastle, member of the famous Baltimore Gun Club. In that hidden and transformed valley, would now be found monsters and pre-humans not to be seen anywhere else.

Such a challenge could not be ignored, and this is the account of Ironcastle's expedition of daring, but inexperienced, amateurs.

Logo No. 188. Cherryh, C.J. (pseud. Carolyn Janice Cherry). *Gate of Ivrel.* Code No. UY1226. First edition. First printing, March 1976. 191 pp. Cover art by Michael Whelan. See *Anatomy of Wonder* 3-185 (1981); *Fantasy Literature*, pp.65-66 (1979). Later published in U.K. by Futura (1977). Still later published by Doubleday (1979) as one novel in the trilogy, *The Book of Morgaine*, which was issued by the Science Fiction Book Club and later published in the U.K. by Methuen (1985). $1.25.

Scattered about the galaxy were the time-space gates of a vanished, but not forgotten, alien race. In their time, long before the rise of the native civilizations, they had terrorized a hundred worlds, not from villainy, but from folly, from tampering with the strands that held a universe together.

Now the task was to uproot these gates, destroy their potency for mischief, and take horror out of the hands of the few who hungered for power by misuse of the gates.

(Bibliographer's note: The author's first book.)

Logo No. 189. Akers, Alan Burt (pseud. Kenneth Bulmer). *Armada of Antares.* Code No. UY1227. First edition. First printing, April 1976. 223 pp. Cover art and illustrations by Michael Whelan. $1.25.

"For sheer pageantry and character development, both major and minor, Akers far outshines any other writer writing this type of story, and the tales of Dray Prescot are a feast for the fan of adventure tales" —The Jackson (Tenn.) Sun

"Here is escapism at its best and most wondrous." —Montreal Star

(Bibliographer's note: The eleventh book in the saga of Dray Prescot and the sixth in the Havilfar Cycle. This book includes a glossary to the Havilfar Cycle, which doesn't duplicate any of the persons, places and things contained in two previous glossaries.)

Logo No. 190. Dickson, Gordon R. *Ancient, My Enemy.* Code No. UW1228. First paperback edition. First printing, April 1976. 206 pp. Cover art by Eddie Jones. Previously published in U.S. by Doubleday (1974). Later published in U.K. by Sphere (1978). $1.50.

Contents:

Ancient, My Enemy	Love Me True
The Odd Ones	Our First Death
The Monkey Wrench	In the Bone
Tiger Green	The Bleak and Barren Land
The Friendly Man	

Logo No. 191. Bradley, Marion Zimmer. *The Shattered Chain.* Code No. UW1229. First edition. First printing, April 1976. 287 pp. Cover art by George Barr. Published later in U.K. by Arrow (1978) and in U.S. in hardcover by Gregg Press (1979). Again published with *Thendara House* in one volume by Doubleday (1983) as *Oath of the Renunciates.* See *Anatomy of Wonder* 4-77 (1987). $1.50.

In this novel, the many colorful threads of Darkover, that part-human, part-alien world, are rewoven. One such thread could be called the Heritage of Ardais, for the heir to the Ardais Domain has vanished and must be found.

The major thread and pattern concerns the role of women. While only women can command the power of the matrix and the secret sciences which keep Darkover from Terran hands, in most respects, they are still chattel; indeed, in some barbaric parts, even kept enchained. Yet there are the strange bands of pledged women known as the Free Amazons, equal to men and outside the laws that keep the rest of their sex subservient.

It is the Free Amazons who provide the key both to the Ardais mystery and the Terran-Darkover dilemma.

(Bibliographer's note: The tenth Darkover novel.)

Logo No. 192. Wollheim, Donald A. with Arthur W. Saha eds. *The 1976 Annual World's Best SF.* Code No. UW1232. First edition. First printing, May 1976. 304 pp. Cover art by Jack Gaughan. See *Anatomy of Wonder* 3-911 (1981). $1.50.

Contents:

Introduction	The Editor
Catch That Zeppelin!	Fritz Leiber
The Peddler's Apprentice	Joan D. Vinge and Vernor Vinge
The Bees of Knowledge	Barrington J. Bayley
The Storms of Windhaven	Lisa Tuttle and George R.R. Martin
The Engineer and the Executioner	Brian M. Stableford
Allegiances	Michael Bishop
Child of All Ages	P.J. Plauger
Helbent 4	Stephen Robinett
The Protocols of the Elders of Britain	John Brunner
The Custodians	Richard Cowper

Logo No. 193. Lee, Tanith. *The Storm Lord.* Code No. UE1233. First edition. First printing, May 1976. 350 pp. Cover art by Gino D'Achille. Published later in U.K. by Futura (1977). See Schlobin, *The Literature of Fantasy* 623 (1979). $1.75.

This novel is an epic story of an unknown planet and of the conflict of empires and peoples on that world. It is the story of a priestess raped and slain, of a baby born of a king and hidden among strangers, and of how that child, grown to manhood, sought his true heritage. There are alien gods and lost goddesses, warriors and wanderers, and vengeance long delayed.

(Bibliographer's note: Collected with *Anackire* and published by the Science Fiction Book Club (1984) as *The Wars of Vis*.)

Logo No. 194. Stableford, Brian M. *The Mind-Riders.* Code No. UY1234. First edition. First printing, May 1976. 143 pp. Cover art by Vincent DiFate. Published later in U.K. by Fontana (1977). See *Anatomy of Wonder* 3-712 (1981). $1.25.

If millions pay today just to watch two men fight for a champion's crown, tens of millions will pay for the additional thrill of being actually within the mind and body of the boxers themselves, to experience *in person* the tension and combat, to throw themselves into punch and counterpunch *without having to feel the pain.*

This is the story of Ryan Hart's final fight. His was not the publicized name of the boxer. Nobody knew him but the insiders, because he was the man who operated the challenger, whose mind handled the boxer's muscles, whose agonies were never felt by the E-linked millions, but who would be, for a few dozen minutes, the embodiment of half the human race!

Logo No. 195. Barrett, Neal Jr. *Aldair in Albion.* Code No. UY1235. First edition. First printing, May 1976. 205 pp. Cover art by Josh Kirby. $1.25.

On the day that Aldair found that his world had abruptly turned upside down, his history-changing quest began. and he didn't even know that it was to be a quest. Aldair had been a true acolyte of the Faith when it happened, and then he found himself an accursed outcast, the one against whom all hands were raised.

His only friends were those who had been his most vicious enemies. His only course led to the lands of horror. His final goal had to be that most forbidden of all lands, the dwelling place of the dead, that island of total terror known as Albion.

(Bibliographer's note: First book in the Albion series.)

Logo No. 196. Norton, Andre. *Perilous Dreams.* Code No. UY1237. First edition. First printing, June 1976. 199 pp. Cover art by George Barr. Part I of this book, "Toys of Tamisen," appeared in *If* in 1969. $1.25.

Would you like to dream high adventure, and have the dream become reality?

One could and did. She was Tamisen the Dreamer, trained to explore other worlds through her genetic ability to transfer herself through dream to their actualities. To a dreamer, all worlds, all times, were open.

But there were risks. There were perils such as no landbound explorer could conceive. For, in an infinity of worlds, there must be an infinity of enemies, of beasts, of personal peril, as well as an infinity of rewards and pleasures.

Contents:

Toys of Tamisen	Get Out of My Dreams
Ship of Mist	Nightmare

(Bibliographer's note: Four connected stories disguised as a novel.)

Logo No. 197. Farmer, Philip Jose. *Flight to Opar.* Code No. UW1238. First edition. First printing, June 1976. 212 pp. Cover art and illustrations by Roy Krenkel. $1.50.

Fabulous Opar, whose ruins and primitive priestess were memorable features of great Tarzan novels, was the birthplace of the warrior-hero Hadon. This was twelve thousand years ago, a time when great inland seas made Central Africa a land of mighty cities and high civilizations. Hadon was the rightful claimant to the throne of that long-forgotten empire, but his was no easy route to power. Instead, he had become the hunted prey of a tyrant's armies, accursed by the tyrant's gods, and fighting for his very life.

(Bibliographer's note: Third and final book in the Ancient Africa series.)

Logo No. 198. Tubb, E.C. *Jack of Swords.* Code No. UY1239. First edition. First printing, June 1976. 152 pp. Cover art by Thomas Barber Jr. Published later in U.K. by Arrow (1979). $1.25.

Dumarest, coming closer to the trail of the mythical Earth, is forced to divert his attention to hunt for a nebulous ghost world. That planet was said to hold on its surface a castle of heart's desire, where every wish would be fulfilled, including, perhaps, the return to Earth itself!

(Bibliographer's note: Fourteenth novel in the series about Earl Dumarest and his quest for lost Terra.)

Logo No. 199. Barbet, Pierre. (pseud. Claude Avice). *The Napoleons of Eridanus.* Code No. UY1240. First U.S. and first English language edition. First printing, June 1976. 157 pp. Cover art by Karel Thole; illustrated by Michael Gilbert. Translated by Stanley Hochman. Original edition entitled *Les Grognards d'Eridan*, published by Editions Fleuve Noir, Paris, France (1970). $1.25.

Supposing yours was an advanced Utopian race on a planet that had eliminated war so long ago that nobody knew how to conduct an adequate defense. And suppose that your solar system were then invaded by a fleet of alien militarists?

This is what happened to a certain planet in the Constellation Eridanus, and what its leaders did to solve their problem was to seek a primitive race that still engaged in warfare. They kidnapped a band of experienced soldiers, Napoleonic veterans fleeing Moscow through the snows of that terrible winter of 1812.

Captain Bernard of the Imperial Dragoons took on the task, but, being a loyal Bonapartist campaigner, he had ambitions that Utopian aliens could not suspect.

(Bibliographer's note: First book of the Eridanus sequence.)

Logo No. 200. Wollheim, Donald A. ed. *The DAW Science Fiction Reader.* Code No. UW1242. First edition. First printing, July 1976. 207 pp. Cover designed by One Plus One Studio. $1.50.

Contents:

Fur Magic	Andre Norton
Warrior	Gordon R. Dickson
The Truce	Tanith Lee
Wizard of Scorpio	Alan Burt Akers
The Martian El Dorado of Parker Wintley	Lin Carter
The Day of the Butterflies	Marion Zimmer Bradley
Captain Fagan Died Alone	Brian M. Stableford

(Bibliographer's note: A special anthology of DAW authors to celebrate the two-hundredth title published by DAW Books.)

Logo No. 201. Edson, J.T. *Bunduki.* Code No. UW1243. First U.S. edition. First printing, July 1976. 204 pp. Cover art by Michael Whelan. Published earlier by Transworld Publishers, Ltd. (1975). $1.50.

Is this a novel about Tarzan of the Apes? No. It's a novel about Tarzan's adopted son.

Is this a novel by Edgar Rice Burroughs? No. It's a novel by J.T. Edson, by special authorization of Burroughs' natural son.

Is this a novel about lost lands and savage beasts? You bet it is!

Is there a beautiful girl in frightful peril? Yes. What's more, she's Tarzan's adopted great-granddaughter.

(Bibliographer's query: Are you sick of these cute consanguineous coincidences? I am.)

Logo No. 202. Landis, Arthur H. *A World Called Camelot.* Code No. UY1244. First edition. First printing, July 1976. 220 pp. Cover art by Thomas Barber, Jr. An earlier and somewhat different version of this novel was published as a serial in 1969 under the title, "Let There Be Magick," as by James R. Keaveny. $1.25.

The natives called Fomalhaut II by the name of Fregis. In Galactic listings, the Adjustors and Watchers called it Camelot for good reasons. For one thing, magic seemed to work. For another, knighthood was the order of the day, and a strict chivalry ruled the lands. For a third, there was evil in the world to be combatted.

Mere observation from orbit no longer sufficed, because now that very evil had assumed menacing and warlike proportions. Armies and huge flying dragons were moving from the sinister southlands to overwhelm this world, much as the legions of legendary Mordor had moved to conquer Middle Earth. It was time for an Adjustor to step in and unravel the mysteries of Camelot, and that task fell to Kyrie Fern, henceforth to be known as Harl Lenti, swordsman and manipulator of a mightier magic: that of galactic science.

(Bibliographer's note: First book of the Camelot in Space series.)

Logo No. 203. Brunner, John. *Quicksand.* Code No. UW1245. First paperback edition. First printing, July 1976. 221 pp. Cover art by Paul Lehr. Published earlier by Doubleday (1967) in the U.S. and by Sidgwick & Jackson in the U.K. (1969). See *Anatomy of Wonder* 3-139 (1981). $1.50.

She appeared in our world naked, defenseless, unable to say a word anyone could understand. Her origin was simply a puzzle at first, then a scientific enigma, and, finally, a series of terrifying surmises that her most fascinated investigator was afraid to probe. But probe he must, for, somehow, he knew that this strange girl was a key to the kind of information science had sought for centuries. However, the more he uncovered from the depths of her mind, the deeper became the quicksand into which his own mind was sinking.

Logo No. 204. Akers, Alan Burt (pseud. Kenneth Bulmer). *The Tides of Kregen.* Code No. UY1247. First edition. First printing, August 1976. 208 pp. Cover art and illustrations by Michael Whelan. $1.25.

Of all the honors that Dray Prescot, Earthman, had won during his fabulous adventures on Kregen, planet of Antares in Scorpio, none were more valued by him than his membership in the Order of the Krozairs of Zy. The Krozairs were the highest order of chivalry on that turbulent planet, dedicated men, warriors of stern convictions and unflinching hearts. Prescot had been ordained a Krozair back at the dawn of his career.

Thus, when the Krozairs, in their hour of need, called on all their far-flung members for aid, he should have come. But he didn't. His return had been blocked by the anger of the mysterious Star Lords. Before Prescot could achieve redemption, he had two armies opposed to him, two warring kingdoms naming him outlaw, and only the tides of the seven moons as a weapon.

(Bibliographer's note: Twelfth book in the saga of Dray Prescot and first in the Krozair Cycle.)

Logo No. 205. Carter, Lin ed. *The Year's Best Fantasy Stories: 2.* Code No. UY1248. First edition. First printing, August 1976. 192 pp. Cover art by George Barr. See *Fantasy Literature*, pp. 191-192 (1979). $1.25.

Contents:

The Year in Fantasy: An Introduction

The Demoness	Tanith Lee
The Night of the Unicorn	Thomas Burnett Swann
Cry Wolf	Pat McIntosh
Under the Thumbs of the Gods	Fritz Leiber
The Guardian of the Vault	Paul Spencer
The Lamp from Atlantis	L. Sprague de Camp
Xiurhn	Gary Myers
The City in the Jewel	Lin Carter
In 'Ygiroth	Walter C. DeBill, Jr.
The Scroll of Morloc	Clark Ashton Smith and Lin Carter
Payment in Kind	C.A. Cador
Milord Sir Smiht, the English Wizard	Avram Davidson

The Year's Best Fantasy Books: An Appendix

Logo No. 206. Van Vogt, A.E. *Earth Factor X.* Code No. UY1249. First paperback edition. First printing, August 1976. 174 pp. Cover art by Deane Cate. Published earlier in the U.S. by Prentice-Hall (1974) and in the U.K. by Sidgwick & Jackson (1975) under the title *The Secret Galactics.* $1.25.

Reality twisted, slightly. Earth shivered in a momentary absence of vibration. For a split second, the solar system wasn't. And then, was again. Less than a billionth of a second, but a time shift occurred for connected persons.

As the shadow ship started to emerge from the time jump, men and aliens were locked in a secret, undeclared war to rule Earth. The aliens, genetically changed, looked exactly like humans. They were everywhere: in government, in business, in finance. Opposed to them were two women and one isolated brain in a mechanical body. But, between them, they possessed the one secret that the aliens had never discerned about the people of Earth.

Logo No. 207. Goulart, Ron. *A Whiff of Madness.* Code No. UY1250. First edition. First printing, August 1976. 156 pp. Cover art by Josh Kirby. $1.25.

Of all the colonized galaxy, the Barnum system was the whackiest. Nobody could ever predict what would be likely to happen there, so it was no surprise to newsman Jack Summer when he was sent to check out the King of Laranja East on the planet Peregrine.

Surprises were waiting for him anyway in the person of the universe's most lecherous photographer, in the weird claimant to the Starbuck fortune, in the highwaywoman known as the Scarlet Angel, and in the numerous angry catmen, scheming lizardmen, and, finally, in the person of the wily King Waldo, who alone could bring justice to the land, even though he, himself, was surely the notorious Phantom of the Fog!

(Bibliographer's note: A novel in the Barnum System series.)

Logo No. 208. Brunner, John. *Interstellar Empire.* Code No. UW1252. First edition. First printing, September 1976. 256 pp. Cover art by Paul Lehr. $1.50.

Contents:

On Standing on One's Own Feet	The Man from the Big Dark
The Altar on Asconel	The Wanton of Argus

(Bibliographer's note: "On Standing on One's Own Feet" first appeared in slightly different form in *Amra* #36. "The Altar on Asconel" first appeared in abridged form under the title "The Altar at Asconel" in *If*, and in full-length form under the present title as half of Ace Book M123 (1965). "The Man from the Big Dark" first appeared in *Science Fiction Adventures*. "The Wanton of Argus" first appeared in *Two Complete Science Adventure* books and was reprinted as half of Ace Book F227, under the title, *The Space-Time Juggler* (1963).)

Logo No. 209. Chester, William L. *Kioga of the Wilderness.* Code No. UW1253. First edition. First printing, September 1976. 303 pp. Cover art by John Hamberger. Published earlier in *Blue Book Magazine* as a serial in 1936. See Sampson, *Yesterday's Faces*, Volume 2, p. 158 (1984). $1.50.

This is the second Kioga novel, sequel to *Hawk of the Wilderness*, which first appeared as a 7-part serial in *Blue Book*, from April through October 1935. Kioga, the Snow Hawk, is a Tarzan imitation, but one of the better ones.

In the original novel, his parents and their Indian friend, Mokuyi, were cast away on a strange land north of Siberia. The climate of Nato'wa, an unmapped wilderness, was endurable due to warming ocean currents and a ring of volcanoes. After the death of his parents, Kioga was adopted and raised by Mokuyi, until, at age six, he was driven from the tribe because of reverse racial prejudice. This book encompasses adventures of Kiowa after he had reached manhood.

(Bibliographer's note: I love commenting about the pulps.)

Logo No. 210. Carter, Lin. *The Immortal of World's End.* Code No. UY1254. First edition. First printing, September 1976. 160 pp. Cover art by Michael Whelan. $1.25.

Here is Ganelon Silvermane, the mighty warrior who was intended by his ancient designers to be the world's Last Hero. Here is the legendary Flying City, self-contained, self-directed, and seeking only inhabitants to fill its luxurious homes. Here is the world's oldest man, the discoverer of immortality, who had probably forgotten more science in his thousands of years than any then living ever knew.

(Bibliographer's note: Here is the third book of the Gondwane epic. An appendix contains a glossary of places mentioned in the text.)

Logo No. 211. Stableford, Brian M. *The Florians.* Code No. UY1255. First edition. First printing, September 1976. 158 pp. Cover art by Michael Whelan. Later published in U.K. by Hamlyn (1978). $1.25.

Once a colony ship has left Earth, it cannot be recalled, and it cannot be contacted. The fate of these vessels and their cargos, designed to be the seeds of new human worlds, remained a tantalizing mystery to those who stayed home. The mission of the scientific recontact ship *Daedalus* was to go out there and find out what happened, and, if necessary, help out the colonists should their developing worlds have taken warped paths.

This novel chronicles the maiden voyage of the *Daedalus* and its crew of seven. On the world of the Florians, they did, indeed, find a planet in trouble, except that the inhabitants refused to admit it.

(Bibliographer's note: First book in the *Daedalus* series.)

Logo No. 212. Cherryh, C.J. (pseud. Carolyn Janice Cherry). *Brothers of Earth.* Code No UW1257. First paperback edition. First printing, October 1976. 254 pp. Cover art by Alan Atkinson. Issued earlier by the Science Fiction Book Club. Later published in the U.K. by Futura (1977). $1.50.

Kurt Morgan's survival capsule brought him down safely on a nameless Earth-type world. He was the only survivor of the battle crew that had just annihilated a planet of the Hanan, the enemy in a bitter galactic war.

The planet was inhabited by humanoids with a pre-technology civilization, a complex religion, and a long history of intricate internal relations. There was one other galactic battle survivor on that world, and she was an officer of the hated Hanan and also the high priestess of the land in which Kurt had found refuge.

Logo No. 213. Berglund, Edward P. ed. *The Disciples of Cthulhu.* Code No. UW1258. First edition. First printing, October 1976. 288 pp. Cover art by Karel Thole. $1.50.

Contents:

Editor's Foreword	Edward P. Berglund
Introduction	Robert Bloch
The Fairground Horror	Brian Lumley
The Silence of Erika Zann	James Wade
All-Eye	Bob Van Laerhoven
The Tugging	Ramsey Campbell
Where Uidhra Walks	Walter C. DeBill, Jr.
The Feaster from Afar	Joseph Payne Brennan
Zoth-Ommog	Lin Carter
Darkness, My Name Is	Eddy C. Bertin
The Terror from the Depths	Fritz Leiber

(Bibliographer's note: If you like this anthology, try *Tales of the Cthulhu Mythos* and *New Tales of the Cthulhu Mythos*, both published by Arkham House and both out of print (therefore expensive!). The latter, edited by Ramsey Campbell, has Stephen King's second Mythos story,

Crouch End." King's first, "Jerusalem's Lot," appears in King's fine collecion, *Night Shift*.)

Logo No. 214. Moorcock, Michael. *Elric of Melnibone*. Code No. UY1259. First U.S. printing of the text authorized by the author. First printing, October 1976. 160 pp. Cover art by Michael Whelan. A version of this novel, e-edited without the author's permission, was published by Lancer Books 1972) under the unauthorized title *The Dreaming City*. See Schlobin, *The Literature of Fantasy* 770 (1979). This text follows that of the U.K. version published by Hutchinson & Co. (1972). $1.25.

For ten thousand years, Melnibone ruled the world. Elric, the 428th Emperor, seemed destined to see that era come to an end. An albino, sustained by rare drugs, it fell to him to confront the rise of the Young Kingdoms, of the monsters and sorceries which were threatening to overwhelm him and his ancient crown.

(Bibliographer's note: First book of the Elric saga.)

Logo No. 215. Smith, George H. *The Second War of the Worlds*. Code No. JY1260. First edition. First printing, October 1976. 174 pp. Cover art by Jack Gaughan. $1.25.

As everyone knows, there are parallel Earths. So, when the Martians failed in their effort to conquer the Victorian world as told in H.G. Wells' famous eye-witness account, they took one short step X-wise and, having immunized themselves against Terran bacteria, tried again.

Earth's parallel world is called Annwn, and it was just slightly behind Victorian England in technology. So when they detected the explosions on the fourth planet, it looked as if, this time, the Martians would succeed. But the Martians had failed to take into account one peculiarity of Annwn. Almost everything was the same as Earth, but there were certain *curious* scientific differences.

(Bibliographer's note: Second book in the Annwn series.)

Logo No. 216. Wallace, Ian (pseud. John Wallace Pritchard). *The World Asunder*. Code No. UW1262. First edition. First printing, November 1976. 252 pp. Cover art by Jack Gaughan. Later published in U.K. by Dobson 1978). $1.50.

This novel depicts a conflict between time epochs, the struggle of demigods, the development of a super-weapon beyond today's, and the creation of the strangest peacekeeping organization ever devised.

(Bibliographer's note: One of the author's Adventures of Minds-in-Bodies series, the novel takes place in 1952 as well as other eras. The other Minds-in-Bodies novels are *Every Crazy Wind*, which is set in 1948, and *Pan Sagittarius*, set in 2509 and prior eras.)

Logo No. 217. Page, Gerald W. ed. *The Year's Best Horror Stories: Series V*. Code No. UY1263. First edition. First printing, November 1976. 208 pp. Cover art by Michael Whelan. See *Horror Literature* 4-289 (1981). $1.25.

Contents:

Logo No. 218. Strugatski, Arkadi & Boris. *The Final Circle of Paradise.* Code No. UY1264. First English language edition. First printing, November 1976. 172 pp. Cover art by Laurence Kresek. Translated by Leonid Renen. Originally entitled *Khischnye Veschi Veka*, published by Young Guard Publishing House, Moscow, Russia (1965). See *Survey of Science Fiction Literature II*, pp. 776-781 (1979). $1.25.

When Ivan Zhilin, interplanetary engineer, returned after years of space work, he wanted a quiet vacation on some sunny restful spot on Earth. At first it seemed he had found the place: a charming seaside city in a "liberated" country.

But somehow, since his long sojourn in far orbits, things had subtly gone wrong. He got disquieting hints of irrational actions, of secret societies of a destructive nature, of events of mass madness, and a constant reference to a mysterious product available only through the "right connections." When he pursued the enigmas, he found himself projected into the final circle of paradise, the ultimate electronic "high."

Logo No. 219. Tubb, E.C. *Spectrum of a Forgotten Sun.* Code No. UY1265. First edition. First printing, November 1976. 157 pp. Cover art by Ray Feibush. Later published in U.K. by Arrow (1980). $1.25.

Mercenaries are gamblers. They fight for pay, but they die without honor. To sell yourself as a soldier in someone else's war makes no sense unless your side wins. No one becomes a mercenary except desperate men, natural killers, and someone like Earl Dumarest. Earl sold himself because he had a quest, and he always needed money to continue his search for the way home, home to Earth, a world in whose existence nobody believed.

Earl's side lost, and Earl, a survivor, had to pay the penalty: more service as a military target or a mission for a ruthless lady who recognized a man of heroic talents when she saw one at her mercy. But there might be an unexpected bonus waiting for Earl at the end of that unwilling mission:

the coordinates of a planet called Terra and just possibly the spectrum of a forgotten sun.

(Bibliographer's note: Dumarest of Terra #15.)

Logo No. 220. Moorcock, Michael. *The Sailor on the Seas of Fate.* Code No. UY1270. First U.S. and first paperback edition. First printing, December 1976. 160 pp. Cover art by Michael Whelan. published earlier in U.K. by Quartet Books, London (1976). See Schlobin, *The Literature of Fantasy* 771 (1979). $1.25.

Elric of Melnibone, last of the emperors of a once mighty land, self-exiled bearer of the sword of power called Stormbringer, found a ship waiting for him on the misty seacoast of an alien land. Boarding it, he learned then that he was to serve a strange quest side by side with other heroes from other times, for this ship sailed no earthly waters and time; for it, time was flexible.

(Bibliographer's note: The second in sequence in the Elric saga.)

Logo No. 221. Akers, Alan Burt (pseud. Kenneth Bulmer). *Renegade of Kregen.* Code No. UY1271. First edition. First printing, December 1976. 192 pp. Cover art by Michael Whelan; illustrated by Jack Gaughan. $1.25.

Never before in his adventurous career under the double suns of Antares had Dray Prescot been in as desperate a situation as he found himself on his second entry into the city of Magdag. Magdag had been the scene of one of Prescot's earliest experiences on Kregen, and he recalled it with loathing as a city of power-lusting slavers, of decadent worshippers of the Green Sun. As one who had been initiated into the chivalric order of Krozairs, he despised all that that city stood for.

But now Prescot was an outcast. Any Krozair, any follower of the Red Sun of his former friends, would slay him on sight. For him there was only one way to recover his home, his children, his self-respect. He would have to perform an act of valor so extreme, so fabulous, that its glory would wash away all that now stained his name. Only by reaching to the very heart of mighty Magdag could he hope to achieve such a suicidal triumph.

(Bibliographer's note: Thirteenth novel in the saga of Dray Prescot of Antares.)

Logo No. 222. Swann, Thomas Burnett. *The Gods Abide.* Code No. UY1272. First edition. First printing, December 1976. 160 pp. Cover art and illustrations by George Barr. See Schlobin, *The Literature of Fantasy* 1016 (1979). $1.25.

In this tale of the time of Rome and the fallen Celtic kingdoms, there is embodied the story of the retreat of the pagan gods and all their array of sprites and nymphs and little folk. Facing the ruthless practicality of the new religion which denied their very right to exist, the varied pre-humans faced utter destruction unless they could find a sanctuary beyond detection.

Logo No. 223. Lake, David J. *Walkers on the Sky.* Code No. UY1273. First edition. First printing, December 1976. 188 pp. Cover art by Richard Hescox. Published later in the U.K. in a revised edition by Fontana (1978). See *Anatomy of Wonder* 3-463 (1981). $1.25.

Sometimes the sky held only clouds, but, at other times, it could get quite busy. It could be full of sailing ships or bands of mounted warriors or even single figures strolling carefully across the empty air.

From the standpoint of those below, they were either apparitions or gods, but, in any case, to be ignored. From the standpoint of the sky walkers, those below were neither phantoms nor gods, yet certainly always beneath their notice. Both viewpoints were wrong.

Because the time had come when one of the sky walkers was going to do the incredible—fall through. And when that happened, all hell was going to break loose. And did!

(Bibliographer's note: Winner of the 1977 Australian Ditmar Award.)

Logo No. 224. Van Vogt, A.E. *Supermind*. Code No. UY1275. First edition. First printing, January 1977. 176 pp. Cover art by Vincent DiFate. Later published in U.K by Sidgwick & Jackson (1978) as first hardcover edition. $1.25.

Research Alpha sought the answer to the ultimate intelligence, and also to certain problems of other intelligent beings sharing our galaxy. Research Alpha sought the reason for humanity's very existence in a vast and apparently hostile cosmos. Research Alpha found answers they never expected. What they found ultimately lead to Point Omega, when man becomes one with totality!

Logo No. 225. Moorcock, Michael. *The Jewel in the Skull*. Code No. UY1276. First printing of the author-revised and authorized edition. First DAW printing, January 1977. 176 pp. Cover art by Richard Clifton-Dey. First published in U.S. by Lancer Books (1967). Unauthorized edition published in 1974. See Schlobin, *The Literature of Fantasy* 756 (1979). $1.25.

Dorian Hawkmoon, late the Duke of Koln, fell under the power of the Runestaff, a mysterious artifact more ancient than Time itself. His destiny, shaped by a vengeful oath sworn by the maddened Baron Meliadus of the Dark Empire, pitted Hawkmoon in battle against his own allies and forced him, by the Black Jewel embedded in his skull, to betray his very heritage.

(Bibliographer's note: First volume in the History of the Runestaff series.)

Logo No. 226. Lee, Tanith. *Drinking Sapphire Wine*. Code No. UY1277. First edition. First printing, January 1977. 175 pp. Cover art by Don Maitz. $1.25.

Four-BEE was an utopian city. If you didn't mind being taken care of all your long life, having a wild time as a "jang" teen-ager, able to do anything you wanted from killing yourself innumerable times, changing bodies, changing sex, and raising perpetual hell, it could be heaven. (Bibliographer's interjection: It sounds good to me.)

But, for one inhabitant, there was always something askew. He/she had tried everything, and, yet, the taste always soured. And then he/she succeeded in committing the one illegal act and was thrown out of heaven forever. But forever is not a term any native of that robotic Utopia understood. So he/she challenged the rules, declared independence, and set out to prove that a human was still smarter than the cleverest and most protective robot.

(Bibliographer's note: Sequel to *Don't Bite the Sun.* The book opens with a Glossary of "Jang" Slang and General Terms and concludes with a Glossary of Conventions, Institutions, and Devices.)

Logo No. 227. Dickson, Gordon R. *Naked to the Stars.* Code No. UW1278. First DAW printing, January 1977. 159 pp. Cover art by Paul Lehr. Published earlier in U.S. by Pyramid Books (1961). Later published in U.K. by Sphere (1978). $1.50.

This is the story of a star soldier who, during a battle against a non-human foe on a far planet, somehow lost sixteen hours from his memory. Discharged for the potential danger those lost hours may have programmed, Cal Truant made it his fixation to uncover the mystery buried in his mind, to find out what happened in those missing hours, and block the peril it might present to his fellow troopers, to his war command, and to the planet for which they fought. Earth.

Logo No. 228. Chester, William. *One Against a Wilderness.* Code No. UW1280. First edition. First printing, February 1977. 172 pp. Cover art by Richard Hescox. Originally appeared in serial form in *Blue Book Magazine* (1937). See Sampson *Yesterday's Faces* Vol. 2, p. 158 (1984). $1.50.

In the far north, warmed by volcanic fires, lies the undiscovered homeland of the people who became the North American Indians. Nato'wa is what they called their land, and, within its forested and lush domain, remained the last great unspoiled wilderness on Earth, a land of green jungles, of wild beasts, and primitive men.

Kioga, the Snow Hawk, son of wrecked explorers, and Tarzan imitation extraordinaire, was raised by the natives and various animals as one of their own.

(Bibliographer's note: The third Kioga book.)

Logo No. 229. Moorcock, Michael. *Legends from the End of Time.* Code No. UY1281. First paperback edition. First DAW printing, February 1977. 175 pp. Cover art by Bob Pepper. Published earlier in the U.S. by Harper & Row and in the U.K. by W.H. Allen (1976). $1.25.
Contents:
Legend the First: Pale Roses
Legend the Second: White Stars
Legend the Third: Ancient Shadows
New novelettes in the series about life at the End of Time, when the universe nears its finale, and a small band of hedonistic, but ingratiating, immortals seek only to amuse themselves with a technology they can no longer understand, although it satisfies their every whim.

(Bibliographer's note: Somewhat connected to the Dancers at the End of Time/Jerry Carnelian series.)

Logo No. 230. Stableford, Brian M. *Critical Threshold.* Code No. UY1282. First edition. First printing, February 1977. 160 pp. Cover art by Douglas Beekman. Later published in U.K. by Hamlyn (1979). $1.25.

The planet called Dendra seemed too good to be true. One vast forest world, marvelous climate, a balanced hospitable ecology: all should have spelled out a good place for a human colony. But the original survey team had registered doubts and listed it as borderline without further explanation. Nevertheless, the politicians had okayed it, and a colony had been landed there, and a hundred and fifty Earthly years had passed without anyone hearing from it. Now the recontact vessel *Daedalus* was coming to check up, and they found the climate as marvelous as before, the forest green and friendly, but the colony was an inexplicable disaster. There was a biological and psychological puzzle that had to be solved for the sake of all human worlds, and, for the crew of the *Daedalus*, it was either crack it or crack up.

(Bibliographer's note: Second book in the *Daedalus* series.)

Logo No. 231. Goulart, Ron. *The Panchronicon Plot.* Code No. UY1283. First edition. First printing, February 1977. 156 pp. Cover art by Josh Kirby. $1.25.

What better way to get rid of your political enemies than to shove them back into the past and maroon them there? It isn't exactly murder, but it sure could raise hob with history.

That was what was happening when they yelled for the Wild Talent Division. The actual time machine was a secret known only to the president, who was apparently the culprit! But someone like Jake Conger would be just weird enough to be able to locate the kind of nut who could travel in time itself.

Logo No. 232. Norman, John (pseud. John Lange). *Slave Girl of Gor.* Code No. UJ1285. First edition. First printing, March 1977. 446 pp. Cover art by Gino D'Achille. Later published in U.K. by Universal (1978). See Schlobin *The Literature of Fantasy* 616 (1979). $1.95.

Tarl Cabot had resumed his allegiance to the Priest-Kings, the non-human, but benevolent, rulers of Earth's orbital twin planet, Gor. Accordingly, Tarl knew that the battle for possession of the planet was under way; the Kurii, the beastlike invaders, had made their plans.

There was a girl, once Judy Thornton of Earth, found in the wilderness of Gor. Captured, as such lovely strangers were apt to be on that ruthless world, she was to undergo the training that would make of her a slave girl of great value.

Unknown to her captors was the fact that she was a tool of the Kurii, and that she carried a programmed message that imperilled the future of Gor. It was for possession of her mind and body that Priest-King and Kur-monster battled, while a planet went its way unsuspecting that its very fate was also locked within the slave collar that graced her neck.

(Bibliographer's note: Check out this cover. You'll understand why they're fighting for Judy's body in the eleventh book of the saga of Tarl Cabot.)

Logo No. 233. Moorcock, Michael. *The Weird of the White Wolf.* Code No. UY1286. First edition. First printing, March 1977. 159 pp. Cover art by Michael Whelan. See Schlobin, *The Literature of Fantasy* 772 (1979). A partial version of this book was previously published by Lancer Books (1967) as *The Stealer of Souls.* This revised version contains two sections presented here in chronological sequence which had been published out of context in a collection titled *The Singing Citadel* and published by Berkley Medallion Books (1970). $1.25.

Imrryr, the dreaming city; Yyrkoon, the hated usurper; Cymoril, the beloved: all had fallen to the fury and unearthly power of the albino prince and his terrible sword. Elric faced, at last, the fate that was to be his in this haunted era: that he must go forth, sword and man as one, and havoc and horror would be forever at his forefront until he found the Purpose that was yet obscured to him.

(Bibliographer's note: The third novel of Elric of Melnibone.)

Logo No. 234. Chandler, A. Bertram. *Star Courier.* Code No. UY1292. First edition. First printing, March 1977. 142 pp. Cover art by Ray Feibush. Later published in U.K. by Hale (1977) as first hardcover edition. $1.25.

In his long and fabulous career as the Captain Hornblower of space, John Grimes was to experience many strange things, rising through the ranks of the Interstellar Federation from triumphs to disaster, and ultimately becoming the most famous of the Rim Runners, far out along the edge of the Milky Way.

But there was a period when Grimes fell between one cosmic empire and another, on his own, commander only of a single deep-space pinnace and looking for work. And that was when he became a God! He thought he was just doing a mailman's job, but the price of the postage turned out to be divinity, with a lovely nude postmistress certified for a goddess!

(Bibliographer's note: Eighth and last book in the John Grimes: Federation Survey Service sequence.)

Logo No. 235. Clayton, Jo. *Diadem from the Stars.* Code No. UW1293. First edition. First printing, March 1977. 235 pp. Cover art by Michael Whelan. $1.50.

Far out among the stars, the masterminds of the spider people had placed their mightiest mysteries in the scientific device called the diadem; when that coronet was stolen, they were prepared to pursue it throughout eternity.

The thief crashed among the nomads of Jaydugar, a semi-barbarian world, and the diadem found its way into the hands and onto the skull of the girl Aleytys. She was herself a strange one, daughter of a sky wanderer, outcast among the people who had raised her out of fear and awe, and the diadem was to prove both her bane and her treasure. For she could not remove it once it had sunk its electronic web into her brain and nervous system, and she did not know how to control the powers that were contained within it.

Yet every moment she wore it, she would be a target for the vengeance of the spider race and the avarice of a thousand worlds.

(Bibliographer's note: First book of the Diadem series.)

Logo No. 236. Foster, M.A. *The Gameplayers of Zan.* Code No. UJ1287. First edition. First printing, April 1977. 445 pp. Cover art by Michael Whelan. Later published in U.K. by Hamlyn (1979). $1.95.

The ler had been genetically created to be a new race of supermen, and the experiment had not been entirely successful. They were superior to normal humans in certain ways, but all too human in others.

Grudgingly, suspiciously, the overpopulated billions of Earth alloted the families of the ler a special reservation: a last wilderness area where they could live their odd lives, contribute their brilliant talents to humanity's desperate needs, and yet be under constant surveillance. For the ler, the situation was precarious, and their future dubious. Then, with the disappearance of a ler girl outside the reservation, the explosion point had been reached.

(Bibliographer's note: Although the second novel to be published in the series chronologically, this is the first book of the "ler" trilogy.)

Logo No. 237. Akers, Alan Burt (pseud. Kenneth Bulmer). *Krozair of Kregen.* Code No. UW1288. First edition. First printing, April 1977. 223 pp. Cover art and illustrations by Josh Kirby. $1.50.

Never before in his fantastic career on Kregen, planet of the twin suns of Antares, had Dray Prescot been in such a desperate predicament. A despised outcast by his friends who wore the red of the sun Zair, he had now been condemned by his old enemies whose battle color was the green of the sun Grodno.

For, while among these slavers and conquerors of the green, searching for a way to turn the tide of war to his own redemption and his friends' advantage, he had personally encountered the deadly animosity of Grodno's king, had betrayed his champion, and had shattered all he had so carefully worked for. But continue he must, for now, in addition to the enormous feat that alone would restore his honor, he had a blood vengeance to achieve that overrode everything.

(Bibliographer's note: The fourteenth book in the saga of Dray Prescot and the third in the Krozair Cycle. Includes a glossary to the Krozair Cycle.)

Logo No. 238. Moorcock, Michael. *The Mad God's Amulet.* Code No. UY1289. First revised edition. First DAW printing, April 1977. 160 pp. Cover art by Richard Clifton-Dey. Published earlier in U.S. by Lancer (1968) and in U.K. by Mayflower (1969) as *Sorceror's Amulet.* See

Schlobin, *The Literature of Fantasy* 757 (1979). $1.25.

Having braved incredible dangers in his battle against the science-sorcery of the Dark Empire, Dorian Hawkmoon was returning to his homeland. But worse fate awaited him. His betrothed Yisselda had been abducted by the Mad God, an evil sorceror who had usurped the Red Amulet of the Runestaff. The amulet gave the power of the Runestaff itself to its possessor, and, now, that mighty force was in the perverted hands of the Mad God. Even as the destructive shadow of the Dark Empire spread across the world, Hawkmoon knew that only he could rescue Yisselda and the Red Amulet from the Red God. But had a mortal man the power to overcome a God?

(Bibliographer's note: Volume two in the History of the Runestaff.)

Logo No. 239. Lake, David J. *The Right Hand of Dextra.* Code No. UW1290. First edition. First printing, April 1977. 176 pp. Cover art by George Barr. See *Anatomy of Wonder* 4-316 (1987). $1.50.

The key to life on Earth is the DNA helix, which determines the characteristics of every living thing. The helix, a series of molecules within the life cell, is a spiral with a left-hand turn.

The planet called Dextra could have been a duplicate of Earth. It teemed with life, both flora and fauna. But, on Dextra, the helix of life had a right-hand thread, and there could be no viable combination between the two life forms: the native and the invading Terran. So it became a battle on the part of the colonists to uproot the native Dextran ecology, purple plants and beasts with surprising intelligence, and replace it with Earth-born green. But the planet fought back in its own way.

(Bibliographer's note: First book of the Dextra sequence.)

Logo No. 240. Wollheim, Donald A. with Arthur W. Saha eds. *The 1977 Annual World's Best SF.* Code No. UE1297. First edition. First printing, May 1977. 280 pp. Cover art by Jack Gaughan. See *Anatomy of Wonder* 3-911 (1981). $1.75.

Contents:

Introduction	The Editor
Appearance of Life	Brian W. Aldiss
Overdrawn at the Memory Bank	John Varley
Those Good Old Days of Liquid Fuel	Michael G. Coney
The Hertford Manuscript	Richard Cowper
Natural Advantage	Lester del Rey
The Bicentennial Man	Isaac Asimov
The Cabinet of Oliver Naylor	Barrington J. Bayley
My Boat	Joanna Russ
Houston, Houston, Do You Read?	James Tiptree, Jr.
I See You	Damon Knight

Logo No. 241. Piserchia, Doris. *Earthchild.* Code No. UW1308. First edition. First printing, May 1977. 204 pp. Cover art by Michael Whelan. Later published in U.K. by Dobson (1979). See *Anatomy of Wonder* 4-412 (1987).

$1.50.

She called herself Reee, and she was the last human being on Earth. This was the one thing she was sure of, because Earth was not a dead planet, not by a long shot. There were all manner of strange plants and bizarre animals, and there were the blue boys who insisted they were human, but she always set fire to them.

There was, however, Indigo, the all-devouring protoplasmic ocean that was literally gobbling up everything in the world. And there was the enigmatic Emeroo to whom she owed her continued existence. There were also the so-called Martians, humans who had fled to Mars and only came back to Earth to scout for survivors and vent their futile furies on the inhospitable homeworld.

Logo No. 242. Tubb, E.C. *Haven of Darkness.* Code No. UW1299. First edition. First printing, May 1977. 173 pp. Cover art by Don Maitz. Later published in U.K. by Arrow (1980). $1.50.

Dumarest had been to many worlds in his long quest for Earth, but none were as dangerous as Zakym. A mere stop on his route, Dumarest had thought, but he had not known then of the things that made Zakym of the double-sun unique. One was the daily recurrence of the dead: the time of delusia when spectres walked and criticized the works of the living. The other was the Pact, the unwritten treaty with an unseen species that divided the world forever. In daytime, it belonged to humanity; after dark, it became a hostile and alien planet.

Dumarest thought Zakym would be a mere stopover on his quest, but the living, the dead, and the invisible decided otherwise.

(Bibliographer's note: The sixteenth book in the saga of Dumarest of Terra.)

Logo No. 243. Carter, Lin. *The Barbarian of World's End.* Code No. UW1300. First edition. First printing, May 1977. 188 pp. Cover art by John Bierley. $1.50.

Ganelon, called Silvermane, was not even remotely akin to True Men. He was a Construct of the Time Gods, an android superman bred to some unknown purpose by an extinct race of unknown savants.

In this adventure, Ganelon has offered himself as hostage to the worst band of barbarians to roam the ancient plains of Earth. Ganelon, as captive of the Horde, rises to greater heights of heroism than ever before and begins to assume the full power of his mighty being.

(Bibliographer's note: The fourth book of the Gondwane epic. An appendix contains a glossary of places mentioned in the text. The first portion of the glossary appeared in *The Immortal of World's End.*)

Logo No. 244. Jakes, John. *The Best of John Jakes.* Edited and with an introduction by Martin Harry Greenberg and Joseph D. Olander. Code No. UE1302. First edition. First printing, June 1977. 252 pp. Cover art by Jack Gaughan. $1.75.

Contents:

Logo No. 245. Moorcock, Michael. *The Vanishing Tower.* Code No. UY1304. First U.S. edition of the authorized text. First printing, June 1977. 175 pp. Cover art by Michael Whelan. Published earlier in U.K. as *The Sleeping Sorceress* by New English Library (1970). See Schlobin, *The Literature of Fantasy* 773 (1979). A re-edited, unauthorized version of this novel, also titled *The Sleeping Sorceress,* was published by Lancer Books (1972). $1.25.

Elric of Melnibone, proud prince of ruins, last lord of a dying race, wanders the lands of the Young Kingdoms in search of the evil sorcerer Theleb K'aarna. His object is revenge. But, to achieve his goal, he must first brave such horrors as: the Creatures of Chaos, the freezing wilderness of World's Edge, the gold-skinned Kelmain hordes, King Urish the Seven-fingered, the Burning God, the Sighing Desert, and the terrible stone-age men of Pio.

Although Elric holds within him a destiny greater than he could ever know and controls the hellsword Stormbringer, stealer of souls, his task looks hopeless until he encounters Myshella, Empress of the Dawn, the sleeping sorceress.

(Bibliographer's note: The fourth book of the Elric saga.)

Logo No. 246. Bishop, Michael. *Beneath the Shattered Moons.* Code No. UW1305. First paperback edition. First printing, June 1977. 189 pp. Cover art by H.R. Van Dongen. Published earlier by Harper & Row (1976) under the title *And Strange at Ectaban the Trees.* Later published in U.K. under this title by Sphere (1978). $1.50.

In the future, on the island of Ongladred, mankind has survived two enigmatic, civilization-destroying setbacks. Now a third holocaust is anticipated. The people fear destruction from invading barbarians, the reappearance of a semi-mythical sea creature, and the devious intervention of the neo-human Parfects.

This imminent disaster is very much the concern of Ingram Marley, a government spy sent to keep surveillance over Stonelore, a secluded haven and the center of free thought on Ongladred, and Gabriel Elk, Stonelore's resident genius.

While panic and fear rage outside, deep inside Stonelore, the mysteries of life are pursued: reanimation of the dead, the invention of powerful laser weapons, and the secrets of "old earth" knowledge.

Logo No. 247. Lake, David J. *The Wildings of Westron.* Code No. UW1306. First edition. First printing, June 1977. 189 pp. Cover art by George Barr. $1.50.

The conflict between man and nature was never more unconditional than on the planet Dextra where the DNA that determines all life runs in reverse from Earth, and where no compromise can exist.

Either the green of Terra must exterminate the purple of Dextra or be exterminated. Yet truce lines were eventually drawn, time did pass, colonies and their governments did arise that seemed stable, until that time had to come when the battle would lead to Armageddon. When it came, it caught the humans in internal warfare, it caught the Dextran world developing a biological super-weapon, and found two humans confronting both crises together.

(Bibliographer's note: The second Dextra novel, sequel to *The Right Hand of Dextra*.)

Logo No. 248. Stableford, Brian M. *The Realms of Tartarus.* Code No. UJ1309. First edition. First printing, July 1977. 448 pp. Cover art by Ron Walotsky. Part One, *The Face of Heaven*, was published in England as a separate book in 1976. $1.95.

They had built Utopia on Earth at last; it was ten thousand years in the making. They built it on a platform that covered the polluted surface of the old world, turned men's eyes away from the unsolved problems of the bad old days, and brought their shining new cities up into the perpetual sunlight.

But, down there, in the lamplit "sky" of the old surface, life had persisted. Men existed, and semi-men, and things that never were men, and nobody in the sunlight above knew of them. Then, disturbing dreams began to intrude, and visions bothered a few sensitive minds.

One man investigated. One man went down to that forgotten basement of the Earth and thereby uncovered the grave of the world that was and let its transformed phantoms glimpse the light above.

Logo No. 249. Moorcock, Michael. *The Sword of the Dawn.* Code No. UY1310. First revised edition. First printing, July 1977. 173 pp. Cover art by Richard Clifton-Dey; maps by John Collier. First published in U.S. by Lancer (1968) and in U.K. by Mayflower (1969). Still later published in U.K. by White Lion (1973) as first hardcover edition. See Schlobin, *The Literature of Fantasy* 758 (1979). $1.25.

In Earth's dim future, the Dark Empire had grown more powerful, so powerful that it threatened to destroy even the well-protected province of the Kamarg. Only the ancient crystal machine of the wraith folk could save the Kamarg's people by warping them into another dimension. But Dorian Hawkwood knew that such a sanctuary was but an illusion. Though his destiny was still ruled by the Runestaff, he was fated to don sword and armor once again, to find himself in a strange, unfriendly land, battling new and powerful enemies.

(Bibliographer's note: The third volume in the History of the Runestaff.)

Logo No. 250. Page, Gerald W. ed. *The Year's Best Horror Stories: Series*

V. Code No. UW*1311. First edition. First printing, July 1977. 237 pp. Cover art by Michael Whelan. See *Horror Literature* 4-290 (1981). $1.50.

Contents:

Introduction	The Editor
The Service	Jerry Sohl
Long Hollow Swamp	Joseph Payne Brennan
Sing a Last Song of Valdese	Karl Edward Wagner
Harold's Blues	Glen Singer
The Well	H. Warner Munn
A Most Unusual Murder	Robert Bloch
Huzdra	Tanith Lee
Shatterday	Harlan Ellison
Children of the Forest	David Drake
The Day It Rained Lizards	Arthur Byron Cover
Followers of the Dark Star	Robert Edmond Alter
When All the Children Call My Name	C.L. Grant
Belsen Express	Fritz Leiber
Where the Woodbine Twineth	Manly Wade Wellman

Logo No. 251. Lee, Tanith. *Volkhavaar.* Code No. UW1312. First edition. First printing, July 1977. 192 pp. Cover art by Michael Whelan. Later published in U.K. by Hamlyn (1981). See *Survey of Modern Fantasy Literature IV*, pp. 2036-2038 (1979); *Fantasy Literature* pp. 108-109 (1979); Schlobin, *The Literature of Fantasy* 624 (1979). $1.50.

A novel of witchcraft and wonders on a world far removed from those we know. Here the gods contend for power, the Dark Forces against the Light, and here an entire city and its land is plunged into the shadow of an evil beyond anything conceivable.

It's the story of Shaina, the slave girl, and of Volk, the outcast, who enslaved himself to cosmic forces to gain total power, and of how they were to meet and clash, with an entire world as their prize.

Logo No. 252. Cherryh, C.J. (pseud. Carolyn Janice Cherry). *Hunter of Worlds.* Code No. UE1314. First paperback edition. First printing, August 1977. 254 pp. Cover art by John Berkey; frontispiece sketch by C.J. Cherryh. Hardcover edition issued by the Science Fiction Book Club (Code H 06 on page 213). Also published in U.K. by Futura (1977). $1.75.

The iduve were the most advanced spacefaring race in the galaxy. They traveled where they pleased in giant city-sized vessels, taking what they pleased, engrossed with their own affairs. The iduves were humanoids, but with a difference: they were predators incapable of human emotions.

Aiela was a world-survey officer who found himself abducted to live and serve the iduve clanship Ashanome. Forcibly mind-linked with two other humans, life became for him a totally different thing, a life lived on three levels and intended for dedication to the service of his captors.

(Bibliographer's note: A glossary of alien terms is included at the back of the book. You'll need to refer to it.)

Logo No. 253. DowDell, Del. *Warlord of Ghandor.* Code No. UW1315. First edition. First printing, August 1977. 253 pp. Cover art and frontispiece by Don Maitz. $1.50.

The fighting men of Ireland were gathering to repel Cromwell's invasion, and with them marched the Dowdalls under their brave young chief, Robert. Master swordsman of Europe, he had returned to lead his kinsmen's steel against the invaders. And then, to the confusion of history, he had vanished.

Here at last is his story, the story of Robert of Eire, who marched to fight an Earthly foe, only to find himself in desperate combat against the beastmen and alien warriors of another world, another Earth, but not the one on which he had been born.

(Bibliographer's note: This has got to be a pseudonym, and I haven't the vaguest idea who the author really is. My guess would be Lin Carter, but I've never known him to write under any name but his own.)

Logo No. 254. Moorcock, Michael. *The Bane of the Black Sword.* Code No. UY1316. First edition thus. First printing, August 1977. 157 pp. Cover art by Michael Whelan. Part of this book originally appeared in a book entitled *The Stealer of Souls*, published in the U.S. by Lancer Books in 1967. This revised version contains a section never previously published in chronological sequence, but which appeared out of context in a collection called *The Singing Citadel*, published by Berkley Medallion Books in 1970. See Schlobin, *The Literature of Fantasy* 774 (1979). $1.25.

High in the wintry sky climbed the dragons as Elric urged his charges westward. Thoughts of love, of peace, of vengeance even were lost in that reckless sweeping across the glowering skies which hung over that Ancient Age of the Young Kingdoms. Elric, proud and disdainful in his knowledge that even his deficient blood was the blood of the Sorcerer Kings of Melnibone, became detached.

He had no loyalties then, no friends, and, if evil possessed him, it was a pure, brilliant evil, untainted by human drivings.

High soared the dragons until below them was the heaving black mass, marring the landscape, the fear-driven horde of barbarians who, in their ignorance, had sought to conquer the lands beloved of Elric of Melnibone.

"Ho, dragon brothers—loose your venom—burn, burn! And in your burning cleanse the world!"

(Bibliographer's note: The fifth novel of Elric of Melnibone.)

Logo No. 255. Bayley, Barrington J. *The Grand Wheel.* Code No. UW1318. First edition. First printing, August 1977. 176 pp. Cover art by Don Maitz. Later published in U.K. by Fontana (1979). $1.50.

Cheyne Scarne was a gambler, and he took the big plunge when he bet his life to get to the inner circle of the Grand Wheel. Because the Wheel was the ultimate syndicate—the final Mafia—that controlled all that was illegal in all the planets under human control.

But Cheyne was not to know whether he had won or lost when he gained his point. Because the Wheel had plans for him, and they made him the historic offer he could not refuse.

There was, it seemed, a similar gambling combine in the rest of the galaxy, bigger by far than the little group of stars held by Earthlings. The Wheel wanted a piece of the action, so Cheyne Scarne found himself selected to be humanity's own player in a game in which nobody knew the value of the cards, and the rules of the game were infinitely variable!

Logo No. 256. Bradley, Marion Zimmer. *The Forbidden Tower*. Code No. UJ1323. First edition. First printing, September 1977. 364 pp. Cover art by Richard Hescox. Later printed in U.K. by Prior (1979) and in U.S. in hardcover by Gregg Press (1979). See *Anatomy of Wonder* 3-127 (1981). $1.95.

This is the novel of four who defied the powers of the matrix guardians, fanatics who protected those powers so that the planet of the ruddy sun might never fall beneath the influence of materialistic Terrans.

The four who found themselves fused into a terrifying unity in that defiance were two men and two women. The men were Damon Ridenow, a Comyn of the ruling caste, and Andrew Carr, the Earthman who had won for himself the right of clan-entry. The women were Ellemir, betrothed of Damon, and Callista, who foreswore her vows to seek the love of the alien from the stars.

All the forces of Ancient Darkover were to combine to resist this "unnatural" alliance.

(Bibliographer's note: This Darkover novel, a 1978 Hugo nominee, is the eleventh in the series.)

Logo No 257. Moorcock, Michael. *The Runestaff*. Code No. UY1324. First revised edition. First printing, September 1977. 158 pp. Cover art by Richard Clifton-Dey; map by John Collier. First published under the title *The Secret of the Runestaff* by Lancer Books (1969). Then published in U.K. by Mayflower (1969) under the present title. See Schlobin, *The Literature of Fantasy* 759 (1979). $1.25.

"As it is written: 'Those who swear by the Runestaff must then benefit or suffer from the consequences of the fixed pattern of destiny they set in motion.'

"And Baron Meliadus of Kroiden had sworn such an oath, had sworn vengeance against all of Castle Brass, had sworn that Yisselda, Count Brass' daughter, would be his. On that day, many months earlier, he had fixed the pattern of fate; a pattern that had involved him in strange destructive schemes, that had involved Dorian Hawkmoon in wild and uncanny adventures in distant places, and that was now nearing its terrible resolution."

—from *The High History of the Runestaff*

(Bibliographer's note: The fourth and final volume in the *History of the Runestaff*.)

Logo No. 258. Geston, Mark S. *The Siege of Wonder*. Code No. UW1325. First paperback edition. First printing, September 1977. 190 pp. Cover art by H.R. Van Dongen. Published earlier by Doubleday (1976). $1.50.

After centuries of fighting wizards, dedicated scientists have found the answer to winning the war: turn magic into science. Reduce it to its final empirical base, to be read and studied. To gather such information, the Special Office decides a transmitter must be implanted in a legendary unicorn, the prize talisman of the most powerful magician. Then it can spy upon the highest councils of sorcery and have the daily transmissions analyzed.

Wearing this electronic eye in place of his own, Aden enters the Holy City and carries out the mission. But it leaves him vulnerable to the wonders of enchantment, and he wanders the middle ground between two warring forces. As scientific rationality picks up momentum, and the enchantment of the enemy crumbles away before it, Aden, and those out to stop him, race to find the unicorn again.

Logo No. 259. Barrett, Neal, Jr. *Aldair, Master of Ships.* Code No. UW1326. First edition. First printing, September 1977. 158 pp. Cover art by Josh Kirby. $1.50.

This novel is a new account of Aldair, the young not-quite-man, and his world. For his world and ours are the same, but his lies in the future and seems destined to parallel the history of our own. Where is humanity? What legacy has true mankind left to its manlike descendants that they must relive our past?

Aldair has been forced into the role of a future Magellan, who must travel down the coasts of unmapped continents, facing monsters, winged lizards and great danger, to find a knowledge older than the history of his entire race. .

(Bibliographer's note: Second book in the Aldair series.)

Logo No. 260. Norvil, Manning (pseud. Kenneth Bulmer). *Dream Chariots.* Code No. UW1238. First edition. First printing, October 1977. 192 pp. Cover art by Richard Clifton-Dey. $1.50.

The world is now aware of the visits of the ancient astronauts to Earth when mankind was first at the dawn of civilization. What was it really like in those marvel days when the gods were physically on Earth, and their "chariots" traversed the skies at will?

The saga of Odan, son of one of those celestial "gods" by a mortal woman, brings to life all the excitement, color and strife of that era, when the cities of the first men were clustered around the Mediterranean basin, before the Flood had destroyed that fertile birthland.

So thrill to those days of yesteryear, when the Space Gods ruled the world, and a Conan imitation struggled for his sky-borne inheritance!

(Bibliographer's note: First book in the Odan series.)

Logo No. 261. Brunner, John. *The Production of Time.* Code No. UW1329. First unabridged U.S. edition of authorized text. First DAW printing, October 1977. 189 pp. Cover art by Don Maitz. Published earlier in U.S. by New American Library (1967) and in U.K. by Penguin (1970). See *Anatomy of Wonder* 3-138 (1981). $1.50.

Murray Douglas had been a theatrical star until he'd hit the bottle once too often. Now he had broken the habit, and, handsome and fit, was ready for a comeback. The most challenging opening available was an avant-garde play where the actors themselves would make up the drama as they went along.

But out at the isolated country estate where the rehearsals were going on, Murray found himself trapped on a real-life day-and-night stage in which nothing was as it seemed, in which inexplicable devices monitored everything, and eerie lures attracted each actor's psychological weakness. Who then was the real sponsor of this terrifying play, and to what alien audience was it to be presented?

(Bibliographer's note: 1968 Nebula nominee.)

Logo No. 262. Scott, Jody. *Passing for Human.* Code No. UW1330. First edition. First printing, October 1977. 191 pp. Cover art by Bob Pepper. $1.50.

Passing for Human or *Who Isn't Afraid of Virginia Woolf?* stars Benaroya, a 36-foot extraterrestial "dolphin" in the role of "Brenda Starr," "Emma Peel," "Mary Worth," Virginia Woolf, and a happy New Guinea hophead. There's an All-Star cast, including: Abraham Lincoln, Jennison, the Kansas Jayhawker, Heidi's grandfather, General George S. Patton, the Los Angeles Police Department, the Prince of Darkness, the Royal Canadian Mounted Police, Ancient Egypt, the Isle of Capri, Interstellar Station 8, four billion newly created people, and several hundred richard nixons.

(Bibliographer's note: I'm intrigued by this book. Aren't you?)

Logo No. 263. Stableford, Brian M. *Wildeblood's Empire.* Code No. UW1331. First edition. First printing, October 1977. 192 pp. Cover art by Michael Whelan. Later published in U.K. by Hamlyn (1979). $1.50.

The colony was successful. That was evident as soon as the recontact ship *Daedalus* had landed. It was successful, prosperous, and everything was due to the genius and work of J. Wildeblood, biochemist and planetary leader. The world even now bore the name of its benefactor, and it was truly his empire, with a grateful, hard-working people heeding every wish of his descendants.

But the suspicious scientific minds of the *Daedalus*'s special crew were very uneasy. Was Wildeblood's Empire all it seemed, or was there a structure invisible to the eye which spelled out something a lot more blood-curdling?

(Bibliographer's note: The third mission of the *Daedalus*.)

Logo No. 264. Moorcock, Michael. *Stormbringer.* Code No. UW1335. First edition of the complete text. First DAW printing, November 1977. 220 pp. Cover art by Michael Whelan. A version of this novel was published in the U.S. by Lancer Books in 1967. The full novel was originally serialized in *Science Fantasy* magazine in 1963-1964. An earlier, abridged edition, with a quarter of the text cut from it, was published in the U.K. by Herbert

Jenkins, Ltd. in 1965, as well as by Lancer. See Schlobin, *The Literature of Fantasy* 775 (1979). $1.50.

"There came a time when there was great movement upon the Earth and above it, when the destiny of Men and Gods was hammered out upon the forge of Fate, when monstrous wars were brewed, and mighty deeds were designed. And there rose up in this time, which was called the Age of the Young Kingdoms, heroes. Greatest of these heroes was a doom-driven adventurer who bore a crooning blade that he loathed.

"His name was Elric of Melnibone, king of ruins, lord of a scattered race that had once ruled the ancient world. Elric, sorcerer and swordsman, slayer of kin, despoiler of his homeland, white-faced albino, last of his line." —from the Prologue

(Bibliographer's note: We're not talking ordinary Mr. Nice Guy here. Oh, yes. The first Elric novel.)

Logo No. 265. Strugatski, Arkadi & Boris. *Monday Begins on Saturday.* Code No. UE1336. First English language edition. First printing, November 1977. 222 pp. Cover art by Bob Pepper. Translated by Leonid Renen. Originally published by the Young Guard Publishing House, Moscow, Russia (1966). $1.75.

The Soviets have been working secretly on the problems of psi powers in a top secret, well-guarded institute in Solovetz where the most intensive research is done to harness the power of black magic, wizardry, and the secrets of super-science and para-normal talents.

This account involves a time-travelling mattress, a man who was two men, a talking cat, an unspendable coin, a golem factory, and other imagination-staggering wonders.

Was it of books such as this that Nikolai Vasilievich Gogol once wrote:
"But what is the strangest, the most incomprehensible of all,
is the fact that authors can undertake such themes—I confess
this is altogether beyond me, really.... No, no, I don't understand it at all."

(Bibliographer's note: An unauthorized translation.)

Logo No. 266. Dickson, Gordon R. *None But Man.* Code No. UE1337. First DAW printing, November 1977. 240 pp. Cover art by Don Maitz. Published earlier in U.S. by Doubleday (1969). Also published in U.K. by Macdonald (1970). $1.75.

Out there, beyond the frontier, beyond the last human settlement in the Pleiades, lay the territory of the Moldaug: alien, menacing things from far, inhuman stars, who were gathering their forces for war. It seemed that the people of the Old Worlds, in unreasonable and unreasoning fear, were preparing to sacrifice the colonies of the New Worlds in a cowardly attempt to avert that war.

But not if frontiersman Cully When had anything to do with it!

Logo No. 267. Carter, Lin ed. *The Year's Best Fantasy Stories: 3.* Code No. UW1338. First edition. First printing, November 1977. 237 pp. Cover art by Josh Kirby. See *Fantasy Literature* p. 191-192 (1979). $1.50.

Contents:

The Year in Fantasy: An Introduction	The Editor
Eudoric's Unicorn	L. Sprague de Camp
Shadow of a Demon	Gardner F. Fox
Ring of Black Stone	Pat McIntosh
The Lonely Songs of Laren Dorr	George R.R. Martin
Two Suns Setting	Karl Edward Wagner
The Stairs in the Crypt	Clark Ashton Smith
The Goblin Blade	Raul Garcia Capella
The Dark King	C.J. Cherryh
Black Moonlight	Lin Carter
The Snout in the Alcove	Gary Myers
The Pool of the Moon	Charles R. Saunders
The Year's Best Fantasy Books: An Appendix	

Logo No. 268. Wollheim, Donald A. ed. *The Best from the Rest of the World: European Science Fiction.* Code No. UE1343. First paperback edition. First DAW printing, December 1977. 316 pp. Cover art by Jack Gaughan. Published earlier by Doubleday (1976). $1.75.

Contents:

Introduction by Donald A. Wollheim
Party Line by Gerard Klein (France)
Pairpuppets by Manuel Van Loggem (Holland)
The Scythe by Sandro Sandrelli (Italy)
A Whiter Shade of Pale by Jon Bing (Norway)
Paradise 3000 by Herbert W. Franke (Germany)
My Eyes, They Burn! by Eddy C. Bertin (Belgium)
A Problem in Bionics by Pierre Barbet (France)
The King and the Dollmaker by Wolfgang Jeschke (Germany)
Codemus by Tor Age Bringsvaerd (Norway)
Rainy Day Revolution No. 39 by Luigi Cozzi (Italy)
Nobody Here But Us Shadows by Sam J. Lundwall (Sweden)
Round and Round and Round Again by Domingo Santos (Spain)
Planet for Sale by Niels E. Nielsen (Denmark)
Ysolde by Nathalie-Charles Henneberg (France)

Logo No. 269. Akers, Alan Burt (pseud. Kenneth Bulmar). *Secret Scorpio.* Code No. UW1344. First edition. First printing, December 1977. 207 pp. Cover art and illustrations by Josh Kirby. $1.50.

The brightest star in the Constellation Scorpio is the brilliant double sun Antares, around which orbits the inhabited planet called Kregen. Kregen is an Earthlike world, but strange, far stranger, than ours, for it is the scene of a conflict between galactic powers who utilize its many human nations and its astonishing variety of humanoid peoples as their warriors.

Dray Prescot of Earth had been a tool of those powers, but courage and ingenuity had won him a high role in the Vallian Empire and a certain independence of his own. Thus, when a mysterious monster cult began to undermine the empire, and, when his own beloved princess became a victim of those secret schemers, Prescot had to go into action.

(Bibliographer's note: The fifteenth adventure in the saga of Dray Prescot.)

Logo No. 270. Swann, Thomas Burnett. *Cry Silver Bells.* Code No. UW1345. First edition. First printing, December 1977. 192 pp. Cover art and illustrations by George Barr. See Schlobin, *The Literature of Fantasy* 1029 (1979). $1.50.

"I am Zoe, Dryad of Crete. Yes, I live in a tree, my ears are pointed, my hair is green (I refuse to disclose my age). But the story I wish to tell is less of me than of Silver Bells, the last of the Minotaurs (except his nephew Eunostos, still a child); and the Humans, Lordon and Hora, who invaded my Country but not to conquer or kill. (Lordon, bless him, will help me to tell my tale, for he knows the human heart.)

"I must also describe the Sphinx, the monster from Egypt, though the tiniest thought of her is like a thunderous wave, which churns you and chokes you and bruises your face with coral; and threatens to drown.

"A good listener never interrupts." —Prologue

(Bibliographer's note: Chronologically, the first Minotaur novel. Published posthumously.)

Logo No. 271. Tubb, E.C. *Prison of Night.* Code No. UW1346. First edition. First printing, December 1977. 160 pp. Cover art by Don Maitz. $1.50.

Urgent message from Central Intelligence to local Cyber agent: "You will proceed to the planet Zakym with the utmost dispatch. Dumarest is not to be killed or his intelligence placed in danger. This is of utmost priority. Once found he is to be removed from the planet immediately. Zakym is approaching a critical state as regards the stability of its present culture. Find Dumarest and move him before he becomes embroiled in a war!"

But Earl Dumarest, seeker of lost Terra, was not ready to leave Zakym, world of the night rulers and the day people. He had a romance to defend, a mystery to be solved, and he had his next step to the mysterious Sol system to be determined.

(Bibliographer's note: The seventeenth novel in the series of Dumarest of Terra.)

Logo No. 272. Lee, Tanith. *Vazkor, Son of Vazkor.* Code No. UJ1350. First edition. First printing, January 1978. 220 pp. Cover art by Gino D'Achille. Later published in U.K. by Futura (1979) as *Shadowfire.* See *Anatomy of Wonder* 3-470 (1981); Schlobin, *The Literature of Fantasy* 626 (1979); *Survey of Modern Fantasy Literature I*, pp. 116-121 (1983). $1.95.

I saw her, hanging in the sky like a flake of the moon. A woman, her face masked by a white shireen, her body by a black shift, but her white arms spread, and her white, white, bone-white hair blowing all around her like a flame composed of smoke. Recognition was immediate. It was my mother.

I shouted at her: "Your son, Ettook's warrior! Do you like what you have made of me? I might have been a prince in Eshkorek Arnor, or in Ezlann. I might have been a king with a great army at my back, beautiful women to please me, and Power to make all men do as I wished. Do you like what you have made?"

It was crystal clear to me, what he had meant for me, my father Vazkor, and what she had robbed me of. I drew from my belt my hunting knife and threw it at her heart.

(Bibliographer's note: Second book of the Birthgrave trilogy.)

Logo No. 273. Chandler, A. Bertram. *The Way Back.* Code No. UW1352. First U.S. edition. First printing, January 1978. 175 pp. Cover art by John Berkey. Published earlier in U.K. by Hale (1976). $1.50.

Lost in space. Lost in time. There can be no more terrifying situation for any spaceman to be in, and such was the problem when Commodore Grimes' Faraway Quest broke free from the mysterious Kinsolving's Planet. Because the universe was vast, and they had been out beyond the Galactic Lens; because time is infinite, and they had slipped beyond their own epoch, and, because, in whatever universe they were in, they could raise no etheric word, no telepathic beacon, no other star vessel.

But, for John Grimes, a veritable Commodore Hornblower of the future space seas, there had to be a way back. The first step was to locate Earth, the launching place for all humanity. But Earth turned out to be legend and myth and faith, and Grimes' rebellious crew were to enact roles already fabled before they were all born.

(Bibliographer's note: A book in the John Grimes: Rim Runners series.)

Logo No. 274. Dickson, Gordon R. *Necromancer.* Code No. UE1353. First DAW printing, January 1978. 189 pp. Cover art by Jack Gaughan from a sketch by Kelly Freas. Published earlier in U.S. by Doubleday (1962) and in U.K. by Mayflower (1963). Also published in U.S. by Macfadden (1963) as *No Room for Man.* See *Survey of Science Fiction Literature I* pp. 330-336 (1979); *Anatomy of Wonder* 3-275 (1981). $1.75.

At the crisis point of humanity's near future, the mysterious cult called the Chantry Guild arose. It was their contention that the computerized world society would fall of its own weight; that it would reduce Earth's billions to a mass of faceless biped ants.

They raised the call of destruction. They called upon alternate laws of science, the powers of nature that men had once called witchcraft, the necromantic anti-science of the past brought forward to save the world by destroying it!

(Bibliographer's note: First novel published in the Childe Cycle and forerunner to the era of the Dorsai.)

Logo No. 275. Clayton, Jo. *Lamarchos.* Code No. UW1354. First edition. First printing, January 1978. 224 pp. Cover art by Michael Whelan. $1.50.

The diadem that crowned the head of Aleytys was in contact with her central nervous system and invisible to outsiders. But even that star-born fugitive herself did not know what the diadem's powers were or what it could do to or for her.

What she did know was that it made her the target of the diadem's unrelenting and non-human owners who had tracked it across space and were still on her trail. She herself had started in search of her own people, but, before she could make progress, she would have to conquer both the unyielding mind-slave band she wore and the menace it held for all in contact with her.

(Bibliographer's note: Second novel in the Diadem series.)

Logo No. 276. Lee, Tanith. *Quest for the White Witch.* Code No. UJ1357. First edition. First printing, February 1978. 317 pp. Cover art by Gino D'Achille. Later published in U.K. by Futura (1979). See *Anatomy of Wonder* 3-470 (1981); Schlobin, *The Literature of Fantasy* 627 (1979); *Survey of Modern Fantasy Literature I* pp. 116-121 (1983). $1.95.

He called himself by the name of the father he had never known, Vazkor, king of a forgotten land. In his veins were mingled the blood of that regal warrior and that of his witch mother, the silver-masked, snowy-haired survivor of the hated Old Race. He had sworn that she would die at his hands in the name of his father and all that his world had become.

Across that barbaric and age-haunted planet, his quest went relentlessly on. As he searched, so grew his own powers, his fearful heritage. Across wide seas, in conquered cities, and among haunted mountains, the hunt took him. As he drew closer to his objective, the clearer became the way she must be slain, the more certain his ability to sunder all her witchcraft and ancient science to rid the world once and for all of his creator, the white witch from the volcano.

(Bibliographer's note: Third book of the Birthgrave trilogy.)

Logo No. 277. Moorcock, Michael. *A Messiah at the End of Time.* Code No. UW1358. First U.S. edition. First printing, February 1978. 192 pp. Cover art by Bob Pepper. Published earlier in U.K. by W.H. Allen (1977) under the title *The Transformation of Miss Mavis Ming.* $1.50.

"I welcome you, people of Earth, to my presence. I cannot say how moved I am to be amongst you again and I appreciate your own feelings on this wonderful day. For the Hero of your greatest legends returns to you. Ah, how you must have prayed for me to come back to you. To bring you Life. To bring you Reassurance. To bring you that Tranquility that can only be achieved by Pain! Well, dear people of Earth, I am back. At long last I am back!"

Unfortunately for the world's self-proclaimed Savior, his hearers were the "Dancers from the End of Time," those decadent, bored inheritors of ultimate power as the world entered its final days. These included that authority on all the ancient faiths, Doctor Volospion; Argonheart Po, the super-cook; My Lady Charlotina; and that impregnable spinster from the 21st Century, Miss Mavis Ming.

The last thing they needed was a messiah. Especially one like the

Fireclown, for that was who it was.

(Bibliographer's note: A book in the Dancers at the End of Time/Jerry Carnelian series.)

Logo No. 278. Leiber, Fritz. *A Specter Is Haunting Texas.* Code No. UJ1359. First DAW printing, February 1978. 220 pp. Cover art by H.R. Van Dongen. Published earlier in the U.S. by Walker (1969) and in the U.K. by Gollancz (1969). See *Anatomy of Wonder* 3-481 (1981). $1.95.

Scully La Cruz was a Thin, a muscleless free-fall phenomenon whose home was the Sack circling the Moon, and who could only support life in Earth-Gravity conditions by having himself encased in a titanium exoskeleton. To the inhabitants of the ravaged post-war Earth, he looked spectrally outlandish.

To Scully, the inhabitants of Earth looked equally odd, because the U.S.A. had disappeared in the aftermath of the atomic conflict and had been replaced by Greater Texas, and Greater Texas was dominated by the Greater Texans, masterful giants created by hormone treatments, who strode lordly about amidst their dwarfish peons and slaves.

To these unhappy underlings, Scully appeared as a Sign, a leader for revolt. To Scully, this reverence sparked his actor instinct sufficiently to make him decide to accept that role.

Logo No. 279. Lake, David J. *The Gods of Xuma, or Barsoom Revisited.* Code No. UW1360. First edition. First printing, February 1978. 189 pp. Cover art by Don Maitz. $1.50.

If the universe is infinite, it follows that there may be somewhere real physical worlds that duplicate those of the imagination. When Tom Carson caught sight of the third planet of 82 Eridani, he recognized at once its resemblance to that imaginary Mars called "Barsoom" by the ancient novelist Burroughs.

Of course there were differences, but, even so, this planet was ruddy, criss-crossed with canals, and its inhabitants were redskinned, fought with swords, and had many things superficially in common with the fantasy Mars of the John Carter adventures. But there were, indeed, vital variations that would eventually trip up the self-deceived science-fiction-reading travelers from 24th Century Earth.

(Bibliographer's note: First novel of the Xuma sequence.)

Logo No. 280. Norman, John (pseud. John Lange). *Beasts of Gor.* Code No. UJ1363. First edition. First printing, March 1978. 444 pp. Cover art by Gino D'Achille. Later published in U.K. by Star (1979). See Schlobin, *The Literature of Fantasy* 617 (1979). $1.95.

On Gor, the other world in Earth's orbit, the term beast can mean any of three things: first, there are the Kurii, the monsters from space who are about to invade that world; second, there are the Gorean warriors, men whose fighting ferocity is incomparable; and third, there are the slave girls, who are both beasts of burden and objects of desire. Tarl Cabot encounters all three as he moves from the canals of Port Kar to the taverns of Lydius, the tents of the Sardar Fair, and to a grand climax among the red hunters of the Arctic ice pack.

(Bibliographer's note: The twelfth book of the saga of Tarl Cabot.)

Logo No. 281. Norvil, Manning (pseud. Kenneth Bulmer). *Whetted Bronze.* Code No. UW1364. First edition. First printing, March 1978. 190 pp. Cover art by Michael Whelan. $1.50.

Before the Mediterranean was a sea, the cradle of civilization lay along the great basin between Europe and Africa. It was then that the astronauts from space, who dominated the sky with their "chariots," ruled barbaric humanity and sowed the roots of civilization. Odan, son of a living god by a mortal woman, had come to Eresh to claim his divine inheritance. But the wily ways of wizards, the schemes of royalty, and the conflicts of rival sky-lords were to test him to the utmost.

(Bibliographer's note: Second book in the Odan the Half-God series.)

Logo No. 282. Moorcock, Michael. *Dying for Tomorrow.* Code No. UW1366. First U.S. edition. First DAW printing, March 1978. 192 pp. Cover art by Michael Whelan. Published earlier in U.K. by Quartet Books (1976) under the title *Moorcock's Book of Martyrs.* $1.50.

Contents:

Introduction	Good-bye, Miranda
A Dead Singer	Flux
The Great Conqueror	Islands
Behold the Man	Waiting for the End of Time ...

Logo No. 283. Goulart, Ron. *Calling Dr. Patchwork.* Code No. UW1367. First edition. First printing, March 1978. 156 pp. Cover art by Josh Kirby. $1.50.

Odd Jobs, Inc. takes assignments that have baffled the best establishments of the rather cockeyed world of the year 2002. If it was wacky, impossible, or simply incredible, it was their oyster.

It was wacky that a stage magician could spring a murder trap for them without any reason. It was impossible that the great talents of dead actors could appear again. It was incredible that the work of the fictional Doctor Frankenstein could be bettered two hundred years later.

So this was a job for Odd Jobs, Inc. Someone was piecing together the best parts of the late greats of stage and pix to make a super-Frankenstein monster that would dominate the entertainment world—and maybe everything else.

(Bibliographer's note: As if it weren't obvious, this is a book in the Odd Jobs, Inc. series.)

Logo No. 284. Cherryh, C.J. (pseud. Carolyn Janice Cherry). *Well of Shiuan.* Code No. UJ1371. First edition. First printing, April 1978. 253 pp. Cover art by Michael Whelan; frontispiece by the author. Later published in U.K. by Magnum (1981). See *Anatomy of Wonder* 3-185 (1981); *Fantasy Literature* p.66 (1979). $1.95.

The world of Shiuan was doomed. Rising waters and shattering earthquakes due to the coming of a vast and strange new satellite had sealed the fate of its peoples, who must flee or die with their world. Their sole escape routes were the Gates, the passages between worlds established by a forgotten race. Just as this knowledge dawned on the desperate tribes and cities, there appeared the woman, Morgaine, whose mission was to seal Shiuan's Gates.

This is the story of Morgaine, her henchman, Nhi Vanye, and of their relentless enemy, Chya Roh, who followed them to the drowning planet.

(Bibliographer's note: Second book of the Morgaine trilogy.)

Logo No. 285. Akers, Alan Burt (pseud. Kenneth Bulmer). *Savage Scorpio.* Code No. UW1372. First edition. First printing, April 1978. 191 pp. Cover art and illustrations by Josh Kirby. $1.50.

Somewhere in the unmapped regions of Kregen, beneath the two suns of Antares, alpha star of the Constellation Scorpio, lies the hidden city of the Savanti. The Savanti were the ones responsible for tearing Dray Prescot away from his native Earth for their struggle against the Star Lords.

Dray had long sought the locale of his original landing, because it would help solve the mystery of his transition. Now the time had come when the search must be completed without delay, for the father of his beloved Delia was a victim of assassins, and only the Savanti could undo the evil that could shatter all that Dray held dear in his second planetary homeland.

(Bibliographer's note: The sixteenth novel in the saga of Dray Prescot and the second in the Vallian Cycle.)

Logo No. 286. Sturgeon, Theodore. *A Touch of Strange.* Code No. UJ1373. First DAW printing, April 1978. 255 pp. Cover art by Hans Arnold. Published earlier in U.S. by Doubleday (1958) and later in the U.K. by Hamlyn (1978). See *Anatomy of Wonder* 3-725 (1981). $1.95.

Contents:

Mr. Costello, Hero	A Touch of Strange
The Touch of Your Hand	The Other Celia
Affair with a Green Monkey	The Pod in the Barrier
A Crime for Llewellyn	The Girl Had Guts
It Opens the Sky	

Logo No. 287. Barbet, Pierre (pseud. Claude Avice). *The Joan-of-Arc Replay.* Code No. UW1374. First U.S. and first English language edition. First printing, April 1978. 189 pp. Cover art by Karel Thole. Translated by Stanley Hochman. Original edition entitled *Liane de Noldaz;* published by Editions Fleuve Noir, Paris, France.(1973). $1.50.

It was the contention of one galactic historian that similar planets must have similar histories. It was the contention of another that this did not imply identical histories. The challenge could be settled only by actual testing in the infinity of the cosmos.

The computer came up with the story of Joan of Arc on the Planet

Earth. Programmed anew, it produced a similar world, the Planet Noldaz of Sigma 32, with a human race rising from medievalism among whom a Maid would appear to lead her country's knights on a war of liberation.

The question: was she inevitably doomed to die at the stake, as Joan had before her? Did identical situations always mean identical conclusions?

Logo No. 288. Wollheim, Donald A. with Arthur W. Saha eds. *The 1978 Annual World's Best SF*. Code No. UJ1376. First edition. First printing, May 1978. 270 pp. Cover art by Jack Gaughan. See *Anatomy of Wonder* 3-911 (1981). $1.95.

Contents:

Introduction	The Editor
In the Hall of the Martian Kings	John Varley
A Time To Live	Joe Haldeman
The House of Compassionate Sharers	Michael Bishop
Particle Theory	Edward Bryant
The Taste of the Dish and the Savor of the Day	John Brunner
Jeffty Is Five	Harlan Ellison
The Screwfly Solution	Raccoona Sheldon
Eyes of Amber	Joan D. Vinge
Child of the Sun	James E. Gunn
Brother	Clifford D. Simak

Logo No. 289. Stableford, Brian M. *The City of the Sun*. Code No. UW1377. First edition. First printing, May 1978. 189 pp. Cover art by Don Maitz. Later published in U.K. by Hamlyn (1980). $1.50.

One of the classical Utopias of philosophy is the *City of the Sun* by Tommaso Campanella, which outlined an ideal community based upon a marvelous Arcadian city encompassing seven levels of advanced humanity.

Utopian groups had emigrated into space to found their ideal communities, and it was on such a colony world, appropriately called Arcadia, that the recontact starship *Daedalus* made its fourth planetfall. There, in all its perfect splendor, stood the fulfillment of Campanella's dream, the seven-circled City of the Sun.

But the city was too literal, the inhabitants too perfect, the world too Arcadian, and, very quickly, the *Daedalus*'s scientists realized that, in this Utopia, the idealists had unleashed a phenomenon that could undermine all human culture on all human worlds.

(Bibliographer's note: Fourth book in the *Daedalus* series.)

Logo No. 290. Chester, William L. *Kioga of the Unknown Land*. Code No. UJ1378. First edition. First printing, May 1978. 222 pp. Cover art by Richard Hescox. Earlier appeared in *Blue Book Magazine* in a six-part serial from March through August 1938. See Sampson, *Yesterday's Faces* Vol. 2, p. 158 (1984). $1.95.

"Blend together a hundred dreams which have haunted man's imagination and given shape to his popular literature: one result is William L. Chester's *Kioga of the Unknown Land*, the fourth and last of the epic adventures of Kioga, the Snow Hawk, in the wilderness of the unknown Arctic continent of Nato'wa, homeland of the American Indian.

* * *

In publishing *Kioga of the Unknown Land*, DAW Books has rescued from the obscurity of the pulp magazines of the 1930s one of the most imaginative and memorable American lost race novels."

— from the Introduction by Thomas D. Clareson

(Bibliographer's note: Fourth book in the Kioga, the Snow Hawk, series.)

Logo No. 291. Moorcock, Michael. *The Warlord of the Air.* Code No. UW1380. First DAW printing, May 1978. 175 pp. Cover art by Gino D'Achille. Previously published by Ace Books (1971) in U.S. and by New English Library (1971) as first U.K. and first hardcover edition. $1.50.

Who has not dreamed of how this Earth of ours could have been had the little incidents of history worked out otherwise? Suppose that a few of our present inventions had been made earlier, in the 19th Century instead of the 20th? Suppose some things had never been discovered at all? Suppose that politics had followed different courses? These things were all possible; are there then Earths where they did work out differently?

(Bibliographer's note: First book of The Nomad of Time series.)

Logo No. 292. Bradley, Marion Zimmer. *Stormqueen!* Code No. UJ1381. First edition. First printing, June 1978. 364 pp. Cover art by Michael Whelan. Later published in U.K. by Arrow (1980) and in U.S. by Gregg Press (1979) in first hardcover edition. $1.95.

The great epic of the world beneath the Bloody Sun known as Darkover did not begin with the coming of the Terrans. It began far earlier, during the dark days of the civilization that came to be known as the Ages of Chaos. In those years, the power of the matrix was first learned and misused in a power struggle between the rising Domains. That mental-physical force created a technology that threatened to make Darkover into a frightening duplicate of all that was bad in far-off Terra.

This novel takes the reader to the days when the matrix was in the hands of ambitious men, when genetic tampering was producing prodigies and wielders of strange powers, and when the heir of the Hasturs met his destiny in the persons of the witch-woman he loved and the mutant girl-child he had pledged to protect.

(Bibliographer's note: The twelfth Darkover novel.)

Logo No. 293. Carter, Lin. *The Wizard of Zao.* Code No. UE1383. First edition. First printing, June 1978. 176 pp. Cover art by Carl Lundgren. $1.75.

"A few years ago it occurred to me that it might be fun to design an entire solar system full of planets, and set a novel on each planet—and not science fiction novels either, as you might logically expect—but heroic fantasy. Not only would it be fun to do, but, since nobody has ever done it before, it could be an original and interesting experiment." —Lin Carter

This novel takes place on a planet revolving around the star Kylix in the Constellation of the Unicorn and is the story of the wandering green wizard, the most powerful wonder-worker of that amazing sphere, of his newly purchased slave girl who knew nothing of civilized ways, and of the mythical beasts and curious humans they encountered. For the wizard did have a purpose to his travels, and thereby hangs the tale!

Logo No. 294. Bayley, Barrington J. *Star Winds*. Code No. UE1384. First edition. First printing, June 1978. 191 pp. Cover art by David Bergen. See *Anatomy of Wonder* 4-47 (1987). $1.75.

The sails were the product of the Old Technology, lost long ago in the depleted Earth, and they were priceless. For, with those fantastic sheets of etheric material, ships could sail the sky and even brave the radiant tides between worlds and stars.

The alchemists who had replaced the scientists still sought the ancient secrets, and Rachad, apprentice to such a would-be wizard, learned that the key to his quest lay in a book abandoned in a Martian colonial ruin long, long ago.

But how to get to Mars? There was one way left: take a sea vessel, caulk it airtight, steal new sails, and fly the star winds in the way of the ancient windjammers.

Logo No. 295. Chandler, A. Bertram. *To Keep the Ship*. Code No. UE1385. First U.S. edition. First printing, June 1978. 175 pp. Cover art by H.R. Van Dongen. Published earlier in U.K. by Hale (1978). $1.75.

Although this was a low point in the ever-changing space career of the legendary John Grimes, it was not without its surprising moments. Between jobs, between loyalties, Grimes was owner and pilot of a small auxiliary vessel whose principal oddity was that it was made of gold. But precious metal or not, Grimes was running errands with it until he fell into the clutches of terrorists.

Susie and her comrades had a Cause, and it was going to take all his efforts to keep the one thing he had to have: his ship. Especially since they left the ship infested with a constantly increasing horde of mini-Susies, vicious little homunculi that looked exactly like their sexy prototype, except that they were hungry, sharp-toothed, and their only Cause was to eat Grimes alive!

(Bibliographer's note: A book in the John Grimes: Rim Runner series.)

Logo No. 296. Dibell, Ansen (pseud. Nancy Ann Dibble). *Pursuit of the Screamer*. Code No. UJ1386. First edition. First printing, July 1978. 270 pp. Cover art by Gino D'Achille. $1.95.

Never defend a Screamer! That was the cardinal rule of the household, and, when Jannus made that mistake, it meant that he, too, would be hunted to the death! Jannus was all-human, a young man, dedicated to the service of his hold, before the pursuit of the Screamer began.

Poli heard the psychic scream best, for she was not entirely human, a warrior-girl of the aboriginal race, doing her service at the household. She, too, was forced to join the Screamer's flight. And the Screamer? What was he? A small boy? A monstrous tiger? An inhuman robotic mind run from a forgotten mechanical monster computer? Or the last king of lost Kantmorie?

(Bibliographer's note: First book of the Kantmorie saga.)

Logo No. 297. Page, Gerald W. ed. *The Year's Best Horror Stories: Series VI.* Code No. UE1387. First edition. First printing, July 1978. 239 pp. Cover art by Michael Whelan. See *Horror Literature* 4-291 (1981). $1.75.

Contents:

Introduction	The Editor
At the Bottom of the Garden	David Campton
Screaming To Get Out	Janet Fox
Undertow	Karl Edward Wagner
I Can Hear the Dark	Dennis Etchison
Ever the Faith Endures	Manly Wade Wellman
The Horse Lord	Lisa Tuttle
Winter White	Tanith Lee
A Cobweb of Pulsing Veins	William Scott Home
Best of Luck	David Drake
Children of the Corn	Stephen King
If Damon Comes	Charles L. Grant
Drawing In	Ramsey Campbell
Within the Walls of Tyre	Michael Bishop

Logo No. 298. Smith, George H. *The Island Snatchers.* Code No. UW1388. First edition. First printing, July 1978. 189 pp. Cover art by Josh Kirby. $1.50.

Flying machines had not yet been invented on Earth's dimensional twin, Annwn. So Dylan MacBride thought it would be a good idea, even if a bit on the crackpot side from the viewpoint of that world's somewhat backward Victorian civilization. But when Dylan and his witch wife Clarinda tried out the machine by flying to Hibernia to attend a wild Irish wedding, they came a-cropper, for the Emerald Isle was not where it ought to be. Instead it was drifting rapidly westward under some strange power.

Now who would hijack a whole land of legends and fair lassies? And how was it done, and why?

(Bibliographer's note: Third book of the Annwn series.)

Logo No. 299. Tubb, E.C. *Incident on Ath.* Code No. UW1389. First edition. First printing, July 1978. 188 pp. Cover art by David Bergen. $1.50.

An art collector seemed an unlikely prospect for information on the galactic coordinates of the forgotten planet Earth. But Earl Dumarest never overlooked any clue, and, when he defended an art devotee named Sardia, he was unexpectedly rewarded by the sight of a painting she sought. For, in its sky, was the unmistakable features of cratered Luna, Earth's equally fabled satellite.

Sardia said the painter of the picture lived on a planet called Ath, and that was significant. So to Ath they went, she to find the painter, and Dumarest to find the source of the accurate lunar presentation.

But Ath was not yet Earth, and, between the painter and the seekers, stood the ominous forces of the Cyclan and of the enigmatic insurrectionists called the Ohrm.

(Bibliographer's note: The eighteenth novel in the saga of Dumarest of Terra.)

Logo No. 300. Cherryh, C.J. (pseud. Carolyn Janice Cherry). *The Faded Sun: Kesrith.* Code No. UJ1393. First paperback edition. First printing, August 1978. 252 pp. Cover art by Gino D'Achille; frontispiece by the author. Issued by the Science Fiction Book Club (first printing has code I 06 on page 247). See *Anatomy of Wonder* 3-186 (1981). $1.95.

This is the story of three people: Sten Duncan, a soldier of humanity; Niun, last warrior of the *mri*, humanity's enemies; Melein, priestess-queen of the final fallen *mri* stronghold.

This is the story of two mighty species fighting for a galaxy: humanity driving out from Earth, and the enigmatic regul struggling to hold their stars with *mri* mercenaries.

This is a story of diplomacy and warfare, of conspiracy and betrayal, and of three flesh-and-blood people who found themselves thrown together in a life-and-death alliance.

(Bibliographer's note: This is the first volume of the Faded Sun trilogy, a 1978 Nebula and 1979 Hugo nominee.)

Logo No. 301. Akers, Alan Burt (pseud. Kenneth Bulmer). *Captive Scorpio.* Code No. UW1394. First edition. First printing, August 1978. 190 pp. Cover art and illustrations by Josh Kirby. $1.50.

Dray Prescot, Earthman on Kregen, that wonder world circling the twin suns of Antares, had risen high in the empire of Vallia, but luck could not always sustain him.

When, at last, all the forces opposed to his lands, his princess, his emperor, and to him personally converged, it was to produce the darkest hour of his long career. For treason struck at the court, while rebel armies marched from the backlands, the war fleets of enemy nations were aloft, and the uncanny wizardry of a master scientist launched a spell of doom for all Prescot held dear.

With his back to the wall, Dray Prescot faced that time of peril with unflinching will, until the cruelest blow of all was struck: his warrior-daughter Dayra rode in the vanguard of his foes.

(Bibliographer's note: The seventeenth book in the saga of Dray Prescot.)

Logo No. 302. Silas, A.E. *The Panorama Egg.* Code No. UE1395. First edition. First printing, August 1978. 224 pp. Cover art by H.R. Van Dongen. $1.75.

His name was Archer, and he thought he was an ordinary man. The collectors of panorama eggs knew better, for Archer was such a collector, and there was a very special find awaiting him: the panorama egg that contained a world.

He was guided in the use of that incredible masterwork by the enigmatic gray woman, Mera Melaklos. That was her name in this everyday world, but her real name could have been something else beyond their space-time continuum. Archer and the gray woman crossed into a world that wasn't Earth and found they had special roles to play in a land where alternate science reigned, and a mission of heroism was the price of existence.

Logo No. 303. Dickson, Gordon R. *Hour of the Horde.* Code No. UW1397. First DAW printing, August 1978. 159 pp. Cover art by Greg Theakston. Published earlier by Putnam (1970). $1.50.

Annihilating everything before it, a horde of monstrous space travelers were advancing through the stars, and Earth lay in their route. To defend their home planets, the worlds that lay in the paths of the monsters created a super task force, asking each planet to contribute one especially talented warrior to help turn the invaders away.

Miles Vander was Earth's man, but when he arrived at the rendezvous point, he found that he was included in the special task force of the less civilized defenders. Nevertheless, in the contest of advanced nuclear weaponry and computer strategy, it turned out to be Vander's group that had the special independent qualities and the raw courage to meet the challenge most effectively.

Logo No. 304. Norton, Andre. *Yurth Burden.* Code No. UE1400. First edition. First printing, September 1978. 158 pp. Cover art and illustrations by Jack Gaughan. $1.75.

The world of Zacar was wracked with storms, and life there was hard. Yet two races shared it with no love between them. The Raski were the first people; the Yurth the late-comers.

This is the story of Elossa, the Yurth girl who followed the Call that every Yurth sensitive must follow when the time came. And this is the story of Stans, the Raski, who had to achieve manhood by blood rite against the hated Yurth. This was a world where ancient injustice had been done and never righted, where brooding evil and age-old vengeance awaited peace-makers, and of two who brought this terror down upon their own heads.

Logo No. 305. Vance, Jack. *Star King.* Code No. UE1402. First DAW printing, September 1978. 160 pp. Cover art by Gino D'Achille. A somewhat different version of this novel appeared serially in *Galaxy Magazine* (1963). Published earlier in U.S. in paperback by Berkley (1964) and as first U.K. and first hardcover by Dobson (1966). Later published by Underwood-Miller (1981) as first U.S. hardcover. $1.75.

The Star Kings were a race of aliens who disguised themselves as human. They sought only power—power over the real men and women they looked upon with both contempt and lust.

Kirth Gersen had been a peace-abiding man until the terrible moment when five of these Star Kings descended upon the planet and home of his parents and viciously wiped them out as an "object lesson." At that news, vengeance became Gersen's sole objective in life; it was his goal to seek out and destroy those five Demon Princes.

First on his hit list was Attel Malagate. His name was probably a fake, his appearance was unknown, but his style was vicious, and his appetite was for human slavery. With only this to go on, Gersen was ready to track him down across a thousand stars.

(Bibliographer's note: The first of the Demon Princes novels.)

Logo No. 306. Clayton, Jo. *Irsud*. Code No. UE1403. First edition. First printing, September 1978. 191 pp. Cover art by Eric Ladd. $1.75.

Sold into slavery, Aleytys's fate was to be worse than that of the usual slave girl's bondage, for her new owners were insectoid, and she was to serve as proxy-mother to the old Queen's successor. In short, like an Earth wasp's prey, she would be both bearer and food for that which was to come.

Had Aleytys been any other human, this would have been the end. But she was the wearer of the diadem, that creation of galactic science that linked her nervous system to powers of strange potency.

(Bibliographer's note: The third book of the Diadem series.)

Logo No. 307. Moorcock, Michael. *The Rituals of Infinity*. Code No. UW1404. First DAW printing, September 1978. 157 pp. Cover art by Michael Mariano. Originally published in U.S. by Ace Books (1967) under the title *The Wrecks of Time* and bound with *Tramontane* by Emil Petaja. Published earlier under this title in U.K. by Arrow (1971). $1.50.

There they lay, outside of space and time, each hanging in its separate limbo, each a planet called Earth. Fifteen globes, fifteen lumps of matter sharing a name. Once they might have looked the same, too, but now they were very different.

One was comprised almost solely of desert and ocean, with a few forests of gigantic, distorted trees growing in the northern hemisphere. Another seemed to be in perpetual twilight, a planet of dark obsidian. Yet another was a honeycomb of multicolored crystal, and still another had a single continent that was a ring of land around a vast lagoon.

These, then, were the wrecks of time, abandoned and dying, each with a decreasing number of human inhabitants, who were, for the most part, unaware of the doom overhanging their worlds. Little did they know that these worlds existed in a kind of subspacial well that was created in furtherance of a series of drastic experiments.

Logo No. 308. Wallace, Ian (pseud. John Wallace Pritchard). *Z-Sting*. Code No UJ1408. First edition. First printing, October 1978. 222 pp. Cover art by H.R. Van Dongen. $1.95.

Croyd brought peace to a warring world by means of his Comcord system. When a nation's discord quotient rose to the boiling point, Comcord would trigger the ultimate peace weapon called Z-Sting.

Z-Sting would encapsulate the war-seeking nation, cutting it off totally from the world and from civilization. Comcord worked, and peace had reigned for a century, until an inexplicable rise in militarism blew the terror whistle.

It was up to Croyd, who had created the system, to find out what had gone wrong, but Croyd was, by then, a very old man. Aided by his great-granddaughter, he sought to prevent the Z-Sting trigger from being falsely activated. To achieve this, they had to:

Bring Croyd back to his youth and vigor.

Uncover the motive behind the war crisis.

Find the trigger that was hidden at the edge of the Solar System.

(Bibliographer's note: Fourth book in the Croyd series.)

Logo No. 309. Vance, Jack. *The Killing Machine*. Code No. UE1409. First DAW printing, October 1978. 159 pp. Cover art by Gino D'Achille. Originally published in U.S. in paperback by Berkley (1964). First U.K. and first hardcover published by Dobson (1967). First U.S. hardcover published later by Underwood-Miller (1981). $1.75.

"My goal is to produce a nightmare quality of fright and to maintain it over an appreciable duration....Once an apparently sensitive area is located, the operator to the best of his ingenuity employs means to emphasize, to dramatize this fear, then augment it by orders of magnitude."

—Kokor Hekkus

Kokor Hekkus was one of the five Demon Princes who had masterminded the massacre of Kirth Gersen's parents and his entire home world. As such, he was on Gersen's list for vengeance.

Though Kokor Hekkus, known as The Killing Machine, was the most dreaded criminal in the universe, wanted and feared by every law agency existing, Kirth Gersen set out to locate him and to prove that this monster in human form could be made to pay in his own coin for his most heinous atrocity.

(Bibliographer's note: The second of the Demon Princes novels.)

Logo No. 310. Carter, Lin. *The Pirate of World's End*. Code No. UE1410. First edition. First printing, October 1978. 173 pp. Cover art by Richard Hescox. $1.75.

Ganelon Silvermane is a massive warrior created by a forgotten genetic science for an unknown purpose. This novel takes place at World's End in the Twilight of Time on Gondwane the Great, Old Earth's last and mightiest continent.

(Bibliographer's note: The fifth book of the Gondwane epic.)

Logo No. 311. Goulart, Ron. *The Wicked Cyborg*. Code No. UW1411. First edition. First printing, October 1978. 156 pp. Cover art by Josh Kirby. $1.50.

The situation bore an alarming resemblance to the classic Gothic situation. But since it was taking place on the planet Esmerelda in the Barnum

System, there were differences. There was a disputed inheritance: an interplanetary robot-making business. There was the uncle who had taken charge, a Cyborg now, fifty per cent human, fifty per cent machine, and one hundred per cent deceit. There was the innocent young heir, the boy, Tad, in the clutches of this uncle and his sinister household. Even the weather was foggy and gloomy, and Tad could find no friend to help him from what seemed certain doom.

That is until he stumbled across the wreckage of the family's greatest engineering triumph, the super-robot Electro. With nothing better to do, he secretly repaired it. Then, once Electro was on his feet and ticking electronically away, wicked cyborg uncle, watch out!

(Bibliographer's note: A novel in the Barnum System series.)

Logo No. 312. Vance, Jack. *Wyst: Alastor 1716*. Code No. UJ1413. First edition. First printing, November 1978. 222 pp. Cover art by Eric Ladd. Later printed in hardcover by Underwood-Miller (1984). See *Anatomy of Wonder* 3-764 (1981). $1.95.

The trouble with Utopia is people. This will remain true even in days to come, even in the Alastor Cluster of thirty thousand inhabited planets, whose sole protector of law was the mysterious person known as the Connatic.

On the planet Wyst, Number 1716 of the Alastor Cluster, there was such a Utopia, or so it claimed. There, in one great city, lived millions of people, sharing alike, working in absolute equality for just a few hours a week. But there was something definitely cockeyed there, and the Connatic finally sent a trusted investigator to bring back the facts even at the risk of his life.

(Bibliographer's note: The third book in the Alastor series.)

Logo No. 313. Lee, Tanith. *Night's Master*. Code No. UE1414. First edition. First printing, November 1978. 188 pp. Cover art and illustrations by George Barr. Later published as a limited edition hardcover by Highland Press (1984). See Schlobin, *The Literature of Fantasy* 622 (1979); *Survey of Modern Fantasy Literature II*, pp. 988-992 (1983). $1.75.

In those days the Earth was not a sphere, and the demons dwelled in vast magical caverns beneath its surface. Wondrous cities dotted the land, and strange peoples and fabulous beasts prowled the deserts and jungles of the world.

Supreme among those mighty demons was Azhrarn, Night's Master. He it was whose pranks made nightmares on Earth, who brought desire and danger to those whom it amused him to visit, and who could grant wonders and create unspeakable horrors.

(Bibliographer's note: The first Master book in the Lords of Darkness series.)

Logo No. 314. Walker, Hugh (pseud. Hubert Strassl). *War-Gamer's World*. First U.S. and first English language edition. First printing, November 1978. 160 pp. Cover art by Michael Mariano. Translated by Christine

Priest. Original edition entitled *Reiter der Finsternis*, and published by Erich Pabel Verlag (1975). See Schlobin, *The Literature of Fantasy* 1003 (1979). $1.50.

The Fellowship of the Lords of the Lands of Wonder! That's the name of the select group who control the struggles and marvels of the world known as Magira, a fantasyland planet created years before war-games were known in America. It was the members of FOLLOW who built up Magira, city by city, island by island, crown by crown, created its continents and oceans, and continue, to this day, to bring ever greater sword-and-sorcery reality to its misty shores.

(Bibliographer's note: First chronicle of Magira in the War-Game series.)

Logo No. 315. Landis, Arthur H. *Camelot in Orbit.* Code No. UE1417. First edition. First printing, November 1978. 175 pp. Cover art by Don Maitz. $1.75.

Fomalhaut II was an inexplicable enigma in the annals of the Galactic Watchers. A world of knights and ladies, of dungeons and dragons, it was truly medieval and, therefore, out of bounds for science-armed Terrans. Yet science seemed thwarted there, for magic really worked, and witchcraft baffled the secret watchers.

Camelot was their name for it, and Kyrie Fern was their Adjustor on its surface. He was a knight in truly shining armor, a champion of chivalry, and the only one who actually stood between the Arthurian natives and the alien being that menaced both their world and the advanced planets that swung unseen through their sky.

(Bibliographer's note: Sequel to *A World Called Camelot* and second book in the Camelot in Space series.)

Logo No. 316. Van Vogt, A.E. *Pendulum.* Code No. UE1423. First edition. First printing, December 1978. 158 pp. Cover art by Penalva. Later published in U.K. by New English Library (1982). $1.75.

Contents:

Pendulum	Footprint Farm
The Male Condition	The Non-Aristotelian Detective
Living with Jane	The Human Operators
The First Rull	The Launch of Apollo XVII

Logo No. 317. Akers, Alan Burt (pseud. Kenneth Bulmer). *Golden Scorpio.* Code No. UW1424. First edition. First printing, December 1978. 207 pp. Cover art and illustrations by Josh Kirby. $1.50.

When you're down, there's no place to go but up. That's the way the brave think, and, if there's anyone on two worlds braver than Dray Pres-...., he has yet to appear.

Because Prescot, who had been a seaman and soldier on distant Earth, ... ~v, on Golden Scorpio's fabulous planet, was claimant to the fallen ....c of a conquered empire, would never give up. Single-handed, if need be, he would be a deadly threat to the enemies of Vallia. But, as he set out on a liberation mission incomparable in the history of two worlds, he knew he would never be alone. There were always the mysterious Star Lords to watch and speculate upon his fate.

(Bibliographer's note: Eighteenth book in the saga of Dray Prescot of Antares and fourth in the Vallian Cycle. Includes a glossary to the Vallian Cycle.)

Logo No. 318. Carter, Lin ed. *The Year's Best Fantasy Stories:4.* Code No. UE1425. First edition. First printing, December 1978. 208 pp. Cover art by Esteban Maroto. $1.75.

Contents:

The Year in Fantasy: an Introduction	The Editor
The Tale of Hauk	Poul Anderson
A Farmer on the Clyde	Grail Undwin
Prince Alcouz and the Magician	Clark Ashton Smith
Nekht Semerkeht	Robert E. Howard & Andrew J. Offutt
The Pillars of Hell	Lin Carter
Lok the Depressor	Philip Coakley
Hark! Was That the Squeal of an Angry Throat?	Avram Davidson
The Cloak of Dreams	Pat McIntosh
The Land of Sorrow	Phyllis Eisenstein
Odds Against the Gods	Tanith Lee
The Changer of Names	Ramsey Campbell
The Year's Best Fantasy Books: an Appendix	The Editor

Logo No. 319. Tubb, E.C. *The Quillian Sector.* Code No. UW1426. First edition. First printing, December, 1978. 158 pp. Cover art by H.R. Van Dongen. Later published in U.K. by Arrow (1982). $1.50.

Take the greatest hunter of a hundred worlds, a man wise to the wiles of beasts and men. Take this professional killer and give him a human target. Take the greatest concentration of brains of a thousand worlds, the Cyclan with its legion of emotionless agents. Take these inhuman monsters and give them a human target.

The target for both was Earl Dumarest. But the rule of the hunt was special. Dumarest must be captured but not killed.

And the place was extra-special: the Quillian Sector, "the place where space goes mad." The Quillian Sector, where Dumarest was searching for lost Terra.

(Bibliographer's note: Nineteenth novel of the saga of Dumarest of Terra.)

Logo No. 320. Bradley, Marion Zimmer and Zimmer, Paul Edwin. *The Survivors.* Code No. UJ1435. First edition. First printing, January 1979. 238 pp. Cover art by Enrich. $1.95.

Dane, Rianna, and the monster Aratak: they were the survivors of the terrible hunt of the Red Moon. Where all others failed, they had lived—to achieve fame and fortune and to find life in the starways unexpectedly colorless, until they were asked to check out a Closed World.

To the combined intelligences, a Closed World was one that held a mystery that science had not cracked and, therefore, held danger. Because the Survivors had become over-confident of their abilities, they took the challenge. But they had not counted on the problem of the only known world with two dominant species living in precarious harmony, and with the dread ghosts of white dragons that seemed bent on destroying that harmony.

(Bibliographer's note: Sequel to *Hunters of the Red Moon* by Bradley, solo.)

Logo No. 321. Moorcock, Michael. *City of the Beast or Warriors of Mars.* Code No. UW1436. First DAW printing, January 1979. 160 pp. Cover art by Richard Hescox. Originally published in U.K. by Compact (1965) and in U.S. by Lancer (1966) as *Warriors of Mars* under the pen-name of "Edward P. Bradbury." Later published in 1970 under the title *City of the Beast* and acknowledged as the work of Michael Moorcock. $1.50.

"I went to Mars...an older Mars, eons in the past, yet still ancient....I encountered a strange romantic civilization totally unlike any we have ever had on Earth....It was beautiful, fantastic, breathtaking—a place where a man could be a man and survive and be recognized for his true qualities of character and prowess....

"And there was a girl, young, ravishingly attractive, an aristocrat from a line that would have made the dynasties of Egypt appear trifling by comparison. She was Princess of Varnal, City of the Green Mists, with its spires and colonnades, its strong, slender people, and the finest fighting men in that martial world...."

Thus spoke Michael Kane, the twentieth-century scientist, who found himself transported through space and time-past.

(Bibliographer's note: First volume of the Warrior of Mars series.)

Logo No. 322. Stableford, Brian M. *Balance of Power.* Code No. UE1437. First edition. First printing, January 1979. 173 pp. Cover art by Don Maitz. Later published in U.K. by Hamlyn (1984). $1.75.

Only the infinite historical experiences of teeming Terra offered a guide to the problems to be faced by the future imitators of Christopher Columbus and Captain Cook.

This was very obvious in the case of the fifth planet-colony to be visited by the recontact ship *Daedalus*. For the struggle for food had become bitter and hard, and the main human colony had slid back to grim fundamentals. The Earth parallel lay in the presence across an "impassable" ocean of another continent, another human colony, long isolated and alienated. The solution was there; the voyage had to rival that of Columbus, and all the clever science brought from far-away Earth would be no substitute for old-fashioned courage and pioneering risk.

(Bibliographer's note: Fifth book in the *Daedalus* series.)

Logo No. 323. Walker, Hugh (pseud. Hubert Strassl). *Army of Darkness.* Code No. UW1438. First U.S. and first English language edition. 155 pp. Cover art by Jad. Translated by Christine Priest. Original edition entitled *Das Heer der Finsternis*, published by Erich Pabel Verlag (1975). See Schlobin, *The Literature of Fantasy* 1003 (1979). $1.50.

"We have plans to make our way into your world, Frankari. You are only the first. The Lion is riding under the Banner of Chaos. I shall take your place as player. This time the fate of Magira is sealed. The rules of the game are changing!"

But the fate of Magira can never be sealed, however vast the power that dared interfere, for that barbaric world with its continents and kingdoms, its hordes of armed warriors, its votaries of fearful religions and monster monarchs, was greater than its creators. Though it had been created by Earth-born men, it existed in a time-space of its own, beyond their ability to destroy, and only leaving men the ability to play out their secretmost desires against the rules of a cosmos not that of Terra!

(Bibliographer's note: Second book of the Magira-War Games series.)

Logo No. 324. Lee, Tanith. *Death's Master.* Code No. UJ1441. First edition. First printing, February 1979. 348 pp. Cover art by David Schleinkofer. Later published in a limited edition hardcover by Highland Press (1984). See Schlobin, *The Literature of Fantasy* 621 (1979); *Survey of Modern Fantasy Literature I* pp. 988-992 (1983). $1.95.

In those days, the world was flat, and demons dwelled beneath who walked among the cities and kingdoms of the surface with powers and mischiefs to please themselves.

Among those demons, there were two who were mighty above all others. One was Azhrarn, Night's Master, and the other was the lord of darkness whose name was Uhlume, Death's Master.

(Bibliographer's note: Second book in the Lord of Darkness series.)

Logo No. 325. Vance, Jack. *The Palace of Love.* Code No. UE1442. First DAW printing, February 1979. 176 pp. Cover art by Gino D'Achille. Originally published in paperback by Berkley (1968). First U.K. and first hardcover edition by Dobson (1968). Later published by Underwood-Miller (1981) as first U.S. hardcover. $1.75.

"The Palace of Love extends over a considerable area and is by no means a single structure but rather a complex of gardens, pavilions, halls, domes, towers, promenades and scenic panoramas. The people of the Palace are all young and beautiful and know no other life; they are the happiest of mortals."

So speaks Viole Falushe. He is said to be fascinated with erotic variations and culminations. One of his favorite games is to rear a beautiful maiden with great care in an isolated cloister. She is trained to the knowledge that some day she will meet a miraculous creature who will love her and then kill her. Then one day she is liberated upon a small island where Viole Falushe awaits.

Viole Falushe was the third of the Demon Princes on the vengeance list of Kirth Gersen. Like the first two, he was elusive, cunning, vicious, and a monster beyond all human nature. Like the others, also, Kirth Gersen would find him no matter in what part of the galaxy or in what isolated distant planet his deadly Palace of Love was hidden.

(Bibliographer's note: Third book of the Demon Princes series.)

Logo No. 326. Moorcock, Michael. *Lord of the Spiders, or Blades of Mars.* Code No. UW1443. First DAW printing, February 1979. 160 pp. Cover art by Richard Hescox. Originally published in U.K. by Compact (1965) and in U.S. by Lancer (1966) as *Blades of Mars* under the pen-name of "Edward P. Bradbury." Later published by Lancer (1970) as *Lord of the Spiders* and acknowledged as the work of Michael Moorcock. $1.50.

Michael Kane was both a scientist and a fighting man, but a laboratory mishap had hurled him through space-time to Mars!

"It was a Mars eons in the past, a Mars that thrived before Man ever walked this planet, a Mars of strange contrasts, customs, scenery—and beasts. A Mars of warring nations possessing the remnants of a once mighty technical civilization—a Mars where Kane had come into his own. An expert swordsman, he had been a match for the master swordsmen of the Red Planet; a romantic, he had rejoiced at the luck which fate brought him."

Now Kane sought only to return to that distant wonder world and the princess he loved. This is the novel of Kane's second coming to the Red Planet, of his discovery that he was in a different and more dangerous part of that world, and that, before he could find his beloved, he must fight and triumph over enemies and obstacles no Earthling had ever before encountered!

(Bibliographer's note: The second Michael Kane, Warrior of Mars, novel.)

Logo No. 327. Chandler, A. Bertram. *The Far Traveler.* Code No. UW1444. First U.S. edition. First printing, February 1979. 174 pp. Cover art by Don Maitz. Originally published in U.K. by Hale (1977). $1.50.

The Far Traveler was hardly the sort of starship to use in the study of lost space colonies. Lost colonies were likely to be desperate, eccentric, and otherwise unappreciative. Besides, *The Far Traveler* was a rich woman's toy, constructed of gold, and directed by an omniscient, dictatorial, and feminine computer known as Big Sister.

John Grimes had become that golden vessel's captain. A captain in name only because nobody could talk back to Big Sister or the haughty beauty who owned everything aboard. But Grimes was a man of many resources, and lost space colonies were places that didn't observe the civilized rules. You could be sure, therefore, that the man known as the Commodore Hornblower of Outer Space would be likely to come through okay, even if the ladies, mechanical and physical, never expected him to!

(Bibliographer's note: A novel in the John Grimes: Rim Runner series.)

Logo No. 328. Norman, John (pseud. John Lange). *Explorers of Gor.* Code

No. UE1449. First edition. First printing, March 1979. 464 pp. Cover art by Gino D'Achille. $2.25.

When the shield ring of the much feared Kurii falls into the hands of a mysterious black explorer, it becomes vital to the Priest-Kings of Earth's planetary twin, barbaric Gor, that Tarl Cabot himself regain that ancient product of an alien science. His quest brings him to the unmapped interior of the great equatorial rain-forests and into new dangers without parallel.

(Bibliographer's note: The thirteenth book of the Saga of Tarl Cabot, and the slave girl on the cover has great lungs. How do I know she's a slave girl? Easy. Almost all of John Norman's female characters are slaves.)

Logo No. 329. Asimov, Isaac and Martin H. Greenberg eds. *Isaac Asimov Presents the Great Science Fiction Stories I (1939)*. Code No. UE1454. First edition. First printing, March 1979. 432 pp. Cover art by Jack Gaughan. $2.25.

Contents:
Introduction

I, Robot	Eando Binder
The Strange Flight of Richard Clayton	Robert Bloch
Trouble with Water	H.L. Gold
Cloak of Aesir	Don A. Stuart
The Day Is Done	Lester del Rey
The Ultimate Catalyst	John Taine
The Gnarly Man	L. Sprague de Camp
Black Destroyer	A.E. van Vogt
Greater Than Gods	C.L. Moore
Trends	Isaac Asimov
The Blue Giraffe	L. Sprague de Camp
The Misguided Halo	Henry Kuttner
Heavy Planet	Milton A. Rothman
Life-Line	Robert A. Heinlein
Ether Breather	Theodore Sturgeon
Pilgrimage	Nelson Bond
Rust	Joseph E. Kelleam
The Four-Sided Triangle	William F. Temple
Star Bright	Jack Williamson
Misfit	Robert A. Heinlein

Logo No. 330. Moorcock, Michael. *Masters of the Pit, or Barbarians of Mars*. Code No. UW1450. First DAW printing, March 1979. 158 pp. Cover art by Richard Hescox. Originally published in U.K. by Compact (1965) and in U.S. by Lancer (1966) as *Barbarians of Mars* under the pen-name of "Edward P. Bradbury." Later published by Lancer (1970) as *Masters of the Pit* and acknowledged to be by Michael Moorcock. $1.50.

The green-death started in Cend-Amrid, turning that once-lovely city into a plague spot, source of a deadly infection that swept Mars and turned men into mindless automatons. Michael Kane had to find the cure, or perish along with the rest of the adopted planet he loved!

The secret lay, he believed, within the untold power of the machines hidden in the vaults of the long-dead superscientific race that had once ruled the Red Planet. When he embarked on his expedition to find this buried horde of knowledge, he expected little trouble, but others had been there before him, and he found that he faced problems of terrifying proportions.

(Bibliographer's note: The third and final Michael Kane, Warrior of Mars, novel.)

Logo No. 331. Goulart, Ron. *Hello, Lemuria, Hello.* Code No. UW1451. First edition. First printing, March 1979. 156 pp. Cover art by Josh Kirby. $1.50.

This novel either is or isn't based on the famous "Shaver Mystery" that agitated the world years before the UFO's appeared in the sky. It also does or doesn't give the real reason for the death of Elvis Presley.

The main accomplishment, however, was that it is destined to be an award winner, being the front-runner for The Goofy at the Annual Convention of the Crackpot Writers of America, which was or will be held at the Sheraton-Nostalgia Hotel, Manhattan, April 2022.

Logo No. 332. Walker, Hugh (pseud Hubert Strassl). *Messengers of Darkness.* Code No UW1452 First U.S. and first English language edition. First DAW printing, March 1979. 156 pp. Cover art by Jad. Translated by Christine Priest. Original edition entitled *Boten der Finsternis* and published by Erich Pabel Verlag (1976). $1.50.

"Do you not want power? The Powers of Darkness are not something one can call up at will—they have their price. I came here because nowhere else in all the continents of the world are the life-forces of the ancient gods still so strong and Darkness so deeply rooted...

"This country has never been free of Darkness. It is within the hearts of men. There was a time when the whole of Ysh was one great temple of Darkness—not a glorious empire as your dreams of the past would have it, but a pestilence on the face of the world, an empire of slaves...

"This time however it will be different!"

And so the battle was joined, the conflict for the heart of Magira, that world outside of time and space, created by the Lords of the Lands of Wonder, but now reaching out to encompass its very creators!

(Bibliographer's note: Third book of the Magira-War Games series.)

Logo No. 333. Cherryh, C.J. (pseud. Carolyn Janice Cherry). *The Faded Sun: Shon'jir.* Code No. UJ1453. First paperback edition. First printing, April 1979. 253 pp. Cover art by Gino D'Achille. Originally issued by the Science Fiction Book Club. $1.95.

Sten Duncan had saved the lives of the last two of humanity's deadliest enemies, during the takeover of the planet Kesrith. Sten, therefore, felt responsible for them and for their future, if any, for though the two *mri* were brother and sister, they represented different power-castes of their ancient warrior-race. Nium was the last of the bred samurai. Melein, though young, was perforce the last priestess-queen.

But struggle and mutual danger had sealed Sten Duncan to their loyalty. As their blood-brother, he would have to help them flee mankind and take the long, long evasion route across the cosmos to a legendary lost planet which might afford the *mri* one more chance.

(Bibliographer's note: Second book of the Faded Sun trilogy.)

Logo No. 334. Page, Gerald W. & Hank Reinhardt eds. *Heroic Fantasy*. Code No. UJ1455. First edition. First printing, April 1979. 320 pp. Cover art by Jad. $1.95.

Contents:

Editors' Introduction

Sand Sister	Andre Norton
The Valley of the Sorrows	Galad Elflandsson
Ghoul's-Head	Don Walsh
First Commentary: Swords and Swordplay	Hank Reinhardt
Astral Stray	Adrian Cole
Blood in the Mist	E.C. Tubb
Second Commentary: Armor	The Editors
The Murderous Dove	Tanith Lee
Death in Jukun	Charles R. Saunders
The De Pertriche Ring	H. Warner Munn
Third Commentary: Courage and Heroism	The Editors
The Hero Who Returned	Gerald W. Page
The Riddle of the Horn	Darrell Schweitzer
The Age of the Warrior	Hank Reinhardt
The Mistaken Oracle	A.E. Silas
Demonsong	F. Paul Wilson
The Seeker in the Fortress	Manly Wade Wellman

Logo No. 335. Prescot, Dray (pseud. Kenneth Bulmer). *A Life for Kregen*. Code No. UE1456. First edition. First printing, April 1979. 215 pp. Cover art and illustrations by Richard Hescox. $1.75.

The world Kregen circles the twin suns of Antares, far distant from the skies of Earth. Yet Kregen is the ground on which the Earthman Dray Prescot must stand and fight for all he holds dear. For Prescot is the unwilling battle arm of the mysterious Star Lords who contend for that planet with the powerful Sevanti.

Still, Prescot's ambitions are his own, for he has inherited the remnant of a shattered empire and must fight to bring hope and freedom to all its peoples. By his side stands his princess, Delia of the Blue Mountains, and a band of stalwart companions of many races and species. Arrayed against him, however, are flying armadas, armed hordes, the wizardry of a super-scientist, and, most shocking of all, the fury and steel claws of his own daughter, Dayra!

(Bibliographer's note: The nineteenth adventure in the saga of Dray Prescot and the first volume of the Jikaida Cycle.)

Logo No. 336. Vance, Jack. *Space Opera.* Code No. UE1457. First DAW printing, April 1979. 168 pp. Cover art by Don Maitz. Published in U.S. in paperback by Pyramid Books (1965) and in U.K. by Coronet (1982). Also published by Underwood-Miller (1984) in first hardcover edition. $1.75.

A space opera is what science fiction readers call an adventure in outer space and on alien planets. But a space opera could also be a true opera, a musical work, that originated in outer space.

This book fits both categories. It starts with the mysterious opera company from the equally mysterious planet Rlaru that arrives on Earth to astonish and infuriate music-lovers and then disappears without a trace! When Roger Wool's wealthy aunt determined to reciprocate by bringing an Earthly operatic team into space and to the unknown world, Rlaru, there unwinds a complex space opera of the first kind.

Logo No. 337. Wollheim, Donald A. with Arthur W. Saha eds. *The 1979 Annual World's Best SF.* Code No. UE1459. First edition. First printing, May 1979. 268 pp. Cover art by Jack Gaughan. $2.25.

Contents:

Introduction	The Editor
Come to the Party	Frank Herbert & F.M. Busby
Creator	David Lake
Dance Band on the Titanic	Jack Chalker
Cassandra	C.J. Cherryh
In Alien Flesh	Gregory Benford
SQ	Ursula K. LeGuin
The Persistence of Vision	John Varley
We Who Stole the Dream	James Tiptree, Jr.
Scattershot	Greg Bear
Carruthers' Last Stand	Dan Henderson

Logo No. 338. Piserchia, Doris. *Spaceling.* Code No. UE1460. First paperback edition. First printing, May 1979. 239 pp. Cover art by George Barr. Issued in hardcover by the Science Fiction Book Club (1978). (First printing has code I 43 on page 244). $1.75.

The ability to see the other-dimensional rings that float in Earth's atmosphere was a late mutation of a few space-age humans. Daryl was under the care of the institution for muters, and she had discovered that, if you jumped through the right ring at the right time, it would land you in another dimensional world and another shape.

This novel tells of Daryl's desperate efforts to unravel the mystery of why she was being held captive and of what was really going on in a certain alien dimension, because she was sure that it was all bad, and that someday everyone would thank her for the revelation. Instead, everyone was engaged in a wild effort to hold her down, to keep her on this Earth, and to keep the world simply intact!

Logo No. 339. Vance, Jack. *City of the Chasch.* Code No. UE1461. First DAW printing, May 1979. 156 pp. Cover art by H.R. Van Dongen.

Originally published in paperback by Ace Books (1968). Later published in U.K. as first hardcover by Dobson (1975) and as first U.S. hardcover by Underwood-Miller (1979). $1.75.

Someone sent distress signals to outer space from the planet Tschai. It was Adam Reith's misfortune to be sent from Earth to investigate. When his ship came close to Tschai, it was torpedoed, and Adam escaped to the surface with his life and nothing else.

Tschai was a vast planet and previously unexplored. Adam, taken as a slave by humans, learned that there were four other intelligent, but non-human, races dominant on that strange world. To find the mystery of the distress call and the vicious attack, he would first have to gain his freedom and then find a safe way to pass the city of the alien Chasch and their treacherous cousins, the Blue Chasch.

(Bibliographer's note: Book One of the Tschai, Planet of Adventure, series.)

Logo No. 340. Petaja, Emil. *Saga of Lost Earths*. Code No. UJ1462. First DAW printing, May 1979. 222 pp. Cover art by Penalva. Previously published by Ace Books (1966). See Schlobin, *The Literature of Fantasy* 874 (1979). $1.95.

"The Force is from outside our time and space, from outside anything we can humanly comprehend. I conceive of a great machine somewhere—alien beyond human thought—sending out tendrils like electric impulses....In the days of the Kalevalan heroes, actually before our present cycle of civilization began, the Force was thrust in on Earth...."

Such is the theme of the author's first novel in his series based on the epic of Finnish lore, the Kalevala ("The Land of Heroes"), a loosely woven song-story which is one of Finland's folk legends.

(Bibliographer's note: This edition of the Kalevala series includes *The Star Mill*, which was also inspired by the Kalevala and published separately by Ace Books (1966).)

Logo No. 341. Cherryh, C.J. (pseud. Carolyn Janice Cherry). *Fires of Azeroth*. Code No. UJ1466. First edition. First printing, June 1979. 236 pp. Cover art by Michael Whelan; frontispiece map by the author. Published later in U.K. by Methuen (1982). See *Anatomy of Wonder* 3-185 (1981); Fantasy Literature pp. 65-66 (1979). $1.95.

Morgaine, the closer of world gates, and her henchman Vanye, came to the land called Azeroth from drowned Shiuan. There was a star gate in Azeroth marked by alien fires, and this, too, Morgaine must seal.

But they brought to that peaceful land devastation and terror, for the hordes of Shiuan were hot on their heels determined to conquer new lands for themselves and to avenge their lost planet upon the legendary White Queen, who was Morgaine. In Azeroth, though, there was a new factor besides mankind. In that third planet, the pre-human *qual* still reigned, and the *qual* were beyond and above human science.

(Bibliographer's note: The third book of the Morgaine trilogy.)

ogo No. 342. Vance, Jack. *Servants of the Wankh.* Code No. UE1467. irst DAW printing, June 1979. 157 pp. Cover art by H.R. Van Dongen. Iriginally published in paperback by Ace Books (1969). Later published as irst U.K. and first hardcover edition by Dobson (1975); first U.S. ardcover published by Underwood-Miller (1980). $1.75.

Marooned on the strange planet Tschai, Adam Reith agreed to lead an xpedition to return the princess Ylin Ylan, the flower of Cath, to her omeland halfway across the globe.

Monsters of land and sea lay before them, and beings, both human and lien, who might rob, kill or enslave them. Tschai was a large planet, an ncient planet, where four powerful alien races struggled for mastery while umans were treated as pawns; nothing would be easy for Reith on this ourney. But the girl's father was enormously wealthy and her homeland :chnologically sophisticated.

If Reith was ever to obtain human aid in returning to Earth, where bet- :r than Cath? If he could only get there alive.

(Bibliographer's note: Book Two of the Tschai, Planet of Adventure, :ries.)

ogo No. 343. Jeter, K.W. *Morlock Night.* Code No. UE1468. First edition. irst printing, June 1979. 156 pp. Cover art by Josh Kirby. $1.75.

Remember the original Time Machine and the Time Traveller's stonishing account of his journey to the far future when humanity had ivided into two races: the worker-bestial Morlocks and the elfin-sheep :loi? Remember also that the Time Traveller went back to that future and ever returned?

What happened to his Time Machine? Did it fall into the hands of the 1orlocks, and did they make use of it to return to the time and place of its rigin, say, perhaps, the England of Wellsian days?

This is the completion of that epic story. This is what happened when ie Time Machine came back, with the Morlocks as its riders and London s their new hunting ground for human cattle!

ogo No. 344. Clayton, Jo. *Maeve.* Code No. UE1469. First edition. First rinting, June 1979. 220 pp. Cover art by Richard Hescox. $1.75.

Aletys, wanderer of the skies, seeker of the home planet of her mother's Jper-race, wearer-slave of the mind-enhancing diadem, is down on 1aeve, forest planet of tree-dwellers and semi-humans. Her aim is to con- nue her quest and to shake her pursuers.

The adventure encompasses guerilla warfare between the tree-folk and ie technology of the Company, and a face-to-face confrontation with the nplacable spider-beings from whom the diadem was stolen.

(Bibliographer's note: Fourth novel of the Diadem series.)

ogo No. 345. Wallace, Ian (pseud. John Wallace Pritchard). *Heller's Leap.* ode No. UE1475. First edition. First printing, July 1979. 317 pp. Cover rt by Tony Roberts. $2.25.

There was only one way to reach Iola where an interstellar distress signal had originated. For Iola belonged to a small group of stars cut off from the rest of the galaxy by the close presence of an all-enveloping black hole. The only way to reach Iola was through that timeless-spaceless cosmic warp.

Klaus Heller answered that call. He leapt, clad in a special, self-sustaining spacesuit, through the black hole.

He returned to the world intact, silent, and secretive, and then he was found murdered where none could have reached him.

(Bibliographer's note: An adventure combining the talents of Claudine St. Cyr, future sleuth, with those of the mastermind Croyd. Thus, the sixth and concluding novel in the Croyd series and the fourth and concluding novel in the Claudine St. Cyr series.)

Logo No. 346. Page, Gerald W. ed. *The Year's Best Horror Stories: Series VII.* Code No. UJ1476. First edition. First printing, July 1979. 221 pp. Cover art by Michael Whelan. See *Horror Literature* 4-292 (1981). $1.95.

Contents:

Introduction	The Editor
The Pitch	Dennis Etchison
The Night of the Tiger	Stephen King
Amma	Charles Saunders
Chastel	Manly Wade Wellman
Sleeping Tiger	Tanith Lee
Intimately, with Rain	Janet Fox
The Secret	Jack Vance
Hear Me Now, My Sweet Abbey Rose	Charles L. Grant
Divers Hands	Darrell Schweitzer
Heading Home	Ramsey Campbell
In the Arcade	Lisa Tuttle
Nemesis Place	David Drake
Collaborating	Michael Bishop
Marriage	Robert Aickman

Logo No. 347. Vance, Jack. *The Dirdir.* Code No. UE1478. First DAW printing, July 1979. 160 pp. Cover art by H.R. Van Dongen. Published earlier in paperback by Ace (1969). First U.K. and first hardcover published by Dobson (1975); first U.S. hardcover published by Underwood-Miller (1980). $1.75.

Getting back to Earth from the planet Tschai involved only stealing a spaceship or having one built to order, for Tschai was the abode of several intelligent star-born races and, as such, had spaceyards. Unfortunately, Adam Reith's problem wasn't so simple.

He'd already been lucky to escape the Chasch and the Wankh, and a dozen different types of humans, and now his course led directly to the Great Sivishe Spaceyards in the domains of the Dirdir.

But the Dirdir were quite different from the other aliens who competed for this world. They were quicker, more sinister, and had an unrelenting thirst for hunting victims like Adam Reith. The closer he came to his objective, the keener their hunting instincts would become!

(Bibliographer's note: Book Three of the Tschai, Planet of Adventure, series.)

Logo. No. 348. Tubb, E.C. *Web of Sand.* Code No. UE1479. First edition. First printing, July 1979. 156 pp. Cover art by Don Maitz. Later published in U.K. by Arrow (1983). $1.75.

Harge was a world wholly owned and controlled by the Cinque, the five families. To them, everyone else was in debt; for them, everyone else must work or starve. There was one way to gather the cost of escape. That was through the singing jewels.

The singing jewels could be found in the burrows of the most vicious monsters on that world of sand dunes. Find a good one, and it would pay your passage out. That was Earl Dumarest's problem. He could fight humans, he could match wits with the implacable Cyclan, but, against that web of sand, would he be just another victim?

(Bibliographer's note: The twentieth novel in the saga of Dumarest of Terra.)

Logo No. 349. Lee, Tanith. *Electric Forest.* Code No. UE1482. First paperback edition. First printing, August 1979. 159 pp. Cover art by Don Maitz. Published by Doubleday and issued by the Science Fiction Book Club (1979). (First printing with Code J 06 on page 149.) $1.75.

The world called Indigo turned upside down for Magdela Cred one unexpected morning. From being that world's only genetic misfit, the shunned outcast of an otherwise ideal society, she became the focus of attention for mighty forces.

Once they had installed her in the midst of the Electric Forest, with its weird trees and its super-luxurious private home, Magdala awoke to the potentials which were opening up all about her. She also realized the peril that now seemed poised above Indigo, which only she, the hated one, could possibly circumvent.

Logo No. 350. Asimov, Isaac and Martin H. Greenberg eds. *Isaac Asimov Presents the Great Science Fiction Stories 2 (1940).* Code No. UE1483. First edition. First printing, August 1979. 350 pp. Cover art by Jack Gaughan. $2.25.

Contents:

Introduction	The Editors
The Dwindling Sphere	Willard Hawkins
The Automatic Pistol	Fritz Leiber
Hindsight	Jack Williamson
Postmarked for Paradise	Robert Arthur
Into the Darkness	Ross Rocklynne
Dark Mission	Lester del Rey
It	Theodore Sturgeon
Vault of the Beast	A. E. van Vogt
The Impossible Highway	Oscar J. Friend

Quietus	Ross Rocklynne
Strange Playfellow	Isaac Asimov
The Warrior Race	L. Sprague de Camp
Farewell to the Master	Harry Bates
Butyl and the Breather	Theodore Sturgeon
The Exalted	L. Sprague de Camp
Old Man Mulligan	P. Schuyler Miller

Logo No. 351. Vance, Jack. *The Pnume.* Code No. UE1484. First DAW printing, August 1979. 158 pp. Cover art by H.R. Van Dongen. Originally published by Ace (1970). Later published as first U.K. and first hardcover by Dobson (1975). $1.75.

The Pnume were an ancient race of the planet Tschai, living underground in a vast network of caverns with their human slave-species, the Pnumekin. The Pnume were the historians of Tschai, collecting its past with ruthless and scholarly dedication. Surface-dwellers never saw the Pnume, if they were lucky.

Adam Reith was not so fortunate. The Pnume had heard rumors of a strange man, claiming to have come from the planet Earth, and they wanted him for Foreverness, the museum of Tschai life. Adam Reith was about to become an alien exhibit.

(Bibliographer's note: The fourth, and final, book of the Tschai, Planet of Adventure, series.)

Logo No. 352. Prescot, Dray (pseud. Kenneth Bulmer). *A Sword for Kregen.* Code No. UJ1485. First edition. First printing, August 1979. 206 pp. Cover art and illustrations by Richard Hescox. $1.95.

The most popular game among the many peoples of Kregen, world of Antares, is one that strongly resembles chess, called Jikaida. Jikaida is a battle of wits and war-game pieces that suited well the tension-charged atmosphere that enveloped Dray Prescot, for reconquering Vallia was assuming the aspect of such a game, move versus countermove, horde versus horde!

Then Dray Prescot found himself no longer in control of just a game; he had become a living chessman on a real-life board at the dreaded arena of Jikaida City. There, every move was accompanied by bloodshed, and behind every game might hang the fate of a city, an island or even a nation!

(Bibliographer's note: The twentieth novel in the never-ending saga of Dray Prescot and the second in the Jikaida Cycle.)

Logo No. 353. Norton, Andre. *Quag Keep.* Code No. UJ1487. First paperback edition. First printing, September 1979. 192 pp. Cover art by Jack Gaughan. Published earlier by Atheneum Press (1978). See Schlobin, *The Literature of Fantasy* 828 (1979). $1.95.

"Do you like war games? Can you believe playing pieces might come alive? Adventure is the keynote offered in this scientific fantasy where the imaginary becomes real.

"Six road companions travel under a wizard's geas to encounter and destroy unknown evil. Descriptive delineation, action and special powers hold the identifying reader in the company of elf Ingrge, bard Wymarc, cleric Deav Dyne, swordsman Milo Jagan, lizardman Gulth, pseudo-dragon Afreeta, berserker Naile Fangtooth, and battlemaid Yevele.

"Go to the edge of Marvel's Axe, a dubious inn on the edge of the Thieves Quarter, in the City of Greyhawk, and look to your own wrist. If you perceive a bracelet and dangling dice, watch for the next throw in the war between Law and Chaos and be prepared to follow the compelling geas." —*Signal* (International Reading Association)

Logo No. 354. Cherryh, C.J. (pseud. Carolyn Janice Cherry). *Hestia.* Code No. UJ1488. First edition. First printing, September 1979. 160 pp. Cover art by Don Maitz. $1.95.

After a hundred pioneer years, the colony on Hestia seemed to be nearing its end. Its holdings on that green and fertile planet were still limited to a single river in one valley. Everywhere else, hostile fauna hedged them in.

Adam could break the deadlock, and they needed an engineer to construct it for them. Sam Merrit was the man who came in answer to their S.O.S., and he wanted out as soon as he had landed. But, once down on Hestia, it was live or die with the colony.

So Sam stayed, only to discover certain anomalies that the hardscrabble colonists had thrust from their minds.

Logo No. 355. Moorcock, Michael. *The Time Dweller.* Code No. UE1489. First DAW printing, September 1979. 172 pp. Cover art by Pujolar. Previously published in U.K. by Hart Davis (1969) and in U.S. by Berkeley (1971). $1.75.

Contents:

The Time Dweller	Consuming Passion
Escape from Evening	The Ruins
The Deep Fix	The Pleasure Garden of
The Golden Barge	Felipe Sagittarius
Wolf	The Mountain

Logo No. 356. Petaja, Emil. *The Stolen Sun.* Code No. UJ1490. First DAW printing, September 1979. 223 pp. Cover art by Segrelles. The title novel was published earlier by Ace (1967). $1.95.

Much of the early history of the Earth is preserved only through the lore handed down by singers and storytellers around primitive campfires. What cosmic secrets are interpreted therein? What mighty events of men and godlike beings are remembered only through the medium of such bards? What historical marvels are concealed in such legendry?

The Kalevala of the Finnish people, whose origins are shrouded in mystery, is a source for science-fictional interpretation in the light of modern speculative astronomy and physics.

(Bibliographer's note: Both the title "novel" and its companion, *Tramon-*

lane, were inspired by the Kalevala legends. The latter was published in a separate edition by Ace (1966).)

Logo No. 357. Foster, M.A. *The Day of the Klesh.* **Code No. UE1492. First edition. First printing, October 1979. 240 pp. Cover art by Michael Whelan. $2.25.**

His name was Meure, and he hired out on an alien ship to see the universe. There were *ler* aboard that vessel, transmuted humans who were partial supermen, and, specifically, there was the *ler* girl, Flerdestar, who had a mission.

When Meure and Flerdestar were marooned on the world called Monsalvat, they were confronted by a planetary enigma involving space and time. For Monsalvat had a myriad human species, all alien to each other, and all in awe of the Mystery that dominated their isolated planet.

(Bibliographer's note: Third book of the *ler* trilogy.)

Logo No. 358. Stableford, Brian M. *The Paradox of the Sets.* **Code No. UE1493. First edition. First printing, October 1979. 176 pp. Cover art by H.R. Van Dongen. $1.75.**

The setup on the colonized planet Geb seemed ideal for humanity. Besides its habitable climate, it also possessed a ready-made slave-labor reserve. There were semi-intelligent natives, humanoid, unaggressive, willing to work. And so the colony thrived.

By the time that the recontact ship *Daedalus* arrived with its trained Earth scientists, things had become less simple. The enigma of the native Sets jarred with the types of life evolved on Geb. It had become obvious that the Sets, with their slave programming, must have originated elsewhere; they might even be an android creation.

That left the *Daedalus* with the greatest and most important problem of their whole cruise. Who were the originators of these Sets? Did Earth have a competitor Out There?

(Bibliographer's note: The final landing of the *Daedalus* mission.)

Logo No. 359. Llewellyn, Edward (pseud. Edward Llewellyn-Thomas). *The Douglas Convolution.* **Code No. UE1495. First edition. First printing, October 1979. 190 pp. Cover art by Don Maitz. $1.75.**

"We are the future. In your heart you are one of us. I want you for your Convolution. The Master of Time. I want you because we share race, language, nation, philosophy."

Ian Douglas of 1980, discoverer of the knot in Time, became Captain Gart of 2170 by accident. Once in that role, he dared not change, for the world was fighting a desperate battle for survival.

The shattered remains of the American East were hanging on grimly in the face of maniacal attacks of bestial men. Across the sea a matriarchal order had grasped the fallen reins of science and provided the last hope for a civilized future. Gart/Douglas, with his forgotten skills, could be their best tool. But, as a tool, he held martial capacities and scientific abilities they could not suspect.

(Bibliographer's note: The author's first SF novel.)

Logo No. 360. Chandler, A. Bertram. *The Broken Cycle.* Code No. UE1496. First U.S. edition. First printing, October 1979. 156 pp. Cover art by Richard Hescox. Published earlier in U.K. by Hale (1975). $1.75.

Being lost in space was no new experience for John Grimes, whose career as an interstellar officer had brought him into many such dilemmas. But being lost inside a colossal alien spacecraft had no precedent.

Complicating the matter was the discovery that the very universe was not their own, but an alternate, and that their captor seemed to be the omnipotent force of that entire other cosmos. As Grimes' only companion was the comely policewoman, Una Freeman, the fate that the Alien God selected for them required the creation of a Garden of Eden. But there were two serpents in this one, both of them bicycles!

(Bibliographer's note: A novel in the John Grimes: Federation Survey Service series.)

Logo No. 361. Vance, Jack. *The Face.* Code No. UJ1498. First English language edition. First printing, November 1979. 224 pp. Cover art by Gino D'Achille. Previously published as *Lens Larque*, in a Dutch translation. Later published by Underwood-Miller (1980) as first hardcover edition. $1.95.

There had been five cosmic villains on Kirth Gersen's vengeance list. There were now just two left. The Demon Prince named Lens Larque was the one who next crossed Gersen's path. As each of the five planet-slayers were different from one another, so, too, was Lens Larque. He was personally ugly, he came from a planet with an appallingly vicious culture, and he was arrogant above all others. (Bibliographer's interjectory note: This man did not drink Shirley Temples.)

Kirth Gersen realized that this was going to be a tough nut to crack. But would it even be possible? For Larque was not only well hidden, he had a mission of villainy that overrode all the other villainies in Gersen's file, and his personal obsession was based upon an enormous and very real foundation in sadistic power.

(Bibliographer's more serious note: The fourth of the Demon Princes novels.)

Logo No. 362. Carter, Lin. *Journey to the Underground World.* Code No. UE1499. First edition. First printing, November 1979. 175 pp. Cover art and illustrations by Josh Kirby. $1.75.

The legends of a fabled land of the lost have floated for centuries around the bazaars of North Africa and the sand-surrounded oases of the vast Sahara. They tell of treasure caravans that have never returned, of weird monsters forgotten by time, and of savage peoples surviving out of antiquity.

Eric Carstairs had heard these tales, but, until he met Professor Potter, he didn't really believe them. But the famous paleontologist had the location of the entrance to the Underground World pinned down and wanted only a man of courage to fly him there.

Carstairs and Potter took the chance and pierced the pit to Zanthodon, a world within the world, where cavemen and cavebeasts roamed side by side with dinosaur-monsters of millions of years ago.

(Bibliographer's note: First volume of a new series of adventures featuring Eric Carstairs in Zanthodon.)

Logo No. 363. Tubb, E.C. *Iduna's Universe.* Code No. UE1500. First edition. First printing, November 1979. 156 pp. Cover art by Michael Mariano. Later published in U.K. by Arrow (1985). $1.75.

It was touch and go for Earl Dumarest when the slavers of the Matriarchy of Onorldi struck his work camp. Had he not captured the Matriarch herself during the fight, it might have spelled his doom when the slavers triumphed.

Even though the odds had turned against him, he was able to strike a bargain. The Matriarch's childdaughter, Iduna, had disappeared into the mind-trap of the Tau. If he could follow, find her, and return with her, he would have his freedom and a chance to locate the lost Earth he sought.

So it was into Iduna's private universe he went, the creation of the Tau under the whims and fancies of a restless and spoiled planetary princess. To escape, Dumarest had to outwit her monster playthings, outfight her hideous horrors, and outdream her satanic fantasies.

(Bibliographer's note: The twenty-first volume in the saga of Dumarest of Terra.)

Logo No. 364. Salmonson, Jessica Amanda ed. *Amazons!* Code No. UE1503. First edition. First printing, December 1979. 206 pp. Cover art and frontispiece by Michael Whelan. $2.25.

Contents:

Introduction: Our Amazon Heritage	Jessica Amanda Salmonson
The Dreamstone	C.J. Cherryh
Wolves of Nakesht	Janrae Frank
Women of the White Waste	T.J. Morgan
The Death of August	Emily Bronte, (edited by Joanna Russ)
Morrien's Bitch	Janet Fox
Agbewe's Sword	Charles R. Saunders
Jane Saint's Travails (Part One)	Josephine Saxton
The Sorrows of Witches	Margaret St. Clair
Falcon Blood	Andre Norton
The Rape Patrol	Michele Belling
Bones for Dulath	Megan Lindholm
Northern Chess	Tanith Lee
The Woman Who Loved the Moon	Elizabeth A. Lynn

Additional Reading compiled with Susan Wood

Logo No. 365. Vance, Jack. *Emphyrio.* Code No. UE1504. First DAW printing, December 1979. 208 pp. Cover art by Gino D'Achille. Previously published by Doubleday (1969). See *Anatomy of Wonder* 3-761 (1981). $2.25.

Halma, where humans were ruled by a race of effete and arrogant Lords; where a feudalistic system banned all work by machines; where a "benevolent" welfare state rewarded talented hand labor with a barely adequate sustaining dole.

Young Ghyl Tarvok, fascinated by the legend of Emphyrio, became a rebel. In a pirated space ship, he began his search through the civilizations of neighboring planets for the key to the origin of his home world's culture and the secret that might change it. Inexorably he moved toward the last desperate hope: the planet his ancestors had left many thousands of years before—the mysterious and terrifying place called Earth.

Logo No. 366. Prescot, Dray (pseud. Kenneth Bulmer). *A Fortune for Kregen.* Code No. UJ1505. First edition. First printing, December 1979. 222 pp. Cover art and illustrations by Richard Hescox. $1.95.

Fame and fortune may await the winners of the life-and-death game called Jikaida, but, for Dray Prescot, his triumphs seemed only to bring infamy and misfortune. An Earthman transposed to the distant world that circles the twin suns of Antares, Prescot had to find a way out of his Jikaida City exile, for his homeland needed him in its hour of danger.

But it seemed that fate now would place him in an even more terrifying game: a treasure hunt played out in the illusion-webbed catacombs of a haunted valley where desperate men came to find fortunes at the risk of their followers' lives and their own sanity.

(Bibliographer's note: The twenty-first book in the saga of Dray Prescot and the third in the Jikaida Cycle.)

Logo No. 367. Purtill, Richard. *The Golden Gryphon Feather.* Code No. UE1506. First edition. December 1979. 160 pp. Cover art and illustrations by George Barr. $1.75.

In those days, the blood of the gods circulated among mortals, and wonderworkers lived side by side with ordinary folk. Chryseis was a princess in whom strange forces and ancient mysteries contended. But she herself had to work out that which confronted her when she was sent as tribute to the legendary isle of Kaphtu.

In that dawnland kingdom, she found herself an object of contention between the human and the non-human forces that had long been in truce. Her major defense was to be the feather of a mythical monster which alone could guide her to an unguessable inheritance.

(Bibliographer's note: The author's first book.)

Logo No. 368. Huntley, Tim. *One on Me.* Code No. UE1508. First edition. First printing, January 1980. 221 pp. Cover art by H.R. Van Dongen. $2.25.

I was the last kid born on Earth—and an embarrassment to my mother. I grew up on a diet of Tri-D serials, wild parties, and screwball "uncles." All I wanted was to get my own wings and have the endless ball that everyone was entitled to in that air-borne Utopia.

But, since Mom hadn't registered my birth with the computers, that was a problem. So she made a deal with me: agree to get a real education, and I would earn my flying wings and all the rest.

However, there was the usual catch. The end product of my eccentric schoolmaster, of the primitive girl who taught me even more, and of the relics of the past that were coming to life around me was a cosmic joke. On me, sure, but what the playboy world didn't know was that ultimately the joke was going to be on them. And it wouldn't be funny!

Logo No. 369. Brunner, John. *The Avengers of Carrig.* Code No. UE1509. First DAW printing, January 1980. 157 pp. Cover art by Gino D'Achille. A considerably shorter version of this novel was published by Ace Books (1962) under the title *Secret Agent of Terra,* as part of an Ace double and bound with *The Rim of Space* by A. Bertram Chandler. Under this title, the book was published by Dell (1969). $1.75.

Once the city of Carrig stood supreme on this planet that had been settled by space refugees in the distant, forgotten past. From every corner of this primitive lost world, caravans came to trade and to view the great King-Hunt, the gruesome test by which the people of Carrig chose their rulers.

Then from space came new arrivals, and with them came their invincible death guns and their ruthless, all-powerful tyranny. Now there would be no King-Hunt in Carrig or hope for the planet, unless a fool-hardy high-born named Saikmar and a beautiful Earthling space-spy named Maddalena, could do the impossible.

(Bibliographer's note: Second book in the Zarathustra Refugee Planet series.)

Logo No. 370. Carter, Lin ed. *The Year's Best Fantasy Stories: 5.* Code No. UJ1510. First edition. First printing, January 1980. 204 pp. Cover art by Penalva. $1.95.

Contents:

The Year in Fantasy:	
An Introduction	The Editor
The Troll	T.H. White
In the Balance	Tanith Lee
The Gem in the Tower	L. Sprague de Camp & Lin Carter
Above Ker-Is	Evangeline Walton
Ms. Lipshutz and the Goblin	Marvin Kaye
Rhian and Garanhir	Grail Undwin
Lord of the Dead	Robert E. Howard
Child of Air	Pat McIntosh
A Malady of Magicks	Craig Shaw Gardner
St. George	David Mallory
Astral Stray	Adrian Cole
Demon and Demoiselle	Janet Fox

The Year's Best Fantasy Books: An Appendix

Logo No. 371. Llewellyn, Edward (pseud. Edward Llewellyn-Thomas). *The Bright Companion.* Code No. UE1511. First edition. First printing, January 1980. 176 pp. Cover art by Don Maitz. $1.75.

When the by-product of the greatest contraceptive ever discovered turned out to be sterility for the next generation, the result was predictable. Within a century, the population of the "civilized" world dropped to a tiny remnant of narrow-minded survivors. Their few communities were ruled by hard-shelled fanatics whose prime need was women who could still bear children.

Anne had been such a trade-off "wife," and, when she slew her captor and fled, there was only one who would help her. This was the young man whose hidden stock of medicines made him a necessity to the isolated homesteads.

(Bibliographer's note: The author's second SF novel. Sequel to *The Douglas Convolution*.)

Logo No. 372. Cherryh, C.J. (pseud. Carolyn Janice Cherry). *The Faded Sun: Kutath.* Code No. UE1516. First paperback edition. First printing, February 1980. 256 pp. Cover art by Michael Whelan. Published earlier by Doubleday (1979) and issued by the Science Fiction Book Club. See *Anatomy of Wonder* 3-186 (1981). $2.25.

Kutath was an ancient world and a dying one. In ages past, its best sons and daughters had gone to the stars to serve as mercenaries in the wars of aliens.

Now the survivors of its star-flung people, the *mri*, had come back: in the form of a single woman, the last priestess-queen Melein, and a single man, the last warrior Niun. And one other—the human Sten Duncan, who had deserted Earth's military to swear service to the foes of his own species.

(Bibliographer's note: The third novel of the acclaimed Faded Sun trilogy.)

Logo No. 373. Bradley, Marion Zimmer ed. *The Keeper's Price and Other Stories.* Logo No. UE1517. First edition. First printing, February 1980. 207 pp. Cover art by Don Maitz. $2.25.

Contents: Introduction: A Word from the Creator of Darkover
I. THE SETTLEMENT

Vai Dom	Diana L. Paxson
The Forest	C. McQuillin

II. THE AGES OF CHAOS

There Is Always an Alternative	Patricia Mathews
The Tale of Durraman's Donkey	Eileen Ledbetter
The Fires of Her Vengeance	Susan M. Shwartz
Circle of Light	Kathleen Williams
The Alton Gift	Elisabeth Waters
The Answer	Jacqueline Lichtenberg and Jean Lorrah

III. UNDER THE COMYN
The Rescue   Linda MacKendrick
The Keeper's Price   Marion Zimmer Bradley
                             and Elisabeth Waters
The Hawk-Master's Son   Marion Zimmer Bradley
A Simple Dream   Penny Ziegler, M.D.
Paloma Blanca   Patricia Mathews
Blood Will Tell   Marion Zimmer Bradley
IV. AFTER THE FALL OF THE COMYN
Ambassador to Corresanti   Linda Frankel
A View from the Reconstruction   Paula Crunk

Logo No. 374. Vance, Jack. *The Five Gold Bands.* Code No. UJ1518. First DAW printing, February 1980. 160 pp. Cover art by Gino D'Achille. Originally published by Toby Books (1953) on pulp paper under the title, *The Space Pirate*; reprinted in an abridged edition in the U.S. by Ace (1963) and in the U.K. by Granada (1980) under the present title. $1.95.

Earth lacked the secret of the intersteller space drive. When it turned out that the galaxy was chock full of wealthy planets and haughty aliens who had the star drive, it made our native world a backward place indeed.

Paddy Blackthorn was an adventurous sort who wasn't going to stand for this. He set off to steal the secret of intersteller flight from the powerful Shauls, who nabbed him and dumped him off on a barren planet as punishment.

Yet it was there that Paddy acquired five golden bands that contained, in code, the very data the Shauls had sought to conceal. Paddy had to keep on the run with the bands until they could be deciphered and, thereby, touched off the greatest manhunt in galactic history!

(Bibliographer's note: The author's second book.)

Logo No. 375. Bayley, Barrington J. *The Garments of Caean.* Code No. UJ1519. First paperback edition. First printing, February 1980. 206 pp. Cover art by H.R. Van Dongen. Published earlier in the U.S. by Doubleday (1976) and in the U.K. by Fontana (1978). $1.95.

Back on Old Earth, there was a saying that clothes make the man. But, on the world called Caean, this became literally true. On that colonized planet, there was a material called Prossim. If your body was in contact with Prossim, your personality changed. You became handsome, you had vast charisma, you had total self-confidence, you were always the power center of every enterprise.

So, throughout the inhabited galaxy, clothing from Caean was the sure key to success, and men would kill to get such a suit. Peder Forbarth was such a man, prepared to turn space pirate to get his hands on some. Instead, he found that, at the risk of worlds, the very secret of Prossim cloth itself was about to open before his eyes.

Logo No. 376. Norman, John (pseud. John Lange). *Fighting Slave of Gor.* Code No. UE1522. First edition. First printing, March 1980. 384 pp. Cover art by Richard Hescox. Later printed in U.K. by Allen (1982) in first hardcover edition. $2.25.

Attempting to save his girl friend from a Gorean slave trap, Jason Marshall found himself kidnapped to that legendary counter-Earth planet. He found himself to be the first "civilized" Earth male to become enslaved in the ruthless chains of Gorean society.

Jason Marshall is made the slave of a haughty woman, then into her fighting champion, and, finally, amid the turmoil of primitive warfare, to seek his liberty in order to search for his lost love amid the slave marts of that alien and turbulent planet.

(Bibliographer's note: The fourteenth book of the Gorean Saga.)

Logo No. 377. Asimov, Isaac and Martin H. Greenberg eds. *Isaac Asimov Presents the Great Science Fiction Stories 3 (1941).* Code No. UE1523. First edition. First printing, March 1980. 352 pp. Cover designed by Jack Gaughan. $2.25.

Contents:

Introduction	The Editors
Mechanical Mice	Maurice A. Hugi
Shottle Bop	Theodore Sturgeon
The Rocket of 1955	C.M. Kornbluth
Evolution's End	Robert Arthur
Microcosmic God	Theodore Sturgeon
Jay Score	Eric Frank Russell
Liar!	Isaac Asimov
Time Wants a Skeleton	Ross Rocklynne
The Words of Guru	C.M. Kornbluth
The Seesaw	A.E. van Vogt
Armageddon	Fredric Brown
Adam and No Eve	Alfred Bester
Solar Plexus	James Blish
Nightfall	Isaac Asimov
A Gnome There Was	Henry Kuttner & C.L. Moore
Snulbug	Anthony Boucher
Hereafter, Inc.	Lester del Rey

Logo No. 378. Van Vogt, A.E. and E. Mayne Hull. *The Winged Man.* Code No. UE1524. First DAW printing, March 1980. 158 pp. Cover art by Douglas Beekman. Previously published in U.S. by Doubleday (1966) and in the U.S. by Sidgwick & Jackson (1967). Originally appeared in *Astounding Science Fiction* in May 1944 as by Hull alone. $1.75.

From the bridge of the submarine *Sea Serpent*, Lt. William Kenlon saw a weird sight. Flying overhead was a huge creature with a wingspread unlike that of any bird the young naval officer had ever seen. When it reappeared to alight on the ship, Kenlon saw that it was a being that was half man and half beast.

Then it happened. A great surge of water, and Kenlon found himself fighting for his life in the cold water of night. When he finally surfaced, it was to find himself at the beginning of a journey thirty thousand years into the future where a grotesque war was being waged between the frightening birdmen and their even more terrifying opponents.

Logo No. 379. Barrett, Neal Jr. *Aldair, Across the Misty Sea.* Code No. UE1525. First edition, First printing, March 1980. 188 pp. Cover art by Josh Kirby. $1.75.

"I have done more than my share of wandering. In a few short years, I have been slave, scholar and master of ships. I have played no small part in the death of two great empires. I have nearly been eaten whole by the shapeless thing that guards the Great River. I have even soared above the Earth like a large, ungainly bird...

"Finally, I have come to know the handiwork of Man, in the sad and fearful land of Merrkia, across the Misty Sea. The terrible secret of that race has come to light at last, though it is a thing I can scarcely fathom even now. And if I have learned nothing more in my travels, I can say in all truth that I am proud to be the beast I am...."

—Aldair, late of the Venicii

The Earth was still green and fully populated. Its "men" were the products of a science that might have begun with the Dr. Moreau of Wellsian legend. Fate had chosen Aldair to seek the truth about Man. Why had Man created these new beast-races, and, above all, where had Man gone?

(Bibliographer's note: Third book of the Aldair series.)

Logo No. 380. Lee, Tanith. *Sabella, or The Blood Stone.* Code No. UE1529. First edition. First printing, April 1980. 157 pp. Cover art by George Smith. See *Anatomy of Wonder* 3-471 (1981). $1.75.

Dracula? A mere figment of superstition, a thing that could not exist.

Sabella? A very real person, an enticing girl of flesh and warmth, who detested the sunlight, who required the blood of young men to feed upon, who was all that Dracula was said to be, except she was never one of the "undead." She lived on Nova Mars, a colony of Earth and very much like the world we know. She knew what she was, and her very existence was a peril to the all-too-human population of that world.

(Bibliographer's note: a Science Fiction/Vampire Novel for those who don't believe that the two are compatible.)

Logo No. 381. Vance, Jack. *The Many Worlds of Magnus Ridolph.* Code No. UE1531. First DAW printing, April 1980. 174 pp. Cover art by David Russell. Previously published in U.S. by Ace (1966) and in U.K. by Dobson (1977). $1.75.

Contents:

The Kokod Warriors	The Spa of the Stars
The Unspeakable McInch	Coup de Grace
The Howling Bounders	The Sub-Standard Sardines
The King of Thieves	To B Or Not To C Or To D

Logo No. 382. Prescot, Dray (pseud. Kenneth Bulmer). *A Victory for Kregen*. Code No. UJ1532. First edition. First printing, April 1980. 224 pp. Cover art and illustrations by Richard Hescox. $1.95.

The windup of Prescot's stark adventures as a living chesspiece in the city of blood-games was to be as terrifying as the perils that had gone before, because now that transposed Earthman had to fight his way back to his embattled Vallian homeland across a sky full of danger and a sea full of death.

And, when he returned, if he could, he would find the combat joined, his son at doom's door, his troops up against superior odds, and a battle he must personally fight that would be two battles in two different places at the same time!

(Bibliographer's note: The twenty-second novel in the saga of Dray Prescot and the fourth of the Jikaida Cycle. Includes a glossary of the Jikaida Cycle.)

Logo No. 383. Tubb, E.C. *The Terra Data*. Code No. UE1533. First edition. First printing, April 1980. 172 pp. Cover art by Michael Mariano. Later published in U.K. by Arrow (1985). $1.75.

That there was ever a planet called Earth only Earl Dumarest believed. He had been seeking it a long time, though nobody else at the crowded galactic center believed in it. He had acquired some bits of information during his search outwards: a Terrestial zodiac, an authentic painting of Luna, a general series of hints that he was getting closer. Then he learned of a man who knew where Earth was and who had the special coordinates that would take a starship directly to it!

The man had lived on Elysius, and his widow knew where his data were. She demanded a price from Dumarest: a chore that involved a mining expedition which would bring her back a fortune and him the information. But, Elysius was not the Elysium its name projected, and the Terra data not so easily come by!

(Bibliographer's note: The twenty-second novel in the saga of Dumarest of Terra.)

Logo No. 384. Wollheim, Donald A. with Arthur W. Saha eds. *The 1980 Annual World's Best SF*. Code No. UE1535. First edition. First printing, May 1980. 284 pp. Cover art by Jack Gaughan. $2.25.

Contents:

Introduction	The Editor
The Way of Cross and Dragon	George R.R. Martin
The Thirteenth Utopia	Somtow Sucharitkul
Options	John Varley
Unaccompanied Sonata	Orson Scott Card
The Story Writer	Richard Wilson
Daisy in the Sun	Connie Willis
The Locusts	Larry Niven & Steve Barnes
The Thaw	Tanith Lee
Out There Where the Big Ships Go	Richard Cowper

Can These Bones Live?   Ted Reynolds
The Extraordinary Voyages
    of Amelie Bertrand   Joanna Russ

Logo No. 385. Van Vogt, A.E. *Rogue Ship.* Code No. UJ1536. First DAW printing, May 1980. 172 pp. Cover art by Greg Theakston. Previously published in U.S. by Doubleday (1965) and in U.K. by Dobson (1967). $1.95.

Centaurus was the ultimate destination of the space ship The Hope of Man. The journey had already taken twenty years, and nine more years remained before Centaurus would be reached.

But the passengers were becoming restless: mutiny was close. Captain Lesbee possessed information not available to anyone else on board. Indeed, the Earth might very well have been obliterated by this time.

So Centaurus was the only hope, and there could be no turning back at this point, no matter how inflammatory the situation became!

Logo No. 386. Tall, Stephen (Pseud. Compton N. Crook). *The People Beyond the Wall.* Code No. UJ1537. First edition. First printing, May 1980. 204 pp. Cover art by Gino D'Achille. $1.95.

Two Alaskan explorers burrow beneath a giant glacier to find themselves beyond the maps of today, where a strong primitive people made life free from crises, wars, and social disasters.

(Bibliographer's note: A modern Lost Race novel.)

Logo No. 387. Henneberg, Nathalie and Charles. *The Green Gods.* Code No. UE1538. First U.S. and first English language edition. First DAW printing, May 1980. 173 pp. Cover art by Don Maitz. Translated by C.J. Cherryh. Original edition entitled *Les Dieux Verts*, published by Librairie Hachette (1961). $1.75.

The long-threatened "greenhouse effect" which scientists have been predicting as a possible outcome of the world's atmosphere crisis is the topic of this novel. Here is the world beneath the greenhouse sky, where vegetation has evolved into huge and intelligent species, and where humanity finds itself, after its own disasters, reduced more and more to servants of these Green Gods and foreseeing their own extinction. Only the daring sea prince Aran and the puppet queen Atlena stand against doomsday.

Logo No. 388. Bradley, Marion Zimmer. *Two To Conquer.* Code No. UE1540. First edition. First printing, June 1980. 335 pp. Cover art by John Pound. Later published in U.K. by Arrow (1982). $2.25.

What forces would operate if there were two objects that were absolutely identical in form and substance? This problem has preoccupied both workers in magic and the scientists of physics and psychology. This is the story of the era when the planet of the Bloody Sun was divided into a hundred warring kingdoms, and civilization teetered on the edge of oblivion.

It's the story of Bard di Asturien, ambitious soldier-outlaw, and of his opponent, Varzil the Good, who struggled to establish the Compact. It's also the story of a man from distant Terra named Paul Harrell who was the exact duplicate of Varzil's enemy.

(Bibliographer's note: The fourteenth Darkover novel.)

Logo No. 389. Vance, Jack. *The Languages of Pao.* Code No. UE1541. First DAW printing, June 1980. 159 pp. Cover art by H.R. Van Dongen. Originally published in book form by Avalon (1958). Later published by Underwood-Miller (1979). See *Survey of Science Fiction Literature III.* pp. 1135-1139 (1979). $1.75.

The people of Pao were docile, much too much so for their own good. They were always easy marks for space pirates and glib-tongued businessmen from commercial worlds.

When one particularly nasty band of ruthless conquerors came down and simply took over the whole planet, the last survivor of Pao's monarchy sought assistance from the scientific wizards of the planet Breakness. Their solution was unprecedented in the history of warfare. They located the basis for the servility of the Paonese and launched a long-term operation that would change human nature there. But they asked a price and failed to take into consideration that a truly reconstructed Pao might not be willing to pay it.

Logo No. 390. Norvill, Manning (pseud. Kenneth Bulmer). *Crown of the Sword God.* Code No. UE1542. First edition. First printing, June 1980. 175 pp. Cover art by Richard Hescox. $1.75.

Odan was his name, called the Half-God. Though raised among barbarians, he laid claim to the throne of the mighty city of Eresh, for he was the son of its queen by the sky-man the city worshipped as its god. It was in that fabled time before recorded history, when the fabled cities of the ancients raised their towers along the fertile valley which was, some day, to become the Mediterranean Sea.

Odan was his name, and it brought terror to many, anger to the foes of Eresh, and hope to some. Wizards conspired against him, and even the mysterious riders of the sky worked their uncanny science to try to defeat him.

(Bibliographer's note: Third book of the Odan the Half-God series.)

Logo No. 391. Carter, Lin. *Zanthodon.* Code No. UE1543. First edition. First printing, June 1980. 188 pp. Cover art and illustrations by Thomas Kidd. $1.75.

Beneath the trackless sands and shifting wastelands of the Sahara, there lies a world unknown to modern man: the underground land of Zanthodon. In its vast unmapped terrain are great jungles, strange seas, and forbidding mountains, and there can be found, as well, many of the beings that have long since vanished from the surface of the earth—dinosaurs, flying monsters, and primitive cavemen.

(Bibliographer's note: The second adventure of Eric Carstairs in the weird world beneath Earth's crust. Includes a short glossary of the characters in Zanthodon.)

Logo No. 392. Piserchia, Doris. *The Spinner.* **Code No. UJ1548. First edition. First printing, July 1980. 176 pp. Cover art by H.R. Van Dongen. Also published as a Science Fiction Book Club selection. $1.95.**

The search for new sources of energy led one man to an accidental breakthrough into a strange parallel world. It was apparently deserted and might have been a good place to prospect until the finder panicked. He tried to shut the dimensional crack that led into that other place.

But the breakthrough had prematurely awakened that world's most predatory inhabitant from hibernation, and, in raging fury, the Spinner slipped through to find itself alone and hungry in an American city loaded with good things to eat. People!

(Bibliographer's query: So where's Spiderman when you need him?)

Logo No. 393. Wagner, Karl Edward ed. *The Year's Best Horror Stories: Series VIII.* Code No. UJ1549. First edition. First printing, July 1980. 221 pp. Cover art by Michael Whelan. See *Horror Literature* 4-308 (1981). $1.95.

Contents:

Introduction: Access to Horror	Karl Edward Wagner
The Dead Line	Dennis Etchison
To Wake the Dead	Ramsey Campbell
In the Fourth Year of the War	Harlan Ellison
From the Lower Deep	Hugh B. Cave
The Baby-Sitter	Davis Grubb
The Well at the Half Cat	John Tibbetts
My Beautiful Darkling	Eddy C. Bertin
A Serious Call	George Hay
Sheets	Alan Ryan
Billy Wolfe's Riding Spirit	Kevin A. Lyons
Lex Talionis	Russell Kirk
Entombed	Robert Keefe
A Fly One	Steve Sneyd
Needle Song	Charles L. Grant
All the Birds Come Home to Roost	Harlan Ellison
The Devil Behind You	Richard A. Moore

(Bibliographer's note: This book is the first with Karl Edward Wagner as editor of what has become the finest horror anthology series in the world.)

Logo No. 394. Clayton, Jo. *Star Hunters.* Code No. UE1550. First edition. First printing, July 1980. 176 pp. Cover art by Michael Mariano. $1.75.

On the world to which the Diadem conveyed her, Aletys must confront, not only the hordes of half-humans who are devastating the planet, but meet head-on the mental force of a madman of her own ancestral race. It's an encounter on several levels, human, inhuman, and superhuman, and she must triumph on all or lose everything.

(Bibliographer's note: Fifth novel in the Diadem series.)

Logo No. 395. Stasheff, Christopher. *A Wizard in Bedlam.* Code No. UJ1551. First paperback edition. First printing, July 1980. 191 pp. Cover art by David B. Mattingly. Previously published in U.S. by Doubleday (1979) and later published in U.K. by Mayflower (1982). $1.95.

Melange was a successful planetary colony—for the very rich. Its population, except for the aristocracy, consisted of miserable serfs and perpetual servants. What was worse, they were all identical. For the underlings were clones: living replicas of the faithful few that had been brought along to serve the masters.

Dirk Dulaine had started life as one of them, but he had been taken offplanet and trained to be a troublemaker. His task was to become the Robespierre of the Melange Revolution, if that was possible. But it wasn't to be easy. Especially since the population had been bred to behave like programmed mechanisms.

Logo No. 396. Cherryh, C.J. (pseud. Carolyn Janice Cherry). *Serpent's Reach.* Code No. UE1554. First edition. First printing, August 1980. 279 pp. Cover art by David B. Mattingly. Also published as a Science Fiction Book Club selection. Later published in U.K. by Macdonald (1981). See *Anatomy of Wonder* 4-132 (1987). $2.25.

The constellation of Hydrus, known as the Serpent, is compact and obscure as seen from Earth's sky. Even in the great era of interstellar colonization, it remained obscure, for it was under strict quarantine, since it harbored an intelligent race, powerful, alien and inhuman. Yet there were human colonies within the Serpent's Reach, cut off from the galaxy beyond, with their own inbred culture, their Families and traditions, and their special relationships to the inhuman *majat.*

This is the story of Raen, the last of the massacred Sul family, and of her lifetime pledge to find vengeance. It was to take her across the worlds of the Reach into the very center of the alien webwork, into the strands of thought and counter-thought that knit the forbidden constellation into a complex of interbred cultures that no outsider could hope to unravel.

Logo No. 397. Prescot, Dray (pseud. Kenneth Bulmer). *Beasts of Antares.* Code No. UJ1555. First edition. First printing, August 1980. 206 pp. Cover art and illustrations by Richard Hescox. $1.95.

Dray Prescot, Earthman on Kregen, the world that orbits the twin suns of Antares in the Constellation Scorpio, once a pawn of cosmic powers, enters a new cycle of his career. He rallies the warriors of Vallia for a final stand against the foes that have encircled them, and, then, in an act of bravado, undertakes single-handedly to rescue three old friends from slavery in a distant land.

(Bibliographer's note: The twenty-third novel in the saga of Dray Prescot, and the first in the Spikatur Cycle.)

Logo No. 398. Carter, Lin. *Lost Worlds.* Code No. UJ1556. First edition.

First printing, August 1980. 176 pp. Cover art by Enrich. $1.95.
    Contents:
    The Introduction: Lost Worlds of Time
    HYPERBOREA;
        The Scroll of Morloc (with Clark Ashton Smith)
        The Stairs in the Crypt (with Clark Ashton Smith)
    MU;
        The Thing in the Pit
    LEMURIA;
        Thieves of Zangabal
        Keeper of the Golden Flame
    VALUSIA;
        Riders Beyond the Sunrise (with Robert E. Howard)
    ANTILLIA;
        The Twelve Wizards of Ong
    ATLANTIS;
        The Seal of Zaon Sathla
    The Afterword: Lost Worlds to Come

Logo No. 399. Goulart, Ron. *Hail, Hibbler.* Code No. UE1557. First edition. First printing, August 1980. 157 pp. Cover art by Josh Kirby. $1.75.
    His name was Adolph Hibbler, and he had escaped the doom of Hitler's Reich by inventing the cryogenic deep freeze long before the rest of the world. As a human icicle, he had been just a circus sideshow for many decades until he finally thawed out—in the 21st Century.
    The trouble began with a series of mysterious events, and the government had to call in Odd Jobs, Inc. But when Jake and Hildy Pace started uncovering the clues, they found an odder job than any previous capers.
    There were the lost cassettes of the world's greatest sex fiend to locate. There were model planes that fired real bullets. There was the army of baby-doll killers. And there were the revolutionary gas station attendants and the Arabian shiek who had ignited them.
    Only Odd Jobs, Inc. could have connected all these cockeyed clues and come up with Hibbler. When it did, it sure looked as if it, and the world, were on a spinoff orbit into infinite disaster!
    (Bibliographer's note: Another wacky adventure in the Odd Jobs, Inc. series.)

Logo No. 400. Norton, Andre. *Lore of the Witch World.* Code No. UJ1560. First edition. First printing, September 1980. 223 pp. Cover art by Michael Whelan. $1.95.
    Contents:
    Introduction by C.J. Cherryh
    Spider Silk
    Sand Sister
    Falcon Blood
    Legacy from Sorn Fen
    Sword of Disbelief

The Toads of Grimmerdale
Changeling
(Bibliographer's note: Twelfth book in the Witch World series, consisting of previously uncollected novelettes and tales of Witch World, including the never previously published novelette, "Changeling.")

Logo No. 401. Lee, Tanith. *Kill the Dead.* Code No. UE1562. First edition. First printing, September, 1980. 172 pp. Cover art by Don Maitz. $1.75.

Kill the dead? How can you slay that which is already slain? Yet, sometimes the dead refuse to stay quiet, for there are times when the dead have a duty that must be fulfilled. There are times when those must walk who defy God and Nature to do so; those are times of horror and haunting.

Then one must call the exorcist. There is work for the slayer of ghosts in the backlands of the world. There is work for Parl Dro, Ghost-Killer.

This is the story of two sisters who defied him. One didn't belong on Earth; one did. But which was the one he must kill? Which was the one he must silence?

Logo No. 402. Vance, Jack. *Nopalgarth.* Code No. UE1563. First DAW printing, September 1980. 272 pp. Cover art by Gino D'Achille. The title novel was published as *The Brains of Earth* by Ace Books (1966) and bound with *The Many Worlds of Magnus Ridolph.* First U.K. and first hardcover edition published by Dobson (1975). *The Houses of Iszm* and *Son of the Tree* were published by Ace (1964), the latter also being separately published in the U.K. by Mayflower (1974). $2.25.

Contents (Three Complete Novels):
Nopalgarth
The Houses of Iszm
Son of the Tree

Logo No. 403. Chandler, A. Bertram. *Star Loot.* Code No. UE1564. First edition. First printing, September 1980. 223 pp. Cover art by Attila Hejja. Later published as first U.K. and first hardcover edition by Hale (1981). $1.75.

In luck and out of luck, John Grimes was a living legend of the spaceways. He had been an officer of the service, he had been the victim of a mutiny, he had discovered lost worlds, he had served under strange masters and on strange ships, but he had never turned space pirate. Until this adventure.

How it happened was a complex story to begin with, but typical Grimes luck. How he became the terror of the star lanes developed, as usual, from his own efforts to make an honest living and other's efforts to use him for devious diversions. This is a story of the loot of the stars, and of how Grimes graduated from operator of a space courier ship to master of a fleet of dreaded carriers of the skull and crossbones!

(Bibliographer's note: Another in the John Grimes a.k.a. SF's answer to Horatio Hornblower series.)

Logo No. 404. Foster, M.A. *Waves.* Code No. UE1569. First edition. First printing, October 1980. 256 pp. Cover art by Ken W. Kelly. See *Anatomy of Wonder* 4-222 (1987). $2.25.

Fraesch arrived on the planet Mulcahen to replace a missing scientist at Halcyon Station. That was the name of the very isolated and weirdly constructed laboratory of Speculations, Inc.

What was going on there wasn't clear, but Fraesch suspected that it had something to do with immortality drugs. So did the owners of the planet, a Russian-Turkish combine, who were shadowing Fraesch from the moment of his arrival.

When Fraesch realized that his predecessor had vanished without trace, and that he was surely going to be next, the situation began to assume its true ominous color. Long life or not, the next wave of the unknown was slated to wash him out, and the station, as well.

Logo No. 405. Asimov, Isaac and Martin H. Greenberg eds. *Isaac Asimov Presents the Great Science Fiction Stories 4 (1942).* Code No. UE1570. First edition. First printing, October 1980. 448 pp. Cover design by One Plus One Studio. $2.50.

Contents:

Introduction	The Editors
The Star Mouse	Fredric Brown
The Wings of Night	Lester del Rey
Cooperate—Or Else!	A.E. van Vogt
Foundation	Isaac Asimov
The Push of a Finger	Alfred Bester
Asylum	A.E. van Vogt
Proof	Hal Clement
Nerves	Lester del Rey
Barrier	Anthony Boucher
The Twonky	Lewis Padgett
QRM-Interplanetary	George O. Smith
The Weapons Shop	A.E. van Vogt
Mimic	Donald A. Wollheim

Logo No. 406. Stableford, Brian M. *Optiman.* Code No. UJ1571. First edition. First printing, October 1980. 190 pp. Cover art by Michael Mariano. Later published in U.K. by Pan (1981) as *War Games.* $1.95.

Warfare between humanity and the Veitch had been going on for hundreds of years with no end in sight. When humans captured the planet Heidra, they found themselves in control of a world with three contending species scrapping over its barren lands. One was the Veitch refugees, one the semi-civilized natives, and one a race of barbaric nomads. For the human adventurer, Remy, it was the last that made his first troubles.

Remy's destination was the uncovering of a lost military installation of a prehistoric galactic race. Assisting him was a newly created genetic-construct warrior, an optiman. Superhuman and sterile, but highly intelligent, optimen could tip the scales in the cosmic conflict if they worked out as planned.

Three-way wargaming is difficult at best, but the unknown factors of the optimen could make it dangerously unpredictable to all sides.

Logo No. 407. Moorcock, Michael. *The Golden Barge.* Code No. UE1572. First U.S. and first paperback edition. First printing, October 1980. 173 op. Cover art by John Pound. Later published in U.K. in hardcover by New English Library (1983). $1.75.

"Then the mist eddied. Out of it, purposefully and with dignity, loomed a great golden barge, a barge which glittered with a light of its own. Tallow was astounded. He looked at the towering shape, agape. He was no longer the integrated and impenetrable thing he had been, for he had not taken the golden barge into account before. He became worried that the barge should not escape as it passed. It disappeared into the mist again...."

(Bibliographer's note: The author's first completed novel (1958), but unpublished for many years. According to Moorcock, it's presented here with minor revisions of the sort that an editor might demand of a first novel.)

Logo No. 408. Lee, Tanith. *Day by Night.* Code No. UE1576. First edition. First printing, November 1980. 316 pp. Cover art by Don Maitz; frontispiece by the author. $2.25.

The planet didn't rotate. On one side eternal day, the sun shining down hotly from the center of the heavens. On the opposite side eternal night, the stars glowing coldly in the black and airless sky. Yet the planet had been colonized. In ages past, civilization had dug into the rock of the darkside and had thrived. Aristocrats vied with aristocrats, and the poor, as ever, struggled to keep home and body together against the ever-encroaching cold surface.

To keep the lower classes happy, Vitra, the storyteller, spun romantic sagas on the popular network. She imagined a strange world on the sunside, inhabited by men and women enmeshed in crime and love, schemes and intrigues. Vitra believed that she was making this up. But was she? Was there really another civilization on the bright side, and could it be that what she related was not fiction, but events which would inevitably send both worlds out of synch to mutual disaster?

Logo No. 409. Piserchia, Doris. *The Fluger.* Code No. UJ1577. First edition. First printing, November 1980. 159 pp. Cover art by H.R. Van Dongen. $1.95.

The Fluger was five meters long, had four thick legs, a body of impenetrable molecular density and numerous teeth capable of chewing diamonds into powder. It was four hundred massive kilos of violence, savagery and hatred.

When the Fluger arrived as unlisted cargo in the enclosed city of Olymous, it launched itself on a murderous rampage which couldn't be halted. It presented that terrified utopian community with the problem of how to stop an irresistible force. The only answer seemed to be a hired alien assassin, an outer-space humanoid about whom the citizens of Olympus knew next to nothing except that he was a professional killer who wouldn't quit until his job was done.

But, when the irresistible force met the immovable object, they turned that fragile city in the sky into a raging battlefield, and their "savior" looked to become as much of a menace as his monster counterpart.

Logo No. 410. Carter, Lin ed. *The Year's Best Fantasy Stories: 6.* Code No. UJ1578. First edition. First printing, November 1980. 191 pp. Cover art by Josh Kirby. $1.95.

Contents:

The Year in Fantasy: An Introduction	The Editor
Garden of Blood	Roger Zelazny
The Character Assassin	Paul H. Cook
The Things That Are Gods	John Brunner
Zurvan's Saint	Grail Undwin
Perfidious Amber	Tanith Lee
The Mer She	Fritz Leiber
Demon of the Snows	Lin Carter
The Pavilion Where All Times Meet	Jayge Carr
Cryptically Yours	Brian Lumley
Red As Blood	Tanith Lee
Sandmagic	Orson Scott Card
The Year's Best Fantasy Books: An Appendix	

Logo No. 411. Tubb, E.C. *World of Promise.* Code No. UE1579. First edition. First printing, November 1980. 160 pp. Cover art by Ken W. Kelly. $1.75.

Ascelius was an academic world, whose primary business was teaching the knowledge of the thousands of worlds, and housing great universities and colleges, populated by students and scholars from all over the galaxy. Such a world was surely the place to learn of the legendary planet called Earth.

Dumarest went to Ascelius, and, indeed, he found that there had once been a study group for Earth lore. To find the remnants of it, to seek out the discarded files of their discussions, wasn't easy. Not when the dreaded Cyber already had a toe-hold on Ascelius, and genetic engineering of man and monster was the latest fad. But Dumarest wasn't a quitter. Whatever the tests might demand, he wouldn't flunk out, although it might mean death for others, and possibly himself.

(Bibliographer's note: The twenty-third novel in the saga of Dumarest of Terra.)

Logo No. 412. Wallace, Ian (pseud, John Wallace Pritchard). *The Lucifer Comet.* Code No. UE1581. First edition. First printing, December 1980. 302 pp. Cover art by Gino D'Achille. See *Anatomy of Wonder* 4-582 (1987). $2.25.

They discovered a vast comet far out between the stars. Within its icy core were two beings, frozen in still life for thousands of years. One was human, a Prometheus figure. But the other, locked with the first in a tableau of eternal combat, was Lucifer.

Lucifer, Satan, the Devil—call him what you will—but there he seemed to be, horns, bat wings, and all, the visible embodiment of all human legendry of all that was evil.

Then they defrosted them. Prometheus was, indeed, the Fire-Bringer. The other was the Old Enemy in person, with powers that baffled even the advanced science of those future days.

Logo No. 413. Prescot, Dray (pseud. Kenneth Bulmer). *Rebel of Antares.* Code No. UJ1582. First edition. First printing, December 1980. 191 pp. Cover art by Ken W. Kelly; illustrated by Jack Gaughan. $1.95.

Lone Earthman on the vivid and intricate world of double-sunned Antares in Scorpio, Dray Prescot had been the pawn of the unseen Star Lords, who had seeded that planet with the offspring of a hundred alien races. But, at last, Prescot had come in sight of the goal which he shared with these space masters, the overthrow of slavers and their evil empires.

On the island kingdom of Hyrklana, his course now seemed clear. Overthrow its decadent queen, lead rebellion against the cruel Arena, and free the princess who was its rightful ruler. It was a hard task, but, for Dray Prescot, against whom sorcerors and swordsmen had contended, it was the only course he could follow. Though it might, this time, lead to his death, there could be no turning back.

(Bibliographer's note: The twenty-fourth adventure in the interminable saga of Dray Prescot.)

Logo No. 414. Barbet, Pierre (pseud. Claude Avice). *Cosmic Crusaders.* Code No. UE1583. First printing, December 1980. 286 pp. Cover art by Oliviero Berni. $2.25.

Contents:

Baphomet's Meteor. This novel was published by DAW Books in December 1972. See Logo No. 35 for complete bibliographical details and a plot summary.

Stellar Crusade. Translated by C.J. Cherryh. First English language edition. Original edition entitled *Croisade Stellaire,* published by Editions Fleuve Noir, Paris, France (1974).

Logo No. 415. Purtill, Richard. *The Stolen Goddess.* Code No. UE1584. First edition. First printing, December 1980. 159 pp. Cover art by Jan Duursema. $1.75.

This is the story of Ducalion of strange parentage and of his initiation into the bull dances and mystic rites of a lost civilization and the intrigues of a court where gods and half-gods were real powers to be reckoned with. This is the story of the quest which was set upon him by Apollo, himself, and of a descent into the fabled regions of darkness and shadow, where the lord of the deathlands had taken the daughter of a jealous goddess.

(Bibliographer's note: The author's second book. Sequel to *The Golden*

Gryphon Feather.)

Logo No. 416. Vance, Jack. *The Book of Dreams.* Code No. UE1587. First edition. First printing, January 1981. 235 pp. Cover art by Ken W. Kelly. $2.25.

Howard Alan Treesong gave a banquet to ten friends. All died in agony, save himself.

Howard Alan Treesong went to his old school reunion to teach his former classmates the meaning of horror.

Howard Alan Treesong was the most elusive of the five Demon Princes upon whom Kirth Gersen had sworn vengeance. A galaxy-wide guessing game proved his undoing.

Howard Alan Treesong wrote his own holy book and called it The Book of Dreams.

(Bibliographer's Query: Would you buy a used car from Howard Alan Treesong?)

(Bibliographer's serious note: The fifth and final Demon Princes novel.)

Logo No. 417. Vance, Jack. *Dust of Far Suns.* Code No. UE1588. First DAW printing, January 1981. 160 pp. Cover art by Paul Chadwick. Originally published as *Future Tense* by Ballantine Books (1964). $1.75.

Contents:

Dust of Far Suns	Ullward's Retreat
Dodkin's Job	The Gift of Gab

Logo No. 418. Vance, Jack. *Trullion: Alastor 2262.* Code No. UE1590. First DAW printing, January 1981. 192 pp. Cover art by David B. Mattingly. Originally published in U.S. by Ballantine Books (1973) and in U.K. by Mayflower (1979) in paperback and later published in hardcover by Underwood-Miller (1984). See *Anatomy of Wonder* 3-764 (1981). $2.25.

Trullion, World 2262 of the Alastor Cluster, was a beautiful waterworld of fens, mists, idyllic islands set in clear oceans whose teeming richness provided food for the taking.

The Trill were a carefree, easy-living race, but violence entered their lives during the raids of the galactic pirates known as the Starmenters. There was also the planetwide game of hussade, and the Trill's ferocious passion for gambling drove them to risk all, even life itself, on the hazardous water-chessboard gaming fields. Their prize? The virginal body of the beautiful sheirl-maiden, the body any Trill is willing to die for.

(Bibliographer's note: The first novel in the Alastor series.)

Logo No. 419. Vance, Jack. *Marune: Alastor 933.* Code No. UE1591. First DAW printing, January 1981. 188 pp. Cover art by David B. Mattingly. Originally published in U.S. by Ballantine Books (1975) and in U.K. by Coronet (1978). Later published in hardcover by Underwood-Miller (1984). See *Anatomy of Wonder* 3-764 (1981). $2.25.

From his palace on Numenes, the Connatic ruled the sprawling Alastor Cluster and kept track of the doings of his trillion or more subjects.

However, there was one man of whom he could learn nothing, for the past life of the wanderer called Pardero was a complete mystery. Pardero set himself two goals. Find out who he was and find the person who had stolen his memory.

Psychologists deduced that his home world must be Marune: World 933 of the Alastor Cluster, a planet lit by four shifting suns. Pardero made his way there and was hailed as the ruler of one of its shadowed realms. Uncovering his lost identity had been comparatively simple. Finding his sworn enemy would be more difficult; there were so many possibilities to choose from!

(Bibliographer's note: The second novel in the Alastor series.)

Logo No. 420. Cherryh, C.J. (pseud. Carolyn Janice Cherry). *Downbelow Station*. Code No. UE1594. First edition. 432 pp. Cover art by David B. Mattingly. Also issued as first hardcover by the Science Fiction Book Club (1981), the first printing being denoted by the code L10 on page 438. Later published in U.K. by Methuen (1983). $2.75.

Pell's Star occupied the central spot in the coming conflict between Earth's tired stellar empire and the tough onslaught of its rebellious colonies. Whoever controlled Pell's Downbelow Station held the key to Earth's defensive perimeter, or a jumping-off point for a Terrestrial offensive to regain the lost empire. But Pell had always been neutral and was determined to remain so.

(Bibliographer's note: First book of the Downbelow Station series. 1981 Hugo Award winner.)

Logo No. 421. Nolane, Richard D. ed. *Terra SF: The Year's Best European SF*. Code No. UE1595. First edition. First printing, February 1981. 268 pp. Cover art by Segrelles. $2.25.

Contents:

Introduction: In Search of European Science Fiction	The Editor
Test Flesh	Gianni Montanari
Parallel Worlds	Paul van Herck
The Fifth Time Out	Bertil Martensson
Drugs'll Do You	Kathinka Lannoy
Opportunities Galore	Gabriel Bermudez Castillo
Fill in the Blank(s)	Michel Jeury
Where Neuroses Thrive	Richard D. Nolane
Back to Earth, Finally	Philip Goy
Take Me Down the River	Sam J. Lundwall
Turnabout	Ingar Knudtsen, Jr.
Aruna	Erwin Neutzsky-Wulff
Red Rhombuses	Lino Aldani
The Many Miniworlds of Matuschek	Thomas Ziegler
End of an Era	Ronald M. Hahn & Jurgen Andreas
The Authors in *Terra SF*	The Editor

145

Logo No. 422. Brunner, John. *To Conquer Chaos.* Code No. UJ1596. First revised edition. First DAW printing, February 1981. 160 pp. Cover art by H.R. Van Dongen. Originally serialized in *New Worlds* (1963) and published in paperback by Ace Books (1964). The present text was revised by the author for this edition. $1.95.

The barrenland lay on the face of the world like a sore, nearly round, more than three hundred miles in circumference. It had been there so long that it was endured, as were the twisted monsters that wandered out of the barrenland and killed.

Conrad, living on the edge, had visions of a time when the barrenland was a rich region full of powerful, magical people: people who traveled to other worlds. He was ruled by a burning need to know what none could tell him: the explanation of the mysterious visions which had plagued him all his life.

Then he met Jervis Yanderman, a soldier who knew of these visions. Yanderman was convinced there was an island in the barrenland where people still clung to life. Yanderman also knew that a man had come out of it—within living memory!

Logo No. 423. Carter, Lin. *Hurok of the Stone Age.* Code No. UE1597. First edition. First printing, February 1981. 192 pp. Cover art and illustrations by Josh Kirby. $1.75.

Beneath the vast and trackless Sahara, there lies a cavern so immense that whole nations could be swallowed up within it. There reside in the eternal subterranean glow the last of the Cro-Magnons and their rivals, the Neanderthals, lost remnants of ancient surface empires, and hordes of beasts and beings from all the ages of prehistory. Into this world, Zanthodon, penetrated the soldier-of-fortune, Eric Carstairs, and immediately became embroiled in tremendous adventures.

Hurok the Neanderthal learned the meaning of friendship from Carstairs and, in return, would lead an expedition of cavemen to the dinosaur-guarded city of Zar where Carstairs had fallen captive to a sadistic queen and her scheming advisors.

(Bibliographer's note: The third adventure of Eric Carstairs in Zanthodon.)

Logo No. 424. Norman, John (pseud. John Lange). *Rogue of Gor.* Code No. UE1602. First edition. First printing, March 1981. 318 pp. Cover art by Richard Hescox. $2.50.

Jason Marshall learned the meaning of manhood and the power of women, both dominant and submissive, when he was kidnapped from Earth to the Counter-Earth called Gor. Winning his freedom, Jason set out single-handedly to win his own place on that gloriously barbaric world on the other side of the sun.

His intent was to find the girl who had been enslaved with him, but that quest thrust him smack in the middle of the war that raged between Imperial Air and the Salerian Confederation and the secret schemes of the pirate armada that sought control of the mighty trading artery of the fighting cities.

(Bibliographer's note: The fifteenth book of the Counter-Earth saga of Gor.)

Logo No. 425. Dibell, Ansen (pseud. Nancy Ann Dibble). *Circle, Crescent, Star.* Code No. UE1603. First edition. First printing, March 1981. 252 pp. Cover art by Ken W. Kelly. $2.25.

Jannus confronts triple danger as the immortal monster Ashai Rey hunts him down, as his protector of the Crescent goes to battle with the dictatress of the Circle, and as the warrior women bands challenge him to deadly combat. The outcome would affect all on that once great, but now declining, planet, and only the power conferred on him as the secret king of Kantmorie held hope against the overwhelming machinations of the Star.

(Bibliographer's note: The Second Book of the Strange and Fantastic History of the King of Kantmorie.)

Logo No. 426. Asimov, Isaac and Martin H. Greenberg eds. *Isaac Asimov Presents the Great Science Fiction Stories 5 (1943).* Code No. UE1604. First edition. First printing, March 1981. 380 pp. Cover design by One Plus One Studio. $2.75.

Contents:

Introduction

The Cave	P. Schuyler Miller
The Halfling	Leigh Brackett
Mimsy Were the Borogroves	Lewis Padgett
Q.U.R	Anthony Boucher
Clash by Night	Lawrence O'Donnell
Exile	Edmond Hamilton
Daymare	Fredric Brown
Doorway into Time	C.L. Moore
The Storm	A.E. van Vogt
The Proud Robot	Lewis Padgett
Symbiotica	Eric Frank Russell
The Iron Standard	Lewis Padgett

Logo No. 427. Johnson, James B. *Daystar and Shadow.* Code No. UE1605. First edition. First printing, March 1981. 206 pp. Cover art by Ken W. Kelly. $2.25.

Daystar was a wanderer in the desertland that had once been America. The terrors of that arid new world were the monster fireworms whose tentacles were death, but they held no horror for him, for he could call upon them for protection.

Daystar was a fugitive from the bands of civilized men who regarded him as a traitor. Nevertheless, Daystar saw himself as their savior, though the evidence was all against him. Shadow was a girl, another wanderer in the wastelands. When the two finally met and joined minds, the world would be transformed, and the final struggle for Earth's dominion would be launched.

Logo No. 428. Stableford, Brian. *The Castaways of Tanagar.* Code No. UE1609. First edition. First printing, April 1981. 319 pp. Cover art by H.R. Van Dongen. $2.50.

A few starships had set out from Earth before civilization ended. One of them found a new world and created a new home for mankind, an ideal intellectual society on Tanager. Humane, its deviants and criminals were sent into space in deep freeze forever.

But then came the rediscovery of Earth, a world now far different from that of the star-voyaging days. The only explorers with guts enough to face that terrifying old world were the very criminals who couldn't abide Tanagar.

Logo No. 429. Lee, Tanith. *Lycanthia or The Children of Wolves.* Code No. UE1610. First edition. First printing, April 1981. 220 pp. Cover art by Paul Chadwick. $2.25.

Even in today's world, there are corners where past evils still cast their terror-haunted shadows. When the young man, Christian, came to his inheritance, a once grand mansion in just such a remote corner of France, he knew only that there was some sort of alternate claim to that ancient building and its lands. Even as the villagers acknowledged him as lord of the manor, there came two from the forest to stake out their interest. With them came fear and desire, terror and love, a combination which could be irresistible, as well as fatal.

Logo No. 430. Mendelson, Drew. *Pilgrimage.* Code No. UE1612. First edition. First printing, April 1981. 220 pp. Cover art by John Pound. $2.25.

As far as anyone knew, all mankind lived in the City. The City, a self-enclosed towering single building, had always moved, generation by generation, across the vast empty landscape.

Brann Adelbran met destiny when his family sector found itself at Tailend. Already the Structors were planning to dismantle his ancestral apartment high on an upper floor of that colossal metropolis. Brann would have to make the pilgrimage to Frontend to re-establish his family there for the generations to come.

But, when tradition was suddenly shattered, Brann was forced to flee, not on the established routes and hallways, but down the forbidden shafts into the lost chambers, corridors, and basements which even legend had forgotten. His pilgrimage became an odyssey of terrors, mysteries, and scientific marvels, all of which led to the end of the world.

Logo No. 431. Tubb, E.C. *Nectar of Heaven.* Code No. UJ1613. First edition. First printing, April 1981. 160 pp. Cover art by Ken W. Kelly. $1.95.

The planet had two unique elements. One was that it produced the galaxy's most elusive and most desirable hallucinatory drug. The other was that it was a stock broker's paradise.

The world was split into rich men's holdings, and every day, every hour, every minute, these were being traded on a continuous stock market. Up and down went values and rights, as men conspired to seize other's properties, to push prices down and costs up. Their money games controlled everything else: the common people, farmers, workers, homes, lives, women, poverty and luxury. All were at the continuous sway of that market of gluttony.

Earl Dumarest went there to find his next stake. Find the drug-gem or manipulate the market: two possibilities. But, behind the scenes, stood the advisors of the inhuman Cyclan, determined to fix the odds against Dumarest.

(Bibliographer's note: Tale 24 in the saga of Dumarest of Terra.)

Logo No. 432. Wollheim, Donald A. with Arthur W. Saha eds. *The 1981 Annual World's Best SF.* Code No. UE1617. First edition. First printing, May 1981. 252 pp. Cover art by Michael Mariano. $2.50.

Contents:

Introduction	The Editor
Variation on a Theme from Beethoven	Sharon Webb
Beatnik Bayou	John Varley
Elbow Room	Marion Zimmer Bradley
The Ugly Chickens	Howard Waldrop
Prime Time	Norman Spinrad
Nightflyers	George R.R. Martin
A Spaceship Built of Stone	Lisa Tuttle
Window	Bob Leman
The Summer Sweet, the Winter Wild	Michael G. Coney
Achronos	Lee Killough

Logo No. 433. Cherryh, C.J. (pseud. Carolyn Janice Cherry). *Sunfall.* Code No. UE1618. First edition. First printing, May 1981. 158 pp. Cover art by Michael Whelan. $2.25.

Contents:
Prologue
The Only Death in the City (Paris)
The Haunted Tower (London)
Ice (Moscow)
Nightgame (Rome)
Highliner (New York)
The General (Peking)

Logo No. 434. Piserchia, Doris. *Doomtime.* Code No. UE1619. First edition. First printing, May 1981. 173 pp. Cover art by H.R. Van Dongen. $2.25.

It all began when someone tried to push Creed into the flesh pool to be ingested. The assassination failed, but Creed was never the same again, because it launched the cliff-dwellers of Creed's colony onto a new course of life, which could lead to humanity's re-emergence as Earth's masters.

In those far future days, Earth's masters were two trees. Not trees as we know them, but two Everest-high growths, whose sentient roots and fast-growing branches dominated every living thing on the world. Men lived between their arboreal combat.

(Bibliographer's note: Joyce Kilmer would have gotten warm all over if he had known about this future Earth.)

Logo No. 435. De Vet, Charles V. & Katherine MacLean. *Second Game.* Code No. UE1620. First edition thus. First printing, May 1981. 158 pp. Cover art by Michael Mariano. A shorter and different version of this novel was published under the title *Cosmic Checkmate* by Ace Books (1962). $2.25.

Mankind's Ten Thousand Worlds had expanded and prospered until they encountered their first aliens. These were people, almost as human as those who had originated on Earth, but with some slight differences. One of their differences was that they would never associate with aliens, never surrender, never compromise. They would conquer the Ten Thousand Worlds or die trying.

The odd thing is that they were able to do so, because they were barbarically cunning warriors with a fanatic military talent, unapproachable by arbitration. Earth's master spy was prepared for this. He would challenge the enemy to two games, and he was prepared to lose the first. But the second would be crucial. On that would depend the lives of billions. It was scientifically inconceivable that he could lose that second game. Until he did.

(Bibliograper's note: Now there's a high roller! Thanks, Mr. Master Spy.)

Logo No 436. Selby, Curt (pseud. Doris Piserchia). *Blood County.* Code No. UE1622. First edition. First printing, June 1981. 176 pp. Cover art by Ken W. Kelly. $2.25.

Blood was what they called that mountain town and the forbidding land around it, and the name was significant. Folks there knew a secret that would have shocked the world, but nobody was ever going to get out of Blood to tell. Not even when Portia Clark arrived, hot on a news story for a national magazine. Especially, not her.

Clint Breen, who had once been in the outside world, tried to save her. But he had to fight a tradition that drove men and women to unspeakable lusts, and that secretly ruled the lives and afterlives of every being in the county. Blood was the place where more men and women walked the night than were ever seen by day. Horror was their heritage, for they were the people that the census dare not count!

(Bibliographer's nostalgic reminiscence: Remember the old radio show, Portia Faces Life?)

Logo No. 437. Landis, Arthur H. *The Magick of Camelot.* Code No. UE1623. First edition. First printing, June 1981. 207 pp. Cover art by Richard Hescox. $2.25.

The planet that the watchers from the stars called Camelot was unique mong all worlds. For there, amid the trappings of medieval chivalry, magic actually worked! It had stumped the secret observers from the Teran worlds for years, until Kyrie Fern brought back the startling answer.

But Kyrie's work wasn't done, for, on the heels of this triumph in leading the knights and ladies and dragonlords to victory, the gate between the universes opened, and the vanguard of a super-science beyond humanity set up its conquering banner on Camelot.

Knighthood may have always been in flower there, but the time had come for warlock spells and high-tech strategies to combine forces, or lose first a world and then the galaxy.

(Bibliographer's note: Third book of the Camelot in Space series.)

Logo No. 438. Dick, Philip K. *Flow My Tears, the Policeman Said*. Code No. UE1624. Reprint of Logo No. 146. This printing, June 1981. 208 pp. Cover art by Oliviero Berni. $2.25.

For comments on this book, see Logo No. 146. This is one of the instances where there has been a reprint with almost everything identical except the new cover and, of course, the price.

(Bibliographer's note: The copyright page, interestingly, continues to refer to the date of first printing as the original "April 1975." However, since its logo number is sandwiched between two books whose dates of first printing are both June 1981, I don't think I'm going too far out on a limb by presuming a June 1981 printing for this book. If I'm wrong, so what; I just renewed my malpractice insurance.)

Logo No. 439. Goulart, Ron. *The Robot in the Closet*. Code No. UJ1626. First edition. First printing, June 1981. 160 pp. Cover art by Josh Kirby. $1.95.

Sara Tenbrook intended to shake down her family tree. She was proud of her distinguished ancestors, and, besides, there was a matter of a lost fortune waiting somewhere among the centuries past. So she rented a time machine and invited her boyfriend along.

The time machine was a robot. It could climb down to any branch of the old Tenbrook family tree and take them with it. What's more, it could also talk, and take on disguises, and had an ego bigger than all creation!

That family tree may have borne some golden apples, but the more that walkie-talkie time robot explored, the more assorted nuts it turned up!

Logo No. 440. Norton, Andre. *Horn Crown*. Code No. UE1635. First edition. First printing, July 1981. 255 pp. Cover art by Michael Whelan. $2.95.

When the Elder People deserted the Witch World, the cosmic Gate opened, and human households migrated in. Though they found the land abandoned, the roads empty and the shrines unattended, they soon became aware that the Old Gods still retained their dread powers.

Elron the Clanless and Galthea the Wise Woman were drawn unwillingly side by side into unexplored realms. Each had a separate quest, but their fates were linked by the unknown. Each sought an unholy alliance; each was in conflict with the other.

(Bibliographer's note: The seminal Witch World novel. Don't you love it when I talk dirty?)

Logo No. 441. Stateham, B.R. *Banners of the Sa'yen.* Code No. UE1636. First edition. First printing, July 1981. 207 pp. Cover art and frontispiece by Ken W. Kelly. $2.25.

He said he was a lost spaceman from the stars. They said he was the Lord's second coming.

He said he knew nothing about their world. They said their prophets foretold the denials.

He said he only wanted to return home. They said he would lead them on a great crusade to restore the Lord's true faith.

Then he found out that the only way to the stars was to uncover the truth about the ancient writers of the prophecies. And so, together, they raised the banner of the Lord Sa'yen to find the path to a forgotten cosmic past.

(Bibliographer's note: This schmuck almost talked himself out of a good deal.)

Logo No. 442. Farmer, Philip Jose. *Hadon of Ancient Opar.* Code No. UE1637. Reprint of Logo No. 100. Date of this printing, July 1981. 224 pp. Cover art by Clyde Caldwell, but Roy Krenkel's interior illustrations retained. $2.50.

(Bibliographer's note: Since the only changes between this reprint and the original printing are the cover and the price, no further comment is necessary. As with *Flow My Tears, the Policeman Said*, the copyright page retained the date of original printing: "April 1974" in this instance. However, sandwiched as it is between two books whose first printing is July 1981, that's the date of first printing that I'm laying my money on.)

Logo No. 443. Brunner, John. *The Repairmen of Cyclops.* Code No. UE1638. First DAW printing, July 1981. 159 pp. Cover art by H.R. Van Dongen. A slightly shorter version of this novel was serialized in *Fantastic Stories* in 1965, which was then reprinted in a paperback edition by Ace Books in 1965. This version was specially revised by the author for this edition. $2.25.

When the star Zarathustra went nova, the desperate survivors spread out in all directions. Those that found habitable worlds were few, and, after hundreds of years, the Zarathustra Refugee Planets were either forgotten or in quarantine.

On Cyclops, an advanced world, an ominous political crisis developed which threatened to oust the Corps Galactica. Something horribly improper was going on; something involving its corps of medical wizards; something that might have to do with an undiscovered Zarathrustra planet. Gus Langenschmidt's job was to save the corps base on Cyclops, but it proved to be a life-and-death task on a multi-planet scale.

(Bibliographer's note: Third book of the Zarathustra Refugee Planet series.)

Logo No. 444. Cherryh, C.J. (pseud. Carolyn Janice Cherry). *Wave Without a Shore*. Code No. UE1646. First edition. First printing, August 1981. 176 pp. Cover art by Don Maitz. $2.25.

Freedom was an isolated planet, off the spaceways track and rarely visited by commercial spacers. It wasn't that Freedom was inhospitable as planets go. The problem was that outsiders such as tourists and traders claimed that the streets were crowded with mysterious characters in blue robes and with members of an alien species.

Native-born humans, however, said that wasn't the case. There were no such blue-robes and no aliens. Such was the viewpoint of both Herrin the artist and Waden the aristocrat, until a crisis of planetary identity forced a life-and-depth confrontation between the question of the reality and the reality of the question.

Logo No. 445. Wagner, Karl Edward ed. *The Year's Best Horror Stories: Series IX*. Code No. UE1647. First edition. First printing, August 1981. 223 pp. Cover art by Michael Whelan. $2.50.

Contents:

Introduction	Karl Edward Wagner
The Monkey	Stephen King
The Gap	Ramsey Campbell
The Cats of Pere Lachaise	Neil Olonoff
The Propert Bequest	Basil A. Smith
On Call	Dennis Etchison
The Catacomb	Peter Shilston
Black Man with a Horn	T.E.D. Klein
The King	William Relling, Jr.
Footsteps	Harlan Ellison
Without Rhyme or Reason	Peter Valentine Timlett

(Bibliographer's note: If you collect modern horror fiction, friends, and you ain't got this series, you ain't got nuthin'.)

Logo No. 446. Prescot, Dray (pseud. Kenneth Bulmer). *Legions of Antares*. Code No. UE1648. First edition. First printing, August 1981. 192 pp. Cover art by Ken W. Kelly; illustrated by Clyde Caldwell. $2.25.

For too long the iron legions of the evil empress of Hamal had devastated the neighboring lands and islands of Kregen. Under the twin suns of Antares, that planet of marvels had been made a scene of carnage, rapine, and death.

Dray Prescot, Earthman transported to Kregen, had battled her all the way, and, at long last, found himself nearing the showdown of his long campaign for his new homeland. Gathering about himself old allies and former enemies, Dray prepared to challenge the empress at the very doors of her capital city, until he discovered that she was about to spring her secret weapon: the super-science of the mad wizard of Loh.

. (Bibliographer recoils in horror: Oh, no, anything but the dreaded super-science of the mad wizard of Loh!)

153

(Bibliographer's mundane note: The twenty-fifth novel in the saga of Dray Prescot.)

Logo No. 447. Phillifent, John T. *King of Argent.* Code No. UE1649. Reprint of Logo No. 46. Originally published in March 1973, with cover art by Kelly Freas. 191 pp. This printing has a cover by David B. Mattingly and appears to have been printed in August, since only three other books were printed that month, not the usual four. $2.25.

(Bibliographer's note: In all respects other than noted above, the two printings are the same.)

Logo No. 448. Lee, Tanith. *Delusion's Master.* Code No. UE1652. First edition. First printing, September 1981. 206 pp. Cover art by Ken W. Kelly. See *Survey of Modern Fantasy Literature II*, pp. 988-992 (1983). $2.25.

When the world was flat, and the gods had not yet restructured the universe, the cities and hopes of mankind hung upon the whims of the immortal lords of all diabolical powers. For these, such as Azhrarn, Night's Master, and Uhlume, Death's Master, the world was a flesh-and-blood playground for all their strangest desires. But among these demonic lords, the strangest was the master of madness, Chuz.

The game that Chuz played with a beautiful woman, with an ambitious king, with an ancient imperial city, was a webwork of good and evil, of hope and horror. But there was always Azhrarn to interfere and to bend delusion to a different outcome, and it was a century-long conflict between two vain immortals with women and men as their terrified pawns.

(Bibliographer's note: The third book in the Master aka the Lords of Darkness aka the Flat Earth series. Ya pays yer money an' ya takes yer cherce.)

Logo No. 449. Chandler, A. Bertram. *The Anarch Lords.* Code No. UE1653. First edition. First printing, September 1981. 208 pp. Cover art by David B. Mattingly. $2.25.

His wild career as a space pirate ended, Grimes faced his toughest assignment. He was "punished" by being made governor of the anarchists' own planet! John Grimes, living legend of the spaceways, had been in and out of some cosmic catastrophes, but this threatened to reach his luck's ultimate breaking point!

An influx of planetary refugees had made that world a paradise of cheap labor, and the original anarchist colonists had become such masters of wealth that no mere outsider could hope to dictate "law and order" to them. They had their own ideas which included slavery, treachery, and utter villainy.

Grimes' first task as governor would be simply to stay alive with a whole world plotting his murder!

(Bibliographer's note: Another in the John Grimes: Rim Runners series.)

Logo No. 450. Dick, Philip K. *Now Wait for Next Year.* Code No. UE1654. First DAW printing, September 1981. 205 pp. Cover art by Michael

Mariano. Published earlier in U.S. by Doubleday (1966) and in U.K. by Panther (1975). $2.50.

In a war-torn world, Dr. Eric Sweetscent was caught between his dope-addicted wife and the world leader who was trying to stave off global catastrophe.

Gino Molinari (known as The Mole) was the ultimate authority over the lives of billions. He possessed the strange ability to die over and over again, and yet be brought back to life by the wizardry of future medicine. As The Mole came to rely more and more on his personal suicides as the political tool to save the rest of humanity, he grew into a grand and tragic figure.

Through his close relationship with Molinari, Eric gradually came to achieve the total vista of a world-spanning viewpoint, and, with that, came the ability to understand at last the aims of the incredible Mole.

Logo No. 451. Carter, Lin. *Darya of the Bronze Age.* Code No. UJ1655. First edition. First printing, September, 1981. 173 pp. Cover art and illustrations by Josh Kirby. $1.95.

Under the trackless sands of the Sahara lies Zanthodon. That vast subterranean realm is the final homeland of the one-time masters of the world's surface: great dinosaurs, mighty jungles, and living bands of primitive peoples from Neanderthals to Ancient Minoans and even Barbary Pirates!

It was into the cruel hands of those feared corsairs that Eric Carstairs' beloved cave-maiden, Darya the Cro-magnon princess, had fallen. It was his mission to save her, as well as to keep his caveman friends and his professor guide from the innumerable dangers spawned in the unmapped wilds of the Underground World.

(Bibliographer's note: Another adventure of Eric Carstairs in Zanthodon.)

Logo No. 452. Bradley, Marion Zimmer. *Sharra's Exile.* Code No. UE1659. First edition. First printing, October 1981. 365 pp. Cover painting by Hannah M.G. Shapero. Chapter two of Book One appeared in slightly different form, as a short story titled "Blood Will Tell" in *The Keeper's Price.* See DAW Logo No. 373. See *Anatomy of Wonder* 4-77 (1987). $2.95.

The most dangerous matrix on all Darkover was the legendary Sharra. Embodied in the image of a chained woman, wreathed in flames, it was the last remaining weapon of the Age of Chaos that had almost destroyed civilization on the planet of the Bloody Sun.

The Sharra had been exiled off-planet among the far stars of the Terran Empire in the custody of Lew Alton, until he found himself called back to his homeworld to contest his rights.

But once the Sharra was back, the flaming image spread far and wide and set in motion events that were to change the land, the domains, and the future of Darkover forever.

(Bibliographer's note: A direct sequel to *The Heritage of Hastur.*)

Logo No. 453. Vance, Jack. *Showboat World*. Code No. UE1660. First DAW printing, October 1981. 188 pp. Cover art and frontispiece by David B. Mattingly. Originally published in U.S. by Pyramid (1975) and in U.K. by Coronet (1975). $2.25.

Vast, beautiful, untamed, Big Planet lay beyond the frontier of terrestrial law. Its inhabitants were eccentric misfits, descended from the original refugees from Earth.

Those that ran the showboats up and down the rivers knew that each port of call hid its own sinister threat. Apollon Zamp and Garth Ashgale were adept at dodging danger. Two of the wiliest rascals in the business, they were deadly rivals to boot. So when Zamp began his perilous journey to compete in the Grand Festival at Nornune, he knew only too well that Ashgale would try to sabotage his plans. And he had the added complication of a mysterious blonde beauty on board.

Logo No. 454. Saha, Arthur W. ed. *The Year's Best Fantasy Stories: 7.* Code No. UE1661. First edition. First printing, October 1981. 191 pp. Cover art, "Elric," by Michael Whelan. $2.25.

Contents:

Introduction	The Editor
The George Business	Roger Zelazny
The Princess and the Bear	Orson Scott Card
Proteus	Paul H. Cook
Spidersong	Susan C. Petrey
The Narrow House	Phillip C. Heath
Wolfland	Tanith Lee
Melpomene, Calliope...and Fred	Nicholas Yermakov
Kevin Malone	Gene Wolfe
Lan Lung	M. Lucie Chin
Keeper of the Wood	Caradoc A. Cador
The Sleep of Trees	Jane Yolen

(Bibliographer's note: First volume in this series under the very capable editorial reins of Arthur W. Saha.)

Logo No. 455. Tubb, E.C. *The Terridae*. Code No. UE1662. First edition. First printing, October 1981. 160 pp. Cover art by Richard Hescox. $2.25.

Zabul was no ordinary world. It was a private religious sanctuary: location secret, visitors unwelcome. It was a world fanatically dedicated to one belief and one goal: the belief that mankind originated on a single world; the goal—to find it.

To find Earth was a goal that Dumarest shared. But how much did he really have in common with the zealot Terridae who slept in caskets decorated with signs of the Zodiac and dreamed of soaring towers of crystal, floating cities and waters of youth?

The Earth they dreamed of was not the world he knew, and, if they were truly searching for Earth, why did the despotic Terridae Guardians refuse to join forces with Dumarest? What were they really after? Dumarest had to find out if they had the vital information he sought, or

die trying!

(Bibliographer's note: The twenty-fifth novel in the saga of Dumarest of Terra and neck-and-neck with Dray Prescot in the Saga derby.)

Logo No. 456. Norman, John (pseud. John Lange). *Guardsman of Gor.* Code No. UE1664. First edition. First printing, November 1981. 304 pp. Cover art by Ken W. Kelly. Later published in U.K. by Star (1982). $2.95.

From kidnapped collegian to a woman's slave, from landless fugitive to warrior-captain, the life of Jason Marshall on Earth's orbital twin was a constant struggle against the naked power and barbaric traditions of glorious Gor.

Now, in the heat of a desperate naval battle against overwhelming odds, Jason faced the pivotal hours of his Gorean career. For him, victory would mean a homeland, a warrior's honors, and the lovely Earthgirl who was the prize he had long sought. Defeat would mean degradation worse than the chains he had once escaped.

(Bibliographer's note: The sixteenth book of the Counter-Earth saga.)

Logo No. 457. Clayton, Jo. *The Nowhere Hunt.* Code No. UE1665. First edition. First printing, November 1981. 208 pp. Cover art and frontispiece by Ken W. Kelly. $2.25.

The Nowhere Hunt was a quest every Hunter refused. Only Aletys, wearer-slave of the mysterious and powerful Diadem, would dare try to slip unseen past starship battalions and land on a world encased in a cosmic shield which rendered all electronic equipment functionless. Avoiding poisonous flora, hostile natives, vicious predators and murderous ransomers, her job was to rescue and transport a massive, semi-intelligent insect queen off planet and save the queen's besieged race from extinction.

A seemingly impossible task, but one Aletys could not refuse, for she had been offered in payment something she desperately needed to continue her own personal quest.

(Bibliographer's note: Sixth book in the Diadem series.)

Logo No. 458. Piserchia, Doris. *Earth in Twilight.* Code No. UE1666. First edition. First printing, November 1981. 156 pp. Cover art by Wayne D. Barlowe. $2.25.

Laredo Space Base hadn't sent a ship to Earth for hundreds of years before the Project Deep Green survey craft was launched. Only one thing was known: the planet humankind had so long ago vacated was a wasteland with nothing on it but poisonous flora and small, murderous denizens.

That's what they taught astronaut Ferrer Burgoyne, and, as a result, he was totally unprepared for the teeming jungle stretching farther than the eye could see. He was even more unprepared for the slightly green humanoids who greeted him. Obviously the scientists of Old Earth had done more in their labs than just mess around mixing human and plant cells. As sure as Ferrer Burgoyne was an astronaut, the new men of Earth were the descendants of those hidden, forbidden experiments.

How then could Burgoyne continue his mission: to defoliate Earth with

the deadly chemical Deep Green and prepare Earth for the return of his species?

Logo No. 459. Saunders, Charles R. *Imaro.* Code No. UE1667. First edition. First printing, November 1981. 208 pp. Cover art by Ken W. Kelly. $2.50.

Imaro was his name: Imaro of the Ilyassai, Imaro the outcast, Imaro the legendary hero of the jungle continent. This novel relates how Imaro achieved manhood, won his rights among the people, and began his long march against the fantastic and unearthly terrors of that alternate-Africa known as Nyumbani.

(Bibliographer's note: First book in the Imaro sequence, with a glossary of alternate-African words used in the novel.)

Logo No. 460. Foster, M.A. *The Morphodite.* Code No. UE1669. First edition. First printing, December 1981. 224 pp. Cover art by Michael Whelan. See *Anatomy of Wonder* 4-221 (1987). $2.75.

How do you destroy a conspiracy without making waves? Because every such underground movement has a key person, the subtle way is to remove that keystone and watch the rest of the organization fall apart.

Their world was ultra-conservative, isolated, opposed to change. Their secret police had tried many means to keep it that way. Now they had contrived their cleverest secret weapon. This was a genetically-patterned, laboratory-raised human genius, the Morphodite.

The Morphodite needed no computors to detect the key to any conspiracy; the know-how was structured into his/her brain. The Morphodite needed no assistance to make a foolproof escape after such an assassination. The know-how was built into his/her body.

But the Morphodite had one defect its "gestapo" parents had not planned. He/she could think for itself, and its thoughts were total subversion.

(Bibliographer's note: First book of the Morphodite series.)

Logo No. 461. Asimov, Isaac and Martin H. Greenberg eds. *Isaac Asimov Presents the Great Science Fiction Stories 6 (1944).* Code No. UE1670. First edition. First printing, December 1981. 368 pp. Cover design by One Plus One Studio. Cover art by Oliviero Berni. $2.95.

Contents:

Introduction

Far Centaurus	A.E. van Vogt
Deadline	Cleve Cartmill
The Veil of Astellar	Leigh Brackett
Sanity	Fritz Leiber
Invariant	John R. Pierce
City	Clifford D. Simak
Arena	Fredric Brown
Huddling Place	Clifford D. Simak
Kindness	Lester del Rey

Desertion	Clifford D. Simak
When the Bough Breaks	Lewis Padgett
Killdozer!	Theodore Sturgeon
No Woman Born	C.L. Moore

Logo No. 462. Prescot, Dray. *Allies of Antares*. Code No. UE1671. First edition. First printing, December 1981. 189 pp. Cover art and illustrations by Clyde Caldwell. $2.25.

Beneath the two suns of Antares, the planet Kregen was truly the wonder of the universe. There, at the inscrutable planning of unseen powers, had been gathered members of the great races of the galaxy, set down among Kregen's lands to become part of the wonderful semi-civilized cities and kingdoms of that world.

There, too, were natural humans, and their strivings and ambitions led the struggle to create a world of peace. Dray Prescot, Earthman, had been brought there as an agent of the Star Lords, but he had made himself into a rallying point of strength in Kregen's colorful history.

Now, when the worst war between the humanoid lands had finally concluded, Prescot again confronts the Star Lords, only to learn that the hard-won peace was just a transition to a great hemispheric invasion that was even then raiding over the horizon.

(Bibliographer's note: For those who are still interested, this is the twenty-sixth novel in the saga of Dray Prescot, and now one ahead of Dumarest.)

Logo No. 463. Lee, Tanith. *The Birthgrave*. Code No. UE1672. See Logo No. 154. Originally printed June 1975, with cover art by George Barr. This printing, with cover art by Ken W. Kelly (who, by the way, does great T & A, for those of us who like that sort of thing), professes to have been done in June 1975. We who know better say it was printed in December 1981. See if you can figure out why I made that statement. $2.95.

(Bibliographer's note: This reprint is pretty much the same as the original, except for the covers, both fore and aft. The preliminary sketch for this cover was for sale at the 1987 Boskone. I passed it by, picking up another Kelly preliminary instead.)

Logo No. 464. Cherryh, C.J. (pseud. Carolyn Janice Cherry). *The Pride of Chanur*. Code No. UE1694. Ostensible first edition. First printing, January 1982. 224 pp. Cover art by Michael Whelan. Also issued in hardcover by the Science Fiction Book Club in (are you ready for this?) December 1981. Therefore, may be only first paperback edition. An abridged version of this novel appeared in *Science Fiction Digest* (1981). Later published in U.K. by Methuen (1983). See *Anatomy of Wonder* 4-131 (1987). $2.95.

No one at Meetpoint Station had ever seen a creature like the Outsider. Naked-hided, blunt-toothed, and blunt-fingered, Tully was the sole sur-viving member of his company, a communicative, spacefaring species hitherto unknown, and he was a prisoner of his discoverer/captors, the sadistic and treacherous *kif*, until his escape onto the *hani* ship, *The Pride of Chanur.*

Little did he know when he threw himself upon the mercy of *The Pride* and her crew, that he put the entire *hani* species in jeopardy and imperiled the peace of the Compact itself. The information that this fugitive held could be the ruin or glory of any of the species at Meetpoint Station.

(Bibliographer's note: First book in the Chanur series.)

Logo No. 465. Van Vogt, A.E. *The Silkie.* Code No. UE1695. First DAW printing, January 1982. 160 pp. Cover art by Wayne Barlowe. Originally published in U.S. by Ace Books (1969) and in U.K. by New English Library (1973). $2.25.

The Silkie. A living spaceship, impervious to heat and cold, virtually indestructible and capable of traveling at supersonic speeds.

The Silkie. Similar to a human being, but not the same. Highly intelligent.

The Silkie. Able to live under the oceans with the ease of a dolphin and the speed of a shark.

The Silkie. A modern angel or a computerized demon?

The Silkie. Friend of Earth, or a pitiless, alien destroyer?

Logo No. 466. Barrett, Neal Jr. *Aldair: The Legion of Beasts.* Code No. UE1696. First edition. First printing, January 1982. 174 pp. Cover art and frontispiece by Ken W. Kelly. $2.25.

It was not given to everyone to meet his Creator face to face, but it was to be the destiny of Aldair and his band of humanoid friends. For the trail to the secret of their existence finally led to the stars and ultimate confrontation with their makers, the last of Earth's humans.

(Bibliographer's note: Fourth book in the Aldair series.)

Logo No. 467. Goulart, Ron. *Upside Downside.* Code No. UE1697. First edition. First printing, January 1982. 156 pp. Cover art by Josh Kirby. $2.25.

Zack Tourney didn't know he'd been murdered. It had happened on Thursday, January 13, 2033, up in the Coldzone, but he didn't have so much as a hint until weeks later. And he wasn't the only one. Half a dozen political and financial figures throughout the world had also been infected with the slow virus which was doing Zack in.

All Zack's friends, the crooks, spies, double agents, sneaks, wild talents, freaks and mewts couldn't do a thing for him. Even Timpany Quarls, Zack's junk food-heiress girlfriend couldn't help him. Where was Timpany, anyway?

Zack had to go it alone. Find his murderers, find the antidote, and, while he was at it, find his girl friend before he dropped in his tracks. After all, it was *his* murder!

Logo No. 468. Wallace, Ian (pseud. John Wallace Pritchard). *The Rape of the Sun.* Code No. UE1704. First edition. First printing, February 1982. 287 pp. Cover art by David B. Mattingly. $2.95.

Dhurk hoped that, if he could win acceptance by his beloved Hreda, it would bring him to the top of his wonder world's most advanced strata. And, in the way of many a fickle folklore princess, Hreda set him a task. Her cosmic museum would not be complete without a star. Bring me that star, place it among my exhibits, and I will be yours, she declared.

But "that star" was Sol, our sun, around which revolved our familiar planets and the Earth. Dhurk accepted the challenge, and strange things began to happen to the sun, to the world's source of heat and light, and to humanity's hopes.

Logo No. 469. Shwartz, Susan M. ed. *Hecate's Cauldron.* Code No. UE1705. First edition. First printing, February, 1982. 256 pp. Cover art by Michael Whelan. $2.95.

Contents:

Introduction: Seasons of the Witch	Susan M. Shwartz
Boris Chernevsky's Hands	Jane Yolen
Mirage and Magia	Tanith Lee
Willow	C.J. Cherryh
Moon Mirror	Andre Norton
The Sage of Theare	Diana Wynne Jones
The Harmonious Battle	Jessica Amanda Salmonson
Science Is Magic Spelled Backwards	Jacqueline Lichtenberg
An Act of Faith	Galad Elflandsson
Witch Fulfillment	Jean Lorrah
Ishigbi	Charles Saunders
Bethane	Katherine Kurtz
The Riddle of Hekaite	Diane L. Paxson
Reunion	Jayge Carr

Bibliography, compiled by Susan M. Shwartz

Logo No. 470. Green, Sharon. *The Warrior Within.* Code No. UE1707. First printing, February 1982. 224 pp. Cover art by Ken W. Kelly. $2.50.

She was one of Earth's most valued Primes, a brilliant and highly trained operative with a special talent for accurately predicting the thoughts and actions of others. He was a barbarian chief from a raw and primitive planet, wise only in the ways of warfare and the schemes of clan domination.

His world had become a much needed key to Earth's space enterprises, and he was prepared to make a deal if the star-people could help him win supreme power. So she was assigned to him.

But the only way she could fulfill her mission was in the full native tradition. She must be locked into the five-banded chains of a warrior's slave girl—and live the role to the hilt.

(Bibliographer's recommendation: Check the cover; the slave girl's wearing pasties in this, the first book of the Terrilian sequence.)

Logo No. 471. Simak, Clifford D. *The Werewolf Principle.* Code No. UE1708. First DAW printing, February 1982. 175 pp. Cover art by Frank

Kelly Freas. Originally published in U.S. by Putnam (1967); reprinted by the Science Fiction Book Club (1968); published in paperback by Berkley (1968). Also published in Canada by Longman's (1967) and in U.K. by Gollancz (1968). $2.50.

Andrew Blake, found in a space capsule on a distant planet, was brought back to an unfamiliar Earth, where antigravity devices had replaced the wheel, and houses talk and even fly! Yet nothing was as strange as Blake's own feelings. Tormented by eerie sensations and a loss of memory, he didn't know who he really was, nor exactly where he came from. His destiny only began to grow frighteningly clear when he met a weird, tassel-eared creature who hinted darkly at the truth about Blake's origins.

Slowly Blake became aware of the long hushed-up "Werewolf Principle," a scientific theory buried in the past, which held the key to Blake's own fate and the future of the entire human race.

(Bibliographer's note: Next to vampires, werewolves are my favorite supernatural critters.)

Logo No. 472. Norman, John (pseud. John Lange). *Savages of Gor.* Code No. UE1715. First edition. First printing, March 1982. 335 pp. Cover art by Ken W. Kelly. Also published in U.K. by Star (1982). $3.50.

The Kur came to Port Kar! Two of the terrible space beasts came to make Tarl Cabot an offer. They, a death squad, sought the renegade Kur commander, the great Half-Ear, whom Tarl had once battled in the Far North.

Tarl refused their offer, for Half-Ear was more valuable to the priest-kings alive than to the Kur dead. And now he knew it was imperative for him to save that monster from the doom that would fast overtake him.

This meant venturing into the forbidden Barrens of Gor, a vast land of plains and prairies whose cruel masters were tribes of savage red riders, and where civilized men were always prey and their women mere trophies of the hunt!

(Bibliographer's note: The seventeenth book of the Tarl Cabot Saga.)

Logo No. 473. Vance, Jack. *The Gray Prince.* Code No. UE1716. First DAW printing, March 1982. 160 pp. Cover art by David B. Mattingly. Published earlier in the U.S. by Bobbs-Merrill (1974) and in the U.K. by Coronet (1976). $2.25.

When Schaine Madduc returned to Koryphon after five years in space, her home planet was not as she left it. The several intelligent species who had lived so long in a sort of symbiotic harmony were at each other's throat. Most prominently, the humanoid Uldra were united in rebellion against the human land-holding community of which Schaine was part.

But Schaine was even more a part than she realized, for the Uldra revolutionary leader and catalyst, a person called the Gray Prince, was Muffin, an Uldra fostered in Schaine's own home, and upon whom Schaine had exerted a profound influence. An influence far more profound than Schaine would have thought possible. An influence possibly powerful enough to smash her home, family, and her entire way of life!

(Bibliographer's note: The copyright page shows the date of printing as March 1981. I show it as March 1982. The copyright page is wrong. I'm right, if anybody's keeping score.)

Logo No. 474. Bayley, Barrington J. *The Pillars of Eternity.* Code No. UE1717. First edition. First printing, March 1982. 159 pp. Cover art by Wayne D. Barlowe. $2.25.

A novel about:

How clones made murder a new sexual experience.

How rebuilding one man's skeleton made him the most sensitive and powerful man in the galaxy.

How a deck of cards was devised that was really programmed to reveal the future.

How a lost planet became the mecca of every treasure-hunter in space.

How Joachim Boaz plotted to derail the entire universe!

Logo No. 475. Farmer, Philip Jose. *Flight to Opar.* Code No. UE1718. First edition. See Logo No. 197. Original printing by DAW was June 1976. That's the date shown on the copyright page of this printing. This printing, however, is, in actuality, the fourth book published in March 1982. Instead of cover art by Roy Krenkel, there's a new T & A cover by Ken Kelly and a new price. $2.50.

Twelve thousand years ago, Africa was the center of world civilization, and mighty cities dotted the shores of its inland seas. Opar the Golden was the capital of its greatest empire, and the warrior-hero, Hadon, claimed its throne.

But Hadon had become the hunted prey of a tyrant's armies, accursed by the tyrant's false gods, and forced to fight for his very life.

(Bibliographer's note: Actually, the above eye-catcher was also changed from the earlier printing. If you're curious, go get Logo No. 197 from your collection. I'll wait. I'm not going anywhere. Got it? Good. Now compare the two. See how cleverly it was altered. I'll bet you thought we bibliographers had it easy.)

Logo No. 476. Lee, Tanith. *The Silver Metal Lover.* Code No. UE1721. First DAW printing, April 1982. 240 pp. Cover art by Don Maitz; frontispiece by Tanith Lee. Published earlier by the Science Fiction Book Club (1981). First printing has code L44 on page 215. See *Anatomy of Wonder* 4-322 (1987). $2.75.

He seemed utterly natural and perfectly human. He had total coordination and beautiful grace. He was handsome; eyes like two russet stars, eyelashes and hair dark cinnamon. Skin pale silver.

He was a robot, and he could do everything a man could do. Yes, everything.

To Jane he was real. Real. He made her all she could be, and some things she thought she couldn't, and she would do anything not to lose him. (Bibliographer's profane interjection: I don't blame Jane. Not if he

163

could do all that.)

But, to society, he was an omen of ultimate threat, a man who excelled men in every way. And society knew how to deal with threats.

What would *you* do if the manufacturer decided to recall the machine who just happened to be your one true love?

(Bibliographer's rhetorical answer: Get a better warranty.)

Logo No. 477. Bradley, Marion Zimmer ed. *Sword of Chaos and Other Stories.* Code No. UE1722. First edition. First printing, April 1982. 240 pp. Cover art and frontispiece by Hannah M.G. Shapero. $2.95.

Contents:

Introduction

AFTER LANDFALL	
A Gift of Love	Diana L. Paxson
THE CYCLES OF LEGEND	
Dark Lady	Jane Brae-Bedell
A Legend of the Hellers	Terry Tafoya
IN THE HUNDRED KINGDOMS	
In the Throat of the Dragon	Susan Shwartz
Wind-Music	Mary Frances Zambreno
Escape	Leslie Williams
Rebirth	Elisabeth Waters
A Sword of Chaos	Marion Zimmer Bradley
BETWEEN THE AGES	
Di Catenas	Adrienne Martine-Barnes
Of Two Minds	Susan Hansen
Through Fire and Frost	Dorothy J. Heydt
IN THE DAYS OF THE COMYN	
The Way of a Wolf	Lynne Holdom
Cold Hall	Aly Parsons
The Lesson of the Inn	Marion Zimmer Bradley
Confidence	Phillip Wayne
THE EMPIRE AND BEYOND	
Camilla	Patricia Mathews
Where the Heart Is	Millea Kenin
Skeptic	Lynn Mims
A Recipe for Failure	Millea Kenin

Logo No. 478. Van Vogt, A.E. *The Darkness of Diamondia.* Code No. UE1724. First DAW printing, April 1982. 176 pp. Cover art by Wayne D. Barlowe. Originally published by Ace Books (1972). Later published in U.K. by Sidgwick & Jackson (1974). $2.25.

Colonel Morton was sent to Diamondia to report on the guerrilla warfare between the Earth colonists and the native warriors of the inhuman Irsk. Something was going terribly wrong; a darkness was setting in, mental confusion was widespread, and there was evidence of Outside interference.

It seemed as if the Outside were deliberately stirring up the planetary pot, mixing minds with minds, and personalities with personalities. When

Morton realized that the only solution might be to find and use the incalculable power of the Lositeen Weapon, he realized also that the decision was too great for any one man—even for all men together—to make.

Logo No. 479. Tubb, E.C. *The Coming Event.* Code No. UE1725. First edition. First printing, April 1982. 160 pp. Cover art by Michael Mariano. $2.25.

The Terridae believed the lost Earth was heaven and utopia combined. In their artificial planet, they moved slowly through the universe in search of it. In their eyes, the rediscovery of Earth was to be the Event.

Now they said the Event was Coming! Earl Dumarest, who was born on Earth and knew the truth, was an unwelcome visitor among them. If they knew of Earth's whereabouts, they weren't telling him, but there were clues aplenty, and Earl wouldn't quit until he had them all.

But another Event was already on its way. A Cyclan ship was rapidly approaching the Terridae's world, sure this time that Dumarest would fall into their heartless clutches. Dumarest wasn't ready to flee, but, if he stayed, there would be no Earth for him, only a long, lingering doom.

(Bibliographer's note: The twenty-sixth in the Dumarest of Terra series.)

Logo No. 480. Wollheim, Donald A. with Arthur W. Saha eds. *The 1982 Annual World's Best SF.* Code No. UE1728. First edition. First printing, May 1982. 304 pp. Cover art by Wayne D. Barlowe. See *Anatomy of Wonder* 3-911 (1981). $2.95.

Contents:

Introduction	The Editor
Blind Spot	Jayge Carr
Highliner	C.J. Cherryh
The Pusher	John Varley
Polyphemus	Michael Shea
Absent Thee from Felicity Awhile	Somtow Sucharitkul
Out of the Everywhere	James Tiptree, Jr.
Slac//	Michael P. Kube-McDowell
The Cyphertone	S.C. Sykes
Through All Your Houses Wandering	Ted Reynolds
The Last Day of Christmas	David J. Lake

Logo No. 481. Clayton, Jo. *Moongather.* Code No. UE1729. First edition. First printing, May 1982. 240 pp. Cover art by Ken Kelly. $2.95.

Serroi had been an outcast. She was a misborn of the windrunners, of small stature with pale olive skin and certain strangely heightened sensitivities. But now she was a *meie,* a woman warrior trained by an exclusive order. She had been with her shieldmate at the Plaz when she overheard the assassination plot against the Domnor. A murder was to take place at Moongather: that time of increased access to the demon world.

But, while trying to escape with the information, Serroi broke her shieldmate oath, a breach of honor which made life unbearable for her and forced her back to search for her betrayed shieldmate and warn the Domnor, although the land itself seemed to be hunting her!

(Bibliographer's note: First book of the Duel of Sorcery trilogy.)

Logo No. 482. Simak, Clifford D. *The Goblin Reservation.* Code No. UE1730. First DAW printing, May 1982. 160 pp. Cover art by Kelly Freas. Originally published in U.S. by Putnam (1968) and in U.K. by Rapp & Whiting (1969). See *Anatomy of Wonder* 3-688 (1981). $2.25.

In those days, interstellar tele-transmission had been perfected. At the same period, time-travel had been mastered. All creatures, real and imaginary, were now free to roam the galaxy.

Professor Peter Maxwell left Earth on his own special mission, but some sort of cosmic error landed him on an unknown crystal planet which turned out to be a storehouse of secret knowledge. When Maxwell returned to Earth filled with the necessity of alerting everyone to this treasure planet, he found, to his astonishment, that nobody would listen. For it seemed that he himself had returned from space a month before with no such story, and had, since then, been accidentally killed.

No one any longer believed that the original Peter Maxwell really existed.

(Bibliographer's note: 1969 Hugo nominee.)

Logo No. 483. Carter, Lin. *Eric of Zanthodon.* Code No. UE1731. First edition. First printing, May 1982. 176 pp. Cover art and illustrations by Josh Kirby. $2.25.

A hidden world lies beneath the shifting sands of the Sahara: the subterranean land of Zanthodon, a vast and varied terrain in which time stands still, and dinosaurs, pirates, heroes, armies, and princesses in peril collide in prehistoric surroundings.

(Bibliographer's note: Fifth and concluding book in the Eric Carstairs in Zanthodon series.)

Logo No. 484. Green, Sharon. *The Crystals of Mida.* Code No. UE1735. First edition. First printing, June 1982. 352 pp. Cover art by Ken W. Kelly. $2.95.

The once-high technological civilization of that world had again fallen to primitive barbarism: walled cities, warring nomadic tribes, and savage chieftains. But none were so fierce as the mythic Midanna Amazons, and none of the Midanna so untamed as Jalav, war leader of the fearsome Hosta clan.

When thieves ransacked the Tower of the Crystal of Mida, slew the warrior guards and stole the holy Crystal, nothing could cool Jalav's fury. Though she led the Hosta to the dreaded slavery-darkened cities and beyond, she cared not, for nothing could halt her in her need to find the thieves, avenge her slain warriors, and bring the Crystal of Mida back to the home-tents of the Midanna.

(Bibliographer's note: First book in the Jalav, Amazon Warrior, series.)

Logo No. 485. Salmonson, Jessica Amanda ed. *Amazons II*. Code No. UE1736. First edition. First printing, June 1982. 239 pp. Cover art by Michael Whelan. $2.95.

Contents:

Introduction: Art, History and Amazons	Jessica Amanda Salmonson
For a Daughter	F.M. Busby
The Battle Crow's Daughter	Gillian Fitzgerald
Southern Lights	Tanith Lee
Zroya's Trizub	Gordon Derevanchuk
The Robber Girl	Phyllis Ann Karr
Lady of the Forest End	Gael Baudino
The Ivory Comb	Eleanor Arnason
The Borders of Sabazel	Lillian Stewart Carl
Who Courts a Reluctant Maiden	Ardath Mayhar
The Soul Slayer	Lee Killough
Nightwork	Jo Clayton
In the Lost Lands	George R.R. Martin

Logo No. 486. Piserchia, Doris. *The Dimensioneers*. Code No. UE1738. First edition. First printing, June 1982. 176 pp. Cover art by Frank Kelly Freas. $2.25.

The orphan had always known she wasn't what people described as "normal." Whether merely precocious, or a mutant freak, she had always been able to link minds with an equally weird mutated lion and skip into the worlds of the fourth dimension.

What the heck, it sure beat staying in school on Earth, until she realized that some of her fellow dimension-hoppers from other planets had more in mind than just a romp in the swamp.

They were launching an inter-dimensional war of imperialism, and she alone held the secret which could save her home world, if she could only escape the truant officer long enough to pull it off!

Logo No. 487. Prescot, Dray (pseud. Kenneth Bulmer). *Mazes of Scorpio*. Code No. UE1739. First edition. First printing, June 1982. 176 pp. Cover art by Richard Hescox. $2.25.

Beneath the emerald and ruby glow of the double suns of Antares, lies a marvelous and brilliant world of savagery and beauty. The planet Kregen, where Dray Prescot, Earthman agent of the superhuman Star Lords, struggles to bring peace to the world which has become his home.

Although his nemesis, the mad empress of Hamal, and her accomplice, the evil wizard of Loh, have been destroyed, Prescot finds that the strands of this enduring battle have not been tied off. An old conspiracy has been given a new and darker impetus which leads him to the jungle continent of Pandahem, where, beneath the dark and sweltering swamps, lies the deadly labyrinth of the Coup Blag, where Prescot clashes with a new and terrible foe.

(Bibliographer's note: Number 27, ho hum, in the saga of Dray Prescot.)

Logo No. 488. Cherryh, C.J. (pseud. Carolyn Janice Cherry). *Merchanter's Luck.* Code No. UE1745. First edition. First printing, July 1982. 208 pp. Cover art by Barclay Shaw. Later published in U.K. by Methuen (1984). See *Anatomy of Wonder* 4-129A (1987). $2.95.

His name was Sandor, and he was the owner and entire crew of a tramp star-freighter that flew the Union planets under false papers and fake names. Her name was Allison, and she was a proud, but junior, member of the powerful family whose mighty starship, *Dublin Again*, was the true queen of the spaceways.

They met at Viking Station, she seeking a night's dalliance, he desperately in search of a spacer assistant. Their fateful meeting was to lead to a record-breaking race to Downbelow Station, thereby catching the calculating eye of the grim commander of the Alliance battlecraft, Norway, and a terrifying showdown at a deadly destination off the cosmic charts.

(Bibliographer's note: Second book in the Downbelow Station series.)

Logo No. 489. Asimov, Isaac and Martin H. Greenberg, eds. *Isaac Asimov Presents the Great Science Fiction Stories 7 (1945).* Code No. UE1745. First edition. First printing, July 1982. 368 pp. Cover design by One Plus One Studio. Cover art by Bernal. $3.50.

Contents:

Introduction

The Waveries	Fredric Brown
The Piper's Son	Lewis Padgett
Wanted—An Enemy	Fritz Leiber
Blind Alley	Isaac Asimov
Correspondence Course	Raymond F. Jones
First Contact	Murray Leinster
The Vanishing Venusians	Leigh Brackett
Into Thy Hands	Lester del Rey
Camouflage	Henry Kuttner
The Power	Murray Leinster
Giant Killer	A. Bertram Chandler
What You Need	Henry Kuttner
De Profundis	Murray Leinster
Pi in the Sky	Fredric Brown

Logo No. 490. Vance, Jack. *The Narrow Land.* Code No. UE1747. First edition. First printing, July 1982. 176 pp. Cover art by Wayne D. Barlowe. Later published in U.K. by Coronet (1984). $2.25.

Contents:

The Narrow Land	Green Magic
The Masquerade on Dicantropus	The Ten Books
Where Hesperus Falls	Chateau D'If
The World-Thinker	

Logo No. 491. Goulart, Ron. *Big Bang*. Code No. UE1748. First edition. First printing, July 1982. 160 pp. Cover art by Josh Kirby. $2.25.

With a whoosh and a bang, various individuals around the world were being annihilated. Here today, then simply nothing tomorrow. Even the Siamese twins, the joint Presidents of the United States, were scared. It could happen to them, and their secret services hadn't a clue.

So, they called in Odd Jobs, Inc. That wizard agency, consisting of Jake and Hildy Pace, had cracked many an uncrackable case. There had to be a motive. There had to be a conspiracy. There had to be something.

For Jake, the case started when he woke up, mind-wiped, on Murderers' Row, awaiting the death sentence.

(Bibliographer's note: An adventure in the Odd Jobs, Inc. series.)

Logo No. 492. Stableford, Brian. *Journey to the Center*. Code No. UE1756. First paperback edition. First printing, August 1982. 176 pp. Cover art by Ken W. Kelly. Issued by Science Fiction Book Club as a Doubleday hardcover (1982). First printing has code M14 on page 152. $2.50.

The galaxy is full of mysteries, and Asgard is one of the most inexplicable. Many different species and many different types of individuals sought answers to the multiple enigmas of Asgard. Anthropologists, fortune hunters, scientists, gangsters, politicians and explorers found reason to congregate on the planet which possibly wasn't a planet. Their purpose was to stand on the artificial surface and wonder how many subcutaneous levels the planet contained, and what, if anything, was at the center.

They also wanted to examine the artifacts on the reachable levels where the temperature approached Absolute Zero; artifacts of a civilization far more advanced than any known spacefaring species of the day; artifacts of a people who still lived at the center, thousands of miles and thousands of levels deeper than any known explorer had set foot.

The general concensus was that Mike Rousseau, an archeological scavenger, might be the only man capable of reaching the center and unraveling the mystery of Asgard. Rousseau didn't quite agree, but, unfortunately, the choice wasn't his.

Logo No. 493. Wagner, Karl Edward. *The Year's Best Horror Stories: Series X*. Code No. UE1757. First edition. First printing, August 1982. 240 pp. Cover art by Michael Whelan. $2.50.

Contents:

Introduction: A Decade of Fear	Karl Edward Wagner
Through the Walls	Ramsey Campbell
Touring	Gardner Dozois, Jack Dann and Michael Swanwick
Every Time You Say I Love You	Charles L. Grant
Wyntours	David G. Rowlands
The Dark Country	Dennis Etchison
Homecoming	Howard Goldsmith
Old Hobby Horse	A.F. Kidd
Firstborn	David Campton

Luna	G.W. Perriwils
Mind	Les Freeman
Competition	David Clayton Carrad
Egnaro	M. John Harrison
On 202	Jeff Hecht
The Trick	Ramsey Campbell
Broken Glass	Harlan Ellison

(Bibliograper's note: "Touring" is my all-time favorite horror story. In case anyone asks, it's my choice for the best horror story ever written. Although it first appeared in *Penthouse*, a more appropriate forum would have been *Rolling Stone*. Check it out. See if you agree. If you don't, who cares? That's why Stephen King and I get the big money.)

Logo No. 494. Van Vogt, A.E. *The Battle of Forever*. Code No. UE1758. First DAW printing, August 1982. 176 pp. Cover art by Wayne D. Barlowe. Published earlier by Ace Books (1971) in paperback and Author's Co-op (1978) in first U.S. hardcover. Also published in U.K. by Sidgwick & Jackson (1972). $2.25.

For thousands of years, mankind had survived in leisure behind the barrier. In miniature form, men had evolved a physiology and a philosophy of peace and contemplation.

Modyun was to be the first to enlarge his body to the massive proportions of ancient times, and, then, to go out to explore the world where animal-men had established their realms. His quest was to lead him to a darkness he had never expected and an uncertain future with which humanity might not be able to cope.

Logo No. 495. Dibell, Ansen (pseud. Nancy Ann Dibble). *Summerfair*. Code No. UE1759. First edition. First printing, August 1982. 272 pp. Cover art by Ken W. Kelly. $2.75.

To bring the dead back to life, to stop the world-wide mutiny of Valde soldiery, to block the conquering ambitions of a Tek of many shapes: these were the problems that converged on Jannus, the secret heir of the crown of lost Kantmorie. Topping off his problems, add the dangerous wanderings of his half-human daughters and the machinations of a spaceship down from orbit.

(Bibliographer's note: The Third Book of the Strange and Fantastic History of the King of Kantmorie.)

Logo No. 496. Bradley, Marion Zimmer. *Hawkmistress!*. Code No. UE1762. First edition. First printing, September 1982. 336 pp. Cover art by Hannah M.G. Shapero. See *Anatomy of Wonder* 4-77 (1987). $2.95.

She had rejected her noble birthright and embraced the freedom only a man could claim. She was Romilly, who lived among the beasts of hill and forest and communicated with them, who tried humanity and turned it down for its evils and jealousies. She had the MacAran gift, the rare laran that conferred mastery over hawk and horse.

There was war in the lands of Darkover, for this was the age of the

Hundred Kingdoms, when usurpers took the throne, and the true king wandered in disguise with a price on his head. Romilly wanted none of all this, but there were those who shared her talents, the men and women of the Towers. For them, Romilly was the key. Whether male-garbed or beast-minded, she was also human. Duty to her own kind pointed her to the ultimate decision.

(Bibliographer's note: Seventeenth Darkover novel.)

Logo No. 497. Selby, Curt (pseud. Doris Piserchia). *I, Zombie.* Code No. UE1763. First edition. First printing, September 1982. 158 pp. Cover art by Ken W. Kelly. $2.25.

When the girl from the asylum drowned in the lake that night, she thought it was the end of her life, but she was wrong. With robots at fifty thousand dollars a unit, it was far more economical to use corpse labor. All it took was a two-thousand-dollar animating pack in the brain, and a zombie worker, under the direction of a helmeted controller, could do just about anything except think.

Or so everyone said. But, in the zombie dorms at night, with only the walking dead for roommates, things were not as they should have been. The girl from the asylum seemed to have more mental ability, not less, and someone was tring to kill her. Kill a dead girl?

Maybe there was more to heaven than an afterlife of manual labor in the company of a bunch of stiffs!

(Bibliographer's note: Contrary to outward appearance, this is science fiction, not horror.)

Logo No. 498. Brunner, John. *Manshape.* Code No. UE1764. First edition thus. First printing, September 1982. 159 pp. Cover art by David B. Mattingly. This novel is based on a novella entitled "Bridge to Azrael," which appeared in *Amazing Stories* (February 1964). Under the title *Endless Shadow*, the same text was published as half of Ace Double F-299 (1964). The present text has been wholly revised by the author and is 50% longer than the original novella. $2.25.

The interstellar Bridge System was the greatest invention in the long history of cosmic humanity. Spread through dozens of planets, men and their societies had drifted apart in isolation until the Bridge came to link together humanity's multifold worlds and had affirmed once more that all men were brothers and sisters under the skin.

The faraway world of Azrael was the exception, the one dissident world that refused the Bridge. It became the task of two agents, a man and a woman, to bring Azrael back into manshape unity and to ferret out the hidden reasons for the stubborn refusal.

Logo No. 499. Lee, Tanith. *Cyrion.* Code No. UE1765. First edition. First printing, September 1982. 304 pp. Cover art by Ken W. Kelly. $2.95.

He came to the The Honey Garden looking for Cyrion. He was a man in grave danger, convinced only one man alive could help him: a man he had heard about in song and story; a man practically everyone knew something about; a man he had never met. Cyrion.

Some said he was the stolen son of a western king, raised by nomads in the desert. A freelance swordsman, a sorceror, a master of disguise, some said he attracted bizarre, uncanny events as some persons attract misfortune.

He, with hair like the sky of earnest sunrise, his fair complexion, his whiplash reactions and quicksilver elegance was like a being from another world. A legend. A myth. But was he for real? And was he for hire?

(Bibliographer's lawyer-type comment: I like the part about whiplash).

Logo No. 500. Cherryh, C.J. (pseud. Carolyn Janice Cherry). *Port Eternity.* Code No. UE1769. First edition. First printing, October 1982. 191 pp. Cover art by Ken W. Kelly. Published later by the Science Fiction Book Club (1983) as first hardcover edition. See *Anatomy of Wonder* 4-130 (1987). $2.50.

Their names were Lancelot, Elaine, Percivale, Gawain, Modred, Lynette and Vivien, but they weren't characters from legend. They were "made people," clone servants designed to suit the fancy of their opulent owner, the Lady Dela Kirn. They worked aboard the *Maid*, an anachronistic fantasy of a spaceship, decorated with swords, heraldic banners, old-looking beams masking the structural joinings, and lamps that mimicked live flame.

They lived in a kind of dream, and had no idea of their origins, their prototypes in those old, old story tapes of romance, chivalry, heroism and betrayal.

One day a wandering instability, a knot in time, a ripple in the "between" sucked them into a spatial no-man's-land from where there seemed to be no escape. They were left alone, with the borrowed personas of their ancient namesakes, to face a crisis those venerable spirits were never designed to master!

Logo No. 501. Saha, Arthur W. ed. *The Year's Best Fantasy Stories: 8.* Code No. UE1770. First edition. First printing, October 1982. 191 pp. Cover art, "Talena," by Oliviero Berni. $2.50. Contents:

Introduction	
When the Clock Strikes	Tanith Lee
Midas Night	Sam Wilson
Unicorn Variation	Roger Zelazny
The Only Death in the City	C.J. Cherryh
The Quickening	Michael Bishop
The River Maid	Jane Yolen
Skirmish on Bastable Street	Bob Leman
A Pattern of Silver Strings	Charles de Lint
A Friend in Need	Lisa Tuttle
Pooka's Bridge	Gillian FitzGerald
The Belonging Kind	John Shirley & William Gibson

Logo No. 502. Simak, Clifford D. *Destiny Doll.* Code No. UE1772. First

DAW printing, October 1982. 208 pp. Cover art by Frank Kelly Freas. Originally published in U.S. by Putnam (1971) and in U.K. by Sidgwick & Jackson (1972). $2.50.

The planet beckoned them from space and closed around them like a Venus Fly Trap!

Assailed by strange perils and even stranger temptations, the little group stumbled towards its destiny: Mike Ross, the pilot; Sara Foster, the big game hunter: blind George Smith; and the odious Friar Tuck.

Before them was a legend made flesh, around them were creatures of myth and mystery, and close behind them stalked Nemesis. The doll, the little wooden painted doll, was to be their salvation or their damnation, for each might choose and find his own Nirvana.

Logo No. 503. Moorcock, Michael. *The Steel Tsar*. Code No. UE1773. First U.S. edition. First printing, October 1982. 160 pp. Cover art by Walter Velez. Published earlier in U.K. by Mayflower (1981). $2.25.

In his epic adventures in the alternative Twentieth Centuries, Chrononaut Oswald Bastable. member of the League of Temporal Adventurers, has crossed and re-crossed many different time-streams. Here, he tells of a world in which the Bolshevik Revolution never happened.

Bastable travels backwards in time from a shell-shocked Singapore to a Russian Empire seething with conflict and preyed on by motley bands of rogues and adventurers. He meets up with fellow-time-traveler Miss Una Persson, and, together, they change the course of a history whose legendary deeds exceed the bounds of everyday imagination and glitter in the exuberant land of the eternal present.

(Bibliographer's comment: Moorcock knocks me out. Check this dedication: "To my creditors, who remain a permanent source of inspiration." That's art for you.)

(Bibliographer's afterthought: A novel in the Oswald Bastable series.)

Logo No. 504. Norman, John (pseud. John Lange). *Blood Brothers of Gor*. Code No. UE1777. First edition. First printing, November 1982. 480 pp. Cover art by Ken W. Kelly. Later published in U.K. by Star (1983). $3.50.

Tarl Cabot, seeking the monsters from the Steel Worlds, found himself among the cruel savages who ruled the vast Barrens. Though himself enslaved, he stood with his comrades and masters against a coming onslaught.

The Kur had united the enemies of the tribe that held Cabot, and death and destruction were unleashed. Out of the plains came riding hordes of feud-driven braves, from the skies came a host of maddened tarn-riders, and, even among the slave girls held by the blood brothers, there was devilish treason.

(Bibliographer's note: The eighteenth book of the Tarl Cabot Saga. Plenty fat book, 480 pages; small print. A bargain.)

Logo No. 505. Landis, Arthur H. *Home-to-Avalon*. Code No. UE1778. First edition. First printing, November 1982. 223 pp. Cover art by Ken W.

Kelly. $2.50.

Avalon, the forbidden world, was the only Terra-type planet ever to be discovered, but, when the scattered remnants of Earth's people sought to migrate there, superstition and politics blocked them.

After two thousand years, the domed colonies of a hundred barren worlds became convinced that Avalon was the one real enemy of their existence. Destroy that mystery planet was the cry!

Jarn Tybalt, Warlord of the Drusus Colony, dared to make the first trip to Avalon in centuries. He found a world teeming with wonders and enigmas: mutants, monsters, medieval knights, science-working dwarves, and a lost city in the Far North where all the answers could be found.

(Bibliographer's note: Fourth and final novel in the Camelot in Space series.)

Logo No. 506. Carter, Lin. *Kesrick.* Code No. UE1779. First edition. First printing, November 1982. 176 pp. Cover art by Keith Stillwagon. $2.25.

Take one young and handsome knight setting out on a Quest and mix in:

A dragon at World's Edge waiting for a knightly meal;

A naked princess staked out for a sea serpent;

A Tartar prince looking for a Flying Garden;

A Super-wizard with a quest all his own;

An angry efreet seeking vengeance;

A fairy godmother with a sharp tongue and a fickle temper. Set them down in Terra Magicka, the world just beyond Terra Cognita, and then stir!

(Bibliographer's note: Subtitled *An adult fantasy.* A "naked princess"? And you thought DAW Books was a family-type operation.)

Logo No. 507. Asimov, Isaac and Martin H. Greenberg eds. *Isaac Asimov Presents the Great Science Fiction Stories 8 (1946).* Code No. UE1780. First edition. First printing, November 1982. 368 pp. Cover design by One Plus One Studio. Cover art by Oliviero Berni. $3.50.

Contents:

Introduction

A Logic Named Joe	Will F. Jenkins
Memorial	Theodore Sturgeon
Loophole	Arthur C. Clarke
The Nightmare	Chan Davis
Rescue Party	Arthur C. Clarke
Placet Is a Crazy Place	Fredric Brown
Conqueror's Isle	Nelson S. Bond
Lorelei of the Red Mist	Ray Bradbury & Leigh Brackett
The Million Year Picnic	Ray Bradbury
The Last Objective	Paul A. Carter
Meihem in ce Klasrum	Dolton Edwards
Vintage Season	Lawrence O'Donnell
Evidence	Isaac Asimov

Absalom	Henry Kuttner
Mewhu's Jet	Theodore Sturgeon
Technical Error	Arthur C. Clarke

Logo No. 508. Shea, Michael. *Nifft the Lean.* Code No. UE1783. First edition. First printing, December 1982. 304 pp. Cover art and frontispiece by Michael Whelan. $2.95.

The adventures of Nifft the Lean, the master thief whose felonious appropriations and larcenous skills will lead you through Stygian realms to challenge your most lurid fantasies and errant imaginings, places where horror, harm and long eerie calms flow past the traveler in endless, unpredictable succession. (Bibliographer's observation: I've lived in worse places.)

Travel with the man whose long, rawboned, sticky fingers and stark length of arm will lead you down to the vermiculous grottos of the demon sea, to stand beneath the subworld's lurid sky and battle monsters who seem the spiritual distillations of human evil itself!

Logo No. 509. Prescot, Dray (pseud. Kenneth Bulmer). *Delia of Vallia.* Code No. UE1784. First edition. First printing, December 1982. 192 pp. Cover art by Ken W. Kelly. $2.35.

The world of Kregen revolving around the double suns of Antares holds many wonders. There are warrior men and warrior beasts with mighty fraternities of valor and courage. There are whispers of similar organizations among the high-born women of many lands. But men knew little of these save the name Sisters of the Rose, and that, somewhere, there was a secret fortress retreat where martial arts were taught that men never learned.

Dray Prescot has, at last, laid bare the story of these fighting sororities in an adventure of Delia of Vallia, leader of a mystic guild, and of her mission to bring justice to one who had betrayed her blood oath and her empress, the traitress Jillian whom she engages in the hidden arena of the whip and the claw.

(Bibliographer's note: Adventure twenty-eight in the always-continuing Dray Prescot series, keeping Prescot ahead of Dumarest by one in the Saga Derby, and this one isn't even about Dray Prescot.)

Logo No. 510. Tubb, E.C. *Earth Is Heaven.* Code No. UE1786. First edition. First printing, December 1982. 160 pp. Cover art by Michael Mariano. $2.25.

All the signals seemed set on "go." Earl Dumarest had found people who believed in the legendary Earth. He had found the coordinates of the Sun and its attendant planets, and he would have the starship with a faithful crew of colonists for whom Earth was the paradise of their dreams.

Before he could reach that ideal moment, Dumarest would have to fight his way out of the demonic Cyclan's master trap as well as unravel a very tricky web of planetary conspiracy. Only if he could achieve those desperate goals would he be able to set sail on what he hoped would be the final lap of his long galactic trek.

If Earth was heaven, then the road there was surely hell itself.

(Bibliographer's note: The twenty-seventh novel in the saga of Dumarest of Terra.)

Logo No. 511. Vance, Jack. *To Live Forever.* Code No. UE1787. First DAW printing, December 1982. 185 pp. Cover art by David B. Mattingly. Originally published in U.S. by Ballantine Books (1956). Also published in U.K. by Sphere (1976). $2.50.

Garven Waylock had waited seven years for the scandal surrounding his former immortal self to be forgotten. He had kept his identity concealed so that he could once again join the ranks of those who lived forever. He had been exceedingly careful about hiding his past. Then he met The Jacynth.

She was a beautiful 19-year-old, and Garven wanted her. But he recognized that a wisdom far beyond her years marked her as one who knew too much about him to live. As far as she was concerned, death was a mere inconvenience. But, once The Jacynth came back, Garven Waylock's life would be an everlasting Hell!

(Bibliographer's note: The author's fourth book.)

Logo No. 512. Green, Sharon. *The Warrior Enchained.* Code No. UE1789. First edition. First printing, January 1983. 352 pp. Cover art by Ken W. Kelly. $2.95.

Terry was Central's Prime Intelligence agent. Her talent made her nearly priceless as an interplanetary operative. Yet there came a time when that price had to be met. The barbarian Tammad demanded it, and Terry's bosses were willing to meet it. She was tricked into returning to a world that considered women the property of their men, and a highly civilized one such as Terry to be a prize possession. (Bibliographer's empathetic comment: I have books I feel that way about.)

But Terry was a warrior at heart, and, though her role called for submission to domination and even bondage, she was prepared to use all her feminine wiles and secret-agent cunning to show a primitive world just who would be its true master.

(Bibliographer's note: Second book in the Terrillian sequence.)

Logo No. 513. Lee, Tanith. *Red As Blood or Tales from the Sisters Grimmer.* Code No. UE1790. First edition. First printing, January 1983. 208 pp. Cover art by Michael Whelan; interior illustrations by Tanith Lee. Also published as first hardcover edition by the Science Fiction Book Club. $2.50.

Contents:
Paid Piper (Asia: The Last Century B.C.)
Red As Blood (Europe: The Fourteenth Century)
Thorns (Eurasia: The Fifteenth Century)
When the Clock Strikes (Europe: The Sixteenth Century)
The Golden Rope (Europe: The Seventeenth Century)
The Princess and Her Future (Asia: The Eighteenth Century)

Wolfland (Scandinavia: The Nineteenth Century)
Black As Ink (Scandinavia: The Twentieth Century)
Beauty (Earth: The Future)
(Bibliographer's note: the title story was a Nebula nominee.)

Logo No. 514. Simak, Clifford D. *Out of Their Minds.* **Code No. UE1791. First DAW printing, January 1983. 175 pp. Cover art by Frank Kelly Freas. Originally published in U.S. by Putnam (1970) and in U.K. by Sidgwick & Jackson (1972). $2.50.**

Out of their minds and the force of their imagination, men have created countless beings, from demons and dragons and monsters of legend to story-book heroes and comic-strip characters.

What if their world were real: if vampires, devils and Don Quixote hob-nobbed with Dagwood Bumstead and Charlie Brown. Such a world would have its fascinations and its dreadful perils—if it existed.

Horton Smith found out that it did exist, and that he was right in the middle of it!

Logo No. 515. Piserchia, Doris. *The Deadly Sky.* **Code No. UE1792. First edition. First printing, January 1983. 176 pp. Cover art by Frank Kelly Freas. $2.50.**

Ashlin had been climbing Mt. Timbrini for more than a decade. Scaling the huge, befogged escarpment, he liked to gaze down upon the city of Emera glittering below like a thousand multi-colored moons.

But, when horrifying visions of gaps in the fabric of sky above the mountain began to plague his nights, and the mysterious appearance of a woman on a section of his heights he knew to be unreachable baffled his daytime ascents, his motivation for climbing began to change.

He didn't realize that his newly motivated enterprise wouldn't bring him peace of mind, but, instead, a dire and dangerous battle for the peace of a world!

Logo No. 516. Clayton, Jo. *Moonscatter.* **Code No. UE1798. First edition. First printing, February 1983. 304 pp. Cover art by Ken W. Kelly. $2.95.**

With skin as pale and eyes as black as death, a blood-red ruby depending from one nostril, he was Ser Noris, the most villainous wizard of all time. He had done it all: slain all adepts worth his scorn, attained immortality, become the dire tyrant of the Sorcerers Isle and a shadow of doom on the lands beyond. But it wasn't enough.

There was yet one opponent he hadn't humbled: She whom men called Maiden; She who was implicit in the alternation of death and birth, the cycling of the seasons, the complex circling of the moons. She who was the phoenix, the spirit of the earth itself!

This is the novel of Serroi, brave warrior-woman of the *meie*, who knows she must overcome the ties set on her by Ser Noris, who raised her as his tool, or see her world crumble. But can she withstand being a pawn in a power game between the most virulent fiend of all time and the spirit of Nature herself?

(Bibliographer's note: The second novel of the Duel of Sorcery series.)

Logo No. 517. Llewellyn, Edward (pseud. Edward Llewellyn-Thomas). *Prelude to Chaos.* Code No. UE1800. First edition. First printing, February 1983. 256 pp. Cover art by David B. Mattingly. $2.75.

Gavin Knox was bodyguard to the President of the United States and witness to a crime which could shake civilization to its foundations. Judith Grenfell was a neurobiologist who discovered a side effect of the most common pharmaceutical on the market which could cause the greatest biological disaster in human history. Both were prisoners in the most advanced maximum-security prison ever devised.

Without their information, the few survivors of biological catastrophe could dissolve in bloody civil war. They had to escape, and fast, to safeguard the survival of the human race, or leave the world barren for eternity.

Logo No. 518. Stableford, Brian. *The Gates of Eden.* Code No. UE1801. First edition. First printing, February 1983. 176 pp. Cover art by Douglas Chaffee. $2.50.

Before the hyper-space vessels could go from planet to planet, stations had to be set up. That meant manned spaceships cut off from Earth for decades. The explorer vessel *Ariadne* had gone toward galactic center and was considered lost, until its call was heard appealing for a xeno-biologist.

Their new world was all swamp. As far as could be seen, there was no intelligent species. Yet this was alarming because all inhabitable planets so far discovered had thinking inhabitants.

But the nature of that planet's "people" turned out to be an enigma that had to be solved, for the alien biology there could spell doom to all the civilizations of the stars: doom, or a terrible unity.

Logo No. 519. Asimov, Isaac and Martin H. Greenberg eds. *Isaac Asimov Presents the Great Science Fiction Stories 9 (1947).* Code No. UE1802. First edition. First printing, February 1983. 366 pp. Cover design by One Plus One Studio. Cover art by Bernal. $3.50.

Contents:
Introduction

Little Lost Robot	Isaac Asimov
Tomorrow's Children	Poul Anderson
Child's Play	William Tenn
Time and Time Again	H. Beam Piper
Tiny and the Monster	Theodore Sturgeon
E for Effort	T.L. Sherred
Letter to Ellen	Chan Davis
The Figure	Edward Grendon
With Folded Hands	Jack Williamson
The Fires Within	Arthur C. Clarke
Zero Hour	Ray Bradbury
Hobbyist	Eric Frank Russell

| Exit the Professor | Lewis Padgett |
| Thunder and Roses | Theodore Sturgeon |

Logo No. 520. Norman, John (pseud. John Lange). *Kajira of Gor.* Code No. UE1807. First edition. First printing, March 1983. 446 pp. Cover art by Ken W. Kelly. Also published in U.K. by Star (1983). $3.50.

Kajira means slave-girl in Gorean. But when Tiffany Collins was kidnapped from Earth and brought to that orbital counter-world, she found herself on the throne of a mighty city as its "queen." Power seemingly was hers, and she didn't realize that her true role was that of a slave puppet of a conniving woman agent of the monstrous Kurii.

Nevertheless, a chained slave she was destined to be, and, in the course of the complex, visible and invisible, struggles between warriors and cities, between Kurii and Priest-Kings, she would play a pivotal role.

(Bibliographer's note: The nineteenth book of the Counter-Earth saga.)

Logo No. 521. Cherryh, C.J. (pseud. Carolyn Janice Cherry). *The Dreamstone.* Code No. UE1808. First edition. First printing, March 1983. 192 pp. Cover art by David A. Cherry. Substantially different versions of portions of this book appeared as "The Dreamstone," published in *Amazons,* DAW Books (1979), and as *Ealdwood,* published by Donald M. Grant (1981). $2.75.

It was that transitional time of the world, when man first brought the clang of iron and the reek of smoke to the lands which before had echoed with inhuman voices. In that dawn of man and death of magic, there yet remained one last untouched place, the small forest of Ealdwood, which kept a time different from elsewhere, and one who dwelt there who had more patience, pride and love of the earth than any other of her kind: Arafel the Sidhe.

(Bibliographer's note: The author has included an afterword in explanation of the derivation of names from their Celt, Welsh and Old English roots.)

Logo No. 522. Dickson, Gordon R. *Mutants.* Code No. UE1809. First DAW printing, March 1983. 224 pp. Cover art by Paul Chadwick. Published earlier by Macmillan (1970). $2.95.

Contents:

Introduction	Roofs of Silver
Warrior	By New Hearth Fires
Of the People	Idiot Solvant
Danger—Human!	The Immortal
Rehabilitated	Miss Prinks
Listen	Home from the Shore

Logo No. 523. Dick, Philip K. *The Three Stigmata of Palmer Eldritch.* Code No. UE1810. First DAW printing, March 1983. 192 pp. Cover art by Bob Pepper. Published earlier in U.S. by Doubleday (1964) and in U.K. by Cape (1966). Reprinted by Gregg Press (1979). See *Anatomy of Wonder* 3-

271 (1981); *Survey of Science Fiction Literature V*, p. 2269 (1979). $2.50.

When the mysterious Palmer Eldritch returned from a distant galaxy, he claimed to have brought a gift for mankind. Chew-Z was a drug capable of transporting people into an illusory world, a world they could live in for years without losing a second of Earth time. For the lonely colonists living out their dreary term on Mars, here was the ultimate trip.

But, in return, Palmer Eldritch exacted a terrible price. He would enter, control, and be a god in everyone's private universe, a universe from which there was no escape.

(Bibliographer's note: 1965 Nebula nominee.)

Logo No. 524. Foster, M.A. *Transformer*. Code No. UE1814. First edition. First printing, April, 1983. 255 pp. Cover art by Michael Whelan. See *Anatomy of Wonder* 4-221 (1987). $2.50.

The Morphodite was a genetically constructed genius who had turned the tables on the police state that had created it. Settled down to a man's quiet life, he contemplated a lifetime of doing good in a liberated world, until a vengeance squad knocked out that hope.

Now, again utilizing that unique talent, the young woman who was now the Morphodite, realized that the job couldn't be finished until the enemies of that planet's society were tracked to their interstellar lair and blasted. Across the planet she went, and finally into outer space in a city-sized spaceship to a final showdown somewhere between the worlds.

(Bibliographer's note: Sequel to *The Morphodite*.)

Logo No. 525. Bradley, Marion Zimmer ed. *Greyhaven*. Code No. UE1815. First edition. First printing, April 1983. 240 pp. Cover art by Victoria Poyser; frontispiece sketch by Diana Paxson. $2.50.

Contents:

Impressions of House Greyhaven	Diana L. Paxson
Greyhaven: Writers at Work (An introduction)	Marion Zimmer Bradley
The Kindred of the Wind	Diana L. Paxson
They Come and Go	Joel Hagen
Cat Tale	Vicki Ann Heydron
Bedtime Story	Anodea Judith
Wrong Number	James Ian Elliot
The Bardic Revel	Marion Zimmer Bradley
From Various Bardic Revels	Diana Paxson, Robert Cook, Ian Michael Studebaker, Fiona Zimmer
Tell Me a Story	Elisabeth Waters
Just Another Vampire Story	Randall Garrett
Wildwood	Adrienne Martine Barnes
The Tax Collector	Phillip Wayne
The Woodcarver's Son	Robert Cook
The Incompetent Magician	Marion Zimmer Bradley
Cantabile	Jon de Cles

Dagger Spring	Susan Shwartz
Lariven	Patricia Shaw Mathews
The Ring	Caradoc A. Cador
The Hand of Tyr	Paul Edwin Zimmer

Logo No. 526. Prescot, Dray (pseud. Kenneth Bulmer). *Fires of Scorpio.* Code No. UE1816. First edition. First printing, April 1983. 173 pp. Cover art by Richard Hescox. $2.50.

Triple trouble always dogged Dray Prescot just when he thought he had things under control. This time, involved with setting things right on the continent of Pandahem, the Star Lords yanked him away from his friends and dumped him, weaponless, at the gates of the terrible temple of the Leem.

To rescue a girl to be sacrificed there was but the start, for, next, he had to help torch the temple and all the others like it, and finally take to the sea to confront the next wave of the fish-headed marauders from Kregen's Southern Hemisphere.

(Bibliographer's note: Twenty-ninth adventure of Dray Prescot and the second novel in the Pandahem Cycle.)

Logo No. 527. Vance, Jack. *The Blue World.* Code No. UE1817. First DAW printing, April 1983. 176 pp. Cover art by David B. Mattingly. First appearance was as a short story titled "King Kragen" in *Fantastic.* (1964). Published earlier in U.S. in book form by Ballantine Books (1966) and in U.K. by Mayflower (1976). Later published by Underwood-Miller (1979) as first hardcover edition. See *Anatomy of Wonder* 3-758 (1981). $2.25.

The Blue World was beautiful. It was a world of water, with floating islands made by the thick, spreading tops of gigantic ocean growths, big enough to support neat houses and sea gardens alive with fish of all kinds, rich with edible water plants, and even communication towers, so that the People of the Floats were not cut off from one another, but could send messages and enjoy festivals and meetings together.

There was one drawback in this paradise, however. The massive abundance of the ocean spawned far more than food for the puny human beings living on its surface. The Floats were in constant danger from the ravaging attacks of monster sea creatures against which there was no defense, merely cowardly propitiation.

The Blue World needed a rebel, one who would give his life, if necessary. They found one. This is his story.

(Bibliographer's note: 1966 Nebula nominee.)

Logo No. 528. Wollheim, Donald A. with Arthur W. Saha eds. *The 1983 Annual World's Best SF.* Code No. UE1822. First edition. First printing, May 1983. 255 pp. Cover art by Vincent DiFate. $2.95.

Contents:

Introduction	The Editor
The Scourge	James White
A Letter from the Clearys	Connie Willis

Farmer on the Dole	Frederik Pohl
Playing the Game	Gardner Dozois & Jack Dann
Pawn's Gambit	Timothy Zahn
The Comedian	Timothy Robert Sullivan
Written in Water	Tanith Lee
Souls	Joanna Russ
Swarm	Bruce Sterling
Peg-Man	Rudy Rucker

Logo No. 529. Clayton, Jo. *Ghosthunt.* **Code No. UE1823. First edition. First printing, May 1983. 189 pp. Cover art by Ken W. Kelly. $2.50.**

A ghost was haunting Cazarit: a kidnapper who snatched the wealthy clientele who vacationed there as if the intensive security didn't exist. Local security was getting desperate. After hundreds of hours and days trying to locate and identify their "ghost," they were no closer to an answer than when they began.

They needed the help of a Hunter, and there was only one who would meet their demands. Aletys, wearer/symbiote of the mysterious and powerful Diadem, had a reputation which preceded her across the galaxy. But little did they know that Aletys already had a good idea who their ghost was, and she didn't want to catch him!

(Bibliographer's note: Seventh novel in the Diadem series.)

Logo No. 530. Lee, Tanith. *Sung in Shadow.* **Code No. UE1824. First edition. First printing, May 1983. 349 pp. Cover art by Victoria Poyser. $3.50.**

In a parallel world, in a Renaissance Italy just a little bit different from that we know, a dashing young man named Romulan met a lovely young lady named Iuletta. But, between their romance, stood the hatred of their feuding families and a witchcraft that really worked.

(Bibliographer's comment: Until we got to the witchcraft part, there was a vague familiarity about this story line.)

Logo No. 531. Simak, Clifford D. *Cemetery World.* **Code No. UE1825. First DAW printing, May 1983. 159 pp. Cover art by Frank Kelly Freas. Originally published in U.S. by Putnam (1973) and then in U.K. by Sidgwick & Jackson (1975). $2.50.**

Earth: graveyard to the galaxy. Those who could afford it shipped the bones of their dead back to Mother Earth, man's ancient birthplace. Ravaged 10,000 years earlier by war, Earth was reclaimed by its space-dwelling offspring as a planet of landscaping and tombstones.

Fletcher Carson came back to Earth to work on an artistic creation of revolutionary design. He was accompanied by a powerful robot, by a talented art-machine, and by a strikingly beautiful treasure hunter whose secret goal was vastly more important than mere gold and jewels.

But for them, the world of the dead was hostile terrain, where the Wolves of Steel dogged their footsteps, where the shrouded Census-taker floated faceless beside them, and where the frightful Shades hovered at landscape's edges.

(Bibliographer's note: By request of the author, the text of the DAW edition follows exactly that of the original magazine serialization, rather than previous book versions.)

Logo No. 532. Green, Sharon. *An Oath to Mida.* Code No. UE1829. First edition. First printing, June 1983. 397 pp. Cover art by Ken W. Kelly. $2.95.

Their world was threatened, torn asunder from within by the primitive warring of bloodthirsty nomadic tribes and threatened from without by mysterious strangers. Jalav, Amazon war leader of the savage Hosta clan, lay dying on a cold battlefield and cared for nothing but her spirit's safe flight to the bosom of Mida, patron goddess of the Midanna Amazons.

But peace was not to be the lot of Jalav. Abducted in her weakness by a tribe of northern barbarian riders, her destination lay in the frozen arctic wastes, far from her beloved sister warriors and the protective embrace of Mida the Golden. For she was the one spoken of in the prophecy of the Snows: the savior who must travel to the glacial hell of Sigurr's Peak and beyond, and, without whom, any mission to save their embattled world would surely fail!

(Bibliographer's Note: The second book in the Jalav, Amazon Warrior, series.)

Logo No. 533. Dick, Philip K. *A Maze of Death.* Code No. UE1830. First DAW printing, June 1983. 191 pp. Cover art by Bob Pepper. Published earlier in U.S. by Doubleday (1970) and in U.K. by Gollancz (1972). $2.50.

Fourteen people came to Delmak-0 in separate one-way space carriers. Their hope was to make new beginnings away from the world where God had made Himself manifest.

Their communication satellite suddenly destroyed, they found themselves each alone on an alien and hostile planet.

Death and mystery and terror became their lot, until they learned the true meaning of the Walker-on-Earth, the Form Destroyer, and the Intercessor.

Logo No. 534. Tubb, E.C. *Melome.* Code No. UE1831. First edition. First printing, June 1983. 160 pp. Cover art by Vincent DiFate. $2.25.

"Welcome to the circus of Chen Wei! A spectacle of marvels culled from a thousand worlds! Things that will amaze you, amuse you, puzzle you, fill you with rapture! A feast for the eye and mind and not one to be missed!"

Dumarest had been on innumerable planets in his long quest, and there could be little that any interstellar circus could surprise him with. But Chen Wei's was special. It held Melome, the girl-child whose song could bring back forgotten data from the logs of lost spaceships and true visions of mythical Terra. Melome was surely the key to Dumarest's next step, but that circus was more than an entertainment. It was a deadly trap set by a monster!

(Bibliographer's note: The twenty-eighth novel in the saga of Dumarest of Terra.)

Logo No. 535. Lake, David J. *Warlords of Xuma*. Code No. UE1832. First edition. First printing, June 1983. 208 pp. Cover art by Oliviero Berni. $2.50.

The planet at first appeared to be a duplicate of old Mars as Burroughs had portrayed it: Barsoom come to life. But the desperate expeditioners from Earth soon found out otherwise. The red "Martians," the flying boats, the warring cities, and the canal network were all parts of an ancient and well-established civilization.

This didn't stop the little human colony from dreaming of conquest. It still seemed possible. Only now it would take cunning diplomacy and the preparation of a few Earth weapons to make themselves masters of that world.

(Bibliographer's note: Sequel to *The Gods of Xuma, or Barsoom Revisited.*)

Logo No. 536. Zahn, Timothy. *The Blackcollar*. Code No. UE1843. First edition. First printing, July 1983. 272 pp. Cover art by Vincent DiFate. $2.95.

Allen Caine had never met any of those superbly trained guerrilla warriors called the Blackcollars, but their exploits in the war against the alien *Ryqril* invaders were legendary.

Chemically augmented with drugs to prolong youth, double speed and reflexes, and enhance memory, they were a special task force trained in hand-to-hand combat against an enemy far more powerful and swift than human soldiers. An ultimate weapon more insidious than the giant Nova-class battle cruisers, the Blackcollars had been the deadliest men in the history of Earth warfare.

But that was 30 years ago in a war that had been lost, and Allen Caine, an operative in Earth's underground Resistance, had a mission to complete. A last-chance effort to overthrow the alien domination of Earth and her colonies would depend on his re-convening a Blackcollar unit, if they still existed, and if he could find them.

(Bibliographer's note: The author's first novel.)

Logo No. 537. Nolane, Richard D. ed. *Terra SF II: The Year's Best European SF*. Code No. UE1844, First edition. First printing, July 1983. 224 pp. Cover art by Oliviero Berni. See *Anatomy of Wonder* 4-661 (1987). $2.95.

Contents:

Preface	The Editor
Shoobeedoowah Across the Universe	Karl-Michael Armer
The Hospital, a Cynical Fable	Daniel Walther
El Pape	Bob Laerhoven
John Henry	Oyvind Myhre
The Biological Truth	Veikko Rekunen
Disslish the Aquamancer	Tais Teng
The Last Atlantean	Francis Carsac

Mikey Turns Three	Merete Kruuse
The Emerald-Studded Scepter	Carlos Saiz Cidoncha
In Search of Aurade	Gianluigi Zuddas
The Ogre's Head	Richard D. Nolane
Haike the Heretic's Writings	Wolfgang Jeschke

Logo No. 538. Chandler, A. Bertram. *Matilda's Stepchildren*. Code No. UE1845. First U.S. edition. First DAW printing, July 1983. 176 pp. Cover art by Ken W. Kelly. Previously published in U.K. by Hale (1979). $2.50.

John Grimes, owner of the deep space pinnace *Little Sister*, couldn't afford to be fussy about whom he carried. But there were compensations, for, if his ship hadn't been chartered to take Fenella Pruin, muckraking reporter, to exclusive New Venusberg, he would never have been able to visit that fabulous pleasure planet.

Unfortunately, there was going to be little pleasure in it for him. Among the visitors was a Shaara princess who owed him vengeance. The planet's authorities were after Fenella's blood to prevent her snooping. Had it not been for the boomerang throwing abilities of two sexy dancers from New Alice, the spaceman and the journalist would have been sacrificed to make a Roman holiday. The spectator sports of the very rich and very depraved involve a high mortality rate among the players.

(Bibliographer's note: A novel in the John Grimes: Rim Runner series.)

Logo No. 539. Kern, Gregory (pseud. E.C. Tubb). *The Galactiad*. Code No. UJ1846. First edition. First printing, July 1983. 128 pp. Cover art by Wayne Douglas Barlowe. $1.95.

The things from beyond the Milky Way galaxy found the intelligent races of our universe amusingly slight. To them, possessors of vast cosmic power, the strivings of various humanoids to outdo each other were a source of contemptuous entertainment.

They established a contest between the worlds. It would be an Olympiad of the whole galaxy, a Galactiad. Let these puny interstellar intelligences meet each other in contest. Pit one against the other, and let the losers beware!

Earth had its team, a mixed group of powerful athletes and genius scientists. Because other worlds didn't always believe in the ideal of good sportsmanship, they had to confront the reality. Win at all costs, or kiss humanity goodbye!

(Bibliographer's note: Guess who's back. Cap Kennedy. And with a logo number all his own!)

Logo No. 540. Cherryh, C.J. (pseud. Carolyn Janice Cherry). *The Tree of Swords and Jewels*. Code No. UE1850. First edition. First printing, August 1983. 254 pp. Cover art by Michael Whelan. $2.95.

They said that Ciaran Cuilean was fey, that he had the touch of the Sidhe on him, and on his lands. And it was true. Elvish blood ran in his veins, and he had been to that other world, that parallel and magical land of Eald, where Arafel, the Lady of Trees, held dominion.

What should have been a blessing was as much a curse, for jealousy and fear grew in the lands of men. Shadows of newly awakened evil swarmed across both landscapes threatening to bring the clang and reek of war from the very hearthstones of the mortal keeps to the silvery heart of Ealdwood. Ciaran knew that he must once again put his humanity aside and reclaim his haunted weapons from the Tree of Swords, or see both his worlds fold into darkness.

(Bibliographer's note: A book in the Arafel saga, sequel to *The Dreamstone*.)

Logo No. 541. Bayley, Barrington J. *The Zen Gun*. Code No. UE1851. First edition. First printing, August 1983. 159 pp. Cover art by Frank Kelly Freas. Later published in U.K. by Methuen (1984). See *Anatomy of Wonder* 4-48 (1987). $2.50.

A novel about:

The absolutely ultimate weapon that can ever exist.

The sub-human who found it and tried to use it.

The beasts who manned humanity's last star fleet.

The widening rip in the space-time continuum.

The brief cosmic empire of the pigs.

The theory of gravitational recession.

The super-samurai who served the zen-gunner.

The colonial girl who defied the galactic empire.

(Bibliographer's note: It's about more stuff, too, but why give it all away?)

Logo No. 542. Bulmer, Kenneth. *The Diamond Contessa*. Code No. UE1853. First edition. First printing, August 1983. 174 pp. Cover art by Ken W. Kelly. $2.50.

Harry Blakey remembered a childhood secret: that there was a room under his folks' home which crossed into another world. (Bibliographer's incredulous query: This is something you can forget?) When, finally, as a war veteran, he came back to the old house, he investigated and found his memory was true. There were, indeed, other Earths and other civilizations and adventures to be had, but at great risks.

When he enlisted in the special commando corps which had been organized to stop the interdimensional warfare, he came up against the terrifying hordes of the Diamond Contessa. She had looted many Earths, and her hunger was always increasing. No mere human heroics would wrest the keys of the worlds away from her; not while her army of monsters held a dozen civilizations in thrall!

(Bibliographer's note: A return to the Keys to the Dimensions series after an eleven-year hiatus.)

Logo No. 543. Asimov, Isaac and Martin H. Greenberg eds. *Isaac Asimov Presents the Great Science Fiction Stories 10 (1948)*. Code No. UE1854. First edition. First printing, August 1983. 287 pp. Cover design by One Plus One Studio. Cover art by Robert Andre. $3.50.

Contents:
Introduction

Logo No. 544. Bradley, Marion Zimmer. *Thendara House.* Code No. UE1587. First edition. First printing, September 1983. 414 pp. Cover art by Hannah M.G. Shapero. See *Anatomy of Wonder* 4-77 (1987). $3.50.

Thendara House was a place on Darkover where the Order of Renunciates dwelled. They were women, known as Free Amazons, who had renounced all subservience to men, and who sought for themselves total equality in all spheres of society. To Thendara House came the Terran Magda in exchange for the Free Amazon Jaelle, who had become the wife of an Earthman and had entered the Terran enclave. The cross-currents of two cultures, one male-dominated, one egalitarian, combined with the human problems of the two who had switched allegiances, brings into focus all the deepest questions of love and marriage, of male and female, and of justice and injustice.

(Bibliographer's note: Eighteenth Darkover novel. Published with *The Shattered Chain*, the tenth Darkover novel, in one volume by Doubleday (1983) under the title *Oath of the Renunciates*.)

Logo No. 545. Kapp, Colin. *Search for the Sun.* Code No. UE1858. First DAW printing, September 1983. 158 pp. Cover art by Vincent DiFate. Originally published by New English Library (1982). $2.25.

"World upon world had been added, each planetary orbit studded with new planets. Planet had been linked to planet, until unimaginably vast concentric shells, spinning, stabilized, surrounded the sun. Each shell teemed with the countless billions of humanity. And always, unceasingly, the work went on."

Out on Mars shell, the question had arisen. Was there really a central sun, or was it just a myth out of the remotest time? To hunt for the sun meant to go through the intervening shells, an expedition that had never been attempted. But there were three who were ready to go: a master assassin, a master illusionist, and a mistress of the erotic arts.

To find the sun, to outwit Zeus, the planet-sized computer that directed the continual expansion of the Solar shells, this would be the greatest adventure of half a million years, and the first of several!

(Bibliographer's note: First book in the Cageworld series.)

Logo No. 546. Dick, Philip K. *Ubik*. Code No. UE1859. First DAW printing, September 1983. 176 pp. Cover art by Bob Pepper. Originally published in U.S. by Doubleday (1969) and in U.K. by Rapp & Whiting (1970). Reissued by Gregg Press (1979). See *Anatomy of Wonder* 3-272 (1981); *Survey of Science Fiction Literature V*, pp. 2350-2356 (1979). $2.50.

What plucked Joe Chip from the year 1992 and sent him spinning crazily back through time to the 1930s?

How could Joe's former boss scrawl ominous messages on washroom mirrors, especially after he'd been killed in a Lunar bomb-blast?

Why was Joe's wayward mistress, with her awesome power of time control, trapped with Joe in a living nightmare she should have been able to end?

Ubik was the answer, and it meant the difference between life and death.

(Bibliographer's note: Philip K. Dick's work is really awesome, and not on the basis of this particular novel alone.)

Logo No. 547. Barbet, Pierre (pseud. Claude Avice). *The Emperor of Eridanus*. Code No. UE1860. First edition. First printing, September 1983. 160 pp. Cover art by Victoria Poyser. Translated by Stanley Hochman. $2.25.

The natives of Eridanus had spaced in veterans of Napoleon's Dragoons to save them from warlike invaders, and the Bonapartists had stayed. In fact, they had followed the tenets of the Little Corporal and had raised their own imperial standards over the conquered stars.

But the path of empire is always uncertain, and the untested vagaries of stellar warfare and of imperial intrigues kept the former Captain Bernard on the edge of his new throne. Enemies among the advanced races of the Milky Way were gathering, and the possibility arose that, for this student of Napoleon, there might also be a Waterloo in his stars.

(Bibliographer's note: Sequel to *The Napoleons of Eridanus*.)

Logo No. 548. Lee, Tanith. *Anackire*. Code No. UE1862. First edition. First printing, September 1983. 414 pp. Cover art by Michael Whelan. $2.95.

The lowland girl seemed to contain fire. Her hair stirred, flickered, gushed upward, blowing flame in a wind that didn't blow. A tower of light shot up the sky, beginning where the girl stood. For half a second, there was only light; then it took form. The form it took was Anackire.

She towered. She soared. Her flesh was a white mountain. Her snake's tail a river of fire in spate. Her golden head touched the apex of the sky, and, there, the serpents of her hair snapped like lightnings. Her eyes were twin suns. The eight arms, outheld as the two arms of the girl had been, rested weightlessly on the air, the long fingers subtly moving.

The girl standing before the well, unblasted by the entity she had released, seemed only quiescent. At last one could see that her face, as it had always been, was the face of Anackire.

(Bibliographer's note: Sequel and companion novel to *The Storm Lord*.)

Logo No. 549. Purtill, Richard. *The Mirror of Helen*. Code No. UE1863. First edition. First printing, October 1983. 192 pp. Cover art by Don Maitz. $2.50.

This is a behind-the-scenes look at Helen of Troy and what it was really like to be involved with that half-goddess whose radiant beauty launched a thousand ships. Here is Helen as a child, kidnapped and held hostage. Here is Helen as a woman, captive in an alien city while the civilized world sought for her and fought for her.

Logo No. 550. Saha, Arthur W. ed. *The Year's Best Fantasy Stories: 9*. Code No. UE1864. First edition. First printing, October 1983. 192 pp. Cover art by Sanjulian. $2.50.

Contents:

Introduction

Influencing the Hell Out of Time and Teresa Golowitz	Parke Godwin
Mirage and Magia	Tanith Lee
"Other"	Jor Jennings
The Horror on the #33	Michael Shea
Another Orphan	John Kessel
Lest Levitation Come Upon Us	Suzette Haden Elgin
Sentences	Richard Christian Matheson
Square and Above Board	R.A. Lafferty
The Malaysian Mer	Jane Yolen
Djinn, No Chaser	Harlan Ellison

Logo No. 551. Trebor, Robert. *An XT Called Stanley*. Code No. UE1865. First edition. First printing, October 1983. 221 pp. Cover art by Kevin Johnson. $2.50.

In orbit at the New Hope satellite, men finally made contact with a civilization in the stars. It came in the form of a complex signal which enabled the building of a super-computer to embody it. Top secret, they called the entity Stanley and allowed it to project a humanoid image to speak for it.

But that XT, that Extra-Terrestrial intelligence, played a cagy game with its interpreters. Possessed of a data bank containing the whole knowledge of an alien super-science, it refused to divulge anything until its own questions about humanity were answered. The battle of wits at New Hope: Stanley versus humanity, scientists versus politicians, and, possibly, planet versus planet, became a growing crisis that could either open up the stars or else put an end to Earth's fondest dreams.

(Bibliographer's note: The author's first novel, written under a pseudonym.)

Logo No. 552. Stone, Charlotte. *Cheon of Weltanland: The Four Wishes.*
Code No. UE1877. First edition. First printing, November 1983. 205 pp.
Cover art by Boris Vallejo. $2.95.

Freed from the tyranny of conquerors and the slavery of the ape-
people, ward and student of a Hyperborean witch, the girl Cheon was to
be granted four wishes. This is what she said:

"That no man shall again do to me as the Bunnish men and the men of
the Dark Place did...

"That I may grow tall and strong and skilled in the use of weapons, that
I may slay me as I please...

"That I may be a witch skilled in sorcery, yet beautiful like the dawn...

"That I may be a queen as my father promised me, the queen of the
Northlands..."

(Bibliographer's note: This is Book One in the saga of Cheon and the
book includes a glossary.)

Logo No. 553. Wagner, Karl Edward ed. *The Year's Best Horror Stories:
Series XI.* Code No. UE1878. First edition. First printing. November 1983.
237 pp. Cover art by Michael Whelan. $2.95.

Contents:

Introduction: One from the Vault	Karl Edward Wagner
The Grab	Richard Laymon
The Show Goes On	Ramsey Campbell
The House at Evening	Frances Garfield
I Hae Dream'd a Dreary Dream	John Alfred Taylor
Deathtracks	Dennis Etchison
Come, Follow!	Sheila Hodgson
The Smell of Cherries	Jeffrey Goddin
Posthumous Bequest	David Campton
Slippage	Michael Kube-McDowell
The Executor	David G. Rowlands
Mrs. Halfbooger's Basement	Lawrence C. Connolly
Rouse Him Not	Manly Wade Wellman
Spare the Child	Thomas F. Monteleone
The New Rays	M. John Harrison
Cruising	Donald Tyson
The Depths	Ramsey Campbell
Pumpkin Head	Al Sarrantonio

(Bibliographer's note: "Cruising" is another personal favorite of mine.)

Logo No. 554. Van Vogt, A.E. *Computerworld.* Code No. UE1879. First
edition. First printing, November 1983. 203 pp. Cover art by Michael
Mariano. Later published as *Computer Eye* by Morrison Raven Hill (1985).
$2.50.

1984 was projected by Orwell to be the year of Big Brother and the
time of Newspeak. But 1984 is at hand, and Big Brother has assumed a dif-

ferent and more real form. Newspeak has been replaced by the new language of the programmers and computer microchips, and the prospects of the years to come now have a more sharply defined and less human form.

Logo No. 555. Simak, Clifford D. *Our Children's Children.* Code No. UE1880. First DAW printing, November 1983. 189 pp. Cover art by Frank Kelly Freas. Published earlier in U.S. by Putnam (1974) and in U.K. by Sidgwick and Jackson (1975). $2.50.

They were our children's children, and they came one day from nowhere, walking through holes in the air into our world. By means of one-way time tunnels, they fled the ravening beasts with teeth, claws and tentacles, that reproduced like bacteria and were intelligent.

They fled to escape the uncontrollable horror of their own far future, and we, their distant ancestors, housed and fed and comforted them, content in their assurance that the tunnel was securely guarded from the beasts, whatever or whoever they were. But then somebody up there slipped, and the beasts were abroad.

Logo No. 556. Lorrah, Jean and Jacqueline Lichtenberg. *Channel's Destiny.* Code No. UE1884. First paperback edition. First printing, December 1983. 208 pp. Cover art by Don Maitz. Originally published by Doubleday (1982). $2.95.

Seth Farris's father had been the first channel, the first Sime to extract selyn, the elixir of life, from a Gen without killing. Seth's life-long ambition had been to emulate his father and to help form a new breed whose special powers would redress the perverse mutation of humanity which had set man against man in a millennium of strife.

If he was to achieve his destiny, his road wouldn't be an easy one. The greatest danger would be in the struggle with his own nature: to resist the kill. For, once a Sime killed, he sought the same sensation every time, an unabating crescendo of bloodlust from which his own mother, a Gen, wouldn't be safe!

(Bibliographer's note: The fifth Sime/Gen novel.)

Logo No. 557. Kapp, Colin. *The Lost Worlds of Cronus.* Code No. UE1885. First U.S. edition. First DAW printing, December 1983. 175 pp. Cover art by Vincent DiFate. Originally published by New English Library (1982). $2.50.

Mercury Shell, Venus Shell, Earth, Mars, Asteroid, Jupiter, Saturn. Each shell was concentric, studded with artificial planets; each planet was imbedded in its shell, spinning like a ball-bearing. The whole was Zeus-created in the service of Man, but now beyond his control.

Mathematics and space physics, converging, suggested another shell, its existence hidden from Man. A shell of utter darkness, cold and silent, where only extreme mutants could survive. To find that shell, the three were journeying again: Maq Ancor, Master Assassin, Magician Cherry, and Sime Anura, Mistress of the Erotic. Together, they were daring the all-seeing, all-sensing hostility of Zeus.

(Bibliographer's note: Second novel in the Cageworld series.)

Logo No. 558. Prescot, Dray (pseud. Kenneth Bulmer). *Talons of Scorpio.*
Code No. UE1886. First edition. First printing, December 1983. 173 pp.
Cover art by Ken W. Kelly. $2.50.

To finish the job of destroying the hideous cult of the Leem was just
one of the problems confronting Dray Prescot, Earthman on Antares'
wonder planet, for he had also to rally all the world's forces to combat the
onslaught that was on its way from the unexplored Southern Hemisphere.

While rescuing kidnapped children from the altars of sacrifice, Dray
found himself fighting side by side with his own worst enemy, his
renegade daughter, Ros the Claw, who had pledged his death. Caught in
the talons of fate, he would first have to unravel that vicious web or be
torn asunder by monstrous adversity.

(Bibliographer's note: Number 30 in the saga of Dray Prescot and third
in the Pandahem Cycle.)

Logo No. 559. Dick, Philip K. and Roger Zelazny. *Deus Irae.* Code No.
UE1887. First DAW printing, December 1983. 192 pp. Cover art by Bob
Pepper. Published earlier in U.S. by Doubleday (1976) and in U.K. by Gol-
lancz (1977). $2.95.

Set in a bizarre future America, you will encounter:

A bunch of backwoods farmers who happen to be lizards;

A tribe of foul-mouthed giant bugs who worship a dead VW sedan;

An automated factory that can't decide whether to serve its customers
or kill them;

Across this nightmare landscape, pursued by an avenging angel on a
bicycle, one man makes a painful pilgrimage in search of the One who
changed the world so drastically: the legendary, but very real, God of
Wrath.

Logo No. 560. Green, Sharon. *The Warrior Rearmed.* Code No. UE1895.
First edition. First printing, January 1984. 253 pp. Cover art by Ken W.
Kelly. $2.95.

Terrilian's ability to project her mind empathically enabled her to control wild animals, but when it came to the human beast, she was in trouble.
Being a desirable object for male lust counterbalanced her skills as an interplanetary agent and created an interplanetary crisis.

Tammad, the barbarian chief who had banded Terry as his, was furious
at her efforts to control his mind. Terry, torn between conflicting loyalties,
sought to break her bonds by escaping. Her flight across a savage world led
her, instead, to a final crisis, when, rearmed, she would fight it out with
everything and everyone that opposed her.

(Bibliographer's note: Third book in the Terrilian Sequence.)

Logo No. 561. Correy, Lee (pseud. G. Harry Stine). *Manna.* Code No.
UE1896. First edition. First printing, January 1984. 239 pp. Cover art by
Vincent DiFate. See *Anatomy of Wonder* 4-149 (1987). $2.95.

On the first day of the 21st Century, the first practical "utopian" state declared its independence. With all the world looking on with skepticism or outright antagonism, the United Mitanni Commonwealth was neither in the capitalist nor the communist bloc. It called itself the first truly free state. To continue to exist, however, it would have to outwit and outfight the entire world.

Alexander Baldwin, former crack U.S Aerospace pilot, had just signed up for the new country's orbital force when the rest of the world began its covert attack. From the start, he was to learn the hard way the real meaning of liberty, the evolving art of space combat, and the priceless value of loyalty and love.

(Bibliographer's note: Included is an appendix detailing the vital statistics of the United Mitanni Commonwealth.)

Logo No. 562. Llewellyn, Edward (pseud. Edward Llewellyn-Thomas). *Salvage and Destroy.* Code No. UE1898. First edition. First printing, January 1984. 256 pp. Cover art by James Gurney. See *Anatomy of Wonder* 4-340 (1987). $2.95.

The quarrelsome, belligerent beings of Earth already had space satellites and planetary probes. Soon, they would find the Ultrons' orbital beacon. The Ultrons, who controlled hundreds of civilized planets, knew that Earth meant trouble; its history proved that. If the beacon transmitting data were found, there'd be no end to mankind's interstellar mischief.

So Lucian of the Ults took on human disguise, manned a space cruiser with tame humans, and set out on a Salvage and Destroy mission. The beacon must be silenced and Earth brought under control, but the problems turned out to be far more complex than any Ult computer or alien commander could ever unravel!

Logo No. 563. Walther, Daniel. *The Book of Shai.* Code No. UE1899. First U.S. and first English language edition. First printing, January 1984. 157 pp. Cover art by Richard Hescox. Translated by C.J. Cherryh. Original edition entitled *Le Livre de Swa*, and published by Editions Fleuve Noir, Paris, France (1982). $2.25.

After science had slipped out of the hands of scientists into the hands of political fanatics, there finally came the time of the Great Burning, followed by centuries of disaster, the tilting of the world's axis, the shifting of the continents, and the slow, horrid rise of a Newer Order of mankind.

Out of one of the last strongholds of stability, the Citadel of the Serpent, came the young man Shai. At first a student believing the fabrications of an unnatural faith, then thrust into the terribly changed world by a catastrophe the Serpent couldn't prevent, Shai's first quest became a testing for manhood among the ruins of the older barbarisms once called Civilization.

Logo No. 564. Roberson, Jennifer. *Shapechangers.* Code No. UE1907. First edition. First printing, February 1984. 221 pp. Cover art by Boris Vallejo. $2.95.

They were the Cheysuli, a race of magical warriors gifted with the ability to assume animal shape at will. For centuries, they had been allies to the King of Homana, treasured champions of the realm, until a king's daughter ran away with a Cheysuli liege man and caused a war of annihilation against the Cheysuli race. Twenty-five years later, the Cheysuli were hunted exiles in their own land. All of Homana was raised to fear them, acknowledge the sorcery in their blood, and call them shapechanger, demon.

This is the story of Alix, the daughter of that ill-fated union between Homanan princess and Cheysuli warrior, and her struggles to comprehend the traditions of an alien race she had been taught to mistrust, to answer the call of magic in her blood, and accept her place in an ancient prophecy she can't deny.

(Bibliographer's Note: Chronicles of the Cheysuli: Book One.)

Logo No. 565. Tubb, E.C. *Angado.* Code No. UE1908. First edition. First printing, February 1984. 159 pp. Cover art by Ken W. Kelly. $2.50.

On Angado's planet, there was a man who knew the whereabouts of the lost Earth, the original planet of mankind. Angado himself was a fellow traveler of Earl Dumarest, the man who had been born on Earth and who sought the way to go home. Because they were comrades in arms, Angado would help Earl find that man for a price.

Angado was returning to a complex of high-tech cunning and high-wealth power, the prodigal son against whom all would plot. The Cyclan, who had put a fabulous price on Dumarest's head, also were closing in. With Angado for a leader and the red-robed fiends for followers, Dumarest was still willing to stick it out to the bitter end, for his priceless reward could be the key to Forgotten Terra.

(Bibliographer's note: Hey, this thing's getting exciting in the twenty-ninth book of the saga of Dumarest of Terra. Did you see the movie, *After Hours*, sure to achieve cult status, about another guy who wanted to go home? I did and thought that it was great.)

Logo No. 566. Saunders, Charles R. *The Quest for Cush.* Code No. UE1909. First edition. First printing, February 1984. 205 pp. Cover art by James Gurney. Portions of this novel previously appeared in altered form in *Fantasy Crossroads* magazine, issues 9 and 14. $2.75.

"The Kandiss of Cush charged me to seek he who was the greatest of all warriors; seek him and return with him to Cush, for the Mashataan, the Demon Gods, are once again astir, and all Nyumbani is in danger. I have witnessed your deeds and I am convinced you are the one the Kandiss meant."

So they told Imaro, and he knew it was true. Why else had he been pursued by death and demons, chased, sought and threatened wherever he went? He knew he must go to Cush. Perhaps there he could finally find the answer to the question which had haunted him and denied him peace for all of his twenty-one rains: the question, "WHO AM I?"

(Bibliographer's note: The second adventure of Imaro in the jungles of alternate Africa.)

Logo No. 567. Van Vogt, A.E. *The Beast.* Code No. UE1910. First DAW printing, February 1984. 176 pp. Cover art by Frank Kelly Freas. Published in U.S. by Doubleday (1963) under this title and in U.K. by Panther (1969) as *Moonbeast.* $2.50.

That strange machine held the potential for peace in all the planets of the galaxy. Jim Pendrake, who found the machine, was only dimly aware of its incredible powers. But others knew, and, in their ruthless efforts, they tried to take it from him.

When the machine disappeared, the sensible thing to do was to let it go and forget about it. Yet Jim's personal future now seemed to depend on solving the machine's riddle, and, so, he began a frantic chase that carried him to a rendezvous with the stars and a showdown with The Beast.

(Bibliographer's stream-of-consciousness at work: If you haven't seen *An American Werewolf in London*, another film destined for cult status, I suggest you do so. Griffin Dunne, the same bloke as in *After Hours*, appears, only in a supporting role rather than the lead. He's the one who gets deep-sixed by the werewolf.)

Logo No. 568. Norman, John (pseud. John Lange). *Players of Gor.* Code No. UE1914. First edition. First printing, March 1984. 396 pp. Cover art by Ken W. Kelly. Published in U.K. by Star (1984). $3.50.

During the holiday revels of Port Kar, an attempt is made on Tarl Cabot's life, which leads Tarl to discover that the Priest-Kings have turned against him. To clear himself of their charge of treason, he must follow the assassin's trail. The way to achieve that was to join, in disguise, a troupe of traveling players, a sort of Gorean carnival, which would give him entry to enemy cities and hostile territories. Life in such a carnival is always a risk in itself. There are monsters in form and monsters in mind among them, and there may be spies of the alien Kurs and the omnipotent Priest-Kings.

(Bibliographer's Note: The twentieth book of the Tarl Cabot saga.)

Logo No. 569. Lee, Tanith. *Tamastara, or The Indian Nights.* Code No. UE1915. First edition. First printing, March 1984. 174 pp. Cover art by Don Maitz. $2.50.

Contents:
First Night: Foreign Skins
Second Night: Bright Burning Tiger
Third Night: Chand Veda
Fourth Night: Under the Hand of Chance
Fifth Night: The Ivory Merchants
Sixth Night: Oh, Shining Star
Seventh Night: Tamastara

Logo No. 570. Brunner, John. *The Jagged Orbit.* Code No. UE1917. First DAW printing, March 1984. 318 pp. Cover art by James Gurney. Originally published in U.S. by Ace Books (1969) and later in U.K. by

Sidgwick & Jackson (1970). See *Anatomy of Wonder* 3-136 (1981). $2.95.

The friendly neighborhood arms salesman lived right next door. But they didn't need anything. The apartment was a fortress, which was only proper and usual in the year 2014, when street-fighting was the norm, and the richest, most powerful force in a very dangerous world was the Gottschalk weaponry combine.

(Bibliographer's note: Winner of the 1971 British SF Award.)

Logo No. 571. Asimov, Isaac and Martin H. Greenberg eds. *Isaac Asimov Presents the Great Science Fiction Stories 11 (1949).* Code No. UE1918. First edition. First printing, March 1984. 317 pp. Cover design by One Plus One Studio. Cover art by Michelangelo Miani. $3.50.

Contents:

Introduction	
The Red Queen's Race	Isaac Asimov
Flaw	John D. MacDonald
Private Eye	Lewis Padgett
Manna	Peter Phillips
The Prisoner in the Skull	Lewis Padgett
Alien Earth	Edmond Hamilton
History Lesson	Arthur C. Clarke
Eternity Lost	Clifford D. Simak
The Only Thing We Learn	C.M. Kornbluth
Private—Keep Out	Philip MacDonald
The Hurkle Is a Happy Beast	Theodore Sturgeon
Kaleidoscope	Ray Bradbury
Defense Mechanism	Katherine MacLean
Cold War	Henry Kuttner
The Witches of Karres	James H. Schmitz

Logo No. 572. Kapp, Colin. *The Tyrant of Hades.* Code No. UE1919. First DAW printing, March 1984. 176 pp. Cover art by Vincent DiFate. Originally published by New English Library (1982). $2.50.

Smoothly, remorselessly, inhumanly, the controlled flow of people continued. As each of the great planetary shells approached population maximum, the surplus mass of humanity was transported out. Inexorably, they filled the space made ready for them by Zeus, the master-minding intelligence.

Mars shell, Asteroid, Jupiter, Saturn, Uranus. At Uranus shell, the flow stopped, and the pressure of the countless billions had pushed the shell to the very edge of breakdown.

Beyond Uranus lay ready Neptune shell, Zeus-designed, Zeus-built, but no longer Zeus-controlled. Another giant intelligence had usurped all power. So it was that Maq Ancor, Master Assassin, Magician Cherry and Sine Anura became the eyes of Zeus as they journeyed to the place where all systems failed and where chaos and the tyrant of Hades ruled.

(Bibliographer's note: Third book of the Cageworld series.)

Logo No. 573. Cherryh, C.J. (pseud. Carolyn Janice Cherry). *Voyager in Night*. Code No. UE1920. First edition. First printing, April 1984. 221 pp. Cover art by Barclay Shaw. Later published in U.K. by Methuen (1985). See *Anatomy of Wonder* 4-134 (1987). $2.95.

Two voyages, two ships. One had been en route for over a hundred thousand years, was the size of an asteroid, and its place of launching had been beyond the trace of any man-made telescope. Its crew was an enigma. The other ship had been out of Endeavor Station just a few months, was a tiny ore-prospector with a crew of three: Rafe, Paul, and Paul's wife, Jillan.

Two ships were on a collision course which neither could avoid in time. The three humans were the first of their species that the master of the monster ship had encountered, but now two were already dead, and one was dying. But that could be remedied and was, many times.

Logo No. 574. Clough, B.W. *The Crystal Crown*. Code No. UE1922. First edition. First printing, April 1984. 223 pp. Cover art by Ken W. Kelly. $2.75.

Liras-ven had never been particularly thrilled to have been chosen from the many royal offspring to ascend the throne of Averidan. To have his mind dominated by the powerful and somewhat frightening Crystal Crown, then to be married off to a barbarian princess whose relatives would like nothing better than to kill him was bad enough! But to have to do battle with the most dangerous and powerful wizard in the land? With allies who could turn to enemies at the drop of a hat?

Liras didn't have much choice. Only the wearer of the Crystal Crown could stand against the evil magus Xerlanthor, and only the King of Averidan could wear the Crystal Crown. No more the quiet life; Liras had to find victory at any cost, or not only lose his life, but the security of his country as well!

Logo No. 575. Dick, Philip K. *A Scanner Darkly*. Code No. UE1923. First DAW printing, April 1984. 222 pp. Cover art by Bob Pepper. Published earlier in U.S. by Doubleday (1977) and in U.K. by Gollancz (1977). See *Anatomy of Wonder* 3-269 (1981). $2.50.

An antidrug novel with its strength in the descriptions of the victims of drugs. Set in 1994, the drug is Substance D, also known as Slow Death, or, if you're in a hurry, simply Death. The protagonist is part agent, part pusher, who's unable to prevent the spread of the drug. A warning story that mirrors the drug scene of today.

(Bibliographer's note: This novel took third place in the running for the 1978 John Campbell Award.)

Logo No. 576. Prescot, Dray (pseud. Kenneth Bulmer). *Masks of Scorpio*. Code No. UE1924. First edition. First printing, April 1984. 175 pp. Cover art by Richard Hescox. $2.50.

For Dray Prescot, the task of burning out the cult of the Silver Leem had been given Star Lords priority. Although he was emperor of Vallia, still he had to work incognito on an enemy island until that task was done. Sided by his warrior daughter, Ros the Claw, and aided by a valiant crew of piratical swashbucklers, Dray invaded the capital of the secret order only to find treachery and terror where he had thought to find treasure and triumph. It became a battle of golden masks against silver masks, and, behind each facepiece, could be hiding the bony features of the Grim Reaper himself!

(Bibliographer's note: Thirty-first book in the saga of Dray Prescot and the fourth in the Pandahem Cycle.)

Logo No. 577. Green, Sharon. *Chosen of Mida.* Code No. UE1927. First edition. First printing, January 1984. 365 pp. Cover art by Boris Vallejo. $2.95.

Having given pledge to the godlike Mida to forge an alliance with the macho males who followed Mida's rival, the man-god Sigurr, the task became Jalav's most difficult assignment. The alliance was needed to stand against the invaders from the stars. Without it, they would all, the yucky, rotten, stinking male-dominated cities and the beautiful, courageous, adorable wild free women of the plains, fall before them.

Jalav set off for Sigurr's stronghold, a lone woman, to challenge the rulers of that harsh city, yucky, rotten and stinking, as aforesaid, to meet her as equals. But double-cross followed double-cross, and she found herself a chained slave in a fortress of scornful masters. Nevertheless, Jalav, though her body, great as it is if Boris's cover is any standard (look, Ma, no pasties), could be conquered, her will could not. Prevail she must if the command of her goddess was to be carried out.

(Bibliographer's note: Sorry, Sharon, only teasing. It was late, and I got silly. See if you can detect my subtle, puckish embellishments. Also, I don't know why the copyright page on this one shows the first printing as January 1984. That would make it noticeably out of natural order, appearing, as it does, with other books published by DAW Books in May 1984. Maybe this will be a trivia question someday. Oh, almost forgot amidst all my banter; this is Book III of the Jalav, Amazon Warrior, series.)

Logo No. 578. Bradley, Marion Zimmer ed. *Sword and Sorceress.* Code No. UE1928. First edition. First printing, May 1984. 255 pp. Cover art by Victoria Poyser. $2.95.

Contents:
Introduction: The Heroic Image of Women:

Woman as Wizard and Warrior	Marion Zimmer Bradley
The Garnet and the Glory	Phyliss Ann Karr
Severed Heads	Glen Cook
Taking Heart	Stephen L. Burns
The Rending Dark	Emma Bull
Gimmile's Songs	Charles R. Saunders
The Valley of the Troll	Charles de Lint
Imperatrix	Deborah Wheeler
Blood of Sorcery	Jennifer Roberson

With Four Lean Hounds	Pat Murphy
House in the Forest	Anodea Judith
Sword of Yraine	Diana L. Paxson
Daton and the Dead Things	Michael Ward
Gate of the Damned	Janet Fox
Child of Orcus	Robin W. Bailey
Things Come in Threes	Dorothy J. Heydt

Logo No. 579. Elgin, Suzette Haden. *Star-Anchored, Star-Angered.* Code No. UE1929. First DAW printing, May 1984. 160 pp. Cover art by Frank Kelly Freas. Originally published by Doubleday (1979). $2.50.

Coyote Jones, secret agent for the Tri-Galactic intelligence service, had a strange handicap. In a universe where every normal being is telepathic, he suffered from almost total mind-deafness. He can project, but he can't receive. When the social system of the planet Freeway began to reel under the force of an alleged female Messiah, Coyote's handicap made him the perfect choice for the assignment: to find out if she's a fake or isn't she?

If Drussa Silver is projecting telepathic illusions instead of performing miracles, Coyote would be immune to them. Since using religion to defraud is a criminal act, he could then bring her back to Mars-Central for trial. If she's the real thing, however, the situation would be utterly different.

(Bibliographer's note: Fourth book in the Coyote Jones series.)

Logo No. 580. Van Vogt, A.E. *The Book of Ptath.* Code No. UE1930. First DAW printing, May 1984. 160 pp. Cover art by Ken W. Kelly. Originally published by Fantasy Press (1947). Reprinted as *Two Hundred Million, A.D.* by Paperback Library (1964). See Schlobin, *The Literature of Fantasy* 1064 (1979). $2.50.

He whose strength is unlimited, who tires not, and knows no fear. He was Ptath, the greatest god the mind of man had ever created. He had returned, but against his will. The goddess, Ineznia, his deadly rival, had thrust him into the dangerous world of two hundred million, A.D. in mortal form.

Would Ptath, with only the limited strengths of a mere man, lose his furious contest with Ineznia? Or was he secretly still the most powerful force in all the worlds of time?

Logo No. 581. Wollheim, Donald A. with Arthur W. Saha eds. *The 1984 Annual World's Best SF.* Code No. UE1934. First edition. First printing, June 1984. 256 pp. Cover art by Vincent DiFate. $2.95.

Contents:

Introduction	The Editor
Blood Music	Greg Bear
Potential	Isaac Asimov
Knight of Shallows	Rand B. Lee
Spending a Day at the Lottery Fair	Frederik Pohl
In the Face of My Enemy	Joseph H. Delaney

The Nanny	Thomas Wylde
The Leaves of October	Don Sakers
As Time Goes By	Tanith Lee
The Harvest of Wolves	Mary Gentle
Homefaring	Robert Silverberg

(Bibliographer's note: The keen-eyed collector will have already noticed that this book has DAW's first wraparound cover. That reminds me of the old advertising jingle: "You'll wonder where the yellow went, When you brush your teeth with Pepsodent.")

Logo No. 582. Lake, David J. *The Ring of Truth.* Code No. UE1935. First DAW printing, June 1984. 192 pp. Cover art by Ken W. Kelly. Originally published in Australia by Cory & Collins (1983). $2.95.

Our cosmos, throughout its enormous length of galaxies, and down to its smallest molecules, obeys the same laws of physics and chemistry from one end to another. It is now suspected that, somewhere in the vast reaches of space, there may well be other universes with completely different natural laws.

Even on those worlds, foreign beyond imagining, there may yet be great adventurers, alien Magellans and Columbuses, whose thirst for exploration can't be assuaged, intelligent beings who would risk anything to know what lies over the horizon beyond the parameters of the known world.

Travel now with Prince Kernin of Palur, just such an explorer in just such an alien universe, and discover wonders upon wonders, in a world very different from our own, as he ventures to the ends of his earth and beyond to find the elusive Ring of Truth!

(Bibliographer's note: There's a short appendix to acquaint the reader with the Shorelandish Calendar.)

Logo No. 583. Chandler, A. Bertram. *The Last Amazon.* Code No. UE1936. First edition. First printing, June 1984. 156 pp. Cover art by Richard Hescox. $2.50.

Originally, Sparta was an all-male planet: an all-male population with everything that implies, such as male babies only, produced by the so-called Birth Machine from an almost unending supply of fertilized ova brought by Sparta's founding father, a dyed-in-the-wool misogynist. (Bibliographer's query: When do we get to the fun part of making babies?). Question answered: unnatural situations rarely stand the test of time, and it wasn't too long before Sparta bowed to Mother Nature.

There was still something rather strange about Sparta when John Grimes landed there to await the arrival of his beloved ship, *Sister Sue.* It seemed to him that, among the recently transplanted women of Sparta, there was a strange movement afoot, and, when the Archon was kidnapped by a group of militant women that the press claimed were men, he knew he couldn't just stand by and watch!

(Bibliographer's note: A novel in the John Grimes: Rim Runners series.)

Logo No. 584. Carter, Lin. *Down to a Sunless Sea.* Code No. UE1937. First edition. First printing, June 1984. 174 pp. Cover art by Ken W. Kelly. $2.50.

Brant's life had been hard after the courts had sent him to the penal colony of Trivium Charontis on Mars. Since working his way to freedom, he had run guns to the High Clan princes, sold them liquor and forbidden tobacco, and peddled narcotics to the soft, timid Earthside clerks. He had stolen, he had cheated at cards, he had killed a man more than once.

Now fleeing from justice across the ancient dust-oceans of Mars, he had no way of knowing that he was running toward the most fantastic adventure any man had ever lived, toward refuge more absolute than any man had ever dreamed of, by the banks of secret rivers, in caverns yet unmeasured by man, on the shore of a sea the sun had never seen!

Logo No. 585. Pohl, Frederik. *Demon in the Skull.* Code No. UE1939. First DAW printing, July 1984. 158 pp. Cover art by Don Maitz. Originally published as *A Plague of Pythons* by Ballantine (1965) and in the U.K. by Gollancz (1966). This is a revised and updated version of that early novel, which, itself, was an expanded version from that which had appeared in *Galaxy* (1962). $2.50.

Something had seized his mind, something that rode his body like a speed-maniac would drive a stolen car. He had committed atrocities against his friends and done unspeakable things; yet his own conscious mind had only stood aside and watched in horror. A demonic intelligence had taken over inside his skull and left him a helpless observer.

He wasn't unique. It was happening all over the world. Society was breaking down in an epidemic of crimes, vicious and senseless, and it would seem as if the world had been invaded by a legion of invisible devils from some interplanetary hell. There had to be a solution, and, when, at last, he found a clue, he set out to pursue it to the bitter end.

Logo No. 586. Barker, M.A.R. *The Man of Gold.* Code No. UE1940. First edition. First printing, July 1984. 367 pp. Cover art by Michael Whelan. $3.50.

Tekumel is a distant world populated by humans who had built up, over thousands of years, a vast and intricate civilization based upon a legion of gods and demons, upon the ways and wiles of alien races who dwelled among them, upon the layered traditions of monarchs, ancient, medieval, or still reigning. Tekumel is a world as real as Earth, where surprise and adventure are as natural as day or night.

(Bibliographer's note: Sub-titled *Tekumel: The Empire of the Petal Throne*, this is the novelization of a fantasy role-playing game created by the author, a professor at the University of Minnesota. Several pages at the end of the book comprise an informal glossary about the languages of the Five Empires.)

Logo No. 587. Purtill, Richard. *The Parallel Man.* Code No. UE1941. First edition. First printing, July 1984. 158 pp. Cover art by Ken W. Kelly. $2.50.

Being a clone can certainly have its advantages. For one thing, it's unlikely that someone would go to the trouble of cloning the average Joe on the street. It's more likely one would seek to duplicate a brilliant statesman, a scientific genius, a famous poet, me, or, perhaps, a legendary king, such as Stephen.

But, then again, being a clone can certainly have its problems. If someone sought to replicate a powerful person from history, it wouldn't be without a reason. There could be scores of Napoleons, dozens of Julius Caesars, or a Caligula or two. But if it was an evil sorcerer who cloned you, and you didn't know his motives, you could be the focal point of disaster.

Prince Casmir thought his life was challenging enough as it was, but, when he discovered the truth about himself, battling firedrakes seemed like child's play, and his life opened like a horrible Pandora's box. Once the secret was out, there was no end to the dangers which double-shadowed his every move!

Logo No. 588. Kapp, Colin. *Star-Search.* Code No. UE1942. First DAW printing, July 1984. 175 pp. Cover art by Vincent DiFate. Originally published by New English Library (1983). $2.50.

To see the stars. This was the great dream: to stand and look upward into space, at the myriad pin-points of light, just as their forebears on Earth had in the long gone days before the building of the planetary shells. Mars, Jupiter, Saturn; shell had succeeded shell, each studded with its captive caged worlds, each progressively populated by men who could look up only into a sky of artificial luminaries and space debris.

Always Zeus, man-created prime mover, was at work behind them, its giant space machines forming and working the next shell. Uranus, Neptune, Pluto. The last shell. Again they journeyed: Maq Ancor, Master Assassin, Magician Cherry and Sine Anura, Mistress of the Erotic, to reach the outer shell, to return to the past when men could see the stars.

(Bibliographer's note: Fourth book of the Cageworld series.)

Logo No. 589. Elgin, Suzette Haden. *Native Tongue.* Code No. UE1945. First edition. First printing, August 1984. 301 pp. Cover art by Jill Bauman. $3.50.

With the defeat of the Equal Rights Amendment in 1982, the women's movement received its first serious setback. In 1991, with the passage of the 25th Amendment, the women's movement received its death blow. That incredible amendment rolled back women's rights two hundred years and assured the supremacy of males in every aspect of life.

Logo No. 590. Shaw, Bob. *The Ceres Solution.* Code No. UE1946. First U.S. edition. First DAW printing, August 1984. 190 pp. Cover art by Vincent DiFate. Originally published in U.K. by Gollancz (1981). $2.95.

This is the story of the collision between two vastly different human civilizations. One is Earth in the early 21st Century, rushing toward self-inflicted nuclear doom. The other is the distant world of Mollan, whose inhabitants have achieved great longevity and the power to transport themselves instantly from star to star. On Earth's side is Denny Hargate, whose indomitable courage drives him to alter the course of history. On their side is Gretana ty litha, working on Earth as a secret observer, who dreams of returning to the delights of her world's high society, but who gets caught up in a cosmic chain of events leading to an explosive climax.

Logo No. 591. Shwartz, Susan ed. *Habitats.* Code No. UE1948. First edition. First printing, August 1984. 220 pp. Cover art by Robert Andre. $2.75.

Contents:

Introduction: There's No Place Like Home	Susan Shwartz
The Folks Who Live on the Hill	Stan Schmidt
A Day in the Skin (or, The Century We Were Out of Them)	Tanith Lee
We Remember Babylon	Ian Watson
In a Cavern	Dean R. Lambe
Government Work	Russell Griffin
"Outcasts"	Graham Diamond
Tree House	Rachel Pollack
Life-Tides	Jeffrey A. Carver
Quarantine	Scott Russell Sanders
Ramadhan	Shariann Lewitt
Earthflight	J.P. Boyd

Logo No. 592. Goulart, Ron. *Hellquad.* Code No. UE1949. First edition. First printing, August 1984. 158 pp. Cover art by Frank Kelly Freas. $2.50.

Years ago an infamous couple had been executed for selling solar secrets to an extra-galactic enemy. Then the sentence was reversed, and the victims resurrected. The two had stashed away a planet's ransom from their treason, and their heiress had long since disappeared with the loot. So Soldiers of Fortune, Inc. went to John Wesley Sand and asked him to find the missing maiden, who was last seen in the Hellquad sector.

To Sand, however, Hellquad meant, in his own words: "slavers, space pirates, welfs, mewts, madmen, psychotic cyborgs, lunatics at large, brokedown andies, lycanthropes, alfies, senile servos, zombies, the dregs of every other planet in the universe." But the money was too good to pass up, and Sand took the job and found everything he had expected, plus some mind-boggling things that he hadn't!

(Bibliographer's note: For some reason, Sand's description of Hellquad reminds me of a high school English class I once taught before going to law school.)

Logo No. 593. Cherryh, C.J. (pseud. Carolyn Janice Cherry). *Forty Thousand in Gehenna.* Code No. UE1952. First DAW printing, September 1984. 445 pp. Cover art by James Gurney; maps by David A. Cherry. Originally published by Phantasia Press (1983). $3.50.

The 40,000 colonists on Gehenna are abandoned for political reasons.

When the re-supply ships fail to arrive, the colony begins to collapse. Over a period of 200 years, the descendants of the colonists who couldn't impose Terran conditions on Gehenna become a part of Gehennan ecology themselves, by entering a partnership with the planet's intelligent natives, the lizardlike, burrowing calibans.

Logo No. 594. Asimov, Isaac and Martin H. Greenberg eds. *Isaac Asimov Presents the Great Science Fiction Stories 12 (1950).* Code No. UE1953. First edition. First printing, September 1984. 319 pp. Cover design by One Plus One Studio. Cover art by Dino Marsan. $3.50.

Contents:

Introduction

Not with a Bang	Damon Knight
Spectator Sport	John D. MacDonald
There Will Come Soft Rains	Ray Bradbury
Dear Devil	Eric Frank Russell
Scanners Live in Vain	Cordwainer Smith
Born of Man and Woman	Richard Matheson
The Little Black Bag	C.M. Kornbluth
Enchanted Village	A.E. van Vogt
Oddy and Id	Alfred Bester
The Sack	William Morrison
The Silly Season	C.M. Kornbluth
Misbegotten Missionary	Isaac Asimov
To Serve Man	Damon Knight
Coming Attraction	Fritz Leiber
A Subway Named Mobius	A.J. Deutsch
Process	A.E. van Vogt
The Mindworm	C.M. Kornbluth
The New Reality	Charles L. Harness

Logo No. 595. Shea, Michael. *The Color out of Time.* Code No. UE1954. First edition. First printing, September 1984. 189 pp. Cover art by Ken W. Kelly. $2.75.

There was something in that lake that was not of this world. A color, indescribable, outside the spectrum, impressed itself upon the eyes and minds of all who approached, and utter evil haunted the vicinity.

(Bibliographer's note: A sequel to H.P. Lovecraft's *The Colour out of Space,* in case you hadn't guessed, set in present-day New England.)

Logo No. 596. Tubb, E.C. *Symbol of Terra.* Code No. UE1955. First edition. First edition. First printing, September 1984. 237 pp. Cover art by Vincent DiFate. $2.75.

Clues from Angado, clues from the lady Govinda, clues of all types, all leading to the lost planet called Earth. But the clues all led first to a collector of ancient wisdom named Tama Chenault. For Dumarest, that was sufficient.

Chenault turned out to be a wily and eccentric man on a planet of feuding nobility. He had assembled a group of strange oddballs about him, he defied the customs of the entrenched powers, and he took Dumarest under his banner. He would reveal the whereabouts of Earth as the reward for Dumarest's allegiance.

Once again Dumarest was pitted against a doubting and hostile world. Once again he had the rare opportunity of winning for himself, not only life and safety, but the road to legendary Terra.

(Bibliographer's note: Number thirty in the saga of Dumarest of Terra.)

Logo No. 597. Saha, Arthur W. ed. *The Year's Best Fantasy Stories: 10.* Code No. UE1963. First edition. First printing, October 1984. 254 pp. Cover art by Jim Burns. $2.75.

Contents:

Introduction

Blue Vase of Ghosts	Tanith Lee
She Sells Sea Shells	Paul Darcy Boles
Green Roses	Larry Tritten
Wong's Lost and Found Emporium	William F. Wu
Huggins' World	Ennis Duling
The Curse of the Smalls and the Stars	Fritz Leiber
The Silent Cradle	Leigh Kennedy
Into Whose Hands	Karl Edward Wagner
Like a Black Dandelion	John Alfred Taylor
The Hills Behind Hollywood High	Avram Davidson & Grania Davis
Beyond the Dead Reef	James Tiptree, Jr.

Logo No. 598. Prescot, Dray (pseud. Kenneth Bulmer). *Seg the Bowman.* Code No. UE1965. First edition. First printing, October 1984. 255 pp. Cover art by Ken W. Kelly. $2.75.

A novel of Dray Prescot's fighting comrade, Seg, the finest archer of two worlds. Seg is a wild and reckless fellow, courageous in the face of any adversity, and this is the account of his greatest challenge. Single-handed, on an enemy island, Seg becomes knight-protector of the mysterious lady Milsi, and, by her side, beats off frightful beasts and inhuman foemen intent on blocking her path to a rightful royal inheritance.

(Bibliographer's note: Number thirty-two in the saga of Dray Prescot.)

Logo No. 599. Brunner, John. *Timescoop.* Code No. UE1966. First DAW printing, October 1984. 239 pp. Cover art by David A. Cherry. Published earlier in the U.S. by Dell (1969) and in the U.K. by Sidgwick & Jackson (1972). $2.50.

Freitas, master of a vast world-wide commercial empire, had commissioned his engineers to build him a device that could ransack the past. All the riches of the ages would be his for the taking, but riches alone were not what Freitas craved. He longed for supreme power, and, from the Pandora's Box of the past, he picked out the cunning men and women who could help him achieve absolute mastery over his rivals.

He hadn't counted on opposition, but there was a major frightening flaw in his scheme: the power these human monsters from the past would have over him; the reign of terror was about to begin.

Logo No. 600. Bradley, Marion Zimmer. *City of Sorcery.* Code No. UE1962. First edition. First printing, October 1984. 423 pp. Cover art by James Gurney. See *Anatomy of Wonder* 4-77 (1987). $3.50.

Haunted by mysterious images of dark, hooded figures and the cawing of strange birds, and drawn by the memory of two lost comrades, Magdalen Lorne, chief Terran operative on Darkover, must pursue her quest, not only to the frozen ends of the physical world, but the perilous limits of the spiritual overworld as well. To find this city that no man had seen, she would be tested as she had never been before, by the evil sorcery of the Dark Sisterhood!

(Bibliographer's note: In the Darkover chronology, this novel takes place approximately seven years after *Thendara House*, which, of course, was published by DAW Books only one year ago. You've been living for that bit of information, haven't you?)

Logo No. 601. Green, Sharon. *Mind Guest.* Code No. UE1973. First edition. First printing, November 1984. 415 pp. Cover art by Ken W. Kelly. $3.50.

Diana Santee woke to find herself helpless on a starcraft bound for nowhere with all its controls destroyed. Beyond all known space, she was saved by the secret outpost of an undiscovered star federation. They needed a girl like her for a desperate mission on a medieval world they were secretly probing. She fit the bill; she volunteered in gratitude.

When she became the unwanted mind guest of a terrified virgin princess, it went beyond anything her space agent training had prepared her for. She had been betrayed into the clutches of a slavery out of the darkest days of a primitive past.

(Bibliographer's note: First book about Diana Santee, Spaceways Agent.)

Logo No. 602. Clayton, Jo. *The Snares of Ibex.* Code No. UE1974. First edition. First printing, November 1984. 320 pp. Cover art by Segrelles. $2.95.

Aletys had searched for her mother across the worlds of the inhabited galaxy. Her mother was of a super-race; her homeworld's location was a secret. But Aletys had become a super star hunter, alert to clues and wary of danger, and she knew that, on Ibex, her ancestral trail must reach its end.

Ibex was an unmapped world banned to outsiders, save for one encircled city. To venture beyond that enclave meant death, for the many alien native tribes were united only in their lust to slay all other-worlders. All the snares of Ibex awaited Aletys beyond the wall, but dare she must if her life were to have any future meaning.

(Bibliographer's note: Eighth book of the Diadem series.)

Logo No. 603. Wagner, Karl Edward ed. *The Year's Best Horror Stories: Series XII.* Code No. UE1975. First edition. First printing, November

1984. 239 pp. Cover art by Segrelles. $2.95.

Contents:

Introduction: Of Fads and Frights	Karl Edward Wagner
Uncle Otto's Truck	Stephen King
3.47 AM	David Langford
Mistral	Jon Wynne-Tyson
Out of Africa	David Drake
The Wall-Painting	Roger Johnson
Keepsake	Vincent McHardy
Echoes	Lawrence C. Connolly
After-Images	Malcolm Edwards
The Ventriloquist's Daughter	Juleen Brantingham
Come to the Party	Frances Garfield
The Chair	Dennis Etchison
Names	Jane Yolen
The Attic	Billy Wolfenbarger
Just Waiting	Ramsey Campbell
One for the Horrors	David J. Schow
Elle Est Trois (La Mort)	Tanith Lee
Spring-Fingered Jack	Susan Casper
The *Flash!* Kid	Scott Bradfield
The Man with Legs	Al Sarrantonio

Logo No. 604. Barrett, Neal Jr. *The Karma Corps.* Code No. UE1976. First edition. First printing, November 1984. 239 pp. Cover art by Les Edwards. $2.75.

Captain Lars Haggart was a soul waiting to be reborn, but, before that blessed event, he had been inducted into the Arm of God Regiment fighting for the Beleaguered Churchers on a newly colonized planet. Their foe were demons who could pop into existence, slay, and pop out of existence the next instant. The demons were winning that war, sending their unborn opponents back to limbo, driving the living colonists back toward extermination.

But this was no fantasy, no business of the religious imagination. The fight was real, blood was blood, and swords cut sharp, for the Unborn were very much alive. Haggart was aware that this was frighteningly contradictory, but, first, he had to fight the demons on their own terms. He had to learn how to appear behind their lines and do to them what they were doing to the humans.

Logo No. 605. Steakley, John. *Armor.* Code No. UE1979. First edition. First printing, December 1984. 426 pp. Cover art by James Gurney. $3.95.

The planet was called simply A-9. The air was unbreathable, the water poisonous. But it had to be conquered, for it was the home world of the most implacable enemies that cosmically expanding humanity had yet encountered.

Body armor had been devised for the commando forces that were to be dropped on A-9, the culmination of ten thousand years of the armorers' craft. A man in that armor would be stronger than a 20th Century tank force. But the enemy had a weapon that was its equal: sheer murderous attack by a horde of thousands of antlike, almost unkillable, beings. Yet there is more to war than battle; there is always the question of the human being within the armor.

Logo No. 606. Lichtenberg, Jacqueline. *RenSime*. Code No. UE1980. First DAW printing, December 1984. 251 pp. Cover art by Jill Bauman. Originally published by Doubleday (1984). $2.95.

Humanity had mutated into two branches: the Simes who must prey on the Gens to survive; the Gens whose bodily energies alone could feed the Simes. Laneff Farris had thought herself an in-between, until the unforgettable day she changed over into Sime form, and, in the energy hunger that overcame her, killed the two who had tried to help her.

When she finally overcame her murderous lust for life-energy, she dedicated herself to finding a way to reunite humanity. Through her biochemical researches, she believed she had found the answers. If her findings were right, it would mean the end of the world's division. But was the world itself ready for this? Extremists said no, and, to prove it, they intrigued to have Laneff kill again. Publicly.

(Bibliographer's note: Sixth Sime/Gen novel. Also contains, as an appendix, a chronology of the Sime/Gen Universe.)

Logo No 607. Carter, Lin. *Dragonrouge*. Code No. UE1982. First edition. First printing, December 1984. 222 pp. Cover art and frontispiece by Ken W. Kelly. $2.50.

Come with us out of this dull, workaday world to Terra Magica, the land beyond the World's Edge, where knights ride out on wonder quests, where beautiful princesses wait for rescue from sea serpents and lustful demons, where sky-high giants seek human morsels for their cookpots, and where a king may seek a champion to set aside his realm's enchantment.

Here again is Kesrick, knight of Dragonrouge, in combat against villainy; at his side the unclothed Scythian princess and a lost nobleman of Tartary. Here be wizards of good and wizards of evil; here be mighty giants and witches of utter meanness. Here be high fantasy.

(Bibliographer's note: Here be Lin Carter with the sequel to *Kesrick*, another "adult fantasy" set on Terra Magica.)

Logo No. 608. Franklin, H. Bruce ed. *Countdown to Midnight*. Code No. UE1983. First edition. First printing, December 1984. 287 pp. Cover art by Vincent DiFate. $2.95.

Contents:

Introduction: Nuclear War and Science Fiction	H. Bruce Franklin
To Still the Drums	Chandler Davis
Thunder and Roses	Theodore Sturgeon
That Only a Mother	Judith Merril
Lot	Ward Moore
I Kill Myself	Julian Kawalec

The Neutrino Bomb	Ralph S. Cooper
Akua Nuten (The South Wind)	Yves Theriault
I Have No Mouth, and I Must Scream	Harlan Ellison
Countdown	Kate Wilhelm
The Big Flash	Norman Spinrad
Everything But Love	Mikhail Yemstev and
	Eremei Parnov
To Howard Hughes: A Modest Proposal	Joe Haldeman

(Bibliographer's note: The copyright page says that this is DAW Collectors' Book No. 600. That's wrong. It's 608. I'm right. Trust me.)

Logo No 609. Cherryh, C.J. (pseud. Carolyn Janice Cherry). *Chanur's Venture*. Code No. UE1989. First DAW printing, January 1985. 312 pp. Cover art and frontispiece by Michael Whelan. Map by David A. Cherry. Originally published by Phantasia Press (1984). $2.95.

Pyanfur Chanur thought she had seen the last of Tully, the lone human who had so disrupted the peace of Meetpoint Station and gained the Chanur Clan the enmity of half a dozen races as well as their own. Yet Tully has returned, bringing with him a priceless trade contract with human space. The contract would mean vast power, riches, and a new hornet's nest for Pyanfur and *The Pride!*

(Bibliographer's note: A longish appendix detailing the Species of the Compact concludes the book.)

Logo No. 610. Gaskell, Jane. *The Serpent*. Code No. UE1990. First DAW printing, January 1985. 320 pp. Cover art by James Gurney. Published earlier in U.K. by Hodder & Stoughton (1963) and in U.S. by St. Martin's Press (1977). $2.95.

In the time-lost world of pre-history, a girl was born to the Dictatress. Was she a goddess? Cija herself believed she was. For seventeen years, her mother had kept her imprisoned in a tower. She released her with one object in view: as a tool to seduce Zerd, the half-man, half-serpent lord of an invading army.

Cija goes off with Zerd to attempt the conquest of fabled Atlantis and enters upon a series of startling adventures that force her into many roles: princess and camp follower, scullion and empress, slave, cook, and heroine warrior.

(Bibliographer's note: The first book of the Atlan saga.)

Logo No. 611. Prescot, Dray (pseud. Kenneth Bulmer). *Werewolves of Kregen*. Code No. UE1991. First edition. First printing, January 1985. 220 pp. Cover art by Richard Hescox. $2.50.

Dray Prescot is an Earthman, seaman and soldier, brought across four hundred light years to a planet of Antares. The Star Lords, a race advanced beyond our ken, needed him on that world called Kregen.

Now, having at last returned to his home empire, to his wife and friends, Dray was to learn that the vengeance of his defeated enemies had launched a final assault, with nine occult curses, against Vallia and all that

Dray held dear. The first curse, the plague of murderous werewolves, took Dray by surprise. Could his valor and courage, though tempered on the battlefields of alien suns, stand up against an unprecedented onslaught of warring witchcraft?

(Bibliographer's note: Thirty-third in the saga of Dray Prescot; the first novel of the Witch War Cycle.)

Logo No. 612. Foster, M.A. *Owl Time*. Code No. UE1992. First edition. First printing, January 1985. 251 pp. Cover art by Frank Kelly Freas. $2.95.

Contents:

The Man Who Loved Owls	The Conversation
Leanne	Entertainment

(Bibliographer's note: Four short novels following an interesting explanatory preface by the author. This is important, so pay attention. "The Man Who Loved Owls" is intended to suggest J.G. Ballard. "Leanne" is after Ray Bradbury or Harlan Ellison—the reader's choice. "The Conversation" reflects a mix of Jorge Borges, Vladimir Nabokov and Franz Kafka. "Entertainment" is intended to emulate Jack Vance. Interesting concept.)

Logo No. 613. Clayton, Jo. *A Bait of Dreams*. Code No. UE2001. First edition. First printing, February 1985. 404 pp. Cover by Ken W. Kelly. $3.50.

They called the gems Ranga Eyes. They were beautiful crystals, cool and smooth. They opened doorways to magical realms, leading to escape, happiness, peace. But they exacted a terrible price, since they were a terrible narcotic. After only a single use, they dragged you in and sucked your soul dry, leaving you to lingering death.

Where did they come from? And what really were they? For Gleia, Shounach, and Deel, it had become a matter of desperate urgency, for each had lost someone to the Eyes, someone they couldn't forget. For them, the source of these damnable jewels must be found and destroyed. Otherwise, the Ranga Eyes would destroy them and all their world.

Logo No. 614. Llewellyn, Edward (pseud. Edward Llewellyn-Thomas). *Fugitive in Transit*. First edition. First printing, February 1985. 302 pp. Cover art by Tim Jacobus. $2.95.

When Peter Ward saw the lone woman standing in the ruins of an obscure temple on a remote Greek island and singing Sappho in the original Aeolic Greek, he may have thought her a goddess, but he would never even have imagined her true identity. Ruth Thalia Adams was a singular entity. Although she appeared as a beautiful, athletic young woman, no one was even sure of her species.

"Alia," as she was called by the Galactic Transit Authorities, had more mysteries than just her species. No one on Earth knew what it was she had done, but, to the Auld Galactic Marshal, she was the most dangerous individual in the spiral arm and had to be caught.

He had chased her through several hundred worlds to no avail, but now he had her cornered, for Earth was the end of the line!

(Bibliographer's note: The author's last book, published posthumously following his death on July 5, 1984.)

Logo No. 615. Lee, Tanith. *The Gorgon and Other Beastly Tales.* Code No. UE2003. First edition. First printing, February 1985. 288 pp. Cover art by Victoria Poyser. $2.95.

Contents:

The Gorgon	Sirriamnis
Anna Medea	Because Our Skins Are Finer
Meow	Quatt-Sup
The Hunting of Death: The Unicorn	Draco Draco
Magritte's Secret Agent	La Reine Blanche
Money's Stagger	

(Bibliographer's note: The title story, "The Gorgon," was the winner of the World Fantasy Award for the best short story of the year.)

Logo No. 616. Young, Robert F. *The Vizier's Second Daughter.* Code No. UE2004. First edition. First printing, February 1985. 203 pp. Cover art by Sanjulian. $2.95.

They sent him into the past to kidnap and bring back Sheherazade, the famous narrator of the Thousand and One Nights. But when he had grabbed a lovely lady out of the Sultan's harem and scooted away on his "magic carpet" time machine, he discovered that he had muffed it, for she was the Vizier's second daughter, Sheherazade's kid sister!

He thought he could rectify that mistake before going back to the 21st Century, but it was already too late, because the ifrits were hot on his trail. Ali Baba had jumped aboard, and the enchanted Castle of Brass awaited his arrival with ghoulish glee.

Logo No. 617. Norman, John (pseud. John Lange). *Mercenaries of Gor.* Code No. UE2018. First edition. First printing, March 1985. 446 pp. Cover art by Ken W. Kelly. $3.95.

War on Gor is a rousing and fearful affair, and, when the armada of Cos landed and began its sweeping arch against the mighty city of Ar, Tarl Cabot was swept up in their drive. Outcast from Port Kar, rejected by the Priest-Kings, Tarl fought now for his own redemption. With comrades at his side, barbarian warriors and daring women, free and slave, his plans went forward, until the mercenaries of Dietrich of Tarnburg disrupted the struggle as a mysterious third force.

(Bibliographer's note: The 21st book of the Tarl Cabot saga.)

Logo No. 618. Hoppe, Stephanie T. *The Windrider.* Code No. UE2020. First edition. First printing, March 1985. 253 pp. Cover art by Les Edwards. $2.95.

Oa had been the prime contender for the throne of Dynast, closer than all the other heirs to holding the reins of Empire, and all the power, intrigue, luxury and illusion that went with them. Then the reigning

Dynast put an insurmountable obstacle in her path; she must kill her true love in the deadly High Dance or forsake her life's ambition.

Avoiding her fate and fleeing downriver to the unknown lands of the west, Oa finds herself on a high plateau where those with power ride remarkable beasts whose soaring flight is like the primeval rush of the wind itself, and whose riders sail between earth and sky. Oa knows that she would fight any battle and face any odds to feel the freedom of speed and space on the untamed back of a Windsteed!

(Bibligrapher's note: The author's first novel.)

Logo No. 619. Gaskell, Jane. *The Dragon.* Code No. UE2021. First DAW printing, March 1985. 240 pp. Cover art by James Gurney. Originally published as part of *The Serpent* by Hodder & Stoughton (1963). Reprinted as a separate title in the U.S. by St. Martin's Press (1977). $2.95.

They called him the Dragon, that blue-skinned semi-human named Zerd. Zerd was indeed the Dragon General whose armies had ravaged Cija's homeland, and who was now preparing his legions to conquer the fabled land beyond the horizon known as Atlan. Cija, girl of fate, loved, loathed, cherished, enslaved, who, even as a child, had tasted all that primeval mankind had to offer from the best to the worst; it was to be Cija who would decide the Dragon's quest: to save Atlan or attend its fall. Fate decreed that Cija would be the instrument of its destiny.

(Bibliographer's note: The second book of the Atlan saga.)

Logo No. 620. Killough, Lee. *Liberty's World.* Code No. UE2023. First edition. First printing, March 1985. 238 pp. Cover art by Segrelles. $2.95.

The planet seemed like salvation for the dying colony ship, *Invictus*, except, within a day of landing, the colonists found the world to be inhabited and themselves caught between two opposing cannibalistic armies. For Liberty Ibarra, who learned languages fast, the situation called for courage, tact, and a blind faith in the aliens' envoy, the brother of the enigmatic emperor, until she learned that her "friend" was also a political schemer with a talent for assassination. Then it began to look as though the humans had dived over the edge of the pan straight into the fire.

(Bibliographer's note: The author's first novel under the DAW imprint.)

Logo No. 621. Brunner, John. *Age of Miracles.* Code No. UE2024. First DAW printing, March 1985. 238 pp. Cover art by Thomas Kidd. Originally published as *The Day of the Star Cities* by Ace Books (1965). Published in U.K. as *Age of Miracles* by Sidgwick & Jackson (1973) and in the U.S. by Ace (1973) in revised form. $2.95.

When the aliens came to Earth, they didn't make contact with its inhabitants. Instead, they set up, overnight, vast shining cities like mountainous gems whose borders men couldn't penetrate, and where nations' bombs and weapons could do no damage. In the impact of these incredible invaders, the world's governments fell apart, and new, ganglike regimes arose.

Reduced to helplessness on what was once their world, men struggle to find a different way of life, free of war, free of national enmities and united only by a burning desire to share in the interstellar Age of Miracles.

Logo No. 622. Shaw, Bob. *Orbitsville Departure.* Code No. UE2030. First U.S. and first paperback edition. First DAW printing, April 1985. 252 pp. Cover art by Bob Eggleton. Originally published in U.K. by Gollancz (1983).

Orbitsville was an artificial world of immense size, built as a shell enclosing its sun, with a landmass equal to five billion Earths. In the two hundred years that passed after its discovery, the majority of the human race had emigrated there.

The question still remained: who built Orbitsville and why? For Garry Dallen back on the semi-deserted Earth, this was to become the ultimate answer to his personal quest for vengeance, a quest which took him across space to confront a cosmic enigma.

(Bibliographer's note: The sequel to *Orbitsville*, winner of the British Science Fiction Award.)

Logo No. 623. Chandler, A. Bertram. *The Wild Ones.* Code No. UE2031. First edition. First printing, April 1985. 253 pp. Cover art by Ken W. Kelly. $2.95.

They called the robomaid "Clockwork Kitty," until she informed them of her right name. She was a triumph of Japan's far-future robotics industry, and she was a present to John Grimes as he set out aboard *Sister Sue* for a voyage to the planet called New Salem.

New Salem was a colony of blue-nosed religious fanatics, and Grimes knew it meant trouble. For, in addition to his sexy-looking robot, he had Shirl and Darleen aboard, two wild ones of Kangaroo ancestry, sure to be problems. As expected, trouble came, not merely from the fire-wielding bigots, but from Grimes' old enemy, Drongo Kane.

(Bibliographer's note: The author died June 6, 1984, shortly after mailing this manuscript to his American agents. Therefore, this is the last John Grimes novel.)

Logo No. 624. Prescot, Dray (pseud. Kenneth Bulmer). *Witches of Kregen.* Code No. UE2032. First edition. First printing, April 1985. 223 pp. Cover art by James Gurney. $2.75.

When his new army was ready to march against the witch hordes, it rained frogs! It was a veritable heavy bombardment from empty skies! That's the sort of thing Dray Prescot was up against during the war of the Nine Unspeakable Curses!

Dray was struggling to gather together his shattered empire when the witchcraft hit. He had wizards on his side, too, and, very soon, it became a battle of sheer courage, quick wits, and fast flying. This was more to the ex-Earthman's liking, for he knew that, this time, the Star Lords might be on his side. Not that he could rely on them, for they were just as likely to toss him back to Earth for a crash course in the old world's learning!

(Bibliographer's note: The thirty-fourth Dray Prescot novel, and the second in the Witch War Cycle.)

Logo No. 625. Walther, Daniel. *Shai's Destiny.* **Code No. UE2033. First edition. First printing, April 1985. 223 pp. Cover art by Richard Hescox. Translated by C.J. Cherryh. Original edition titled** *Le Destiny de Swa* **and published by Editions Fleuve Noir, Paris, France (1982). $2.75.**

"Arise, Wind of Darkness! Cone to me, Wind of Night! Come to me shadow and fire, poison, cold, bile and blood!"

And the nightwind answered, for he was the fighting arm of the Great Serpent, the guardian of hateful tradition. His army stirred and marched. Their quarry was the traitor who had swept away the ashes of the old world and who sought to raise a new and cleaner order amidst the ruins of the ancient disasters. Shai was his name.

(Bibliographer's note: The second book of Shai.)

Logo No. 626. Green, Sharon. *The Will of the Gods.* **Code No. UE2039. First edition. First printing, May 1985. 383 pp. Cover art by Ken W. Kelly. $3.50.**

To alert her world to the coming of the strangers from space, the gods had given Jalav the mission to bring truce between the men of the cities and the women of the plains. Now she must venture among the latter, herself a war chief of the Midanna, going among her tribal enemies, the amazons of the feuding clans. But go she must, and behind her came the macho warriors of Sigurr whom she thought she had tamed, but whose real intentions were an unsuspected secret!

(Bibliographer's note: Fourth book in the Jalav, Amazon Warrior, series.)

Logo No. 627. Moorcock, Michael. *Elric at the End of Time.* **Code No. UE2040. First DAW printing, May 1985. 221 pp. Cover art by Michael Whelan. $2.95.**

Contents:

Introduction	Sojan the Swordsman
Elric	Jerry Cornelius and Co.
Elric at the End of Time	New Worlds—Jerry Cornelius
The Last Enchantment	In Lighter Vein
The Secret Life of Elric of Melnibone	The Stone Thing

(Bibliographer's note: Although somewhat disguised as a novel, as publishers are wont to do, even fine ones like DAW Books, for the reason that novels sell better than collections or anthologies, this book collects previously published, but uncollected, fiction and non-fiction, not all of which involves Elric.)

Logo No. 628. Bradley, Marion Zimmer ed. *Sword and Sorceress II.* **Code No. UE2041. First edition. First printing, May 1985. 287 pp. Cover art by Ilene Meyer. $2.95.**

Contents:

A Night at Two Inns	Phyliss Ann Karr

The Red Guild	Rachel Pollack
Shadow Wood	Diana Paxson
Unicorn's Blood	Bruce D. Arthurs
The Unshadowed Land	C.J. Cherryh
Shimenege's Mask	Charles Saunders
The Black Tower	Stephen Burns
The Lady and the Tiger	Jennifer Roberson
Fireweb	Deborah Wheeler
Cold Blows the Wind	Charles de Lint
Sword of the Mother	Dana Kramer Rolls
Hunger	Russ Garrison
On First Looking into Bradley's Guidelines, or Stories I Don't Want to Read Either	Elizabeth Thompson
The Chosen Maiden	Paul Reyes
Red Pearls	Richard Corwin
Wound on the Moon	Vera Nazarian

Logo No. 629. Goulart, Ron. *Brainz, Inc.* Code No. UE2402. First edition. First printing, May 1985. 205 pp. Cover art by Tim Jacobus. $2.75.

Sylvie Kirkyard was co-owner of Brainz, Inc., makers of the world's finest androids. So when she was murdered, she came directly to Odd Jobs, Inc. to find out who had done it. It seems that her firm had perfected a personality chip that guaranteed immortality, and that her own android was now her.

For Hildy and Jake Pace, it wasn't all that simple. How do you prove the second Sylvie was legally the first? How do you find out what super-whiz had penetrated Brainz's secrets and aimed for life-and-death control? How do you stay alive when the billion-dollar firm was bent on wiping out your own tapes?

(Bibliographer's note: Another odd job for Odd Jobs, Inc.)

Logo No. 630. Wollheim, Donald A. with Arthur W. Saha eds. *The 1985 Annual World's Best SF.* Code No. UE2047. First edition. First printing, June 1985. 302 pp. Cover art by Frank Kelly Freas. $2.95.

Contents:

Introduction	The Editor
The Picture Man	John Dalmas
Cash Crop	Connie Willis
We Remember Babylon	Ian Watson
What Makes Us Human	Stephen R. Donaldson
Salvador	Lucius Shepard
Press Enter	John Varley
The Aliens Who Knew, I Mean, *Everything*	George Alec Effinger
Bloodchild	Octavia E. Butler
The Coming of the Goonga	Gary W. Shockley
Medra	Tanith Lee

Logo No. 631. Sladek, John. *Tik-Tok.* Code No. UE2048. First DAW printing, June 1985. 254 pp. Cover art by Peter Gudynas. Originally published in U.K. by Gollancz (1983). $2.95.

"A robot shall not injure a human being, or through inaction allow a human being to come to harm." —Asimov's First Law of Robotics

Tik-Tok was one of the finest domestic robots ever made, but his asimov circuits were defective. He could injure people as much as he pleased, and he pleased to do it often. But the life of a robot (if that isn't a contradiction) is still all service and unpaid labor. Tik-Tok served many masters, all of whom came to a bad end. Happily he went on gathering steam with a trail of catastrophes getting bigger and bigger, destined to culminate with his campaign for the vice-presidency of the United States.

Logo No. 632. Gaskell, Jane. *Atlan*. Code No. UE2049. First DAW printing, June 1985. 334 pp. Cover art by James Gurney. Originally published in the U.K. by Hodder & Stoughton (1965). First U.S. edition published by St. Martin's Press (1977). See Schlobin *The Literature of Fantasy* 691 (1979). $3.50.

A goddess. So Cija believed herself to be.

A hostage. Delivered over to the great Dragon-General Zerd.

A fugitive. Fleeing from Zerd's clutches with the help of her lover.

An empress. Wedded to Zerd, conqueror and lord in the fabled land of Atlan.

Again Cija is plunged into peril as war blazes across the secret continent, and Zerd must fight to keep his captive land, while the women in his life conspire against him. But the enchanted land plots its own magic to bring the moment when Ancient Atlan will wake to rid itself of the invaders.

(Bibliographer's note: Second part of the Atlan saga as originally published in the U.K., but the third book as reprinted in the U.S.)

Logo No. 633. Carter, Lin. *Found Wanting*. Code No. UE2050. First edition. First printing, June 1985. 220 pp. Cover art by Tim Jacobus. $2.75.

He knew his name, Kyon. He wore the garb of a gardener; therefore, he was a gardener. But that was all he knew. The city was a maze of wonders and terrors. The people were strangers, condescending and sometimes spiteful. Kyon had to do something, to go somewhere, but none would tell him. And it was important!

Urbs, the ultimate city, was on the scales of history. It would be up to Kyon whether all it represented, the flowering of science, would be found wanting.

Logo No. 634. Van Vogt, A.E. *Null-A Three*. Code No. UE2056. First edition. First printing, July 1985. 254 pp. Cover art by Tim Jacobus. Also published in U.K. by Sphere (1985). $3.50.

Gilbert Gosseyn, the man with the extra brain who staved off disaster for the Solar System, is launched on his greatest challenge, a showdown with the originators of cosmic civilization.

(Bibliographer's note: This book is the third and last book in the Null-A

˒ universe sequence, that began with *The World of Null-A*, which first appeared in *Astounding Stories* in 1945 as a three-part serial.)

Logo No. 635. Roberson, Jennifer. *The Song of Homana*. Code No. UE2057. First edition. First printing, July 1985. 352 pp. Cover art by James Gurney. $3.50.

For five long years, the land of Homana had been strangling in the grasp of a usurper king. Its people were ravaged by strife, poverty and despair, and its magical race, the Cheysuli, had been forced to flee or face extermination at the hands of their evil counterparts, the sorcerous Ilhini.

The time had come for Prince Carillon, Homana's rightful ruler, to return from exile with his Cheysuli shapechanger liege man, free his land from the evil domination of the tyrant Bellam and his villainous magicians, restore the Cheysuli to their rightful position of grace, and claim his birthright. To do this, he would not only have to raise an army, but overcome the fear and prejudice of an ignorant population and answer the call of a prophecy he never chose to serve.

(Bibliographer's note: Book two of the Chronicles of the Cheysuli.)

Logo No. 636. Asimov, Isaac and Martin H. Greenberg eds. *Isaac Asimov Presents the Great Science Fiction Stories 13 (1951)*. Code No. UE2058. First edition. First printing, July 1985. 337 pp. Cover design by One Plus One Studio. Cover art by Cesare Reggiani. $3.50.

Contents:

Null-P	William Tenn
The Sentinel	Arthur C. Clarke
The Fire Balloons	Ray Bradbury
The Marching Morons	C.M. Kornbluth
The Weapon	Fredric Brown
Angel's Egg	Edgar Pangborn
"Breeds There a Man—"	Isaac Asimov
Pictures Don't Lie	Katherine MacLean
Superiority	Arthur C. Clarke
I'm Scared	Jack Finney
The Quest for St. Aquin	Anthony Boucher
Tiger by the Tail	Alan E. Nourse
With These Hands	C.M. Kornbluth
A Pail of Air	Fritz Leiber
Dune Roller	Julian May

Logo No. 637. Tubb, E.C. *The Temple of Truth*. Code No. UE2059. First edition. First printing, July 1985. 222 pp. Cover art by Ken W. Kelly. $2.95.

The quest for lost Earth had taken Earl Dumarest across the galaxy and through numerous perilous worlds. People scoffed at the legend of Terra. There were no records of it. Still, he hunted for the astronomical data that could take him to that mythical place from which a thousand colonized planets had originated.

In relentless pursuit of Earl, seeking the body-switching formula which would make them masters of the universe, came the emotionless minions of the Cyclan, determined to seize Dumarest alive to gain his secret.

It all came together on the world of the Guardians, where, in the great temple of their fanatic faith, the true whereabouts of Earth was listed. There, the Cyclan and Dumarest struggled together, while the fate of all humanity hung in the balance.

(Bibliographer's note: Thirty-first book in the saga of Dumarest of Terra.)

Logo No. 638. Clayton, Jo. *Changer's Moon.* Code No. UE2065. First edition. First printing, August 1985. 352 pp. Cover art by Jody Lee. $3.50.

The two contenders tossed the dice for the final contest. The Noris drew the Runner, the Sword, the Sorcerer, the Eye. He was pleased. The armies could march. The valley and all that was in it would be his.

The Indweller drew the Kingfisher, the Poet-warrior, the Priestess, the Magic Child. "The mix as before," she said, "but with a change." She pointed to the priestess. She still had a chance. And the chance was Serroi, once the puppet of the Noris, now moving through the people like an electric current, against the patriarchs, to serve the Changer, for the Coyote was the one who could alter the rules; who could make the incredible credible and the impossible possible.

(Bibliographer's note: The final novel of the Duel of Sorcery trilogy.)

Logo No. 639. Chandler, A. Bertram. *Kelly Country.* Code No. UE2066. First U.S edition. First DAW printing, August 1985. 348 pp. Cover art by Ken W. Kelly. Originally published in Australia by Penguin (1983). $3.50.

The United States won its independence in 1776, and the world has never been the same since. What if Australia had followed suit? How would our world have been different? In the famous outlaw, Ned Kelly, was there the possibility of an Australian George Washington?

Ned Kelly wasn't just a lawless bushranger. He was a man of unusual imagination who created his own armor, gathered a band of Irish rebels, and took arms against the frontier law of old Australia. Now, by time machine and calculated interference, a certain 20th Century John Grimes goes back and alters history. Kelly survives! Kelly utilizes the hidden discoveries of science, and an Australian-Irish Republic arises Down Under.

(Bibliographer's note: An If-of-History novel.)

Logo No. 640. Bayley, Barrington J. *The Forest of Peldain.* Code No. UE2068. First edition. First printing, August 1985. 223 pp. Cover art by Ken W. Kelly. $2.75.

Life wasn't possible on that watery world, except on the Hundred Islands. The Empire of Arelia ruled them all—all except one. Peldain was entirely covered with a forest so impenetrable and so deadly that all attempts to explore it were disastrous. Then a man came out of that jungle, a human, who told the Arelians that, at the center of the island, a secret kingdom flourished.

There was nothing for it but to organize an expedition. However deadly the alien forest might be, if one man could get out, an army could get in. So Lord Vorduthe landed and began the assault on the great green enemy. Nobody could have foreseen the horrors with which the forest defended itself. Nobody could have foreseen the price that would be paid by Vorduthe's men. Only Vorduthe, himself, would learn the incredible secret of the island, if his mind could stand it!

Logo No. 641. Prescot, Dray (pseud. Kenneth Bulmer). *Storm Over Vallia.* Code No. UE2069. First edition. First printing, August 1985. 254 pp. Cover art by Tim Jacobus. $2.95.

Drak, Crown Prince of Vallia, Dray Prescot's son, was sore beset on three sides. For one, he was leading an army of liberation against the usurper Alloran who had seized part of Vallia, and who was grinding Drak's troops down with blackest magic and most villainous mercenaries.

For two, he was the target of a marriage plot by an allied queen, whose forces he needed desperately.

For the third, he was in love with Silda, daughter of his father's loyal friend, Seg the Bowman. But Silda was even now in Alloran's camp, a black-leather swordswoman commanding the usurper's do-or-die Amazon guards.

Magic, mystery, treason, warfare and romance make a heady concoction, and, before this adventure was over, Drak would have his fill of it all.

(Bibliographer's note: Thirty-fifth tale in the Dray Prescot saga.)

Logo No. 642. Bradley, Marion Zimmer. *Warrior Woman.* Code No. UE2075. First edition. First printing, September 1985. 205 pp. Cover art by James Gurney. $2.95.

They called her Zadieyek of Gyre, which meant "dreaded woman." She was a fighter, dangerous to confront. Dreaded. The distant city of Gyre trained such women, so they thought she came from there and called her Zadieyek of Gyre.

If she had a real name and a true birthplace, she couldn't remember them. Her life had apparently begun with her sale to the Arena for a brief stardom fighting vicious men and savage beasts. Because she was truly a skilled gladiator, she became an object of value. Bids were made for her body, by those who wanted a winner or a valued slave. For herself, she was determined to get to Gyre, to find her freedom and her heritage. This is her story, a mystery of fiery passions, of fierce conflict and forbidden ambitions, and the flickering memory of alien wonders and unearthly things.

Logo No. 643. Barker, M.A.R. *Flamesong.* Code No. UE2076. First edition. First printing, September 1985. 412 pp. Cover art by Richard Hescox. $3.50.

This novel is the chronicle of a commander of the Petal Throne and what occurred when he captured a high-ranking woman officer of the enemy, who was in possession of a horrendous weapon from the forgotten ages of the past. Isolated in the uncharted subterranean speedways of that past, they are forced to travel together to unknown lands and undiscovered monster species, taking with them the means of their doom and the means of their mutually exclusive rewards.

(Bibliographer's note: The second in the series of Tekumel, the Empire of the Petal Throne, the novelization of the detailed role-playing game devised by the author.)

Logo No. 644. Steele, Linda. *Ibis*. Code No. UE2077. First edition. First printing, September 1985. 221 pp. Cover art by J. Chiodo. See *Anatomy of Wonder* 4-535 (1987). $2.95.

When Padrec Morrissey and the crew of his Planetary Exploration ship crashlanded on Ibis 2, they realized quickly that they weren't the first human ship to have landed there. The native Ibisians were not only sentient, but strangely human. However, unlike most of the early colonies, the denizens of Ibis deviated widely from the mammalian norm.

The natives displayed a highly organized societal behavior like that of certain Terran insects, and their behavior mirrored their physiological changes. As in a beehive, 95% of Ibisians were neuter, workers or warriors. Very few were truly male or female, and, of these, only the true females, the "Queens," were intelligent.

Padrec faced a triple problem: how to explain to his "queen" captor that he was an individual; how to escape a future of mindless hive servitude; and how to save his crewmen's lives.

(Bibliographer's note: The author's first novel.)

Logo No. 645. Clough, B.W. *The Dragon of Mishbil*. Code No. UE2078. First edition. First printing, September 1985. 189 pp. Cover art by Segrelles. $2.95.

The trouble with the city of Mishbil was water, for the city got its life from the waters of the Dragon, and the Dragon was under an enchantment.

Zaryas was the Shan King's viceroy in Mishbil and called upon the great magician Xerlanthor to set the Dragon right. Xerlanthor, however, had schemes of his own and, besides, wasn't much on hydromancy. So, when he set the Dragon wild, and Zaryas saw her city going underwater, she realized this would cost her her head! As for Xerlanthor, his double-game was working out just fine, for a black magician.

But, in the land of Averidan, nothing works out the way it's planned, especially under the high fantasy reign of the Crystal Crown.

(Bibliographer's note: The author has included a one page appendix in explanation of the breakdown of the Viridese year. Why?)

Logo No. 646. Cherryh, C.J. (pseud. Carolyn Janice Cherry). *Cuckoo's Egg*. Code No. UE2083. First DAW printing, October 1985. 319 pp. Cover art by Michael Whelan. Originally published by Phantasia Press (1985). See *Anatomy of Wonder* 4-127 (1987). $3.50.

They named him Thorn. They told him he was of their people, although he was so different. He was ugly in their eyes, strange, sleek-skinned instead of furred, clawless, different. Yet he was of their power class: judge-warriors, the elite, the fighters, the defenders.

Thorn knew that his difference was somehow very important, but not important enough to prevent murderous conspiracies against him, against his protector, against his caste, and, perhaps, the peace of the world. But when the crunch came, when Thorn finally learned what his true role in life was to be, that on him might hang the future of two worlds, then he had to stand alone to justify his very existence.

(Bibliographer's note: This novel was also a selection of the Science Fiction Book Club.)

Logo No. 647. Gaskell, Jane. *The City*. Code No. UE2085. First DAW printing, October 1985. 276 pp. Cover art by James Gurney. Originally published in U.K. by Hodder & Stoughton (1966). Reprinted in U.S. by St. Martin's Press (1977). See Schlobin *The Literature of Fantasy* 692 (1979). $3.50.

"I have, in a sense, come to the only place I can call home....

"I had visited the City and the Tower again. I had been the General's bride, and he the new Emperor of North and South and Atlantis-across-the-Ocean. The city had been any city to a conqueror, sheeted in flags, misted in wine. I had not recognized it, this third bitter time, but this is the City I was born in.

"This is the dictatorship ruled by my Mother, where the High Priest is the man who fathered me, who fathered my brother and lover Smahil on the witch Ooldra, and must surely kill me, the living proof of his betrayal of his vows of lifelong celibacy."

(Bibliographer's note: Third part of the Atlan saga.)

Logo No. 648. Wagner, Karl Edward ed. *The Year's Best Horror Stories: Series XIII*. Code No. UE2086. First edition. First printing, October 1985. 251 pp. Cover art by Michael Whelan. $2.95.

Contents:

Introduction: 13 Is a Lucky Number	Karl Edward Wagner
Mrs. Todd's Shortcut	Stephen King
Are You Afraid of the Dark?	Charles L. Grant
Catch Your Death	John Gordon
Dinner Party	Gardner Dozois
Tiger in the Snow	Daniel Wynn Barber
Watch the Birdie	Ramsey Campbell
Coming Soon to a Theatre Near You	David J. Schow
Hands with Long Fingers	Leslie Halliwell
Weird Tales	Fred Chappell
The Wardrobe	Jovan Panich
Angst for the Memories	Vincent McHardy
The Thing in the Bedroom	David Langford
Borderland	John Brizzolara
The Scarecrow	Roger Johnson

The End of the World	James B. Hemesath
Never Grow Up	John Gordon
Deadlights	Charles Wagner
Talking in the Dark	Dennis Etchison

Logo No. 649. Saunders, Charles R. *The Trail of Bohu.* Code No. UE2087. First edition. First printing, October 1985. 222 pp. Cover art by James Gurney. $2.95.

The magic of the Demon Gods was mobilized for vengeance and was crying out: "We will strike in lands of the Abamba. We will strike along the East Coast. We will strike in Punt and Axum. And we will strike in the heart of Cush itself!

"Yes, in Cush! And in Cush we will destroy Imaro and avenge his slaying of Chitendu and Chikanda! With the Ilyassai gone, the rest of our tasks will be easy to accomplish...."

Imaro was the key. Imaro was the obstacle to all their evil plans. Yet Imaro was but a man, a man of strength and power, but still a man. Could he stand against all of a continent's evil?

(Bibliographer's note: Third novel in the saga of Imaro. Includes a glossary of strange words contained in the text.)

Logo No. 650. Norman, John (pseud. John Lange). *Dancer of Gor.* Code No. UE2100. First edition. First printing, November 1985. 479 pp. Cover art by Ken W. Kelly. $3.95.

Doreen Williamson appeared to be a quiet shy librarian, but, in the dark of the library, after hours, she would practice, semi-nude, her secret studies in belly-dancing. One fateful night, the slavers from Gor kidnapped her.

On that barbarically splendid counter-Earth, Doreen drew a high price as a dancer in taverns, in slave collar and ankle bells, Soon each of her owners became aware that their prize dancer was the target of powerful forces; that, in the tense climate of the ongoing war between Ar and Cos, two mighty empires, Doreen was too dangerous to keep.

(Bibliographer's note: This is the 22nd book of the Counter-Earth saga of Gor. Doreen has a great body as depicted on the cover by Ken W. Kelly. I like Kelly's artwork. At the 1987 Boskone, I bought one of his preliminary sketches. Ironically, it wasn't a preliminary DAW cover, and, unfortunately, it wasn't even a T & A cover. It was for a Robert Adams Horseclans novel, but was the best of the sketches offered. I've got my eye out; next time it's got to be a John Norman or Sharon Green cover. Slaves and amazons—good clean fun!)

Logo No. 651. Lee, Tanith. *Days of Grass.* Code No. UE2094. First edition. First printing, November 1985. 250 pp. Cover art by Michael Whelan. $3.50.

The free humans lived underground, secretive, like rats. Above, the world was a fearsome place for them, the open sky a terror, the night so black, and the striding machines from space so laser-flame deadly.

Esther dared the open; she saw the sky; she saw the Enemy, and she was taken, captive, to the vast alien empty city. Surrounded by the marvels of a science not born on Earth, Esther didn't know what they wanted of her. There was mystery in the city, dread in the heavens, and magic in the handsome alien man who came to her.

Logo No. 652. Foster, M.A. *Preserver.* Code No. UE2095. First edition. First printing, November 1985. 253 pp. Cover art by Ken W. Kelly. Cited in *Anatomy of Wonder* 4-221 (1987). $2.95.
   Teragon: planet of darkness revolving around a white dwarf sun. Teragon, a world that, by all the rules of science, had no right to exist, a planet where law and order were an individual matter, and only the strong, the quick and the clever could long survive.
   This was Demsing's adopted home, the place that had made him all he had become, or had it? For Demsing, master of illusion and manipulator of his fellow humans, held within him the deadliest secret in the starways, the secret of the Morphodite, and, if he ever learned how to unlock this deeply buried knowledge, he could change the entire destiny of his world.
   (Bibliographer's note: The third book of the Morphodite trilogy.)

Logo No. 653. Saha, Arthur W. ed. *The Year's Best Fantasy Stories: 11.* Code No. UE2097. First edition. First printing, November 1985. 238 pp. Cover art by Segrelles. $2.95.
   Contents:
   Introduction

Draco, Draco	Tanith Lee
The Harvest Child	Steve Rasnic Tem
Love Among the Xoids	John Sladek
Stoneskin	John Morressy
Unmistakably the Finest	Scott Bradfield
The Foxwife	Jane Yolen
Golden Apples of the Sun	Gardner Dozois, Jack Dann and Michael Swanwick
My Rose and My Glove	Harvey Jacobs
Strange Shadows	Clark Ashton Smith
A Little Two-Chair Barber Shop on Phillips Street	Donald R. Burleson
Taking Heart	Stephen L. Burns
The Storm	David Morrell
A Cabin on the Coast	Gene Wolfe

Logo No. 654. Shea, Michael. *In Yana, the Touch of Undying.* Code No. UE2080. First edition. First printing, December 1985. 318 pp. Cover art by Terry Oakes. $3.50.
   Bramt Hex is a student of ancient lore until a chance meeting at an inn opens infinite pathways of possibility. Touched by destiny, Bramt abandons his ivory tower for the greater world, hoping to become a maker of legends in his own right. But the world is a fearful place peopled by cun-

223

ning nobles and wily wizards, demons and ogres, vampires and vengeful ghosts, sword-wielding warriors and flesh-craving giants. Soon, Bramt's quest for fame and wealth becomes a battle for survival and a desperate, magic-led search for a treasure far greater than gold, the secret of immortality which can only be found in the dangerous, illusive realm called Yana.

Logo No. 655. Green, Sharon. *Gateway to Xanadu.* Code No. UE2089. First edition. First printing, December 1985. 413 pp. Cover art by Ken W. Kelly. $3.95.

Special Agent Diana Santee had beat the odds, returning alive and well from what the slaver, Radman, had meant to be a one-way trip to the fringes of space. With her new partner, the alien Val, Diana was only too eager to pick up Radman's trail again, this time to complete her mission as the slaver's judge, jury and executioner.

When Diana and Val tracked their enemy to the pleasure world of Xanadu, they found themselves trapped in a land where excess and ecstacy were the only rules. Finding a slaver in a realm of slaves and lords became a deadly game where a single misstep could turn Diana from hunter to hunted, from top level agent to unwilling slave.

(Bibliographer's note: Second book in the series featuring Diana Santee, Spaceways Agent.)

Logo No. 656. Prescot, Dray (pseud. Kenneth Bulmer). *Omens of Kregen.* Code No. UE2090. First edition. First printing, December 1985. 222 pp. Cover art by Richard Hescox. $2.95.

Striving to save his strife-torn empire of Vallia from the Nine Unspeakable Curses, Dray Prescot has faced a plague of murderous werewolves and attack by the witch hordes.

Now he must conquer the bloodthirsty forces of the would-be king of North Vallia, while, at the same time, protecting the realm from the evil witch Csitra and her sorcerous son. Journeying to the witch's dark Maze of Coup Blag, Dray and his comrades must meet the challenge of this realm of traps and treasures, where death waits around every turn, and a wizardly battle of destruction is the price of winning free.

(Bibliographer's note: Thirty-sixth novel in the Dray Prescot saga and third of the Witch War Cycle. Wow!)

Logo No. 657. Bradley, Marion Zimmer ed. *Free Amazons of Darkover.* Code No. UE2096. First edition. First printing, December 1985. 304 pp. Cover art by Richard Hescox. $3.50.

Contents:

Introduction: About Amazons	Marion Zimmer Bradley
The Oath of the Free Amazons	Walter Breen
The Legend of Lady Bruna	Marion Zimmer Bradley
Cast Off Your Chains	Margaret Silvestri
The Banshee	Sherry Kramer
On the Trail	Barbara Armistead

To Open a Door	P. Alexandra Riggs
The Meeting	Nina Boal
The Mother Quest	Diana L. Paxson
Child of the Heart	Elisabeth Waters
Midwife	Deborah Wheeler
Recruits	Maureen Shannon
A Different Kind of Courage	Mercedes Lackey
Knives	Marion Zimmer Bradley
Tactics	Jane M.H. Bigelow
This One Time	Joan Marie Verba
Her Own Blood	Margaret Carter
The Camel's Nose	Susan Holtzer
Girls Will Be Girls	Patricia Shaw-Mathews
Growing Pains	Susan Shwartz
Oath of the Free Amazons: Terran, Techno Period	Jaida n'ha Sandra

Logo No. 658. Cherryh, C.J. (pseud. Carolyn Janice Cherry). *The Kif Strike Back.* Code No. UE2104. First DAW printing, January 1986. 299 pp. Cover art and map by David A. Cherry. Originally published by Phantasia Press (1985). $3.50.

When the *kif* seized Hilfy and Tully, *hani* and human crew of *The Pride of Chanur*, they issued a challenge Pyanfar, captain of *Pride*, couldn't ignore, a challenge that was to take Pyanfar and her shipmates to Mkks station and into a deadly confrontation between *kif, hani, mahendo'sat,* and human. What began as a simple rescue attempt soon blossomed into a dangerous game of interstellar politics, where today's ally could become tomorrow's executioner, and where methane breathers became volatile wild cards playing for stakes no oxy breather could even begin to understand.

(Bibliographer's note: The third book in the Chanur saga, with a short afterword by the author educating the reader as to the reason the saga has been divided in this fashion, as well as the games publishers (DAW Books happily not included) and booksellers play.)

Logo No. 659. Watson, Ian. *The Book of the River.* Code No. UE2105. First U.S. edition. First DAW printing, January 1986. 256 pp. Cover art by Jael. Originally published in U.K. by Gollancz (1984). $2.95.

Ever since she was a child, that had been Yaleen's goal in life, to join the powerful River Guild, and ply the waters, learning about all the towns of the eastern bank. Now she was a riverwoman at last, one with the water, one with the mysterious, sentient black current which granted women the rule of the river, yet called men forth to madness or death.

But when her only brother joined the male organization, the Observers, and lured her to aid him with knowledge of the seemingly unattainable western shore, Yaleen found herself caught by a destiny beyond her control, a destiny that would put her beyond the laws of her guild and lead her on to challenge the black current itself.

(Bibliographer's note: The first book of the Yaleen the Riverwoman trilogy.)

Logo No. 660. Asimov, Isaac and Martin H. Greenberg eds. *Isaac Asimov Presents the Great Science Fiction Stories 14 (1952).* Code No. UE2106. First edition. First printing, January 1986. 352 pp. Cover design by One Plus One Studio. Cover art by Tony Roberts. $3.50.

Contents:

Introduction	Martin H. Greenberg
The Pedestrian	Ray Bradbury
The Moon Is Green	Fritz Leiber
Lost Memory	Peter Phillips
What Have I Done?	Mark Clifton
Fast Falls the Eventide	Eric Frank Russell
The Business, As Usual	Mack Reynolds
A Sound of Thunder	Ray Bradbury
Hobson's Choice	Alfred Bester
Yesterday House	Fritz Leiber
The Snowball Effect	Katherine MacLean
Delay in Transit	F.L. Wallace
Game for Blondes	John D. MacDonald
The Altar at Midnight	Cyril Kornbluth
Command Performance	Walter M. Miller, Jr.
The Martian Way	Isaac Asimov
The Impacted Man	Robert Sheckley
What's It Like Out There?	Edmond Hamilton
Sail On! Sail On!	Philip Jose Farmer
Cost of Living	Robert Sheckley

Logo No. 661. Adams, Terry A. *Sentience.* Code No. UE2108. First edition. First printing, February 1986. 381 pp. Cover art by James Gurney. $3.50.

They thought themselves the lords of the universe and looked upon D'neerans, the only human telepaths, as being not quite human, not quite trustworthy. But a few true-humans could see the promise and possibilities of the D'neerans. So when Jameson, true-human master of manipulation, launched the exploratory starship, *Endeavor,* one D'neeran, the lady Hanna, a navigator and telepath who had studied the known sentient races, was part of the crew.

The *Endeavor* began its star search, broadcasting a message of greeting and hope, but, when an answer finally came, it was meant for the single D'neeran aboard and upon her would rest the fate of all humankind.

Logo No. 662. Lorrah, Jean. *Ambrov Keon.* Code No. UE2109. First edition. First printing, February 1986. 256 pp. Cover art by Walter Velez. $2.95.

When Sime killed Gen, it was the normal way of things. Gens weren't people, after all. They existed to produce the life-giving selyn, which, taken at the moment of death's fear, gave Simes renewed existence.

Then Sime Risa Tigue, shipwrecked, injured and needing selyn,

226

stumbled on the trail of the Gen called Sergi ambrov Keon. Sergi was a Companion, a Gen who could control the transfer of selyn so both Gen and Sime survived. In Risa, Sergi saw a Sime with the potential to become that rarest of beings, a Channel, a true giver of life. But Risa was a born killer, not a life-giver. Could she survive the transformation from one to the other? And, even if she did, could she, Sergi and the Simes and Gens of Keon survive the deadly enmity of a land of killer Simes?

(Bibliographer's note: A Sime/Gen novel, part of a universe created by Jacqueline Lichtenberg.)

Logo No. 663. Elgin, Suzette Haden. *Yonder Comes the Other End of Time.* Code No. UE2110. First edition. First printing, February 1986. 302 pp. Cover art by Richard Courtney. $2.95.

The Communipaths have traced a mind message of incredible strength to a seemingly empty sector of space, and now Tri-Galactic Federation agent Coyote Jones must find an invisible planet and bring back the unknown telepath who threatens to disrupt the entire Communipath system.

Bursting through a Spell of Invisibility and straight into Brightwater Kingdom on the planet Ozark, Coyote discovers a realm ruled by an iron-willed young woman named Responsible, perhaps the very telepath he seeks. But, on this world where Magicians of Rank can call up a storm or cure a wounded and unwelcome offworlder with equal ease, will Coyote's psience or Ozark's spells prove the stronger?

Logo No. 664. Norman, John (pseud. John Lange). *Renegades of Gor.* Code No. UE2112. First edition. First printing, March 1986. 444 pp. Cover art by Ken W. Kelly. $3.95.

As the bloody tide of war spread over Gor, Tarl Cabot, outcast by the Priest-Kings, became deeply enmeshed in the military combat between the empire of Ar and the invaders from Cos. His fate would depend upon which proved victorious in the coming confrontation at Ar's besieged river port. It looked like Tarl himself might prove the deciding factor that would tip the scales of destiny for one side or the other.

(Bibliographer's note: The 23rd book of the Tarl Cabot saga.)

Logo No. 665. Lee, Tanith. *Dark Castle, White Horse.* Code No. UE2113. First DAW printing, March 1986. 302 pp. Cover art by Ken W. Kelly. *The Castle of Dark* was originally published in U.K. by Macmillan (1978) and *Prince on a White Horse* by Macmillan (1982). $3.50.

Contents:

The Castle of Dark

Prince on a White Horse

Dark Castle, White Horse

(Bibliographer's note: Combined edition of several of the author's juvenile novellas.)

Logo No. 666. Gaskell, Jane. *Some Summer Lands.* Code No. UE2114.

First DAW printing, March 1986. 365 pp. Cover art by James Gurney. Originally published in U.K. by Hodder & Stoughton (1977). Later published in U.S. by St. Martin's Press (1979). $3.50.

Seka, the Voiceless One: she who hears all, yet speaks not. Daughter to the goddess Cija and the Dragon Lord Zerd, it is she who is the heart of hope, the enemy of despair, the secret guardian of the greatest treasure and most fearsome threat of that fabled paradise, Atlan.

But now the magical strands of fate are weaving a final pattern for Seka and all those she holds dear. As the Dragon Lord leads his armies forth to new conquest, Seka and Cija must search for victory in a far different kind of war, a timeless battle that will change the very fate of their world.

(Bibliographer's note: The fourth volume of the Atlan saga as published by Hodder & Stoughton, and the fifth as published by St. Martin's Press and DAW Books.)

Logo No. 667. For those collectors who are losing their minds trying to locate this book, fear not. You're as sane as I am, unfortunate ones. There is no Logo No. 667. The number was inadvertently skipped while Don Wollheim was ill and never recaptured. If you happen to be compulsive about the orderliness of your universe, write to DAW and insist that the number be used. After all, there's no sense in letting a perfectly good logo number go to waste. If that suggestion makes sense to you, you're in trouble. I say it's spinach, and the hell with it.

Logo No. 668. Clayton, Jo. *Drinker of Souls.* Code No. UE2123. First edition. First printing, April 1986. 335 pp. Cover art by Segrelles. $3.50.

She was Brann, the Drinker of Souls, from whom all but the very brave and the very foolish fled in fear. Bonded to twin demonic shape-shifters, she roved the land in search of rich life source to feed her demons' need.

But Brann, too, had a need that couldn't be denied, a quest to free her family from the evil king who had enslaved them, a quest that would lead Brann and her unearthly allies into magical realms ruled by witches and werewolves, lawless lords and murderous villains, and the ever-present ghosts of the restless dead.

Logo No. 669. Roberson, Jennifer. *Legacy of the Sword.* Code No. UE2124. First edition. First printing, April 1986. 384 pp. Cover art by Julek Heller. $3.50.

For decades, the magical race of shapechangers called the Cheysuli have been feared and hated exiles in their own land, a land they rightfully should rule. Victims of a vengeful monarch's war of annihilation and a usurper king's tyrannical reign, the Cheysuli clans have nearly vanished from the world.

Now, in the aftermath of the revolution which overthrew the hated tyrant, Prince Donal is being trained as the first Cheysuli in generations to assume the throne. But will he be able to overcome the prejudice of a populace afraid of his special magic and succeed in uniting the realm in its life-and-death battle against enemy armies and evil magicians?

(Bibliographer's note: Third book of the Chronicles of the Cheysuli.)

Logo No. 670. Harness, Charles L. *Redworld*. Code No. UE2125. First edition. First printing, April 1986. 229 pp. Cover art by Angus McKie. See *Anatomy of Wonder* 4-251 (1987). $2.95.

The treaty that ended the civil war decreed that the men of science and the followers of the gods would split all of society between them. Yet, Guild apprentice Pol was torn between the logic of science and the lure of faith, unaware that destiny had already chosen a very special role for him to play. Pol was about to encounter a woman of unique power, the mistress of a mysterious, forbidden castle, who would lead him down the pathways of prophecy to a strange and frightening new world.

Logo No. 671. Green, Sharon. *To Battle the Gods*. Code No. UE2128. First edition. First printing, May 1986. 446 pp. Cover art by Ken W. Kelly. $3.50.

The gods have spoken, and Jalav, warrior woman, has heeded their command, joining together her Midanna warriors with the male fighters of the dark lord Sigurr to stand against the prophesied "strangers from the stars." Yet, even as she marshals her forces, Jalav wonders how long the uneasy truce between male and female warriors will hold if the prophecy of coming battle proves false.

What if the strangers from the stars are not truly Jalav's enemies? What if her greatest challenge comes not from some distant stellar realm, but from the gods themselves?

(Bibliographer's note: Fifth, and concluding, book in the series featuring Jalav, Amazon Warrior, unless the author changes her mind.)

Logo No. 672. Cherryh, C.J. (pseud. Carolyn Janice Cherry). *Visible Light*. Code No. UE2129. First edition. First printing, May 1986. 348 pp. Cover art by David A. Cherry. See *Anatomy of Wonder* 4-133 (1987). $3.50.

Contents:

Author's Introduction	A Thief in Korianth
Cassandra	The Last Tower
Threads of Time	The Brothers
Companions	Endpiece

(Bibliographer's note: The cover, executed by the author's brother, depicts a spacer whose face bears a remarkable resemblance to the author. Coincidence? Sure. And I've got this bridge I'd like to sell you.)

Logo No. 673. Watson, Ian. *The Book of the Stars*. Code No. UE2130. First U.S. edition. First DAW printing, May 1986. 252 pp. Cover art by Jael. $2.95.

Yaleen, heroine of the River War, was the only one who truly understood the secret of the Black Current and of the entity that was its heart and mind. Now she must pay the price of that forbidden knowledge, forced to become the Black Current's spy, and to abandon her body and her world for a celestial journey to the inner sanctum of its mysterious, seemingly all-powerful foe, the Godmind.

Yet could Yaleen discover the Godmind's plans for cosmic conquest? And, if she did, was the Black Current a strong enough defender to stand against this omnipotent enemy in the coming interstellar conflagration?

(Bibliographer's note: Second book of the Yaleen the Riverwoman trilogy.)

Logo No. 674. Lee Tanith. *Delirium's Mistress.* Code No. UE2135. First edition. First printing, June 1986. 416 pp. Cover art by Michael Whelan. $3.95.

In the age of demons, when the Earth was still flat, a daughter was born to a mortal beauty and Azhrarn, Demon Lord of Night. This daughter of the Night was called Azhriaz, and she was hidden away on a mist-shrouded isle, spirit-guarded, to spend her life in dreams. But Azhriaz was destined for more than dark dreaming, for, if her father was the Lord of Night, her mother was descended from the Sun itself.

Her beauty and power soon called to another mighty demon lord, Azhrarn's enemy, Prince Chuz, Delusion's Master, who worked a magnificent illusion to free Azhriaz from her prison and transform her into Delirium's Mistress.

As Mistress of Madness and Delirium she would become known in realms of both demon and humankind. Her destiny would make her goddess, queen, fugitive, champion, seeress, and her to whom even the very Lord of Darkness would one day bow down.

(Bibliographer's note: Fourth book in the Flat Earth series.)

Logo No. 675. Wollheim, Donald A. with Arthur W. Saha eds. *The 1986 Annual World's Best SF.* Code No. UE2136. First edition. First printing, June 1986. 303 pp. Cover art by Vincent DiFate. $3.50.

Contents:

Introduction	The Editor
Earthgate	J. Brian Clarke
On the Dream Channel Panel	Ian Watson
The Gods of Mars	Gardner Dozois, Jack Dann and Michael Swanwick
The Jaguar Hunter	Lucius Shepard
Sailing to Byzantium	Robert Silverberg
Webrider	Jayge Carr
With Virgil Oddum at the East Pole	Harlan Ellison
The Curse of Kings	Connie Willis
Fermi and Frost	Frederik Pohl
Pots	C.J. Cherryh

Logo No. 676. Clough, B.W. *The Realm Beneath.* Code No. UE2137. First edition. First printing, June 1986. 256 pp. Cover art by Walter Velez. $2.95.

Liras-ven had been touched by destiny, chosen despite his own wishes to be the wearer of the Crystal Crown and, thereby, named king of the

Shan. As king, he had withstood a mighty wizard's deadly attack and saved his people from a terrifying doom.

Yet, now, a far worse doom awaited Liras-ven and the people of Averidan, for the barbarian Cayd were invading, overwhelming the Shan in bloody battle. As the Cayd warlord threatened to break down the final fortress gates, Liras and his mage and warrior allies sought even the most desperate means to protect their imperiled lands. But, did a king, still un-tutored in the true magic of the Crystal Crown, dare to use it to surrender himself to the powers of the Realm Beneath, the otherworld of godly forces from which a true Shan king drew strength, but in which an ill-prepared lord could lose his very identity?

(Bibliographer's note: Third book in the Averidan series.)

Logo No. 677. Clayton, Jo. *Quester's Endgame.* Code No. UE2138. First edition. First printing, July 1986. 372 pp. Cover art by Michael Whelan. $3.50.

Across the years and through endless star systems, Aletys had searched for her mother Shareem and for her long-denied heritage: the chance to claim her rightful place as a member of the nearly immortal super-race, the Vrya. Now, at last, Aletys was about to rendezvous with Shareem for a journey to the secret homeworld of her people.

But, even at Aletys' moment of triumph, she faced her deadliest chal-lenge. On Vrithian waited Kell, blood enemy, mastermind of treachery, who held an entire planet hostage in fear, and who wouldn't rest until he'd destroyed Aletys and any who dared ally with her.

(Bibliographer's note: Ninth and concluding novel of the Diadem Saga.)

Logo No. 678. Bradley, Marion Zimmer ed. *Sword and Sorceress III.* Code No. UE2141. First edition. First printing, July 1986. 285 pp. Cover art by Jael. $3.50.

Contents:

Introduction: The Evolution of Women's Fantasy	Marion Zimmer Bradley
Dragon-Amber	Deborah Wheeler
Enter the Wolf	A.D. Overstreet
Valley of the Shadow	Jennifer Roberson
The Song and the Flute	Dorothy J. Heydt
Journeytime	Dana Kramer-Rolls
Orpheus	Mary Frances Zambreno
Scarlet Eyes	Millea Kenin
The River of Tears	Anodea Judith
Fresh Blood	Polly B. Johnson
The Mist on the Moor	Diana L. Paxson
Bargains	Elizabeth Moon
A Woman's Privilege	Elisabeth Waters
Talla	J. Edwin Andrews
Tupilak	Terry Tafoya
Sword Sworn	Mercedes Lackey

A Tale from Hendry's Mill	Melissa Carpenter
S.A.R.	Patricia B. Cirone
More's the Pity	L.D. Woeltjen
Marwe's Forest	Charles R. Saunders
The Hunters	Mavis J. Andrews

Logo No. 679. Llewellyn, Edward (pseud. Edward Llewellyn-Thomas). *Word-Bringer.* Code No. UE2142. First edition. First printing, July 1986. 222 pp. Cover art by James Gurney. $2.95.

Richard Ryan, attorney, patent investigator, engineer, was a man with clients ranging from the United States government to corporations at the forefront of technological development. His clients valued him for his unique ability to sense deceit, especially in the form of scientific cover-ups. Some thought his talent was empathy, some clairvoyance or telepathy, but Ryan himself would only admit to a well-developed power of observation.

Then Ryan was hired to uncover the source of some incredible scientific breakthroughs, and he stumbled on a truth he couldn't deny, for Richard Ryan did, indeed, have a special kind of mind power, a power which could open the way to communication with the first emissary from the stars. But, was this alien ambassador offering humanity the riches of the universe, or the trigger for Earth's destruction?

(Bibliographer's note: A posthumously published novel, the author having died July 5, 1984.)

Logo No. 680. Cherryh, C.J. (pseud. Carolyn Janice Cherry). *Angel with the Sword.* Code No. UE2143. First paperback printing, August 1986. 295 pp. Cover art by Tim Hildebrandt. Maps by Pat Tobin. Originally published in hardcover by DAW (1985). $3.50.

Merovingen is where gutsy young canaler Altair Jones earns her livelihood on the danger-filled byways of the canals and the dark "lower city," always staying just the right side of the law and keeping out of trouble until the night she rescues a high-born stranger from drowning. Then, suddenly, Altair is catapulted into the world of upper-level politics, where games of power are played for keeps, and where a canaler must use all her wit and skill just to survive.

(Bibliographer's note: Merovingen is a colony created by the author for use as a vehicle around which she and other writers may set novels and stories. It appears to be similar to the concept of the popular Thieve's World series. A 45-page appendix includes a history of the Merovin, its vital statistics and detailed maps.)

(Bibliographer's second note and first query: The copyright page indicates the date of printing as "October 1986"; so, how come it was published in August 1986? Must be another of life's little mysteries.)

Logo No. 681. Green, Sharon. *The Warrior Challenged.* Code No. UE2144. First edition. First printing, August 1986. 382 pp. Cover art by Ken W. Kelly. $3.50.

In this barbaric land ruled by men, women are meant only to serve. But Terril, an empathic agent from an advanced interstellar society, owes her first allegiance to her masters from the stars and can never be completely ruled by any man, not even Tammad, the barbarian lord she has come to love.

Yet, when Terril joins Tammad on a rescue expedition to the distant female-dominated city of Vediaster, neither she nor Tammad can foresee that they are riding straight into a trap that may claim both their lives. Will Terril's rapidly growing skills of both body and mind prove powerful enough to meet the deadly challenge of the tyrant of Vediaster?

(Bibliographer's note: The fourth book of the Terrilian Series.)

Logo No. 682. Lichtenberg, Jacqueline and Jean Lorrah. *Zelerod's Doom.* Code No. UE2145. First edition. First printing, August 1986. 277 pp. Cover art by Walter Velez. $3.50.

Earth, the day after tomorrow, when a bizarre mutation has split humanity between Simes and Gens. Two kinds of humans, deadly enemies, the Simes are forced to slay Gens to gain the life-giving selyn which only Gens produced.

In the territory of the Simes, small groups of Simes and Gens have gathered into Householdings, working together to prevent the long-predicted day of Zelerod's Doom when, with one Gen left for every Sime to kill, the final destruction of all humankind will begin. With drought and disease rampant, with Freeband Raider Simes and Wild Gens roaming the land bent on murder, and, with the Gen Army mobilizing for a desperate invasion of Sime territory, can even legendary Householdings like Zeor and Keon find the means to save this world gone mad?

(Bibliographer's note: The end of the book contains a cast and description of characters and a glossary of terms and other descriptive guides to understanding the Sime/Gen Series.)

Logo No. 683. Zahn, Timothy. *The Backlash Mission.* Code No. UE2150. First edition. First printing, September 1986. 288 pp. Cover art by Vincent DiFate. $3.50.

The War Drug! That was what Backlash was, the secret formula which turned ordinary soldiers into the legendary Blackcollars, the super warriors who, decades after Earth's conquest by the alien *Ryqril*, remained humanity's one hope to regain its freedom. But the Backlash drug had been used up in the war effort, and, unless Allen Caine and his commando team could discover where the formula was hidden, there would be no new generation of Blackcollars to carry on the battle against the tyrannical *Ryqril*.

The Blackcollars had pinpointed one spot on Earth as the possible cache for Backlash: Aegis Mountain, an impregnable fortress which even the enemy had never been able to crack. But Aegis was in the heart of *Ryqril*-run territory, and, even with the aid of the last surviving Blackcollars, could Caine evade the enemy long enough to take on the challenge of the deathtrap called Aegis Mountain?

(Bibliographer's note: Sequel to *The Blackcollar*.)

Logo No. 684. Roberson, Jennifer. *Sword-Dancer*. Code No. UE2152. First edition. First printing, September 1986. 286 pp. Cover art by Kathy Wyatt. Map by Elizabeth T. Danforth. $3.50.

He was Tiger, born of the desert winds, raised as a slave and winning his freedom by weaving a special kind of magic with a warrior's skill. Now he was an almost legendary sword-dancer, ready to take on any challenge, if the price was right, or the woman pretty enough.

She was Del, born of ice and storm, trained by the greatest of Northern sword masters. Now, her ritual training completed, and steeped in the special magic of her own runesword, she had come South in search of the young brother stolen five years before.

But even Del couldn't master all the dangers of the deadly Punja alone. Meeting Del, Tiger couldn't turn back from the most intriguing challenge he'd ever faced, the challenge of a magical, mysterious sword-dancer of the North.

Logo No. 685. Watson, Ian. *The Book of Being*. Code No. UE2153. First U.S. edition. First DAW printing, September 1986. 252 pp. Cover art by Jael. Originally published in U.K. by Gollancz (1985). $2.95.

As the Black Current's agent against the power of the Godmind, Yaleen the Riverwoman has faced death and rebirth to learn the truth about the Godmind's plan to destroy the universe. Yet now, back on her home world, Yaleen's own people refuse to heed her warnings of the terrifying fate which awaits them if the Godmind isn't stopped.

Only her old ally, the Black Current, offers Yaleen the help she so desperately needs. But is the Current truly trying to save humankind? Or does it seek to use Yaleen to destroy the Godmind, and humanity as well?

(Bibliographer's note: Concluding novel of the Yaleen the Riverwoman trilogy.)

Logo No. 686. Bradley, Marion Zimmer. *Lythande*. Code No. UE2154. First edition. First printing, October 1986. 237 pp. Cover art by Walter Velez. $3.50.

Contents:

The Secret of the Blue Star	Sea Wrack
The Incompetent Magician	The Wandering Lute
Somebody Else's Magic	Looking for Satan by Vonda N. McIntyre

(Bibliographer's note: This bibliography game gets tougher all the time. Whereas C.J. Cherryh's *Angel with the Sword*, Logo No. 680, showed an October 1986 printing date, even though, chronologically, it seems to be an August publication, the obverse appears here. Could it be that the two books are changelings, destined always to exist in an identity vacuum/time-space warp? Or am I overreacting?)

Logo No. 687. Correy, Lee. *A Matter of Metalaw*. Code No. UE2155. First edition. First printing, October 1986. 256 pp. Cover art by John Harris. $2.95.

234

When a Metalaw Investigation Team mysteriously vanishes while on a top-secret assignment, Peter Starbuck and his crack crew are called in to finish the mission and discover the fate of their missing comrades.

What they uncover may well prove the toughest case of their career: an incredible interstellar invasion plan spearheaded by a genetically altered race out to spread its unique brand of madness to other worlds, and ready to destroy any obstacle, even the agents of Metalaw, to fulfill its dreams of conquest.

Logo No. 686. Wagner, Karl Edward ed. *The Year's Best Horror Stories: XIV*. Code No. UE2156. First edition. First printing, October 1986. 291 pp. Cover art by Michael Whelan. $3.50.

Contents:

Introduction: Nurturing Nightmares	Karl Edward Wagner
Penny Daye	Charles L. Grant
Dwindling	David B. Silva
Dead Men's Fingers	Phillip C. Heath
Dead Week	Leonard Carpenter
The Sneering	Ramsey Campbell
Bunny Didn't Tell Us	David J. Schow
Pinewood	Tanith Lee
The Night People	Michael Reaves
Ceremony	William F. Nolan
The Woman in Black	Dennis Etchison
...Beside the Seaside, Beside the Sea	Simon Clark
Mother's Day	Stephen F. Wilcox
Lava Tears	Vincent McHardy
Rapid Transit	Wayne Allen Sallee
The Weight of Zero	John Alfred Taylor
John's Return to Liverpool	Christopher Burns
In Late December, Before the Storm	Paul M. Sammon
Red Christmas	David S. Garnett
Too Far Behind Gradina	Steve Sneyd

(Bibliographer's note: I particularly liked Schow's "Bunny Didn't Tell Us," a nice blend of horror and humor, a difficult thing to accomplish successfully.)

Logo No. 689. Williams, Tad. *Tailchaser's Song*. Code No. UE2162. First paperback edition. First printing, November 1986. 375 pp. Cover art by Braldt Bralds. Originally published in hardcover by DAW Books (1985).

Meet Fritti Tailchaser, a ginger tom cat of rare courage and curiosity, a born survivor in a world of heroes and villains, of powerful feline gods and whiskery legends about those strange furless, erect creatures called M'an. Join Tailchaser on his magical quest to rescue his catfriend Hushpad, a quest that will take him all the way to cat hell and beyond.

(Bibliographer's note: H.P. Lovecraft loved kitties, too.)

Logo No. 690. Saha, Arthur W. ed. *The Year's Best Fantasy Stories: 12*.

Code No. UE2163. First edition. First printing, November 1986. 226 pp. Cover art by Julek Heller. $2.95.

Contents:

Introduction

Unferno	George Alec Effinger
Dinner in Audoghast	Bruce Sterling
Fortunes of a Fool	Nicholas Yermakov
Preliminary Notes on the Jang	Lisa Goldstein
The Red House	Robert R. McCammon
Flight	Peter Dickinson
The Castle at World's End	Chris Naylor
The Persistence of Memory	Gael Baudino
The Face in the Cloth	Jane Yolen
The Last Dragon Master	A.A. Attanasio
Paladin of the Lost Hour	Harlan Ellison

(Bibliographer's note: The usual capable selection by a very capable anthologist.)

Logo No. 691. Shaw, Bob. *Fire Pattern*. Code No. UE2164. First DAW printing, November 1986. 189 pp. Cover art by Tony Roberts. Originally published in U.K. by Gollancz (1984). $2.95.

It's the year 1996, and science reporter Rayner Jerome has been assigned to investigate a case of spontaneous human combustion. Setting out to prove the incident is some sort of giant hoax, Ray learns, to his growing horror, that spontaneous combustion does, indeed, occur, and, further, that its cause is extraterrestrial in origin. This knowledge catapults Rayner on a nightmare journey of discovery, a journey stretching from a quiet, backwater town on Earth to the heart of an alien stronghold. As Rayner uncovers a frightening, centuries-in-the-making plot to invade Earth, he is plunged into the midst of a titanic struggle between two super-human factions, one bent on finding a peaceful means of coexisting with mankind, the other determined to enslave all of humanity!

Logo No. 692. Clayton, Jo. *Skeen's Leap*. Code No. UE2169. First edition. First printing, December 1986. 320 pp. Cover art by Jody Lee. $3.50.

Skeen had prowled the spaceways for more years than she cared to remember, keeping one step ahead of the law, searching the ruins of many a world for priceless artifacts. Yet now Skeen was afraid she'd finally gone too far, as, fleeing the local authorities on a backwater world, she stumbled through a bizarre "Gateway," a door into an unknown world where eight separate races dwelt together in uneasy peace.

Here Skeen found treasures beyond her wildest imagining just waiting to be plucked from the unwary. But here, too, waited danger-filled traps for newcomers to these lands. Skeen was soon entangled in a double-dealing web of intrigue, pursued by vengeful shape-changers and a bloodthirsty warrior clan, as she desperately sought the legendary creators of the Gateway: the only beings who could open the way back to her own universe.

(Bibliographer's note: The first book of a projected Skeen trilogy.)

Logo No. 693. Felice, Cynthia. *Downtime.* Code No. UE2170. First paperback edition. First DAW printing, December 1986. 252 pp. Cover art by Richard Hescox. Originally published by Bluejay Books (1985). $2.95.

Life eternal, the dream of all-too-mortal humankind, became a reality with the discovery of the longevity elixir. But as humans sent ever more starships downtime to colonize new planets, there wasn't enough elixir to meet everyone's needs. So the Decemvirate ran a lottery, rationing the precious substance to maintain peace everywhere.

Yet there was a traitor among this elite ruling group, a tyrant who would destroy whole worlds to realize ambitions of power and conquest. Calla, Commander of the Guard, for whom the longevity elixir was poison, not cure, had been chosen to catch the betrayer before it was too late. But, when her mission reunited her with her long-lost love, could Calla sacrifice their newly regained happiness to end the tyrant's reign?

Logo No. 694. Asimov, Isaac and Martin H. Greenberg eds. *Isaac Asimov Presents the Great Science Fiction Stories: 15 (1953).* Code No. UE2171. First edition. First printing, December 1986. 352 pp. Cover art by Tony Roberts. $3.50.

Contents:

Introduction

The Big Holiday	Fritz Leiber
Crucifixus Etiam	Walter M. Miller. Jr.
Four in One	Damon Knight
Saucer of Loneliness	Theodore Sturgeon
The Liberation of Earth	William Tenn
Lot	Ward Moore
The Nine Billion Names of God	Arthur C. Clarke
Warm	Robert Sheckley
Impostor	Philip K. Dick
The World Well Lost	Theodore Sturgeon
A Bad Day for Sales	Fritz Leiber
Common Time	James Blish
Time Is the Traitor	Alfred Bester
The Wall Around the World	Theodore R. Cogswell
The Model of a Judge	William Morrison
Hall of Mirrors	Fredric Brown
It's a Good Life	Jerome Bixby

Logo No. 695. Cherryh, C.J. (pseud. Carolyn Janice Cherry). *Chanur's Homecoming.* Code No. UE2177. First DAW printing, January 1987. Cover art by Michael Whelan. Map of Compact Space by David A. Cherry. Originally published by Phantasia Press (1986). $3.95.

When those enigmatic entities called humans sent their first exploration ship into Compact space, all the traditional power alliances of the seven Compact races were totally disrupted. Giving shelter to Tully, the only surviving human, Pyanfar Chanur and her *hani* crew were pitched into the center of a galactic maelstrom, key players in a power game they scarcely understood.

Now, with space stations destroyed by rival factions, unwillingly "allied" with the most devious and trustworthy *kif*, and forced to doubt their own long-time champions, the *mahendo'sat*, Pyanfar and her space-going comrades had become the last desperate hope of the entire *hani* race. For, as a one-planet race among whom only the females were allowed into space, the *hani* were in the direct path of a running space battle which might wipe the very memory of their world from the galactic maps.

(Bibliographer's note: Concluding book of the Chanur tetralogy.)

Logo No. 696. Morwood, Peter. *The Horse Lord.* Code No. UE2178. First U.S. edition. First DAW printing, January 1987. 268 pp. Cover art by Neal McPheeters. Originally published in U.K. by Century (1986). $3.50.

Centuries ago, the Horse Lords had ridden into Alba to defeat the evil sorcerer Kalarr cu Ruruc and banish magic from the land. Now an ambitious lord has once again meddled with dark forces, unleashing the power of Kalarr cu Ruruc on the unsuspecting and unprotected Horse Lords.

With Castle Dunrath besieged and overrun by sorcery, only the young warrior and heir Aldric survives to seek vengeance on the enemies who have slain his clan and stolen his birthright. But, alone, even Aldric stands little chance. To fight dark magic, he, too, must make alliance with magic, and, rescued from pursuers by an aging wizard, Aldric finds the ally he seeks, and a quest that will send him to challenge a dragon's wrath in hopes of winning the one weapon of power which can destroy a creature that's five hundred years dead.

(Bibliographer's note: First book of The Book of Years trilogy.)

Logo No. 697. Carter, Lin. *Mandricardo.* Code No. UE2180. First edition. First printing, January 1987. 223 pp. Cover art by Walter Velez. $2.95.

Terra Magica, fabulous land next door to our own, where trolls and monsters, wizards and warriors vie over virtuous maidens and the wealth of kingdoms. Here waits adventure beyond your wildest imaginings, here in this sorcerous world where a misplaced wish can condemn a doughty knight to the midst of a broiling desert or spirit a beautiful Amazon to a watery domain.

So, welcome one and all on the quest of the stalwart knight Mandricardo, who, in searching for his lost Amazonian love, will tame a flying carpet, rescue a forlorn princess, and take on the challenge of any hero's lifetime, a fiery, feisty Salamandre bent on burning its way through all of Terra Magica.

(Bibliographer's note: Third book in the Terra Magica sequence. Included is an appendix designated The Notes to Mandricardo.)

Logo No. 698. Bradley, Marion Zimmer and the Friends of Darkover. *The Other Side of the Mirror and Other Darkover Stories.* Code No. UE2185.

First edition. First printing, February 1987. 303 pp. Cover art and border design by Richard Hescox. $3.50.

Contents:

Introduction	Marion Zimmer Bradley
The Other Side of the Mirror	Patricia Floss
Bride Price	Marion Zimmer Bradley
Everything but Freedom	Marion Zimmer Bradley
Oathbreaker	Marion Zimmer Bradley
Blood Hunt	Linda Frankel and Paula Crunk

Logo No. 699. Eldin, Suzette Haden. *The Judas Rose.* Code No. UE2186. First edition. First printing, February 1987. 363 pp. Cover art by Jill Bauman Versandi. Wild grape vine wreath logo by Randy Farran. $3.50.

It is said that in language lies power. On a future Earth, where genetically bred linguists hold the key to the planet's economic survival, because only they can serve as translators between human and alien traders, language has, indeed, become the way to power. But what this future Earth's male-dominated society does not yet realize is that ordinary women as well as linguists can wield this weapon of the mind.

While mankind vies to claim its place in an alien-ruled universe, womankind strives in a unique battle back on Earth, spreading the knowledge of Laadan, the secret language of women. For, in Laadan, lies women's one hope for regaining their freedom and for saving all humankind.

(Bibliographer's note: Second book of the Native Tongue series.)

Logo No. 700. Brunner, John. *More Things Than Heaven.* Code No. UE2187. First edition. First printing, February 1987. 221 pp. Cover art by John Harris. $2.95.

When the exploratory spaceship *Starventure* had soared to the stars in search of new worlds for mankind, top science journalist David Drummond had been proud that his own brother Leon had been part of the crew. Now *Starventure* was back in the solar system, heading for its long awaited rendezvous with Earth.

Suddenly, the logical, scientific foundations of David's world were falling apart. For, though he knew his brother was still millions of miles away, David also knew that he had seen Leon walking the streets of Earth that very day. Before long, the whole world would know what David was about to discover. Something was terribly wrong aboard *Starventure*, something that could change the entire future of all humankind.

(Bibliographer's note: This book is based on an earlier work by the author published by Ace Books (1963) as *The Astronauts Must Not Land.*)

Logo No. 701. Norman, John (pseud. John Lange). *Vagabonds of Gor.* Code No. UE2188. First edition. First printing, March 1987. 495 pp. Cover art by Ken W. Kelly. $3.95.

As treachery and betrayal become the prime weapons in the war between Ar and Cos, Tarl Cabot is trapped in the siege of Ar's Station, and, when Ar's Station falls to the warriors of Cos, it's only with the aid of the loyal Vosk League that Tarl and other survivors make their escape from the defeated port.

But, with the forces of Cos now readying to continue on their devastating march of conquest, Tarl must go undercover as a spy within the enemy camp, hoping to discover their plans and send word to Ar's army before it's too late.

(Bibliographer's note: 24th book of the Tarl Cabot Saga.)

Logo No. 702. Lackey, Mercedes. *Arrows of the Queen.* Code No. UE2189. First edition. First printing, March 1987. 320 pp. Cover art by Jody Lee. $2.95.

Chosen by the Companion Rolan, a mystical, horse-like being with powers beyond imagining, Talia, once a runaway, has become a trainee Herald, destined to become one of the Queen's own elite guard. For Talia has certain awakening talents of the mind that only a Companion like Rolan can truly sense.

As Talia struggles to master her unique abilities, time is running out. Conspiracy is brewing in Valdemar, a deadly treason which could destroy Queen and kingdom. Opposed by unknown enemies capable of both diabolical magic and treacherous assassination, the Queen must turn to Talia and the Heralds for aid in protecting the realm and insuring the future of the Queen's heir, a child already in danger of becoming bespelled by the Queen's own foes.

Logo No. 703. Greenberg, Martin H. and Charles G. Waugh eds. *Vamps.* Code No. UE2190. First edition. First printing, March 1987. 365 pp. Cover art by Jill Bauman Versandi. $4.95.

Contents:

Introduction

One for the Road	Stephen King
She Only Goes Out at Night	William Tenn
Heredity	David H. Keller
Clarimonda	Theophile Gautier
The Cloak	Robert Bloch
For the Blood Is the Life	F. Marion Crawford
The Last Grave of Lill Warran	Manly Wade Wellman
The Girl with the Hungry Eyes	Fritz Leiber
Ken's Mystery	Julian Hawthorne
Restless Souls	Seabury Quinn
The Drifting Snow	August Derleth
When It Was Moonlight	Manly Wade Wellman
Luella Miller	Mary Wilkins Freeman
Dress of White Silk	Richard Matheson
Red As Blood	Tanith Lee
Carmilla	Sheridan Le Fanu

(Bibliographer's note: Vampires are my favorite creatures.)

Logo No. 704. Cherryh, C.J. ed. *Festival Moon*. Code No. UE2192. First edition. First printing, April 1987. 300 pp. Cover art by Tim Hildebrandt; maps by Pat Tobin. $3.50.

Contents:

Festival Moon	C.J. Cherryh
First Night Cruise	Leslie Fish
Festival Moon (reprised)	C.J. Cherryh
Two Gentlemen of the Trade	Robert Lynn Asprin
Festival Moon (reprised)	C.J. Cherryh
Cat's Tale	Nancy Asire
Festival Moon (reprised)	C.J. Cherryh
Deathangel	Mercedes R. Lackey
Festival Moon (reprised)	C.J. Cherryh
Sword Play	Janet and Chris Morris
Festival Moon (reprised)	C.J. Cherryh
First-Bath	Lynn Abbey
Festival Moon (reprised)	C.J. Cherryh
Night Action	Chris Morris
Festival Moon (reprised)	C.J. Cherryh

Appendix
Sea Floor Maps
Merovingen Ecology
Index to City Maps
Merovingian City Maps and Merovin Hemispheric Maps
Merovingian Songs

(Bibliographer's note: Merovingen Nights #1. Tales set in the world of Merovin, which was introduced by the editor in *Angel with the Sword*.)

Logo No. 705. Roberson, Jennifer. *Track of the White Wolf*. Code No. UE2193. First edition. First printing, April 1987. 375 pp. Cover art by Julek Heller; Cheysuli map by Liz Danforth. $3.50.

Niall, Prince of Homana, key player in a prophecy that spans generations, should have been the treasured link between Cheysuli and Homanan. Yet neither of the peoples he is destined to someday rule feel anything but suspician of Niall. Homanans fear him for his Cheysuli heritage, while Cheysuli refuse to accept him as their own, because he has acquired neither a lir-shape nor the lir companion which is the true mark of the Cheysuli shapechangers.

Now, despite his precarious situation within the kingdom, Niall must undertake a journey to fulfill yet another link in the ancient prophecy. He must travel through war-torn lands to claim his bride, a mission which may well prove his doom. As he searches for both his destiny and his lir, Niall is about to be plunged into a dangerous maelstrom of intrigue, betrayal, and deadly Ihlini sorcery.

(Bibliographer's note: Fourth book of the Chronicles of the Cheysuli.)

Logo No. 706. Lee, Tanith. *Night's Sorceries*. Code No. UE2194. First edition. First printing, April 1987. 287 pp. Cover art by Michael Whelan.

$3.50.

In the age of demons, when the Earth was still flat, Prince Chuz, Delusion's Master, stole Azhriaz, daughter of the Demon Lord of Night, from the underworld citadel meant to be her eternal prison. Pursued by the vengeful Lord of Night, Chuz and Azhriaz fled to the world above, to the lands of mortal men, seeking a haven for their love.

Yet when demons dwell in the realm of men, terror and wonders were bound to result. And so it was for all who came in contact with Chuz, Azhriaz, and their dread pursuer. As all three worked their powerful sorceries, men and women, from the highest lords to the lowest peasants, were led into new kingdoms of enchantment where a man could learn to commune with beasts, where magicians found their spells recast, where a woman's kindness could turn back time, and where a mortal might fulfill a prophecy that would place the very sun and moon within his grasp.

(Bibliographer's note: Book Five of Tales from the Flat Earth.)

Logo No. 707. Friedman, C.S. *In Conquest Born*. Code No. UE2198. First edition. First printing, May 1987. 511 pp. Cover art by Michael Whelan. $3.95.

Braxi and Azea, two civilizations fighting an endless campaign over a long-forgotten cause, two peoples born of the ancient human species and genetically bred over countless generations into super-races following opposite roads to power. The Braxana: created to become the ultimate warriors. The Azeans: raised to master the powers of the mind, using telepathy to penetrate where mere weapons cannot.

Now, at last, the final phase of their war is approaching, the time when whole worlds will be set ablaze by the force of ancient hatred, the time of Zatar and Anzha, master Braxana and Azean generals, who have made this battle a personal vendetta, and who will use every power of body and mind to claim the vengeance of total conquest.

(Bibliographer's note: The wraparound cover art depicts the generals, one male, one female, one on the front cover, one on the back cover. Why am I telling you such an obvious thing? Well, two forms of the book exist; one with the male on the front cover and the female on the back cover. The other, if you haven't wised up yet, is just the reverse. On a less mundane level, this is the author's first book, one that was ten years in the making.)

AUTHOR-TITLE INDEX

This index includes all authors and editors, together with the titles of their respective books. Short fiction contained in collections and anthologies has not been indexed. Entries are cited by Logo numbers, not page numbers.

The Pride of Chanur, 464
Serpent's Reach, 396
Sunfall, 433
The Tree of Swords and Jewels, 540
Visible Light, 672
Voyager in Night, 573
Wave Without a Shore, 444
Well of Shiuah, 284
Cherryh, C.J. ed.
Festival Moon, 704
Chester, William L.
Kioga of the Unknown Land, 290
Kioga of the Wilderness, 209
One Against a Wilderness, 228
Chilson, Robert
As the Curtain Falls, 98
The Star-Crowned Kings, 161
Clayton, Jo
A Bait of Dreams, 613
Changer's Moon, 638
Diadem from the Stars, 235
Drinker of Souls, 668
Ghosthunt, 529
Irsud, 306
Lamarchos, 275
Maeve, 344
Moongather, 481
Moonscatter, 516
The Nowhere Hunt, 457
Quester's Endgame, 677
Skeen's Leap, 692
The Snares of Ibex, 602
Star Hunters, 394
Clement, Hal
Ocean on Top, 57
Clough, B.W.
The Crystal Crown, 574
The Dragon of Mishbil, 645
The Realm Beneath, 676
Compton, D.G.
The Unsleeping Eye, 102
Coney, Michael G.
Friends Come in Boxes, 56
The Hero of Downways, 70
The Jaws That Bite, The Claws That Catch, 144
Mirror Image, 31
Monitor Found in Orbit, 120
Rax, 170

249

ARTIST-TITLE INDEX

References in this index, as in the Author-Title Index, are to Logo numbers, not page numbers. In the case of multiple authorship and editorship, only the name of the first author or editor is listed. The titles have not been alphabetized, but are, instead, chronologically listed by Logo number under the artist's names which have, of course, been alphabetized.

Andre, Robert
Isaac Asimov Presents the Great Science Fiction Stories 10 (1948) (Asimov), 543
Habitats (Shwartz), 591
Arnold, Hans
Can You Feel Anything When I Do This? (Sheckley), 99
The Year's Best Horror Stories: Series II (Davis), 109
Spacehawk, Inc. (Goulart), 132
A Touch of Strange (Sturgeon), 286
Atkinson, Alan
Brothers of Earth (Cherryh), 212

Barber, Thomas, Jr.
Jack of Swords (Tubb), 198
A World Called Camelot (Landis), 202
Barlowe, Wayne D.
Earth in Twilight (Piserchia), 458
The Silkie (Van Vogt), 465
The Pillars of Eternity (Bayley), 474
The Darkness of Diamondia (Van Vogt), 478
The 1982 Annual World's Best SF (Wollheim), 480
The Narrow Land (Vance), 490
The Battle of Forever (Van Vogt), 494
The Galactiad (Kern), 539
Barr, George
The Day Star (Geston), 6
At the Seventh Level (Elgin), 10
Green Phoenix (Swann), 27
Hunters of the Red Moon (Bradley), 71
Games Psyborgs Play (Barbet), 83
A Quest for Simbilis (Shea), 88
How Are the Mighty Fallen (Swann), 94
The Weathermonger (Dickinson), 104

267

272

279

TITLE INDEX

This index was prepared to allow the user direct access to a title when the user doesn't know or is unsure of the author's name. The Author-Title Index includes the information from the Title Index and should be consulted when the author's name is known. As with the Author-Title Index and the Artist-Title Index, reference is to the Logo number, not the page number.

Printed in Great Britain
by Amazon

55849321R00179